STATE OF THE
WORLD
1998

Other Norton/Worldwatch Books
Lester R. Brown et al.

State of the World 1984

State of the World 1985

State of the World 1986

State of the World 1987

State of the World 1988

State of the World 1989

State of the World 1990

State of the World 1991

State of the World 1992

State of the World 1993

State of the World 1994

State of the World 1995

State of the World 1996

State of the World 1997

Vital Signs 1992

Vital Signs 1993

Vital Signs 1994

Vital Signs 1995

Vital Signs 1996

Vital Signs 1997

ENVIRONMENTAL ALERT SERIES

Lester R. Brown et al.
Saving the Planet

Alan Thein During
How Much is Enough?

Sandra Postel
Last Oasis

Lester R. Brown
Hal Kane
Full House

Christopher Flavin
Nicholas Lenssen
Power Surge

Lester R. Brown
Who Will Feed China?

Lester R. Brown
Tough Choices

Michael Renner
Fighting for Survival

STATE OF THE WORLD

1998

A Worldwatch Institute Report on Progress Toward a Sustainable Society

PROJECT DIRECTOR
Lester R. Brown

ASSOCIATE PROJECT
DIRECTORS
Christopher Flavin
Hilary F. French

EDITOR
Linda Starke

CONTRIBUTING RESEARCHERS
Janet N. Abramovitz
Chris Bright
Lester R. Brown
Seth Dunn
Christopher Flavin
Hilary F. French
Gary Gardner
Anne Platt McGinn
Jennifer Mitchell
Michael Renner
John Tuxill

W·W·NORTON & COMPANY
NEW YORK   LONDON

Copyright © 1998 by Worldwatch Institute

All rights reserved.

Printed in the United States of America.

The STATE OF THE WORLD and WORLDWATCH INSTITUTE trademarks are registered in the U.S. Patent and Trademark Office.

The views expressed are those of the authors and do not necessarily represent those of the Worldwatch Institute; of its directors, officers, or staff; or of its funders.

The text of this book is composed in ITC New Baskerville, with the display set in Caslon. Composition by Worldwatch Institute; manufacturing by the Haddon Craftsmen, Inc.

First Edition

ISBN 0-393-04565-X
ISBN 0-393-31727-7 (pbk)

W. W. Norton & Company, Inc., 500 Fifth Avenue, New York, N.Y. 10110
http://www.wwnorton.com

W. W. Norton & Company Ltd., 10 Coptic Street, London WC1A IPU

1 2 3 4 5 6 7 8 9 0

This book is printed on recycled paper.

Acknowledgments

The production of *State of the World* every year is a team effort. And the team includes numerous individuals whose names do not appear on the cover. We take the opportunity here to extend our sincere thanks to all the committed, hard-working people within and outside the Institute who have made this volume possible.

Worldwatch staff researchers play a key role in producing the book. Among other things, they gather and analyze data, track down obscure numbers and citations, and review draft manuscripts with a critical eye. Jennifer Mitchell not only coauthored Chapter 10, she also helped with the research for Chapters 1 and 5. Ashley Mattoon and Payal Sampat joined the staff at midyear, and were quickly immersed in *State of the World* research. Ashley applied her biology training to work on Chapter 2, and Payal brought her background in international development to bear on Chapter 9. In addition, Molly O'Meara cheerfully helped *State of the World* researchers with last-minute details while writing a feature article for *World Watch* magazine.

Work on a forthcoming Worldwatch Environmental Alert Series book prevented Senior Researcher David Roodman from contributing a chapter this year, but he made up for it by his vigorous participation in our annual staff review meeting, which helped strengthen many of the chapters. Senior Fellow Sandra Postel, now working on water issues from Amherst, Massachusetts, contributed her experience and expertise by reviewing several chapters, while former Senior Researcher John Young also reviewed much of the manuscript.

Worldwatch interns also provide invaluable research help at the Institute. This year, Candace Chandra helped with the research on Chapter 2, Sophie Chou and Michael Strauss assisted with Chapter 4, Yasmin Daikh and Giovanna Dore with Chapter 6, Daniel Schwartz with Chapter 8, and Yumi Katagiri with Chapter 9. Matthew St. Clair and Brian Halweil joined us late in the year, in time for Brian to help with the proofing of galleys. We thank all of them for their assistance and their esprit de corps.

The job of managing the flow of information into the Institute that underpins the analysis in *State of the World* falls to Research Librarian Lori Brown and Library Assistant Laura Malinowksi. In addition, Lori prepares the Worldwatch Database Disk, which includes all the quantitative information included in this year's book, and manages our Web site.

Once the book is in draft, we face the challenge of turning our often-rough initial efforts into smooth, concise prose. For editing the book and managing this unwieldy process, we were fortunate once again this year to be able to turn to the only editor *State of the World* has ever had, Linda Starke. Linda also edits *Vital Signs*, our other annual report, and the Worldwatch Environmental Alert books. To keep things interesting for her, we did the layout for *State of the World* in-house for the first time this year. Thanks for this go to Designer Elizabeth Doherty, who managed to remain unflappable while simultaneously producing *State of the World* and the January-February issue of *World Watch* magazine. Once Liz finished with the book and Ritch Pope of Dexter, Oregon, indexed it, the manuscript was placed in the trusty hands of Iva Ashner, Nomi Victor, and Andrew Marasia at W.W. Norton & Company, who have managed in recent years to have *State of the World* off the presses in less than two months.

Even before the completed book is sent to Norton, the Worldwatch Communications Department is busy planning our outreach efforts, to ensure that *State of the World's* message is disseminated as widely as possible around the globe. This undertaking is spearheaded by Director of Communication Jim Perry, in cooperation with Deputy Director Denise Byers-Thomma, Press Officer Mary Caron, and Administrative Assistant Amy Warehime.

Also key to *State of the World's* worldwide reach is Worldwatch's publications staff, who ensure that thousands of orders for the new book are filled as quickly as possible. Publications Sales Coordinator Millicent Johnson heads up this effort, while also ably serving as our in-house photographer. She is aided by Publications Assistant Joseph Gravely and Receptionist Sharon Lapier.

Once again this year, Reah Janise Kauffman was integral to the publication of *State of the World*. She plays many positions on the Worldwatch team, among them Corporate Secretary and Assistant to the President, while helping with fundraising and managing our computer system and our arrangements with foreign publishers. Major thanks are also due to Assistant Treasurer Barbara Fallin for keeping us all in line (not to mention managing the Institute's finances), and to

Administrative Assistant to the Vice Presidents for Research Suzanne Clift, for the numerous contributions she makes to keeping the research staff on track, including ensuring that day-to-day responsibilities are not neglected while authors scurry to complete their chapters.

While *State of the World* deadline pressures mount, *World Watch* magazine continues to roll off the presses. This is due largely to the determination and talent of our magazine staff: Editor and Editorial Director Ed Ayres, Senior Editor Chris Bright, and Assistant Editor Curtis Runyan. We are also grateful to independent editor Jane Peterson for keeping Worldwatch Papers flowing to the printer throughout the year.

Outside the Institute, numerous individuals made important contributions to *State of the World*. We thank the following for either reviewing drafts or helping us to obtain data: Josefina Mena Abraham, Dean Anderson, Peter Auster, Phyllis Bennis, Dirk Bryant, Michelle Chan-Fishel, Sidonie Chiapetta, Ben DeAngelo, Dominick DellaSala, Laurie Drinkwater, Nigel Dudley, Masataka Fujita, Robert Goodland, Michael Grubb, Don Hinrichsen, Nels Johnson, Michael Klare, Florentin Krause, Dan MacMeekin, Gerhard Magreiter, William Mankin, William H. Mansfield III, Jeffrey McNeely, Carmini Luther Michelitsch, Sascha Muller-Kraenner, Norman Myers, Laura Orlando, Scott Paul, Maurizio Perotti, Richard Pollnac, Gareth Porter, Mark Ritchie, Julie Velasquez Runk, Frances Seymour, David Wedin, and Ray Weil.

We are also indebted to those who support the Institute financially, thus making *State of the World* possible. The Curtis and Edith Munson Foundation supported the research on fisheries that led to Chapter 4. Other private foundations that fund our work include the Nathan Cummings, Geraldine R. Dodge, Ford, W. Alton Jones, William and Flora Hewlett, John D.

and Catherine T. MacArthur, Charles Stewart Mott, Rasmussen, Summit, Surdna, Turner, Wallace Genetic, Winslow, and Weeden Foundations. Other funders include The Pew Charitable Trusts, the Rockefeller Brothers Fund, Rockefeller Financial Services, the United Nations Population Fund, and the Wallace Global Fund.

This year we would also like to gratefully acknowledge the help of our Council of Sponsors, a newly established group of individuals who provide $50,000 per year in support of the Institute's work. The charter members of this group include Toshishige Kurosawa (Ikari Institute for Environmental Culture), Kazuhiko Nishi (ASCII), Roger and Vicki Sant, and Robert Wallace.

Lester R. Brown, Christopher Flavin,
and Hilary F. French

Contents

Acknowledgments   vii

List of Tables and Figures   xiii

Foreword   xvii

1 **The Future of Growth,** *by Lester R. Brown*   3

ECONOMY OUTGROWING ECOSYSTEMS
MORE SYSTEMS STARTING TO COLLAPSE
LEARNING FROM CHINA
FOOD SCARCITY: THE WAKE-UP CALL
A LEGACY OF TOUGH CHOICES

2 **Sustaining the World's Forests,** *by Janet N. Abramovitz*   21

TRENDS IN FOREST AREA AND QUALITY
RISING PRESSURES ON FORESTS
THE IMPACT OF NATIONAL POLICIES
SUSTAINABLE FOREST MANAGEMENT
FORGING A NEW RELATIONSHIP WITH
   FORESTS

3 **Losing Strands in the Web of Life,** *by John Tuxill and Chris Bright*   41

BIRDS: THE CLEAREST OF ALL
   INDICATORS
MAMMALS: A DARKER PICTURE
REPTILES AND AMPHIBIANS: THE
   HIDDEN FAUNA
FISH: THE DARKEST PICTURE OF ALL
HALTING THE DECLINES

4 **Promoting Sustainable Fisheries,** *by Anne Platt McGinn*   59

EXTENT OF THE MARINE BIOLOGICAL
   CRISIS
THE IMPACT OF FISHING GEAR
HOW OVERCAPACITY DRIVES
   OVERFISHING
SOCIAL AND ECONOMIC RIPPLE
   EFFECTS
MANAGING THE FISHERS
SETTING A NEW COURSE

5 **Struggling to Raise Cropland Productivity,** *by Lester R. Brown*   79

ONLY TWO OPTIONS
SOURCES OF HIGHER PRODUCTIVITY
RAISING GRAIN YIELDS
FACING BIOLOGICAL REALITY
THE EMERGING POLITICS OF
   SCARCITY

6 **Recycling Organic Wastes,** *by Gary Gardner*   96

ORGANIC MATERIAL FLOWS
THE COST OF BREAKING THE
   LOOP
COMPOSTING URBAN GARBAGE
REROUTING HUMAN WASTE
RESCALING MANURE PRODUCTION
RETURNING TO OUR ORGANIC
   ROOTS

7 **Responding to the Threat of Climate Change,** *by Christopher Flavin and Seth Dunn* 113

UP THE EMISSIONS MOUNTAIN—AND
DOWN AGAIN?
FINDING THE RIGHT PRICE FOR
CARBON
BOOSTING EFFICIENCY
SUPPORTING NEW ENERGY SUPPLIES
THE CHALLENGE OF KYOTO

8 **Curbing the Proliferation of Small Arms,** *by Michael Renner* 131

WARS AND PRIVATIZED VIOLENCE
LIKE BUYING FISH IN THE MARKET
FEEDING THE HABIT
TAKING WEAPONS OUT OF
CIRCULATION
REGISTERS, CODES, AND CONTROLS

9 **Assessing Private Capital Flows to Developing Countries,** *by Hilary F. French* 149

FOLLOWING THE MONEY
NATURAL WEALTH
MANUFACTURING ABROAD
THE INFRASTRUCTURE BOOM
THE POWER OF THE PURSE
THE RULES OF THE GAME

10 **Building a New Economy,** *by Lester R. Brown and Jennifer Mitchell* 168

A NEW ECONOMY
STABILIZING POPULATION
STABILIZING CLIMATE
STEERING WITH TAX POLICY
CROSSING POLITICAL THRESHOLDS

Notes   189
Index   245

Worldwatch Database Disk

The data from all graphs and tables contained in this book, as well as from those in all other Worldwatch publications of the past two years, are available on disk for use with IBM-compatible or Macintosh computers. This includes data from the State of the World *and* Vital Signs *series of books, Worldwatch Papers,* World Watch *magazine, and the Environmental Alert series of books. The data are formatted for use with spreadsheet software compatible with Lotus 1-2-3 version 2, including all Lotus spreadsheets, Quattro Pro, Excel, SuperCalc, and many others. For IBM-compatibles, a 3 1/2 inch (high-density) disk is provided. Information on how to order the Worldwatch Database Disk can be found at the back of this book.*

List of Tables and Figures

LIST OF TABLES

Chapter 2. Sustaining the World's Forests

2–1   Principles and Criteria for Forest Stewardship   34

Chapter 3. Losing Strands in the Web of Life

3–1   Conservation Status of Birds, 1996   43
3–2   Conservation Status of Mammals, 1996   47
3–3   Conservation Status of Reptiles Surveyed, 1996   50
3–4   Conservation Status of Amphibians Surveyed, 1996   51
3–5   Conservation Status of Fish Surveyed, 1996   52

Chapter 4. Promoting Sustainable Fisheries

4–1   Size of World's Fishing Fleet, by Region, 1970 and 1992   68
4–2   Value of Imports and Exports, Top 10 Countries, 1995   71
4–3   Selected Marine Protected Areas and National Legislation   76–77

Chapter 5. Struggling to Raise Cropland Productivity

5–1   Annual Wheat Yield Per Hectare in Key Producing Countries, 1994–96   85
5–2   Annual Rice Yield Per Hectare in Key Producing Countries, 1994–96   86
5–3   Annual Corn Yield Per Hectare in Key Producing Countries, 1994–96   87
5–4   Annual Change in World Grain Yields by Decade, 1950–95   89

Chapter 6. Recycling Organic Wastes

6–1   Domestic Consumption of Domestically Grown Grain Nutrients by Humans and Animals, by Continent, Mid-1990s   98
6–2   Grain Exports from Seven Largest Exporters, 1995   98
6–3   Nutrients in Organic Municipal Solid Waste Compared with Nutrients in Fertilizer, Selected Countries, Early 1990s   103
6–4   Nutrients in Human Waste Compared with Nutrients in Fertilizer, Selected Countries, Mid-1990s   105
6–5   United States: Concentration of Livestock Production, Mid-1990s   110

Chapter 7. Responding to the Threat of Climate Change

7–1   Fossil Fuel Subsidies in Selected Developing Countries and Countries in Transition, 1990–96   118
7–2   Carbon/Energy Taxes, Industrial Countries, 1997   119
7–3   Industry Covenants, Selected Industrial Countries, 1997   122
7–4   Policies to Promote Renewable Energy, Selected Industrial Countries, 1997   125

Chapter 8. Curbing the Proliferation of Small Arms

8–1   Private Security and Public Police, Late 1980s, and Military Armed Forces, 1995, Selected Countries   135
8–2   Selected Examples of Commodities-for-Arms Transactions, 1980s and 1990s   141
8–3   Selected Examples of Gun Buy-Back Programs, 1990s   145

Chapter 9. Assessing Private Capital Flows to Developing Countries

9–1   International Private Capital Flows, Top 10 Developing-Country Recipients, 1995   151
9–2   Private Capital Flows to Developing Countries, 1996   152

Chapter 10. Building a New Economy

10–1   Sixteen Countries with Zero Population Growth, 1997   174
10–2   Tax Shifts from Work and Investment to Environmentally Damaging Activities   182

LIST OF FIGURES

Chapter 1. The Future of Growth

1–1   Grain Production in Saudi Arabia, 1960–97   6
1–2   Grain Area in Kazakhstan, 1960–97, With Projections to 2000   9
1–3   World Paper Production, 1950–94   10
1–4   Average Temperature at the Earth's Surface, 1866–1996   11
1–5   Grain Consumption in China and the United States, 1960–97   13
1–6   Grain Used for Feed in China, 1960–97   15
1–7   World Grain Carryover Stocks, as Days of Consumption, 1961–98   16

Chapter 2. Sustaining the World's Forests

2–1   Forest Area, by Region, 1996   22
2–2   Global Distribution of Population and of Paper and Paperboard Consumption, Selected Countries and Regions, 1994   25

Chapter 4. Promoting Sustainable Fisheries

4–1   World Fish Harvest, Fish Catch, and Aquaculture Production, 1950–96   60

Chapter 5. Struggling to Raise Cropland Productivity

5–1   Grain Area Per Person Worldwide, 1950–97, With Projections to 2030   81
5–2   Rice Yields for Japan, 1878–1997, and Wheat Yields for United States, 1866–1997   82
5–3   Wheat Yields in France, China, and United States, 1950–97   84
5–4   Rice Yields in Japan, China, and India, 1950–97   87
5–5   Corn Yields in United States, China, and Brazil, 1950–97   88
5–6   World Wheat Prices, 1950–96   92
5–7   U.S. Grain Yield Per Hectare, 1950–97   93

Chapter 6. Recycling Organic Wastes

6–1   Natural and Human Sources of Nitrogen Fixing   100

Chapter 7. Responding to the Threat of Climate Change

7–1   World Carbon Emissions from Fossil Fuel Burning, by Economic Region, 1950–96   114
7–2   Carbon Emissions Trends, Selected Industrial and Former Eastern Bloc Countries, 1990–96   115
7–3   Carbon Emissions Trends, Selected Developing Countries, 1990–96   116

Chapter 8. Curbing the Proliferation of Small Arms

8–1   Number of Armed Conflicts, 1946–95   133
8–2   Deaths in Armed Conflicts, by Five-year Period, 1946–95   134
8–3   U.S. Firearms Production, 1946–95   137

Chapter 9. Assessing Private Capital Flows to Developing Countries

9–1   International Capital Flows to Developing Countries, 1970–96   150

Chapter 10. Building a New Economy

10–1   Grain Production and Consumption in the European Union, 1961–97   170
10–2   World Beef and Poultry Production, 1950–97   173
10–3   Population of Pakistan and Bangladesh, 1950–97, With Projections to 2050   175
10–4   World Bicycle and Automobile Production, 1950–96   178
10–5   Sales of Compact Fluorescent Bulbs Worldwide, 1988–95   179
10–6   World Wind Energy Generating Capacity, 1980–97   179

Foreword

As we work to complete this fifteenth edition of *State of the World* in the autumn of 1997, we are confronted with new evidence of the urgency of the problems we write about—and of widespread failure to summon the political will needed to solve them. In recent months, a plume of smoke larger than the continental United States has spread across Southeast Asia, turning the skies dark and leaving at least 20 million people choking on air that has become a toxic soup, killing hundreds outright. The areas affected include Brunei, Indonesia, Malaysia, Papua New Guinea, the Philippines, Singapore, Thailand, and Viet Nam.

Residents of cities such as Bangkok and Kuala Lumpur have become accustomed to breathing the exhaust of millions of cars and motorbikes, but they were unprepared for the additional burden of the massive forest and peat fires that have swept Borneo and Sumatra this fall—sending life-threatening pollution to cities more than 1,000 kilometers away. People around the region have been reduced to wearing face masks, and many foreign embassies have sent diplomats and their families home. For the region's unique wildlife, the disaster is more profound and long-lasting: some of the world's most diverse tropical forests are going up in smoke, threatening the

Sumatran tiger, Malaysian tapir, proboscis monkey, and hundreds of less well known species.

The Southeast Asian fires are a powerful reminder of the interconnected dangers we face—threads of which are found virtually throughout *State of the World 1998*. One cause of the fires was El Niño—a recurring weather phenomenon that causes severe droughts as well as floods, and allows the annual burning practiced by many loggers and farmers to get out of control. But El Niño also reminds us of our growing vulnerability to climatic extremes. Unless we reduce our dependence on fossil fuels and accelerate reliance on new energy and transportation options, the climate will become more erratic over time, and all of the Earth's ecosystems will be threatened.

In their natural state, tropical forests do not usually burn, which provides strong evidence that the conflagrations of 1997 reflect deeper instabilities—including massive timber cutting and the expansion of agriculture and tree farms into areas once covered by natural forests. This year's book examines the state of the world's forests in detail for the first time in five years, and shows that deforestation in Southeast Asia is a global phenomenon. In fact, the record-setting forest fires in Brazil in 1997 were actually greater than those in Indonesia, but received less attention because they were in a more remote area; northern countries such as Canada and Russia are also failing to protect their remaining forests. Altogether, an estimated 16 million hectares of forest are now being cleared of trees each year, either by fire or chainsaw, equivalent to twice the entire land area of Nigeria.

Many of the deeper forces behind the Southeast Asian fires are discussed elsewhere in *State of the World 1998*. The growing demand for food, pulp, and other commodities of an increasingly affluent population of nearly 6 billion is putting more and more pressure on the land. According to one estimate, the demand for food alone will require an additional 90 million hectares by 2010—equivalent to half the area of Indonesia. Perhaps half of that could come from the world's already threatened forests.

The unprecedented ecological and health crisis that has enveloped Southeast Asia has received far less attention than the financial meltdown in the region that it coincided with. But economies will not be healthy for long unless the natural environments that underpin them remain healthy as well. This is a theme that has recurred annually in *State of the World*, but that figures particularly prominently in this year's book. Several chapters deal with the intricate links between forests, animal wildlife, other natural systems, and the human communities that depend on them. And in the last chapter, we explore what it would take to build an economy that does not rely on the one-time pollution of the atmosphere, clear-cutting of forests, and overpumping of aquifers. Such an economy is not only within reach, we believe, but in the end would be more economical—and productive—than the one that supports us today.

In this year's book, we also look closely at one aspect of that challenge: the growing pressure exerted by the $244 billion of private capital that flowed from industrial to developing countries in 1996. Much of that capital is being invested in natural-resource-based or heavily polluting industries, as poor countries strive to develop on the western model. One of the great challenges faced in the coming decades is to shift that flow of capital to more sustainable—and ultimately more productive—investments in areas such as renewable energy, regenerative agriculture, and closed-loop, zero-emission factories. This is a far more intricate challenge than that of changing the policies of national governments and international institutions, the traditional targets of environmental reformers.

The twentieth century has been extraordinarily successful for the human species—perhaps too successful. As our population has grown from 1 billion to 6 billion and the economy has exploded to more than 20 times its size in 1900, we have overwhelmed the natural systems from which we emerged and created the dangerous illusion that we no longer depend on a healthy environment. As a result, humanity now faces a challenge that rivals any in its history: restoring balance with nature while expanding economic opportunities for the billions of people whose basic needs—for food and clean water, for example—are still not being met.

In a 1997 review of a new biography of the author Rachel Carson, Robert Semple, editorial writer of the *New York Times*, noted that, "Carson's dismal scenario of a 'silent spring,' where robins and other birds would not appear, did not in fact come to pass. But one powerful reason that her predictions were wrong was that her diagnosis was right." In fact, society heeded her warning, enacting necessary reforms such as bans on the use of DDT, thus avoiding—at least so far—the silence she predicted.

As we go to press, representatives of

some 160 nations are about to gather in Kyoto for a historic effort to strengthen the Framework Convention on Climate Change, a signal achievement of the Earth Summit nearly six years ago. Although at this writing we do not yet know the outcome of that meeting—and its ultimate success cannot be known for years—its significance is clear. Unless humanity stabilizes the global atmosphere that we have been steadily altering for more than a century, virtually every ecosystem on Earth will be at risk. By focusing on the magnitude of this threat—and on the means for addressing it—we hope to have played a small role in spurring governments to action.

Anniversaries are a time for taking stock, as well as for looking ahead. When we launched the first *State of the World* report 15 years ago, we had high hopes for its impact, but did not anticipate that it would become semiofficial, widely used by government officials, U.N. agencies, corporate planners, educators, and environmental activists around the world. Similarly, while we hoped publishers in other languages would be interested in *State of the World*, never in our fondest dreams did we anticipate that it would one day appear in some 30 languages. We hoped that it would one day be published at least in the major languages, such as French and Chinese, but we did not anticipate that it would also appear in Persian and Thai. And this past year, we launched a second Chinese edition, this one in Taiwan, thanks to the efforts of Carolyn Hansen of Earthplace.

We had hoped that *State of the World* would sell well. We did not anticipate that one day the first printing in the United States would be 100,000 copies. Nor did we expect that we would be on the best seller list in Finland and Argentina. We thought that *State of the World* might be useful to policymakers, but did not antici-

pate that it would be used by college and university courses worldwide, including 795 in the United States alone in 1997.

Changes have also occurred over the past decade and a half in how *State of the World* is produced. In the early years, we sent W.W. Norton, our U.S. publisher, a paper copy of the manuscript, which they then set in type. Page proofs came back to us for review, revisions, and update. Then for some years we sent an electronic disk with the final copy to Norton for publishing and to our foreign publishers for translation. Now, we produce camera-ready copy of the entire book, including figures and tables, in-house, and send it on a disk to Norton. We also e-mail final electronic copy directly to many of our more than 20 publishers in other languages, enabling some of them to get *State of the World* into bookstores within a few weeks of the U.S. edition, which appears in early January.

Next year, *State of the World 1999* will be our millennial edition. We will release it in 1999 so that it can serve as a source of long-term environmental thinking for the millions of readers and hundreds of publishers who will be anticipating the coming of a new millennium. If you have any comments or suggestions for this special edition, please let us know by letter, fax (202-296-7365), or e-mail (<worldwatch@ worldwatch.org>). We also hope you will visit our Web site at <http://www.world watch.org>.

Lester R. Brown
Christopher Flavin
Hilary French

Worldwatch Institute
1776 Massachusetts Ave., NW
Washington, DC 20036

December 1997

STATE OF THE
WORLD
1998

1

The Future of Growth

Lester R. Brown

In its spring 1997 semiannual economic assessment, the International Monetary Fund (IMF) projected the global economy would grow 4.4 percent in 1997, the fastest in a decade. Further, it forecast that the rapid expansion would continue in 1998. There were few signs of trouble: inflation was low, budget deficits were shrinking in the leading economies, and international trade and capital flows were expanding. The report was, as the *Financial Times* observed, "one of the most glowing accounts of global economic prospects in decades."[1]

The appraisal came near the end of a remarkable half-century, one that witnessed unprecedented global economic growth. The global output of goods and services grew from just under $5 trillion in 1950 to more than $29 trillion in 1997, an expansion of nearly sixfold. From 1990 to 1997, it grew by $5 trillion—matching the growth from the beginning of civilization

to 1950. This brought widespread economic and social progress. Worldwide, life expectancy climbed from 47 years in 1950 to 64 years in 1995. Literacy levels rose on every continent. Throughout much of this period, diets were improving.[2]

Even with the financial turmoil in Southeast Asia, the IMF's fall 1997 assessment still estimated that the global economy would expand 4 percent in 1997. Occasional disruptions notwithstanding, the IMF report seemed to imply that such growth could continue indefinitely. But can it? Can China, the world's fastest-growing economy during the 1990s, achieve U.S. consumption levels? Can people everywhere expect to one day live like Americans?[3]

As the economy grows, pressures on the Earth's natural systems and resources intensify. From 1950 to 1997, the use of lumber tripled, that of paper increased sixfold, the fish catch increased nearly fivefold, grain consumption nearly tripled, fossil fuel burning nearly quadrupled, and air and water pollutants multi-

---

Units of measure throughout this book are metric unless common usage dictates otherwise.

plied severalfold. The unfortunate reality is that the economy continues to expand, but the ecosystem on which it depends does not, creating an increasingly stressed relationship.[4]

While economic indicators such as investment, production, and trade are consistently positive, the key environmental indicators are increasingly negative. Forests are shrinking, water tables are falling, soils are eroding, wetlands are disappearing, fisheries are collapsing, rangelands are deteriorating, rivers are running dry, temperatures are rising, coral reefs are dying, and plant and animal species are disappearing. The global economy as now structured cannot continue to expand much longer if the ecosystem on which it depends continues to deteriorate at the current rate.

The ideology of growth has permeated every corner of the globe.

"Growth for the sake of growth," notes environmental writer Edward Abbey, "is the ideology of the cancer cell." Just as a continuously growing cancer eventually destroys its life-support systems by destroying its host, a continuously expanding global economy is slowly destroying its host—the Earth's ecosystem.[5]

The ideology of growth knows no geographic boundaries. It has permeated every corner of the planet. Political leaders in developing countries often denounce the high levels of consumption in industrial countries, but none have talked about eventual limits on their own consumption as they modernize. No national political leader of an industrial country, no matter how affluent, has announced plans to stabilize demands on the Earth's ecosystem once people's basic needs for food, shelter, and health care

are satisfied. The challenge facing the entire world is to design an economy that can satisfy the basic needs of people everywhere without self-destructing. (See Chapter 10.) The enormity of this task is matched only by its urgency.

ECONOMY OUTGROWING ECOSYSTEMS

While economists may be oblivious to the relationship between the global economy and the Earth's ecosystem, environmental scientists are not. For them, evidence of mounting stresses can be seen on every hand as more and more sustainable yield thresholds are crossed and as waste absorptive capacities are overwhelmed.

Once the sustainable yield threshold of a natural system is crossed, growth in consumption can continue only by consuming the resource base itself. When the amount of fish caught surpasses the sustainable yield of a fishery, for instance, fish stocks begin to shrink. If fishing continues, the fishery eventually collapses. It may or may not recover. A similar situation exists with forests. Once the demand for forest products exceeds the sustainable yield of the forest, it begins to shrink. As the excess of demand over sustainable yield widens, deforestation accelerates. Within scarcely a generation, countries like Mauritania, Ethiopia, and Haiti have been almost entirely deforested, largely by the local demand for firewood.[6]

When rising consumption crosses these thresholds, several changes are set in motion. If, for example, the growing consumption of water exceeds the sustainable yield of an aquifer, the water table begins to fall. If the demand for water continues to grow, the gap between it and the sustainable yield of the aquifer widens and the fall of the water table accelerates. When the aquifer is depleted, the rate of pumping automatically falls to the rate of recharge. If an aquifer is being pumped at, say, double the recharge rate when it is finally depleted, then the pumping rate is cut in half. Wherever water tables are falling, cutbacks in pumping lie ahead. Exactly when these cuts will come or how precipitous they will be depends on the particular situation. But the story is the same in one ecosystem after another: fishery collapses, deforestation, and aquifer depletion are now beginning to affect global economic prospects.

Marine biologists at the U.N. Food and Agriculture Organization who monitor oceanic fisheries report that nearly all fisheries are now being fished at or beyond capacity. After increasing from 18 million tons in 1950 to nearly 90 million tons in 1990, the oceanic catch has fluctuated around the same level during the last seven years, showing little sign of increase or decrease.[7]

The generation born before mid-century enjoyed a doubling of seafood catch from 8 kilograms per person in 1950 to 17 kilograms in 1990. If the warning advice of marine biologists some 20 years ago that the oceans could not likely sustain a catch of more than 100 million tons had been heeded, and if world population had been stabilized, consumption could remain at 17 kilograms. Unfortunately, however, while the last generation benefited from a steady growth in the seafood catch per person, the next can expect a steady decline and a rise in seafood prices that will likely last until world population growth comes to a halt.[8]

If we have "hit the wall" in oceanic fisheries, future growth in fish supplies can only come from fish farming. But once fish are put in ponds or cages, they have to be fed. Fish ponds are, in effect, marine feedlots, competing with humans and producers of poultry, pork, and beef for grain.

As long as there were more fish in the oceans than we could hope to catch, managing oceanic fisheries was a simple matter. But with some fisheries already collapsing, such as the Canadian cod fishery off the coast of Newfoundland, the sturgeon fishery in the Caspian Sea, and the U.S. West Coast salmon fishery, and with other fisheries facing imminent collapse, the management challenge of allocating the catch among competing nations and protein-hungry populations is infinitely more difficult. (See Chapter 4.) Sustaining even the 90-million-ton catch annual average of the 1990s will require unprecedented levels of cooperation.

Even among countries accustomed to working together, such as the members of the European Union (EU), the challenge of negotiating catch limits at sustainable levels can be difficult. But in April 1997, after prolonged negotiations, agreement was announced in Brussels to reduce the fishing capacity of EU fleets by 30 percent for endangered species, such as cod, herring, and sole in the North Sea, and 20 percent for overfished stocks, such as cod in the Baltic Sea, the bluefin tuna, and swordfish off the Iberian peninsula. The good news is that the EU finally reached agreement on reducing the catch. The bad news is that these cuts, even if successfully implemented, may not be sufficient to arrest the decline of the region's fisheries.[9]

Perhaps one of the most underrated issues facing the world as it enters the third millennium is spreading water scarcity. As water use has tripled since mid-century, it has led to massive overpumping. Water tables are falling on every continent—in the southern Great Plains and the southwestern United States, in southern Europe, in North Africa, in the Middle East, in Central Asia, in southern Africa, on the Indian subcontinent, and in central and northern China. A matter of growing concern for many governments, water scarcity is often considered separately from food scarcity. But 70 percent of all the water pumped from underground or drawn from rivers is used for irrigation, so if we face a future of water scarcity, we also face a future of food scarcity.[10]

Much of the growth in irrigation in the southern Great Plains of the United States since mid-century has relied on wells drilled into the vast Ogallala aquifer, which stretches from Nebraska south through the Texas panhandle. Unfortunately, this is essentially a fossil aquifer— a body of underground water deposited during a previous geological era, with limited recharge. The Ogallala is deeper in the northern end, whereas in the southern end it is quite shallow. The pumping of the last few decades has depleted the aquifer in some of its southern reaches, forcing cutbacks in irrigation. Even with an impressive effort to boost irrigation efficiency, Texas lost 11 percent of its irrigated area between 1982 and 1992. Irrigated area is also shrinking in Oklahoma, Kansas, and Colorado. The large green circles of irrigated crops formed by center-pivot irrigation systems that are visible from airplanes over the region are starting to diminish in number.[11]

Another country that turned to the wholesale use of fossil water is Saudi Arabia, home to nearly 20 million people. After the oil embargo of the 1970s, the Saudis realized they would be vulnerable to a grain embargo and so decided to subsidize grain production in order to become self-sufficient in the production of wheat and barley, their leading food and feedgrains. In 1980, grain production totaled 260,000 tons. But after increasing every year for the next 14 years in response to a government procurement price for wheat of $24 a bushel—easily six times the world market price—grain production reached nearly 5 million tons in 1994, roughly a 20-fold increase.[12]

At this point, the aquifer was nearly depleted, underlining the futility of subsidies. In response, subsidies were cut as irrigation pumping fell precipitously.

Within two years, production dropped by more than half, and the country turned to imports to satisfy the needs of its fast-growing population. (See Figure 1–1.) Although few cutbacks in irrigation from overpumping are likely to be as abrupt as this one, the Saudi experience does give a sense of the declines in irrigation and agricultural production that lie ahead where aquifers are being depleted.[13]

Irrigation cutbacks from overpumping aquifers will have the greatest effect on food production in China and India, which rank first and third in world grain production (the United States is second), and which rely on irrigation for most of their food. A water assessment by the National Environmental Engineering Research Institute, one of India's premier research organizations, reports that "in every state and in every city, exploitation of below-surface water has been extensive and reckless, with no regard for what is sustainable and without any plans for replenishment. And it is getting worse at an increasing rate." Groundwater levels are declining in much of the country as some 6 million pumps lift water for irrigation. Among the states incurring huge water deficits from overpumping are

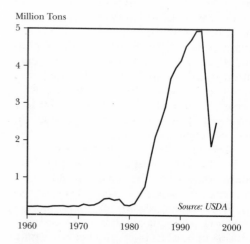

Figure 1–1. Grain Production in Saudi Arabia, 1960–97

Gujurat, Haryana, Karnataka, Maharashtra, the Punjab, and Rajasthan. In the Punjab, India's breadbasket, the water table in much of the state is falling roughly two thirds of a meter per year.[14]

China's problems are equally serious. A 1996 study from Beijing indicates that water tables are falling virtually everywhere that the land is flat as pumps pull water from underground aquifers for agricultural, industrial, and residential uses. They are falling fast in the densely populated provinces of central and northern China. In much of centrally located Hebei Province, the water level is dropping by one meter per year. In Shandong Province, which produces one fifth of China's wheat and one seventh of its corn and which relies on underground sources for half its irrigation water, a third of the wells in the province were not pumping during a severe drought in mid-1997, apparently because of aquifer depletion. In an area of north central China inhabited by roughly 100 million people, the water table has fallen some 30–35 meters over the last two or three decades. For a country that gets most of the food for its 1.2 billion people from irrigated land, the prospective cutbacks in irrigation are a matter of deep concern.[15]

As countries begin to press against the limits of their water supplies, the competition between the countryside and cities intensifies. In this battle, the cities almost always win, diverting water from irrigation to higher-priority industrial and residential uses. As water is taken from agriculture, grain imports typically rise. To import one ton of grain is to import 1,000 tons of water. Indeed, for countries facing water deficits, the most efficient way to import water is to import grain, leaving the available water to satisfy residential and industrial needs.[16]

As a result, water scarcity is beginning to shape international grain trade patterns, much as land scarcity has historically. North Africa and the Middle East, the region stretching from Morocco to Iran, is now the world's fastest-growing grain import market, growing faster even than East Asia. Egypt and Iran, each importing more than 7 million tons of wheat in 1997, led the world in imports of this traditional food staple. The region's incendiary combination of rapidly growing populations, incomes boosted by oil wealth, and irrigation water shortages is driving grain imports upward at a record pace. The water required to produce the grain and other farm commodities imported into the region each year already equals the annual flow of the Nile.[17]

In many countries, water diversion from rivers has now reached the point where some of them no longer make it to the sea. The Colorado, the major river in southwestern United States, is now drained dry to irrigate cropland and to satisfy industrial and residential needs in Colorado, California, and Arizona, rarely ever reaching the Gulf of California, the point at which it used to enter the sea. And the Huang He (Yellow River) in China, which flows through eight provinces, has run dry for part of each of the last eight years. As the provinces upstream divert more and more water for industrial and residential uses, the dry period grows longer. For several weeks in 1996, the river ran dry before reaching Shandong Province, the last one it flows through en route to the sea. In 1997, it went dry a week earlier than the preceding year. Unfortunately, the farmers in Shandong Province depend on the Huang He directly for half of their irrigation water and indirectly for underground water as it helps recharge the province's aquifers.[18]

A somewhat similar situation exists with the Ganges River in the Indian subcontinent. Originating in the Himalayas and providing much of the irrigation water in northeastern India, it has little left when it reaches Bangladesh. This has created serious problems for the

Bangladeshis, who desperately need irrigation water and who are faced with the incursion of sea water as the river's freshwater flow diminishes. And from the Nile River, with Sudan and Egypt using nearly all its water, only a small amount of recycled irrigation water is left to flow into the Mediterranean. If Ethiopia, which controls part of the head waters of the Nile, decides to develop irrigation to feed its swelling population—59 million people growing at 3 percent a year—Egypt, which already imports 40 percent of the wheat for its 65 million people, will face cutbacks in irrigation.[19]

Rivers running dry signal not only water scarcity, but also ecological disruption. Rivers that no longer reach the sea obviously cannot be used by freshwater-spawning oceanic species, such as salmon. In the grand scheme of the Earth's ecosystem, oceans and continents have a symbiotic relationship, with the oceans watering the continents and the continents nourishing the oceans. The water that is carried overland by clouds fed with evaporation from the oceans falls on the land and then carries nutrients with it as it flows back to the sea. This steady flow of nutrients nourishes the oceanic food chain that supports fisheries. Thus, rivers running dry not only deprive key species of spawning opportunities, they also rob fisheries of nutrients.

Rangelands, too, are being denuded, by overgrazing. The vast rangelands that are used to support herds of cattle and flocks of sheep and goats are not suitable for farming. Roughly double the area of world cropland, this land supports 1.32 billion cattle and 1.72 billion sheep and goats. With growth of these herds and flocks tracking the growth in human populations, the growing demand for meat, milk, leather, and other livestock products has led to extensive overgrazing. As Africa's population has grown by leaps and bounds, so have its livestock numbers.[20]

Some of the most severe overstocking of rangelands comes in areas where people depend on cattle, sheep, and goats for their livelihoods, including much of Africa, the Middle East, Central Asia, the Indian subcontinent, and much of western and northern China. For example, Iran, with more than 8 million cattle and a staggering 77 million sheep and goats—the source of the wool for its fabled rug-making industry and most of its meat—is faced with a steady deterioration of rangeland because of overstocking. With rangelands now being pushed to their limits and beyond, future growth in the supply of beef and mutton can only come from feedlots, which in turn puts additional pressure on the world's cropland.[21]

As the consumption of grain and other agricultural products has tripled since mid-century, farmers have extended agriculture onto marginal lands, some of it in areas where rainfall is low and soils are vulnerable to wind erosion. Nowhere is this more visible than in Kazakhstan. Originally part of the Soviet virgin lands expansion in the mid-1950s, much of the wheatland of semiarid Kazakhstan has eroded to the point where it can no longer support cropping. After peaking at nearly 26 million hectares around 1980, the area sown to grain, mostly wheat, dropped to 16 million hectares in 1997. (See Figure 1–2.) Scientists at the Institute for Soil Management in Alma Alta believe that grain cultivation is sustainable on only 13 million hectares, roughly half the area sown in 1980.[22]

Once producing and exporting nearly as much grain as Australia, Kazakhstan may soon be struggling to feed itself. Just as Saudi Arabia overextended its grain production, based on the unsustainable use of water, so Kazakhstan overextended its production based on the unsustainable use of land. These are but two among the scores of countries with part of their agricultural production based on the unsustainable use of land, water, or both.

The thin mantle of topsoil that supports plant life accumulated over long

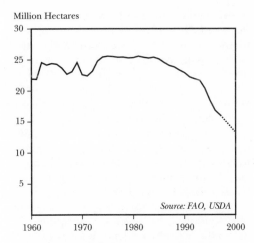

Million Hectares

Source: FAO, USDA

Figure 1–2. Grain Area in Kazakhstan, 1960–97, With Projections to 2000

stretches of geological time as evolving plant vegetation held soil in place, protecting it from erosion. Throughout most of the Earth's history, soil formation exceeded soil erosion. Now a combination of overplowing, overgrazing, and deforestation has reversed that relationship. In effect, another threshold has been crossed. With soil erosion exceeding soil formation in many areas, parts of the Earth are slowly being drained of their inherent fertility.

In Africa, a continent where soils are shallow to begin with, soil losses can disproportionately shrink the grain harvest. Its rapid population growth and rapid soil erosion (perhaps the fastest of any continent) are on a collision course. Rattan Lal, an internationally noted agronomist at Ohio State University's School of Natural Resources, has made the first estimate of yield losses due to soil erosion for the continent. Although the data are incomplete, he concludes that the excessive erosion of recent decades reduced Africa's 1989 grain harvest by 8.2 million tons, or roughly 8 percent. Further, he expects the loss to climb to 16.5 million tons by 2020 if soil erosion continues unabated.[23]

Among the countries in Africa suffering heavy soil losses are Botswana, Lesotho, Madagascar, Nigeria, Rwanda, and Zimbabwe. Nigeria, Africa's most populous country, is suffering from extreme gully erosion. Lal reports gullies 5–10 meters deep and 10–100 meters wide. Unfortunately, not one of these governments is addressing the soil erosion threat effectively. As a result, the next generation of farmers in Africa will try to feed not the 719 million people of today, but 1.45 billion in the year 2025—and with far less topsoil.[24]

MORE SYSTEMS STARTING TO COLLAPSE

The demand for forest products, like that of many other resources, has increased several times as the world economy has expanded. Since mid-century, lumber use has tripled, paper use has increased sixfold, and firewood use has soared as Third World populations have multiplied. (See also Chapter 2.) In West Africa, the economy of Côte d'Ivoire flourished in the 1960s and 1970s in large part because of timber exports, but since the timber was not harvested on a sustainable basis, export earnings from forest products have now plunged to nearly zero. Nigeria, once an exporter of tropical hardwoods, is now a net importer of forest products. In Southeast Asia, deforestation has converted the Philippines and Thailand into net importers of forest products. The timber companies that initially helped deforest much of Southeast Asia and West Africa are now shifting their attention to Latin America.[25]

The soaring demand for paper (see Figure 1–3) is contributing to deforestation, particularly in the northern temperate zone. Canada is losing some 200,000 hectares of forest a year. Siberia is losing

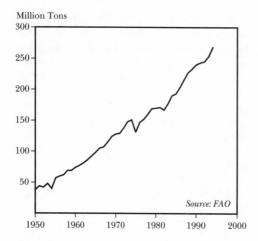

Million Tons

Figure 1–3. World Paper Production, 1950–94

Source: FAO

far more. At the same time, forests have receded from cities and towns in many parts of the Third World in response to the growing demand for firewood. In India, the demand for fuelwood is now six times the sustainable yield of its remaining forests, forcing the burning of cow dung and crop residues for cooking, thus depriving the soil of nutrients and organic matter. Satellite photographs of India show forests receding from virtually every city in the country. A similar phenomenon exists in many cities in Africa, particularly those in the Sahelian zone and in eastern and southern Africa, all semiarid regions.[26]

Over the last century, the world has lost close to half of its original forest area. As forest cover has shrunk, rainfall runoff has increased, contributing to flooding and soil erosion and reducing the amount that percolates downward to recharge aquifers. In effect, deforestation can exacerbate the aquifer depletion described earlier.[27]

As fossil fuel use has increased nearly fivefold since 1980, carbon emissions have far exceeded nature's capacity to fix carbon dioxide (CO_2). As a result, atmospheric concentrations of CO_2 have climbed to the highest level in 150,000 years. And as the computer models that

simulate the effects of rising concentrations of CO_2 and other greenhouse gases in the atmosphere have projected, temperatures are rising. The 13 warmest years since recordkeeping began in 1866 have occurred since 1979. (See Figure 1–4.) Within these 13, the four warmest years have occurred since 1990.[28]

Leaders in the insurance industry, perhaps the first major sector of the economy to be severely affected by climate change, are deeply concerned about the greenhouse effect. Hotter surface waters, particularly in the tropics and subtropics, release more heat into the atmosphere to drive storm systems. As a result, storms are more frequent, more intense, and more destructive. Worldwide, weather-related insurance claims have climbed from $17 billion during the 1980s to $66 billion thus far during the 1990s. One consequence of greater property damage from storms is higher insurance rates. In Florida, located in the heart of the U.S. hurricane belt, homeowner insurance premiums have climbed 72 percent since 1992.[29]

Unfortunately, the higher temperatures that threaten the liquidity of insurance companies may now be starting to affect food security as well, as record heat waves reduce harvests in major food-producing countries such as China, the Ukraine, and the United States. In July 1995, one such heat wave not only reduced the U.S. corn harvest, it claimed 465 lives in Chicago. Three of the last 10 U.S. grain harvests have been reduced by severe heat. If the trend of rising temperatures over the last 15 years continues, higher temperatures may soon lead to higher food prices.[30]

Another consequence of an expanding economy based on fossil fuels is worsening air pollution, especially in Third World cities, such as Bangkok, Beijing, and Mexico City—where the air literally is unfit to breathe. In Southeast Asia in the late summer and early fall of 1997, smoke from the burning of forests in Indonesia

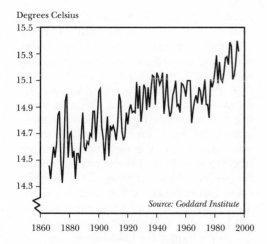

Degrees Celsius

Source: Goddard Institute

**Figure 1–4. Average Temperature at the
Earth's Surface, 1866–1996**

and Malaysia, combined with the on-going pollution from automobiles and industrial sources, closed airports because of a lack of visibility. Schools and businesses were shut down because of air pollution so severe that people were left physically sick. In India, the Tata Energy Research Institute estimated in 1997 that the combination of indoor and outdoor air pollution was causing 2.5 million premature deaths a year in that country. The industrial world is not exempt from this problem. In Washington, D.C., authorities issued several red-alert warnings during the summer of 1997, indicating the air was unhealthy; they urged even healthy individuals not to exercise and asked the elderly and infirm to stay in their homes.[31]

As our fossil-fuel-based global economy continues to expand, water pollution is now spiraling out of control in developing countries, where industrialization is proceeding at a record rate but without adequate controls. Nowhere is this more evident than in China, where water pollution is rendering part of the nation's water supply unfit even for irrigation, much less for direct human consumption. One survey showed that water in 11 percent of

China's 85,000 kilometers of rivers was classified as unsuitable for irrigation. In Shanxi Province, rice consumed in the provincial capital of Taiyuan contains excessive levels of the heavy metals lead and chromium. Its cabbage, a staple winter food in northern China, is described as "loaded with cadmium." At some point, the usable water supply is reduced not only by physical scarcity, but also by pollution so severe that it cannot be used even for irrigation or by industry.[32]

The expanding economy not only damages our life-support systems, it also threatens the very existence of other forms of life with which we share the planet. For example, of the nearly 10,000 species of birds on the planet, more than 1,000 are officially threatened with extinction. For mammals, where some 1,100 species out of 4,400 are threatened with extinction, the numbers are even more alarming. Among mammals, the 232 species of primates—our closest relatives—are most at risk, with the survival of nearly half of them in question. As our numbers go up, their numbers go down.[33]

The threat to fish may be the greatest of all, with one third of all species—freshwater and saltwater—now threatened with extinction. (See Chapter 3.) In North America, 37 percent of all freshwater species are either threatened or already extinct. In Europe, the figure is 42 percent. In South Africa, two thirds of the 94 fish species are expected to disappear in the absence of special efforts to protect them. In semiarid regions of Mexico, 68 percent of native and endemic species have disappeared. As various life forms disappear, they affect the entire ecosystem and particularly the basic services provided by nature, such as pollination, seed dispersal, insect control, and nutrient cycling. This loss of species is weakening the web of life, and if it continues, it could tear huge gaps in its fabric, leading to irreversible changes in the Earth's ecosystem.[34]

Although these symptoms of economies outgrowing ecosystems are numerous and highly visible, they do not seem to catch the attention of traditional economists. In a report released in September 1997, the World Bank projected that five developing countries—Brazil, China, India, Indonesia, and Russia— would become economic superpowers by 2020. In an upbeat economic forecast, the Bank projected that the Chinese economy would grow to more than five times its current size, that of India four times, Indonesia five times, and Brazil three times. Income rises of this magnitude among low-income consumers in these societies, along with population growth, could dramatically boost grain consumption and the use of climate-altering fossil fuels. What is not explained is what this means in, for example, China and India, where water tables are already falling in large areas. The Bank alludes to the possibility of scarcity-induced grain price rises, but dismisses that prospect as unrealistic. If the global economy is already overrunning its natural capacities, what happens as China, India, and other fast-developing countries strive to emulate the American lifestyle?[35]

LEARNING FROM CHINA

China is not only the world's most populous country, containing one fifth of humanity, but during the 1990s it has also been the fastest-growing economy. Since 1980, it has doubled in size every eight years. From 1992 through 1995, it registered double-digit economic growth rates each year—12 percent, 14 percent, 11 percent, and 10 percent. This streak ended in 1996 as growth dropped to 9 percent. Using purchasing power parity to measure output, China's 1995 gross national product of more than $3 trillion

exceeded Japan's $2.8 trillion and trailed only the U.S. output of $7.1 trillion. If the Chinese economy continues to double every eight years, it will likely overtake that of the United States by 2010.[36]

Because China is growing at such an extraordinary rate, it is in effect telescoping history, enabling us to better understand a future in which other developing countries reach the development levels likely to be achieved in the not-too-distant future in China. It provides a window on a future where other countries may also grow rapidly as they learn how to attract both foreign capital and technology. (See Chapter 9.) Like China, they can draw on an enormous backlog of available technology.

Many commentators often note that the United States, with only 5 percent of the world's people, consumes 40 percent or more of the world's resources. This was certainly true for a long period after World War II, but it no longer is. In the consumption of such basic items as grain, red meat, fertilizer, steel, and coal, China has already passed the United States and become the world leader.[37]

While it is not particularly surprising that China's total consumption of some basic resources has now overtaken that of the United States, given its population size, it is startling that it has surpassed the United States in consumption per person of some basic goods such as pork and eggs. Although China's grain use per person, both direct and indirect, is still only some 300 kilograms compared with roughly 800 kilograms in the United States, this is up from 200 kilograms in 1978. As a result, consumption of all grain in China now totals 380 million tons, compared with 245 million tons in the United States. (See Figure 1–5.) As incomes continue to rise in China, so too will grain consumption per person.[38]

Now that China has closed the pork gap, what if it closes the beef gap as well? If per capita consumption there, current-

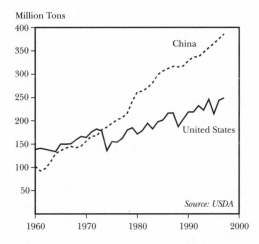

Million Tons

Source: USDA

Figure 1–5. Grain Consumption in China and the United States, 1960–97

ly only 4 kilograms per year, were to match that in the United States (45 kilograms), the Chinese would eat an additional 49 million tons of beef each year. Produced in feedlots, this would take some 343 million tons of grain, equal to the entire U.S. grain harvest. While there is obvious reason to doubt whether China will ever close this particular gap, its consumption of beef has already more than doubled during the 1990s. If the economy continues to expand rapidly, China's need for imported grain could quickly exceed the exportable supplies of the United States and other countries.[39]

In Japan, the other densely populated Asian country that has industrialized, the growth in the demand for animal protein that accompanied rising incomes historically was satisfied by eating fish. As population pressure built in Japan, the limited land available for cropping was used to produce rice, the food staple, while the country turned to the oceans for its animal protein. In 1996 Japan, with a population of just over 125 million people, consumed 10 million tons of seafood. If China's 1.2 billion were to consume at the same rate, they would eat 100 million tons

of seafood, slightly more than the entire oceanic fish catch.[40]

Three years ago, the Ministry of Heavy Industry in China decided that the automobile industry would be one of the five "pillar" industries (along with telecommunications, petrochemicals, machinery manufacture, and construction) that would be the engines of economic growth over the next few decades. Beijing invited major automobile manufacturers from abroad, such as Volkswagen, General Motors, and Toyota, to invest in automobile manufacturing in China. If China continues along this automobile-centered path, patterned after that of the western industrial economies and Japan, and if car ownership and oil consumption per person there reach U.S. levels, the country would need 80 million barrels of oil per day. In 1996, the world produced 64 million barrels per day.[41]

China is teaching us that the western industrial model is not viable, simply because there are not enough resources.

China is teaching us that the western industrial development model is not viable for China or for the world as a whole, simply because there are not enough resources. Global land and water resources are not sufficient to satisfy the growing grain needs in China if it continues along the current development path. Nor will the oil resources be available, simply because world oil production is not projected to rise much above current levels in the years ahead as some of the older fields are depleted, largely offsetting output from newly discovered fields. If carbon emissions per person in China ever reach the current U.S. level, this alone would roughly double global emissions, accelerating the rise in temperatures that now appears to be under way.[42]

Although consumption levels in China are still relatively modest, the country is already paying a high environmental price for its booming economy. Its heavy reliance on coal, for example, has led to some of the worst air pollution anywhere. As a result, respiratory disease has become endemic in China and deadly. In October 1996, the National Environmental Protection Agency of China reported a staggering 3 million deaths in cities during the preceding two years from "chronic bronchitis...as a result of urban air pollution." Visitors to Beijing in the winter complain about throat irritation and coughing within hours of arriving in the capital. Crop yields are suffering as well.[43]

Even with pollution controls, China faces a formidable challenge simply because of the density of its population. Although it has a total land area that is almost exactly the same as the United States, most of China's 1.2 billion people live in a 1,500-kilometer strip on the eastern and southern coasts. Most of the vast northwestern region of the country is uninhabited, simply because it is largely desert. For Americans to understand the density of population in China, it would be necessary to squeeze the entire U.S. population into the area east of the Mississippi and then multiply it by five. That would be comparable to the density in the inhabited region of China. Even the rather stringent U.S. pollution controls would lead to intolerable concentrations of air and water pollution.[44]

Interestingly, the relevance of the western industrial development model for China is being challenged from within. A group of prominent scientists, including many in the Chinese Academy of Sciences, have written a white paper questioning the government's decision to develop an automobile-centered transportation system. They point out that China does not have enough land both to feed its people and to provide the roads, highways, and parking lots needed to accommodate the automobile. They also note with concern the heavy dependence on imported oil that would be required and the potential air pollution and traffic congestion that would result if they strive for a car in every garage.[45]

If the western development model is not viable for China, then it is not viable for India's 960 million or for the other developing countries, home to another 2 billion people. And in an integrated, global economy, it will not be viable for western industrial countries themselves over the long term. China is demonstrating that the world cannot remain for long on the current economic path. It is underlining the urgency of restructuring the global economy, including the economies of the industrial world.

FOOD SCARCITY: THE WAKE-UP CALL

We know that the economy cannot continue to expand if the environmental support systems on which it depends continue to deteriorate. But how will these divergent trends be reconciled? What exactly will disrupt growth? No one knows for sure, but the most likely prospect appears to be food scarcity, since nearly all the trends of environmental deterioration cited earlier make it more difficult to expand the food supply rapidly.

Feeding 80 million more people each year means expanding the grain harvest by 26 million tons, or 71,000 tons a day. Not only is the world now adding 80 million people annually, but it is projected to add nearly this number for the next few decades, reaching 9.4 billion in 2050.[46]

Rising affluence is also expanding the demand for grain as consumers use additional income to diversify diets, moving away from heavy dependence on a starchy staple, such as rice, for most of their calories and consuming more meat, milk, and eggs. In some countries with particularly rapid economic growth, rising affluence is generating more additional demand for food than population growth does. There is no precedent for the scale on which incomes are rising today in Asia. The area from Pakistan through Japan contains 3.1 billion people. Excluding Japan, the economy in this region has been growing nearly 8 percent a year over the last five years. By comparison, when a grain-based livestock and poultry economy began to evolve in the United States right after World War II, there were 160 million Americans. When Western Europe went through a similar stage at about the same time, it had 280 million people.[47]

Not only does Asia's population dwarf that of western industrial societies, but so do its economic growth rates. While China's economy is growing at 10 percent a year during the 1990s, its income per person is rising at nearly 9 percent annually. India is also beginning to pick up the economic pace, averaging 5–6 percent a year in the mid-1990s. Pakistan and Bangladesh are growing at a comparable rate. Indonesia is expanding at some 7 percent a year. South Korea, Viet Nam, Malaysia, and Thailand averaged 8–10 percent a year for several years. Assuming that the Southeast Asian economic crisis of 1997 is short-lived, rapid growth could continue for some time.[48]

As Asia's billions move up the food chain, consuming more beef, pork, poultry, eggs, milk, beer, and other grain-intensive products, the demand for grain is soaring. In China, rising affluence—generating demand for livestock products and the grain to produce them (see Figure 1–6)—has accounted for easily two thirds of the country's growth in demand for grain during the 1990s, overshadowing that from population growth. As the

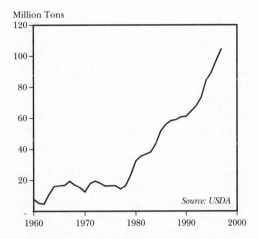

Million Tons

Figure 1–6. Grain Used for Feed in China, 1960–97

Source: USDA

consumption of grain climbs in China and other Asian countries, outstripping the region's production, grain imports also climb, intensifying the pressure on land and water resources in the rest of the world.[49]

Even as the global demand for food grows at a record pace, growth in the supply of food is slowing. If, as noted earlier, the oceanic fish catch is no longer increasing, then all future growth in the food supply must come from land-based sources. The 2-million-ton annual addition to the world's animal protein supply that used to come from growth in the fish catch must now come from fish farming, poultry production, or some other source. And it will require at least 4 million tons of additional grain for feed each year. The same is true with rangelands. If the Earth's grazing capacity is being pushed to the limit and often beyond, future growth in beef and mutton production can come only from feedlots.

Meanwhile, on the land, growth in the grain harvest is slowing. Farmers who have faced a scarcity of new land to plow since mid-century are now also facing water scarcity as scores of countries suffer cutbacks in irrigation as aquifers are depleted. Prominent among the countries that are likely to offset irrigation water losses with greater imports of grain are China, Egypt, India, Iran, Mexico, Pakistan, and Saudi Arabia.

While many people are aware of the limits of fisheries and of aquifers, few are aware of an even more pervasive limit—the capacity of existing crop varieties to use fertilizer. After increasing from 14 million tons in 1950 to more than 140 million tons in 1989, world fertilizer use is no longer growing as fast. In several industrial countries use has leveled off as crop yield response to the use of additional nutrients has diminished. While fertilizer use has plateaued or declined in North America, Western Europe, the former Soviet Union, and Japan, use in developing countries has continued to climb, surpassing that of industrial countries. By 1997, farmers in China were using 29 million tons of fertilizer compared with only 21 million tons in the United States, suggesting that fertilizer usage there might also be approaching the absorptive limits of crops.[50]

The old formula of combining increasing amounts of fertilizer with higher-yielding varieties to steadily raise land productivity and expand the grain harvest is no longer working very well in many countries. Unless agricultural scientists can quickly find a new formula, it may not be possible to restore rapid growth in the world grain harvest.

All key indicators of food security show a decline in recent years. As the worldwide rise in land productivity has slowed during the 1990s, all U.S. cropland idled under commodity programs has been returned to production. As growth in the world grain harvest has slowed during the 1990s, carryover stocks of grain have declined, falling to the equivalent of 52 days of consumption in 1996, the lowest level on record. (See Figure 1–7.)[51]

In 1996, the world grain harvest

climbed to a record 1.87 billion tons, well above the previous record set in 1992. It was a year of favorable growing weather almost everywhere, with many regions and countries achieving record yields simultaneously. But even with this exceptional harvest, world grain stocks were rebuilt by only 5 days of consumption. This raises a disturbing question. If depleted world grain stocks cannot be rebuilt substantially in a year with a bumper harvest, when can they? The 1997 world grain harvest was about the same, but since consumption rose, grain stocks dropped slightly, falling from 57 to 55 days of consumption. At least 70 days of carryover stocks are needed to cushion even one poor harvest.[52]

Rising world grain prices may be the first global economic indicator to tell us that the world is on an economic and demographic path that is environmentally unsustainable. Over most of the last half-century, world grain prices have fallen, reflecting technological gains that have increased the overall efficiency of grain production. Among other things, this has made it possible for low-income people to buy more food, thus reducing

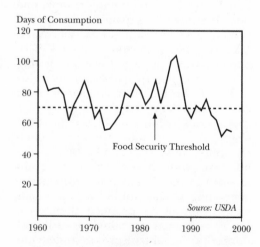

Figure 1–7. World Grain Carryover Stocks, as Days of Consumption, 1961–98

the worldwide incidence of hunger. Between 1950 and 1993, world prices of wheat, corn, and rice fell in real terms by 67, 83, and 88 percent, respectively. Despite fluctuations, the annual price of wheat fell by more than 2 percent a year, corn by more than 3 percent a year, and rice by nearly 4 percent a year.[53]

Since 1993, however, the trend has been reversed. The world price of wheat climbed from a low of $3.97 per bushel in 1993 to $5.54 in 1996, a gain of 39 percent. (See Figure 5–6 in Chapter 5.) During this same time, rice prices climbed by 30 percent and corn was up by 58 percent. The price of each of the grains reached either its all-time low or close to it in 1993, and all three have risen since then. While three years do not make a new long-term trend, this rise is what would be expected with strong continuing growth in demand and slower growth in production. And notably, the price rises of the last three years occurred during a period when idled cropland was being returned to production.[54]

If grain prices were to double their 1993 levels, as wheat and corn prices did temporarily in the spring of 1996, and if they were to remain at this level for an extended period, the situation could create economic and political stresses on an unprecedented scale. For those living in industrial countries, it would not be a major threat since a relatively small share of income is spent on food. Consumers are also isolated from commodity prices by the processing of the products they buy. If a loaf of bread costs a dollar, it may contain less than 10¢ of wheat. Thus a doubling of wheat prices would add only 10¢ to the price of the loaf.[55]

But for the 1.3 billion people who, according to the World Bank, live on a dollar a day or less and who do not grow their own food, a doubling of grain prices would be life-threatening. People who were unable to buy enough food to keep their families alive would hold their governments responsible. They would likely take to the streets, creating unprecedented political instability in Third World cities. At this point, political instability could begin to affect economic progress. This, in turn, would affect the earnings of multinationals, the performance of stock markets, and the earnings of pension funds. The stability of the international monetary system would be at risk. It would become clear that the world is on a demographic and economic path that is environmentally unsustainable.[56]

Rising world grain prices may be the first economic indicator that the world is on a path that is environmentally unsustainable.

The world is now moving into uncharted territory on the food front, facing a set of problems on a scale that dwarfs those of the past. But these are simply the more visible manifestations of the need to restructure the economy and quickly stabilize population. Without a massive mobilization by governments to reverse the trends that are threatening future food security, future political instability may well disrupt economic progress.

A Legacy of Tough Choices

As a species, we seem to have an infinite capacity to postpone difficult decisions. But since these decisions are inevitable, we are simply leaving the next generation with far more difficult ones than any we now face. Decisions are being postponed in societies at all levels of industrial development and of every political persuasion, suggesting that this may be an innate human trait, one that affects us as a species. In effect, we are behaving as though we have no children, as though there will not be a next generation.

Are we congenitally unable to respond to long-term threats that accumulate gradually, such as population growth, rising CO_2 levels, or soil erosion? If we cannot fashion a response to some of the environmental threats to our future when we have only 5.8 billion people, will our children in 2020 do any better when our numbers will be approaching 8 billion and the threats will be even more difficult to manage?[57]

If we were both intelligent and capable of exercising foresight, we would carefully note when we are approaching sustainable yield thresholds, adjusting our demands before setting in motion the decline or collapse of the natural systems on which we depend. Governments would calculate the sustainable yield of aquifers, fisheries, forests, and rangelands, noting the commitment to future generations not to exceed these yield levels. We would make certain not to plow land so erodible that it would become wasteland. Instead we would leave the land in grass or in forest, productive uses that are sustainable. We would reduce fossil fuel use before carbon emissions destabilize the Earth's climate.

Nowhere is this tendency to ignore sustainable yields more obvious than with aquifer depletion. In a country where the demand for water is approaching the recharge rate of aquifers, the only responsible action is to restrict water use before the sustainable yield threshold of the aquifer is crossed, thus maintaining the resource base. For example, when the demand for water began to exceed the recharge rate of the aquifer in the Punjab, India's breadbasket, it was largely ignored. India could have adopted more-efficient irrigation practices or shifted cropping patterns away from rice to sorghum, millet, or other less water-intensive crops, in effect buying some time to

accelerate the effort to stabilize population before the demand for water irrevocably exceeded the sustainable yield of the aquifer.

Unfortunately for the coming generation in India, this did not happen. As a result, the amount of water used each year increases, further widening the gap between consumption and the sustainable yield of the aquifer. This leaves the next generation with an extraordinarily difficult problem, one that will be far harder to deal with simply because the gap between water use and the sustainable aquifer yield will be so great. What if the aquifer under the Punjab is depleted in 2025, when India has 1,330 million people, and the rate of pumping is three times the rate of recharge? When that point is reached, pumping will be cut abruptly by two thirds. How will India feed itself then?[58]

India is not alone in facing this dilemma: scores of countries face irrigation cutbacks at some time in the future. As a result of aquifer depletion, some have already begun. Irrigated area is now shrinking in Saudi Arabia, in Texas and California, and in the Chinese provinces of Shandong and Hebei, to cite just a few prominent examples.

Oceanic fisheries have collapsed not just off the coasts of developing countries, which may have lacked the capacity to collect biological information on sustainable yields, but also off those of industrial countries. Governments find it almost impossible to come to grips with the sustainable yield thresholds of fisheries. As a result, Canada's cod fishery off Newfoundland collapsed, leading to a total fishing ban and the loss of some 30,000 jobs among fishers and those working in the fish-processing industry. The United States, unable to learn from this lesson, was in short order faced with the collapse of its own cod and haddock fisheries off the coast of New England. (See Chapter 4.)[59]

A similar situation exists with soil erosion. This natural process does not pose a serious problem unless the rate of soil erosion exceeds the rate of new soil formation through natural processes. Once this threshold is crossed, soil losses from erosion begin to reduce productivity. If this excessive loss continues indefinitely, the productivity of the land drops to the point where it is no longer economical to farm, forcing abandonment at some time in the future, when the demand for food will be far greater than it is today. Unfortunately, few national governments are responding to this threat to the food security of the next generation.

No one who was around when the Industrial Revolution began two centuries ago expressed concern about the rise in carbon emissions from the explosive growth in coal burning, which began in the United Kingdom and quickly spread to Western Europe and the United States. A century and a quarter lapsed between the design of the steam engine by James Watt and the discovery of the greenhouse effect by chemist Svante Arrhenius in 1896. Since then, the world has made the transition from coal-fired steam engines to the gasoline-powered, internal combustion engine, but the global excess of carbon emissions over nature's capacity to fix CO_2 continues to widen.

Since 1959, atmospheric CO_2 concentrations have been carefully measured. During each year since then they have risen, making this one of the world's most predictable ecological trends. The greenhouse effect, as first outlined at the beginning of the century, is not debated in the mainstream scientific community. What is debated is how fast the warming will proceed, what the precise local effects might be, and the extent to which sulfate aerosols (also from fossil-fuel burning) and more water vapor in the atmosphere will ameliorate the greenhouse effect. Even after nearly two decades of rising temperatures, most governments are still not responding to the threat of global warming. (See Chapter 7.) The response of the United States, the leading source of carbon emissions and of climate instability, has been embarrassingly inadequate. As a result, the next generation will face far more disruptive climate change and far more difficult challenges in trying to stabilize climate.[60]

In effect, we are behaving as though we have no children, as though there will not be a next generation.

We are changing things faster than we realize and sometimes without even knowing that we are doing so. Ecologist Jane Lubchenco at Oregon State University describes it well: "We're changing the world in ways that it's never been changed before, at faster rates and over larger scales, and we don't know the consequences. It's a massive experiment, and we don't know the outcome."[61]

Our inability to respond effectively to the threats outlined in this chapter raises a series of questions. Are we accumulating a backlog of problems that will become unmanageable, undermining confidence in our political institutions, leading to their collapse and to social disintegration? Are we, as a species, unable to evolve fast enough and develop the discipline and foresight to respond to gradually building threats or to develop the intelligence needed to understand the complex interactions between the Earth's ecosystem, the global economy, and our political systems? Are we not able to control either our material acquisitiveness or our reproductive behavior?

Despite the unfettered optimism of economists assessing the economic prospect, this analysis suggests that business-as-usual will not continue for much longer. What is not clear is whether the trends undermining our future will be arrested and reversed because we quickly adjust policies and shift priorities, or whether the situation will change because continuing environmental deterioration raises food prices to the point where political instability disrupts economic growth, thus alleviating the unsustainable pressure on ecosystems.

2

Sustaining the World's Forests

Janet N. Abramovitz

For millennia, humankind has influenced forests, although much of the impact was hard to see. In recent decades, however, the scale and impact of our footprint on the world's forests has changed. Almost half the forests that once covered the Earth are gone, and deforestation is expanding and accelerating. The health and the quality of remaining forests are declining.

Mechanization of forestry and agriculture has allowed large areas to be harvested quickly and converted to other uses, so old frontiers are being abandoned and new ones are being exploited. Globalization and free trade allow corporations to roam the world seeking more profitable forest opportunities. Huge fires—conflagrations visible from space—are destroying vast areas and sickening millions of people. Pollution blows in from distant autos and industries, and the buildup of greenhouse gases has ushered in an era of climate change that further threatens forests.

A major force driving these trends is the explosive growth in the global consumption and trade in forest products, in part due to rising affluence. Since 1950, the demand for wood has doubled, and paper use has increased more than five-fold. In the next 15 years, demand for paper is expected to almost double again as industrial countries continue their already high levels of consumption and as demand in developing countries grows.[1]

Our relationship to forests has evolved in some positive ways as well, however. In some places there has been a shift from unrestrained boom-and-bust forest exploitation and conversion to more sustainable forest management for a wider range of goods and services. People who have lived in and near the forest for generations are being recognized as forest managers in many places, not forest destroyers. New ways of satisfying the need for forest products less wastefully are also being pursued.

Sustaining forests for the next century

and beyond calls for changes in the way forestry is practiced on the ground. It also calls for reforming policies and pricing, reducing waste and overconsumption, and strengthening land tenure and equity. And it will mean recognizing that the real wealth of the forests lies in healthy forest ecosystems—and appreciating how much we depend on them.

TRENDS IN FOREST AREA AND QUALITY

Today, forests cover more than one quarter of the world's total land area (excluding Antarctica and Greenland). Slightly more than half of the world's forests are in the tropics; the rest are in temperate and boreal (coniferous northern forest) zones. Seven countries hold more than 60 percent of the world's forests: in order of forest area, they are Russia, Brazil, Canada, the United States, China, Indonesia, and the Democratic Republic of Congo (formerly Zaire).[2]

The world's forest estate has declined significantly in both area and quality in recent decades. As noted earlier, almost half the forests that once blanketed the Earth are gone. Each year another 16 million hectares of forest disappear as land is cleared by timber operations or converted to other uses, such as cattle ranches, plantations, or small farms.[3]

The extent of forest loss and fragmentation was made clear in a recent study by the World Resources Institute that identified what it calls "frontier forests"—areas of "large, ecologically intact, and relatively undisturbed natural forests." The study found that only 22 percent of the world's original forest cover remains in these large expanses, about evenly divided between boreal and tropical forest. More than 75 percent of the frontier forest is in three large areas: the boreal forest of Canada

and Alaska, the boreal forest of Russia, and the tropical forest of the northwestern Amazon Basin and the Guyana shield (Guyana, Suriname, French Guiana, northeastern Brazil, Venezuela, and Colombia). (See Figure 2–1.)[4]

Until recent decades, most forest loss occurred in Europe, North Africa, the Middle East, and temperate North America. By the early part of the twentieth century these regions had been largely stripped of their original cover. Now forest cover in Europe and the United States is stabilizing, as secondary forests and plantation forests fill in. In the last 30–40 years, in contrast, the vast majority of deforestation has occurred in the tropics, where the pace has been accelerating. Indeed, between 1960 and 1990, one fifth of all tropical forest cover was lost. Asia lost one third of its cover, and Africa and Latin America lost about 18 percent each.[5]

Broad regional overviews such as these can mask even more severe forest loss that is taking place in some countries and forest types. Half of the tropical deforestation during the 1980s took place in just six countries: Brazil, Indonesia, the

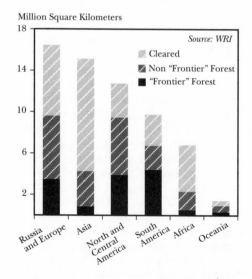

Figure 2–1. Forest Area, by Region, 1996

Democratic Republic of Congo, Mexico, Bolivia, and Venezuela. Tropical dry forest types, mangrove forests, and the temperate rainforests of North America have also experienced very high losses.[6]

Deforestation is not the only threat. Serious declines in forest quality are affecting much of the world's forests. Ironically, while many people in northern countries look at tropical forests with concern, they may be unaware that the temperate forests in their own backyards are the most fragmented and disturbed of all forest types. For example, 95–98 percent of forests in the continental United States have been logged at least once since settlement by Europeans. And in Europe, two thirds of the forest cover is gone, while less than 1 percent of old growth remains.[7]

The secondary forest and plantations that are filling in are a very different type than the original. The mix of tree and understory species has changed, and the age is more uniform. The forests are highly manipulated and highly fragmented. Plantations and even-aged stands occupy substantial areas of forestland. In the last 15 years, the area covered by forest plantation has doubled globally. And it is expected to double again in the next 15 years. Worldwide, at least 180 million hectares of forest have been converted to forest plantations. These altered ecosystems usually cannot support the full array of native species and ecological processes that characterize natural forests. Many nonnative species—from tree species to vines to insect and animal pests—have invaded these woodlands.[8]

Atmospheric pollution is also taking a toll on forest quality. Exposure to pollution weakens trees and makes them more vulnerable to the effects of pests, diseases, drought, and nutrient deficiencies. This is especially evident in Europe, North America, Asia, and cities throughout the world. More than a quarter of Europe's trees show moderate to severe defoliation from these stresses, according to regular surveys by the U.N. Economic Commission for Europe.[9]

As troubling as the statistics on forest loss and declining quality are, the true picture of the global forest situation is undoubtedly much worse. A major obstacle to assessing forests is the quality of the data assembled by U.N. Food and Agriculture Organization (FAO), the most widely used source. FAO relies on self-reporting by governments, and many countries do not have the capacity to carry out systematic forest assessments. Nor is there a system of independent monitoring in place—either by satellite or by ground-truthing.

FAO also uses inconsistent and confusing definitions, which in turn can result in some misleading conclusions. "Natural forest" is estimated, and forest quality is not measured at all. Deforestation is defined by FAO as the conversion of forests to other uses such as cropland and shifting cultivation. Forests that have been logged and left to regenerate are not counted as deforested, nor are forests converted to plantations. Thus, some of the land reported by countries as forest actually has no trees on it at all. According to FAO definitions, 80–90 percent of forest cover can be removed by logging without "deforesting" an area. Then when small-scale farmers reduce the remaining forest cover the next few percent they have, according to the official definition, "deforested" the land. This is why "slash-and-burn" farmers are often blamed for deforestation for which they are not responsible.[10]

RISING PRESSURES ON FORESTS

Widespread reports that poor agriculturalists and fuelwood gatherers are responsible for the rapid loss of the world's forests are greatly exaggerated. Closer examination reveals a different—and more complex—picture. The rising appetite for forest products and trade is a major driving force behind the logging and conversion of many of the world's forests to other uses. Policies and subsidies that encourage conversion (for timber harvest or agriculture and settlements) also drive the process. This holds true in the temperate and boreal forests of Canada, the United States, and northern Siberia as well as in the tropical forests of the Amazon, Central Africa, and Southeast Asia.[11]

Trade in forest products—both legal and illegal—is a strong economic force. Although less than 8 percent of timber and 26 percent of paper production are traded internationally, the legal and recorded trade of $114 billion a year in timber, pulp, and paper makes forest products one of the most valuable sectors in the global marketplace. Tropical timber has received much attention, but nearly 90 percent of the legal and recorded international timber trade comes from temperate and boreal forests.[12]

The demand for forest products has grown rapidly in recent decades. The global production of roundwood—the logs cut for industrial lumber and paper products or used for fuelwood and charcoal—has more than doubled since 1950. Population growth, however, is not the primary cause of rising demand. In fact, most industrial roundwood use takes place in wealthier countries, where population is relatively stable. Over half of the world's timber harvested for industrial use is consumed by the 20 percent of the world who live in Western Europe, the United States, and Japan.[13]

According to FAO statistics, about half of the wood cut worldwide is used for fuelwood and charcoal, mostly in developing countries. In some areas, especially in the dry tropics, the portion is even higher, up to 80 percent. But in moist tropical nations such as Malaysia, the vast majority of trees cut are for industrial timber. Most of the live trees that are cut for fuel are used to make charcoal or in other industrial applications, such as brick-making and tobacco-curing, and in cities. This commercial fuelwood collection, especially when concentrated near cities, can cause significant local deforestation. On the other hand, the fuelwood collected by rural households is usually dead wood, which does not contribute to deforestation.[14]

Consumption of paper (including newspaper and paperboard) is increasing faster than any other forest product. The world uses more than five times as much paper today as it did in 1950, and consumption is expected to double again by 2010. About two thirds of the paper produced worldwide is made from virgin logs; only 4 percent is made from non-wood sources such as cotton or rice straw. The rest comes from wastepaper. Soon paper production is expected to account for more than half of the global industrial wood harvest.[15]

Paper consumption is not evenly distributed around the globe. (See Figure 2–2.) More than 70 percent of the world's paper output is used by the 20 percent of the world living in North America, Western Europe, and Japan. While global per capita use of paper stands at about 46 kilograms a year, the U.S. average is 320 kilograms (the world's highest), Japan's is 232, and Germany's is 200, while in Brazil the figure is 31 kilograms, in China it is just over 24, and in India the average is only 3 kilograms.[16]

Forest management for commercial exploitation is causing a number of fundamental changes in the world's forests and adding to the pressures already described. Clear-cutting and selective harvesting, and the activities used to support them, result in simplification, fragmentation, and degradation of forests. So, too, does conversion to forest or agricultural plantations and pasture. These changes diminish the ability of forests and lands to provide the full range of goods and ser-

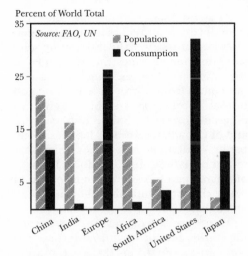

Percent of World Total

Source: FAO, UN

Population
Consumption

China India Europe Africa South America United States Japan

Figure 2–2. Global Distribution of Population and of Paper and Paperboard Consumption, Selected Countries and Regions, 1994

vices humankind depends on—from non-timber forest products to the regulation of water supplies and climate.[17]

Many of these fundamental changes are brought about as harvesting and roads create a checkerboard of disconnected forest fragments. And roads, highways, waterways, and pipelines all open the forest for exploitation and change brought by timber and agriculture operations, mining, hunters, landless settlers, and invasive species.[18]

The network of roads built into forests is extensive. One square kilometer of forest can have up to 20 kilometers of roads. In federally managed U.S. National Forests, for example, there are more than 600,000 kilometers of roads—enough to circle the globe nearly 15 times, and 2.4 times the length of the national highway system. And in one large timber concession in Indonesia, building 500 kilometers of logging roads cleared 40,000 hectares more than was directly logged.[19]

Throughout Brazil, as elsewhere, the rapid and extensive deforestation of recent decades has been concentrated near roads. During the 1950s and 1960s the Brazilian government began building roads and infrastructure to spread population and economic activity into its vast, untapped interior. The first big project was the highway to Brasília, the new national capital. Several million settlers were encouraged to relocate along the highway, and soon vast areas were cleared for cattle. At first, little of the wood was marketed, and billions of dollars of timber was simply burned. As settlement and infrastructure developed, and as transportation costs fell in the 1980s, timber extraction began to play a major role in the deforestation process. Since then, timber production in the Brazilian Amazon has increased 34 times. Transportation corridors are also facilitating the conversion of forests to produce agricultural commodities bound for Europe. As a result of the ambitious road building and integration program, the area deforested in the Amazon increased from 30,000 square kilometers in 1975 to at least 600,000 square kilometers today, with twice as much area affected biologically.[20]

As forests are opened up by roads and logging, they become drier and more prone to fires. Over the last 20 years a new phenomenon is occurring in the moist tropical forests: forest fires, previously rare in wet forest types, have become common. Fires that raged in Indonesia and Brazil in 1997 are part of this new ecological pattern.[21]

In Southeast Asia, the fires ignited regional and global concern as Indonesia, Malaysia, Singapore, Brunei, and southern Thailand and the Philippines were blanketed in smoke and haze for many months in 1997. The fires were started by pulp, palm oil, and rubber plantation owners to clear natural forest in Indonesia, and then they spread to at least 2 million hectares of forest and underground peat deposits. Tens of millions of people were sickened, hundreds died, and schools, transportation, and businesses were shut down. Enormous amounts of carbon dioxide—perhaps as much as emitted in the United Kingdom in one year—were added to the atmosphere. The fire recalled the first great humanmade conflagration on the island of Borneo in 1983, when Indonesia alone lost more than $5 billion in standing timber.[22]

Governments often look to their forests as a standing asset that can be liquidated to solve financial problems.

As tree cover is lost, a forest's watershed protection services are impaired. Year-round water supplies can become seasonal streams, flooding during some periods and dry during others. The costs of lost services can illustrate just how valuable forests' free services really are. Deforestation in India's Ganges river valley has caused heavier flooding and property damage of $1 billion per year. In the U.S. Pacific Northwest, where many hundreds of landslides now occur each year, a study found that 94 percent originated from clear-cuts and logging roads. The torrents of water and debris from degraded watersheds caused billions of dollars in damage in 1996 alone.[23]

A major force behind the large-scale forest exploitation and infrastructure developments just described are large transnational logging corporations, which have long been heavily involved in the timber trade, and which are now expanding their reach. As noted earlier, most internationally traded timber comes from temperate and boreal forests, and it is harvested by companies from those nations. A new trend, however, is the increasing role of companies based in southern countries, especially in Asia.[24]

As some Asian nations have depleted their forest resources, they have turned elsewhere to satisfy their domestic consumption needs and the demands of their forest industries. Some of the timber comes from northern temperate and boreal forests—as in the logging of Siberian forests by South Korean firms and of Canadian forests by Japanese companies—but much of it comes from other southern nations. In 1996 alone, the area of Amazonian forest under concession to Asian timber companies quadrupled to more than 12 million hectares.[25]

There are several reasons for the rising influence of roving international companies. First, in the past decade international trade restrictions and tariffs have been eased and global and regional trade agreements have expanded. Domestic policy measures—such as logging and log export bans, subsidies to timber processing industries, and even better law enforcement and tax collection—have led companies to look beyond their home countries to find raw materials and higher profits. By operating in nations with less restrictive laws, lower fees, and lax enforcement, timber companies can reap higher profits from their legal—and sometimes illegal—timber harvest.[26]

The size and power of the timber companies and the often desperate economic situation of host countries allows the companies to dictate very favorable terms. In the Solomon Islands, for example, landowners were paid $2.70 per cubic meter for timber that foreign companies then sold for $350 per cubic meter. In Suriname, companies from Indonesia, Malaysia, and China proposed investments of more than $500 million— an amount nearly the size of that nation's annual economic output. Yet what may appear to be a short-term boost to the national economy (and to the few individuals who benefit legally or illegally) often turns out to be both an economic and an ecological loss long after the logging operations have departed.[27]

THE IMPACT OF NATIONAL POLICIES

National laws, policies, and attitudes have enormous influence on how forests are managed, and on who benefits from their use or misuse. Where governments control a significant portion of the forest estate—such as in Canada, where 94 percent of forestland is publicly owned, or in Indonesia, where the state controls 74 percent—the role of government is obvious. But even without direct ownership, government trade and economic policies, management regulations, and agriculture and land tenure polices exert significant influence over the fate of forests.[28]

One common attitude that profoundly influences the future of this life-support system is the undervaluing of benefits provided by intact natural forests. These are often viewed as vast uninhabited spaces that are valuable only when converted to agriculture or mined for timber. Standing forest is seen as wasted and unproductive. The economic benefits of forest exploitation or conversion are routinely overestimated, in large part because the ecological and economic costs of the exploitation are ignored. Ironically, while governments consistently overestimate the benefits of the extractive timber industry, at the same time they underprice timber and other forest resources. The combined effect is to encourage rapid forest exploitation, depletion, and waste, and to sacrifice public revenues and benefits from intact forest.[29]

Forests are routinely sold at prices far below what the timber alone is worth. In Canada, stumpage rates are half of what they are in the United States, with large companies paying even less than small ones. And in Indonesia, an independent assessment of timber concessions concluded that in 1990 alone the government collected less than one fifth of the potential revenues—a loss of $2.5 billion.[30]

Just as a small landowner will sell a few trees for cash during hard times, governments often look to their forests as a standing asset that can be liquidated to solve financial problems. In Russia, some cash-strapped municipalities are paying creditors with forestland, and its Far East has been opened up to resource exploitation by outside companies. The economically desperate South American nations of Suriname and Guyana considered bids that would give away half of their forests to Asian timber companies for pennies per hectare. When Indonesia's military government came to power in the late 1960s, it took over a country with massive debt and high inflation. The new leaders put in place a series of policies—from underpricing logs to subsidizing timber processing to give-away concessions—that precipitated the deforestation of Indonesia. By 1991, concessions to 41 percent of the nation's forestland had been granted to a small number of companies.[31]

The extent of underpricing and lost revenue from timber on public land even in wealthy countries would astound most people. The subsidies can be so large that governments are in effect paying private interests to take public timber. In the United States, for example, 117 of 122 National Forests returned less money to the treasury than the Forest Service spent preparing the concessions for sale in 1995. From 1992 to 1994, the timber sales program lost $1 billion in direct costs alone. And this figure does not include the costs of reforestation, stream erosion, loss of fisheries and water supply, loss of recreation, and so on. The most heavily subsidized logging is in the coastal rainforests of Alaska. Even though timber sales from federal lands have turned a profit in only 3 of the last 100 years, Congress continually mandates high harvest levels.[32]

Governments also underprice their forests by levying a flat charge for timber rather than differentiating between more and less valuable timber species. And they may base fees on the volume of timber removed from a site rather than the volume available. This encourages concessionaires to remove and pay for only the most valuable species. Meanwhile, more forest is degraded and less revenue is returned to the government. Short concession terms, where the loggers have no incentive to ensure that forests regenerate because they will not be there to re-harvest, also encourage a cut-and-run approach.

One way that governments have attempted to raise revenues and promote employment from forest industries has been to encourage value-added domestic timber processing. This can also be a way to reduce the pressure on forests. Unfortunately, in too many cases, the effect has actually been to reduce revenues and fuel deforestation.

In Indonesia, for instance, the government banned the export of raw logs in 1985 and gave heavy financial incentives to stimulate the development of processors such as plywood mills. Without these inducements and tax concessions, timber processing in Indonesia would not have been profitable. The effort to add value to timber exports backfired as logs were reduced in value in inefficient mills, and more forest was needed to meet mills' demands. Even with illegal logging, some mills cannot operate at full capacity. Despite clear timber shortages and a 1993 World Bank assessment that harvests were 50 percent above sustainable levels, the Indonesian government continues to encourage domestic processing, plans to raise harvest levels by 57 percent, and is pushing its timber companies into remaining forest frontiers and into looking overseas for additional timber.[33]

Another manifestation of the failure to recognize the value of intact forest is laws that grant ownership and tax and credit benefits to those who "improve" forest by clearing it, and even provide subsidies to do so. A series of policies begun in the 1960s to spur investment in the interior of Brazil sparked the deforestation that has affected so much of that nation's forests. Roads built deep into the country's interior, generous tax holidays, credit with negative interest rates, and other subsidies encouraged the conversion of millions of hectares of forest to cattle ranches that would otherwise not have been profitable. By 1980, 72 percent of the forest conversion detected by satellite was due to cattle pasture. After 1990, four times as much deforestation came from subsidized ranches as from nonsubsidized ranches, and about a quarter of the pasture was already abandoned. Brazil lost more than valuable forest. By 1988, the fiscal cost of all 470 subsidized ranches was $2.5 billion. Despite some tax reforms, taxes are still higher and less credit is available on land with forest cover, and Brazil is pushing even more ambitious infrastructure and agriculture expansion plans.[34]

Governments also use forests as safety valves, to reduce pressure in heavily populated areas by siphoning people off to new areas. Indonesia's transmigration program moved settlers from Java to the nation's less populated islands. During the 1970s and 1980s, 6 million people were relocated. Nearly all these people were settled in forested areas, much of it already occupied by native Dayak tribes. An estimated 3 million hectares—5 percent of the country's forest—were converted during this scheme. The cost to the government was about $10,000 per family, an enormous amount in a nation where the per capita gross national product was only $530. Despite the massive infusion of funds, the ill-conceived resettlement scheme fell far short of its objectives. Many of the settlements have already been abandoned, and the people have moved on or returned to Java. Similar resettlement programs have also failed in Malaysia and Brazil.[35]

Too often, forests are seen as vast uninhabited spaces. When forest dwellers are acknowledged at all, they are usually considered impediments to development and encroachers in the forest. Rarely is the distinction made between shifting cultivators—who have a long history of successful forest management, like the Dayak of Indonesia—and shifted cultivators, settlers who have been relocated to forest areas often without knowledge of how the forests should be managed.[36]

Few forest communities have been successful in gaining recognition for their customary rights to the very resource they have often managed sustainably for generations. Their occupancy has been made illegal in some cases, and disregarded in others. Even when laws are passed allowing for the demarcation of tribal lands (as in Brazil) or community forest management (as in India), they are often not enforced, and encroachment by individuals and industry is tacitly allowed. In Brazil, hard-won indigenous reserves have been invaded by miners and loggers. Sometimes loggers, miners, and settlers will rush to stake a claim on land in anticipation of indigenous claims. In nation after nation, communities have lost their ability to control access to their forestlands, to the detriment of both.[37]

In Indonesia, the government declared in 1967 that it had sole legal jurisdiction over the nation's forests—74 percent of the land area. Customary rights, which had evolved as a complex and sustainable management system over many generations, were not legally recognized. As elsewhere, by removing power from local communities, a real life "tragedy of the commons" was created—the government, which has the authority, is unable to police the nation's vast forests, and the communities who are in the forest have no power to stop exploitation by outsiders. One analysis concluded that "the traditional...rights of millions of people...have been handed over to a relatively small number of commercial firms and state enterprises."[38]

Despite clear timber shortages, the Indonesian government is pushing its timber companies into remaining forest frontiers.

Little of the economic benefits from forest exploitation in Indonesia or elsewhere return to the communities who lost access to forest resources. In fact, their standard of living has declined. Most of the profits benefit a few powerful industries or families. The liquidation of 90 percent of the Philippines' primary forest during the Marcos regime, for instance, made a few hundred families $42 billion richer, but impoverished 18 million forest dwellers.[39]

Domestic policies can also have unintended consequences on the forests of other nations. After the devastating floods and landslides of 1985 that originated in its deforested highlands, Thailand enacted a logging ban. Although legal domestic logging ended, domestic consumption did not, fueling logging (much of it illegal) in neighboring Myanmar and Cambodia. Some of the activity was aided by the army. Indonesia's and Malaysia's policies that encouraged rapid and wasteful exploitation of domestic timber spurred the growth of large companies and overcapacity in the industry. Now the companies roam the world looking for timber to feed their mills and coffers.[40]

All too often, governments do not have the capacity or the will to enforce their own forest laws and policies. Logging beyond the boundaries of concessions and in sensitive river and stream areas, tax evasion, and falsification of boundaries, log volume, and grades are all common practices in timber concessions around the world. So too are the harvesting of protected species, exceeding quotas, and not mapping and reforesting as required. Penalties, such as they are, are too light and too rarely applied and paid to be a genuine deterrent. Companies see bribes and fines as a very minor business cost.[41]

Two thirds of Canada's coastal rainforest has been degraded by logging and development.

Many nations lose significant portions of their forests and potential revenues as a result of failure to enforce existing laws. Papua New Guinea's losses from unmonitored log exports alone, for example, were estimated at $241 million a year in 1994. In Ghana, about one third of timber is harvested illegally. If the current situation continues, Ghana will lose $65 million a year and 10,000 jobs. The Brazilian government reports that 80 percent of timber extraction in the Amazon is done illegally.[42]

In Cambodia, the amount lost to the national treasury as a result of illegal logging alone is equal to the entire national budget. The co-prime ministers and the military control the nation's forests and timber trade—most of which is illegal. Profits bypass the official budget, and go directly to a parallel budget that funds the factions in the ongoing civil war. The two prime ministers awarded timber concessions for the nation's remaining forests in 1995, also in violation of the law. And logging restrictions have been violated by the Khmer Rouge guerrillas, who were making $10–12 million a month selling timber to Thai logging firms from the areas under their control. Based on the amount of timber known to be exported in 1995

and 1996, for example, $400 million should have been generated, yet only $10 million came to the treasury. The losses to the people of Cambodia who depend on the forests and fisheries is far higher. The forests are expected to be depleted in the next decade, and the Tonle Sap—the great lake, which is one of the world's richest fishing grounds and the source of much of the nation's water and protein—will be silted up in 25 years if deforestation continues.[43]

Nations with weak laws or enforcement capabilities or prone to corruption are vulnerable targets for domestic or foreign companies looking for cheap timber. Suriname—where the forest service has a budget of $20,000–30,000, a few staff, and just one vehicle to monitor nearly 150,000 square kilometers of forest—has little capacity to enforce even minimal contractual and environmental standards on the proposed timber concessions that would have covered up to 40 percent of the country had they gone through. Even in nations with a relatively well staffed, funded, and monitored forest service, enforcement problems can occur. In the United States in early 1990s, it was discovered that timber companies were stealing hundreds of millions of dollars in trees from federal lands each year, sometimes with the knowledge of Forest Service agents. The Forest Service eventually won a multimillion-dollar lawsuit in court, but the money recovered was a small fraction of the value of the timber lost.[44]

In many nations, timber concessions, subsidies, and contracts are used to ensure political and familial patronage. They enrich powerful families, strengthen political power, and maintain the support of the military. Philippine dictator Ferdinand Marcos granted vast timber concessions to his allies, who deforested the nation in the 1960s and 1970s. The Philippines went from being the second largest log exporter in the world to a net timber importer today. Strong ties between politicians and their families, the military, and extractive industries thrive in many nations today, including Malaysia and Indonesia.[45]

Government policies and enforcement can be easily influenced or subverted by powerful interests. Money from Indonesia's reforestation fund is routinely diverted by President Soeharto for non-forest uses, such as aircraft manufacturing, or for projects that benefit loggers. In 1997, he ordered $115 million transferred from the fund to build a paper factory for timber magnate "Bob" Hasan, who also had a hand in crafting Indonesia's forest policy and is a business partner of the president's son. In Cambodia, forest department officials who have tried to implement legally mandated forest reforms have been dismissed, intimidated, and murdered.[46]

In Canada, especially in the forest-rich province of British Columbia, the forest industry is a powerful force in the economic and policy arena. More than $30 billion worth of forest products are exported each year—making Canada by far the world's largest exporter. Government-owned "crown lands" account for 94 percent of the forests, and more than three quarters of all timber revenues from Canadian crown lands come from British Columbia. Forests are leased to timber companies, and high-volume logging is stipulated.[47]

In 1995, British Columbia enacted a Forest Practices Code in response to widespread international concern over the rapid degradation of the province's rich temperate rainforest through industrial clear-cutting. Cutting has tripled in the last 30 years and is well above sustainable levels—earning the province the label of "Brazil of the North." Two thirds of Canada's coastal rainforest, which is a rare and threatened ecosystem, has already been degraded by logging and development. The province also serves as an important habitat for salmon—of which 140 stocks are already extinct and

624 are at high risk. Salmon depend on intact forested watersheds and streams for survival and reproduction.[48]

An audit by Canada's Sierra Legal Defense Fund of timber cutting plans for 10,000 forest blocks approved by the Ministry of Forests after the Forest Practices Code became law found a vast difference between the letter of the code and the plans approved. Contrary to the code, clear-cutting was the harvest method on 92 percent of the blocks, including landslide-prone slopes; 83 percent of streams were clear-cut to the banks; fish-bearing streams were misclassified or unidentified by the companies; and destructive yarding—dragging logs through streambeds—was approved and common. The annual cut was not reduced as promised, and harvest blocks were more than twice the allowable size. None of the special areas for wildlife and biodiversity protection or old-growth management called for in the code had been designated. Of the million-dollar fines promised, only 9 of 120 fines levied were over $10,000.[49]

These findings and others led many to conclude that the Forest Practices Code's standards were inadequate and that too much of the responsibility for identifying and protecting sensitive areas was left to the discretion of logging companies, who abused this obligation. Despite the lax rules and apparently laxer enforcement, the industry complained that the code was too burdensome and was hurting its profits and market share. In June 1997, the government eased the Forest Practices Code.[50]

SUSTAINABLE FOREST MANAGEMENT

Management for timber commodities and conversion of forests to other uses has reduced or curtailed the ability of forests to provide many other benefits and services. These include producing nontimber materials such as food, fodder, fish, and medicines; purifying and regulating water supplies; absorbing and decomposing wastes; cycling nutrients; creating and maintaining soils; providing pollination, pest control, habitat, and refuge; regulating disturbances; and regulating local and global climates. Forests also provide educational, recreational, aesthetic, and cultural benefits. They provide sustenance and livelihoods for hundreds of millions of people, including those who are excluded from the formal economy.[51]

Many consumers want their buying habits to be part of the solution to forest decline rather than its cause.

Despite this array of benefits and beneficiaries, all too often it is assumed that the greatest value that can be derived from a forest is maximizing timber and pulp production or converting it to agriculture. In fact, not only are other uses more valuable, they can also be sustained over the long term and benefit more people. In one illustration of this truth, alternative management strategies for the mangrove forests of Indonesia's Bintuni Bay were compared. When fish, locally used products, and erosion control were included in the calculations of the economics of forest use, the most profitable strategy was to keep the forest standing, yielding $4,800 per hectare. In contrast, cutting the timber yielded only $3,600 per hectare. Not cutting down the forest would also ensure continued local uses of the area worth $10 million a year, providing 70 percent of local income, and would protect fisheries worth $25 million a year.[52]

Still, it is clear that the world will continue to need timber products, and that

much of that need will be satisfied through commercial forest management. Thus a major focus of attention by foresters, ecologists, and economists has been reforming forest practices. When many foresters use the term "sustainable forestry" today they usually mean "sustained yield"—that is, a continuous supply of timber and fiber. Even by that weak standard, so far forestry has been failing to sustain the resource base. For example, when the last estimate was made, in the late 1980s, less than one tenth of 1 percent of tropical forests were managed for sustained yield. Since then, some in the industry have accepted principles of sustainable forestry that incorporate other goals, yet timber production remains the bottom line.[53]

Sustainable forest management (SFM), on the other hand, recognizes that forests must be managed as complete ecosystems to supply a wide array of goods and services for current and future generations. As Kathryn Kohm and Jerry Franklin of the University of Washington College of Forest Resources put it: "If 20th century forestry was about simplifying systems, producing wood, and managing at the stand level, 21st century forestry will be defined by understanding and managing complexity, providing a wide range of ecological goods and services, and managing across broad landscapes...managing for wholeness rather than for the efficiency of individual components." In recent years, progress has been made in understanding the complexity of forests, defining SFM, and describing how it can be applied in various forest types and nations. Some of this effort has gone into developing international criteria and indicators to assess conditions in tropical, temperate, boreal, and dry forests, such as the Helsinki and Montreal Criteria and Indicators of Sustainable Forest Management, the Tarapoto Proposal of the Amazonian Cooperation Treaty, and the Dry-Zone Africa Initiative.[54]

While the concept of sustainable forest

management continues to evolve, some elements are common to most definitions. First is that forests should be managed in ways that meet the social, economic, and ecological needs of current and future generations. These needs include nontimber goods and ecological services. Management should maintain and enhance forest quality, and look beyond the stand to encompass the much larger landscape so that biodiversity and ecological processes are maintained. When trees are cut, the rotation period should follow the longer natural cycle of a forest rather than a shorter financial cycle.[55]

Sustainable forest management seeks to mirror the conditions in natural forests that are heterogeneous, with many species, ages, and sizes. Natural disturbances are enabled and mimicked. (While industry often claims that its management and harvesting practices mimic natural disturbances, such claims generally cannot be supported.) Sensitive areas like streams and important habitat such as dead tree "snags" are protected. Since forest species are interdependent, species that were once considered "pests," such as fungi and insects, are kept because they are important to ecosystem functioning. Finally, sustaining forests requires the active and meaningful participation of all stakeholders, especially local communities.[56]

At the same time that foresters and ecologists have been redefining the science of forestry, many consumers have indicated they want their buying habits to be part of the solution to forest decline rather than its cause. This concern is shared by a growing number of commercial buyers and retailers. In response, there has been a proliferation of "ecolabels" for forest products and self-certification schemes by industry and government, some of which amount to little more than "greenwashing." Many claims have been made—"five trees planted for each one harvested," "made from plantation grown trees," "environmentally friendly," "sus-

tainable"—that create confusion in the marketplace. Unsupported claims also put producers using more sustainable methods at a competitive disadvantage.[57]

It became clear that for claims to be meaningful and credible, independent auditing and verification were necessary. To accomplish this, environmental groups, foresters, timber producers and traders, indigenous peoples' groups, and certification institutions established the Forest Stewardship Council (FSC) in 1993. This group has developed "Principles and Criteria for Forest Stewardship" (see Table 2–1) that apply to tropical, temperate, and boreal forests managed for forest products. Detailed standards based on these principles are being developed by national and local councils. FSC accredits certifiers who, at the request of companies wishing to use the FSC logo, audit forest management practices and certify products for the entire chain of custody, from forest to transport to processing. By using globally consistent principles and an easily recognizable single label, FSC certification can help ensure consumer confidence and improve market access for timber from well-managed forests around the world.[58]

The FSC is a promising initiative that has had a small but growing impact in its first few years. In 1996, just under 3 percent of the wood traded internationally was certified timber, double the amount in 1994. Since worldwide demand for certified wood exceeds supply, there is room for considerable growth.[59]

Companies that pledge to produce, market, and purchase wood products certified to FSC standards have said they do so because they believe their customers expect it and because they believe it makes good business sense. Commitment by industry can in turn promote better forest management by their suppliers. The 75 companies in the "UK-1995 Plus" buyers group, for example, that have pledged to phase out wood products that

Table 2–1. Principles and Criteria for Forest Stewardship

Forest management shall respect all applicable laws of the country in which they occur, and international treaties and agreements to which the country is a signatory, and comply with all FSC Principles and Criteria.

Long-term tenure and use rights to the land and forest resources shall be clearly defined, documented and legally established.

The legal and customary rights of indigenous peoples to own, use and manage their lands, territories, and resources shall be recognized and respected.

Forest management operations shall maintain or enhance the long-term social and economic well-being of forest workers and local communities.

Forest management operations shall encourage the efficient use of the forest's multiple products and services to ensure economic viability and a wide range of environmental and social benefits.

Forest management shall conserve biological diversity and its associated values, water resources, soils, and unique and fragile ecosystems and landscapes, and, by so doing, maintain the ecological functions and the integrity of the forest.

A management plan—appropriate to the scale and intensity of the operations—shall be written, implemented, and kept up to date. The long-term objectives of management, and the means of achieving them, shall be clearly stated.

Monitoring shall be conducted—appropriate to the scale and intensity of forest management— to assess the condition of the forest, yields of forest products, chain of custody, management activities and their social and environmental impacts.

Primary forests, well-developed secondary forests and sites of major environmental, social or cultural significance shall be conserved. Such areas shall not be replaced by tree plantations or other land uses.

Plantations shall be planned and managed in accordance with [these] Principles and Criteria.... While plantations can provide an array of social and economic benefits, and can contribute to satisfying the world's needs for forest products, they should complement the management of, reduce pressures on, and promote the restoration and conservation of natural forests.

SOURCE: Forest Stewardship Council, in WWF-UK, *World Wildlife Fund Guide to Forest Certification 1997*, Forests for Life Campaign (Godalming, Surrey, U.K.: 1997).

do not come from well-managed forests as defined by FSC principles represent about 25 percent of the U.K. market.[60]

So far the greatest impact of certification has been in the United States and Europe—which is significant because these regions are major producers and consumers. Consumer demand for certified forest products has barely surfaced in the important Asian market. The certification concept has recently been introduced in Japan, which is by far the world's largest importer of industrial roundwood—37 percent of all wood traded internationally ends up there. Raising

awareness and demand for certification in this region could have a major positive impact on the world's forests.[61]

Certification is not a panacea, of course. It is not a substitute for reducing wasteful consumption or for sound legislation and policies. It does provide a voluntary market-based approach to fostering sustainable forest management and trade. It also provides a positive alternative to bans, which can boomerang and make alternative land uses, such as ranching or agriculture, more profitable than maintaining forests. These voluntary standards can complement the other national and international initiatives noted earlier.[62]

FORGING A NEW RELATIONSHIP WITH FORESTS

Clearly, people need forest products. But the majority of the world's forests are managed in a way that precludes the other goods and services that people also need and value from forests. Governments, citizens, and nature pay too high a price for the continued misuse and undervaluation of forests. With the demand for forest products expanding and forests declining in area and quality, how can we ensure that our needs for forest resources and services are met? By forging a new relationship with forests— one that ensures conservation, sustainable use, and the fair and equitable sharing of benefits from forests.

Elements of this new relationship include halting forest degradation and conversion, restoring forest health, improving management, reducing waste and overconsumption combined with making consumption more equitable, getting the market signals right, returning the control of forests to communities, reforming and strengthening national policies as well as international agreements, and improving research and monitoring.

An overarching goal of the new relationship is to halt degradation of remaining primary forest and restore forest cover and health. Mining new frontiers and clearing natural forests to establish tree plantations or agricultural land has no place in the twenty-first century relationship. Sustainable forest management is a long-standing practice in some communities, and now in some small commercial forest enterprises. These practices need to be expanded in scale. A proposal to raise the area under certifiable sustainable management from 4.5 million hectares today to 200 million hectares by 2005 has recently been endorsed by environmental and business groups as well as by the World Bank.[63]

One strategy for maintaining and restoring healthy forests is to expand the protected areas network to ensure adequate ecological representation of all forest types. Protected areas today serve a much broader array of social and ecological functions than the scenic beauty parks of the past. The World Wide Fund for Nature and the World Conservation Union have proposed that a minimum of 10 percent of each forest type be in protected areas by 2000. Currently only 6 percent of the world's forests fall in this category, and in many cases that protection is in name only. (See also Chapter 3.)[64]

Rehabilitating and restoring forests will become increasingly important as nations seek to regain the social and environmental benefits that forests provide. To be successful, rehabilitation will need to be different from current practices of planting large areas of single (often exotic) species with little consideration to local needs or environmental services. The restored forests of tomorrow should use a mix of native species and provide multiple benefits. Preventing the accidental or intentional introduction of exotic species is also an important part of restoring forest health. Intensive plantations have a role to play, if they follow these guidelines and are established on degraded land. One of the stated rationales for plantations—that they reduce pressure on natural forests—does not hold true if they convert natural forest or push people who depended on the land further into remaining forestland.

Improving management techniques will be of limited success unless the excessive levels of waste during harvesting and processing are lowered and overconsumption and waste by consumers is reduced. One source of valuable wood is the high percentage of trees that are currently damaged and left on the ground in many commercial forest operations around the world—50 percent collateral damage is common. Better road placement and mapping of tree location and felling direction can reduce damage in the forests.[65]

A study in Brazil found that only one third of each harvested log is turned into sawn wood; the rest is discarded.

Many species that are currently discarded have high potential value. In the tropics, only a few of the many hardwood species are currently marketed. One forest consultant stated that the "junk" woods that are used to make rough shipping crates for forest products in the tropics are often more valuable than the contents of the crate and have promise as valuable specialty woods. In the forests of the U.S. Pacific Northwest, the yew tree once discarded as trash was found to yield taxol, an important cancer-fighting drug.[66]

Reducing the waste in processing also has enormous potential for diminishing pressures on the forest and improving economic returns at the same time. In the United States, more than half the wood brought to a sawmill leaves as "waste" such as chips and sawdust, and about three fourths of this is used for pulp or fuel. Globally, there has been some success in increasing industrial output with less roundwood input by recycling more materials and residues, according to FAO. The organization suggests that if developing countries used this approach, it could provide for growth in consumption "without placing unnecessary stress on the forest resource." A study by IMAZON in Brazil found that only one third of each harvested log is turned into sawn wood (the wood used to make finished products); the rest is discarded. Improving equipment maintenance and training workers alone could increase processing efficiency by 50 percent. Combined with better forest management practices, companies could use one third as much forestland to produce the same amount of lumber.[67]

Lowering waste and overconsumption by consumers would yield substantial benefits for forests and economies without sacrificing quality of life. As noted earlier, more than half of the world's industrial timber and more than 70 percent of the paper is consumed by the 20 percent of the world who live in the United States, Western Europe, and Japan. Reducing their consumption and waste by even a small fraction would ease pressures on forests significantly. In the United Kingdom, for example, 130 million trees' worth of paper is discarded each year. A German survey found that 98 percent of secondary product packaging is unnecessary. Nearly a fifth of all lumber in the United States is used to make shipping crates and pallets, most of which are discarded after use. In fact, they account for 40 percent of all wood waste.[68]

Unless industrial nations reduce waste and overconsumption as developing nations expand their use of paper, even greater pressures will be placed on the world's forests. If everyone in the world consumed as much today as the average American (who consumes more than anyone else in the world—320 kilograms a year), the world would be using nearly seven times as much paper. And by 2050 it would need more than 11 times as much. If, on the other hand, paper use stabilizes at today's global average—47 kilograms a year per person—and it were distributed more equitably, paper consumption in 2050 could be held to 1.7 times today's level.[69]

Recycling has been expanding and there is plenty of room for continued growth. In the United States, 45 percent of paper and paperboard is now recovered and recycled, up from 29 percent in 1987 (when industry began to record these statistics), thanks to high participation rates by homeowners and municipalities. The U.S. industry has a goal of 50-percent recovery by 2000, a standard already met in many countries. The major obstacles to meeting this target is low participation by offices and businesses, who are the largest source of high-quality wastepaper, and uneven enforcement of laws mandating recycled content. Not recovering and recycling waste paper also stresses waste disposal systems—in the United States, for example, paper accounts for 30–40 percent of the waste sent to landfills and incinerators.[70]

Reducing the amount of wood consumed for fuel is also possible. As noted earlier, most of the live trees cut for fuel in developing countries are for industrial and urban fuel users. Shifting these sectors to clean, renewable energy sources (such as wind and solar) could greatly reduce the pressures on the forests and improve air quality.

Much forest mismanagement, waste, and overconsumption results from the fact that only a fraction of forest goods are counted when they enter the marketplace, and that forest services—the life-support systems—are not counted at all. The profit from deforesting land is counted as an addition to the national economy, but the depletion of timber, fisheries, or watershed and climate services is not subtracted. This sends misleading economic signals to decisionmakers at all levels. As environmental consultant Norman Myers puts it, "our tools of economic analysis are far from able to apprehend, let alone comprehend, the entire range of values implicit in forests."[71]

Incorporating the full costs of management and production into the cost of forest products would encourage more judicious use by producers and consumers. To do this, many perverse incentives and subsidies need to be eliminated, such as below-cost timber sales, give-away forest concessions, and subsidized forest conversion. These subsidies waste money and degrade the environment. Other policies, such as granting land titles to those who clear the forest, also need serious reform in order to ensure that they do not contribute to forest degradation.[72]

In the last few years, a new breed of economists—ecological economists—has been trying to find ways to correct misleading economic signals and better estimate the contributions of nature. Alternative measures of gross domestic product and methods for calculating the benefits from forests and nature are being developed. Capturing the value of a forest's ecological services to support sustainable rural development in places like the Amazon represents an important step forward. These new tools can help the market better reflect the value of nature and guide decisionmaking.[73]

A recent landmark study helps illuminate the importance of nature's services in supporting human economies. It provides a first-ever overall estimate of the current economic value of the world's ecosystem services and natural capital. The findings of more than 100 studies were synthesized to compute the value of each of the services that the world's major ecosystem types provide. Robert Costanza of the University of Maryland and colleagues from around the world calculated that the current economic value of the world's ecosystem services is at least $16–54 trillion per year, exceeding the gross world product of $28 trillion (in 1995 dollars). If every service for each ecosystem type were measured, the figure would by much higher. Fixing a more accurate price for the benefits from forests is essential, but so too is acknowledging that not everything has a price. Much of a forest's value is quite literally beyond measure.[74]

Frequently the financial benefits from

forest exploitation go to private individuals or entities, while the economic, social, and environmental losses are distributed across society. Economists call this "socializing costs." Simply put, while a small segment of society profits from unsustainable forest exploitation, the rest of society (and future generations) pays the costs. Thus there is little economic incentive for those exploiting a resource to use it judiciously or in a manner that maximizes public good. In addition to the reasons noted earlier, one explanation for this is that over time, control over the forests has shifted from communities who have a direct stake in the health of forests to the state and to corporate entities, where short-term thinking often prevails.[75]

A proven way to reconnect the costs and benefits of forest management is by returning—or devolving—control of forests to communities. Community control can improve the prospects for the sustainability of the forests and the quality of life of people in and near the forest. In India, for example, when the state assumed control over forests from local communities over a century ago, they removed the only successful safeguard from overexploitation, and the condition of forests declined. After the policy was modified in the late 1980s, thousands of communities regained control over state forestlands. Communities now protect and control—and benefit from—the forests that they manage and rehabilitate. In Indonesia, reinstating customary rights could help reverse the degradation and poverty caused by the last few decades of state and industrial control over the forests.[76]

Community forest control can also improve the quality of forests and communities in industrial countries. In British Columbia, a shift from the current corporate control of public forestlands to community-based control has been proposed. Current laws and regulations require high-volume, commodity-export-driven forestry, which has led to the problems described earlier. A proposed "Forests in Trust" act would allow communities and First Nations in British Columbia to determine management practices and objectives and allow them to manage forests for ecosystem health and long-term economic and community stability.[77]

There is significant room for improvement in national laws and policies governing forests, as noted earlier. Eliminating subsidies that encourage forest degradation or conversion, reforming tenure policies, and improving revenue collection from public lands are important elements. So, too, is better enforcement of existing national laws, including preventing illegal logging and trade. These changes make good economic and ecological sense.

Yet too often, illogical and inequitable resource use continues in the face of evidence that it is ecologically, economically, and socially unsustainable. The reason is that powerful interests are able to shape or ignore government policy by legal or illegal means, through corruption and favoritism. Future progress will be difficult if the current breakdown in the rule of law governing forests and forest products is allowed to continue.

Although most of the action on forests needs to take place at the national level, there is also a role for international agreements, institutions, and initiatives. Forests are a global issue. They cross political boundaries, as do many of the threats and problems. And many of the services forests provide—such as storing carbon, regulating the climate, and sustaining biodiversity—are shared globally.

Governments need to renew the commitments made in Rio de Janeiro in 1992 and to accelerate action. In the years leading up to the 1992 Earth Summit, tropical forests were a major focus of international concern. When it came time to negotiate a binding forest convention, southern nations were concerned that northern governments would use a convention to impose controls on tropical forests that northerners were unwilling to accept at home—a tension that persists today. At the eleventh hour a set of non-legally binding "Forest Principles" that applies to all forests was adopted.[78]

Nations did agree to two legally binding instruments that provide significant opportunities for cooperation and meaningful action on forests—the Framework Convention on Climate Change and the Convention on Biological Diversity. The latter treaty, signed by 169 nations in the five years since the Earth Summit, has the conservation and sustainable and equitable use of biodiversity—including forests—as its mandate. Forests will be a major agenda item when the signatories meet in May 1998.[79]

Agenda 21—the plan of action that emerged from the Earth Summit—contains a chapter called "Combating Deforestation" that also provides guidance for action. Nations agreed to sustain the multiple roles of all types of forests, to enhance sustainable management and conservation, to rehabilitate degraded forests, to value and use forest goods and services more fully, and to improve the quality and availability of information about forests.[80]

Given the lack of progress on combating deforestation since Rio—indeed, the situation has grown worse—the United Nations set up an Intergovernmental Panel on Forests (IPF) in 1995. Its goal was to facilitate discussion by governments on a broad—some say too broad—range of issues and provide concrete recommendations for moving forward. A separate World Commission on Forests and Sustainable Development was also set up, consisting of scientists, policymakers, and others.[81]

At the United Nations' five-year review of progress since the Earth Summit, a successor to the IPF was designated to implement its proposals for action and deal with issues left pending. After its first

meeting in October 1997, the new Intergovernmental Forest Forum urged nations to examine the underlying causes of deforestation and develop strategies to address them.[82]

Powerful interests are able to shape or ignore government policy by legal or illegal means, through corruption and favoritism.

One initiative still under consideration is a global forest convention. Ironically, a forest convention could delay action, as negotiating and ratifying an international treaty can take a decade, plus further years for substantive action to begin once the treaty is "in force." With few exceptions, governments have been unwilling to accept international agreements that have "teeth," so it is likely that a forest convention would formalize weak, nonbinding standards. Not coincidentally, many of the nations that now support a forest convention have powerful timber industries. Given the political realities and the urgency of the forest problem, the most effective course of action is to use existing mechanisms and legal instruments, such as the biodiversity and climate change conventions.[83]

There are also opportunities for international cooperation in regional environmental and trade agreements and forums. To date, many of these trade alliances have been driving forest destruction. In the future, they could be used to secure a better future for their economies and environments. Existing trade treaties such as the International Tropical Timber Agreement, for example, could be reformed to cover the entire timber trade, not just tropical timber—a step that the parties failed to take when it was renegotiated in 1994. Likewise, the laudable goals of its Guidelines for the Sustainable Management of Natural Tropical Forests by the year 2000 could be expanded to apply to the temperate and boreal forest products trade, and be made binding. The Convention on International Trade in Endangered Species of Wild Flora and Fauna has had some success in halting the decline of a few listed species (such as elephants), but the record for tree species has not been as good.[84]

International lending and donor agencies also have a role to play by ensuring that their loans and grants encourage positive reforms and sustainable practices rather than deforestation. So, too, do the private investors who are now responsible for the majority of financial transfers. (See Chapter 9.) Loans for dams, road building, and agriculture and resettlement schemes are examples of projects that contribute to deforestation. On the positive side, however, the World Bank announced that it will help client nations meet the goals of having 10 percent of each forest type in protected areas and expanding the area under certified sustainable forest management by 200 million hectares by 2005. Recently, the United Nations, the International Monetary Fund, and the World Bank made their future aid to Cambodia conditional on reforming and adhering to national forest laws and not violating the laws of neighboring nations.[85]

More investment in forest research and management is also needed. Funding for forest-related research is a small fraction of agriculture research, and both are inadequate to meet the challenges of tomorrow. There is still much to learn about forest species, functioning, and dynamics and about the best management practices. Many nations do not have the budgets or resources to monitor and manage their forest estates adequately. More investment and a building up of these nations' capacities for forest management would reap substantial benefits in ensuring the long-term health of the world's forests.[86]

A key opportunity for international cooperation is through improving monitoring of global forest conditions and threats. As noted earlier, major weaknesses exist in the data on forest conditions and extent gathered by national governments and FAO. In order to assess the state of the world's forests accurately, data collection procedures and classifications need to be improved, satellite monitoring used, in-country capacity strengthened, and an independent monitoring mechanism put in place.

Ultimately, the effectiveness of policy, management, and market reforms will be determined by whether the decline of the world's forests is arrested and reversed, and the quality of life of people who depend on them is improved. And by whether future generations inherit healthy forests.

3

Losing Strands in the Web of Life

John Tuxill
Chris Bright

Ask three doctors with different medical backgrounds about the health of a patient and you will probably get three different opinions—diagnoses that agree in general but differ considerably in emphasis and detail. Ask three environmental scientists about the health of the planet and you may hear something similar. Some environmental assessments will track changes in biogeochemical cycles—rates of soil erosion, freshwater depletion, or fluctuations in the composition of Earth's atmosphere. Others might measure the harvest and regrowth of key biological resources, such as forests, fisheries, and grasslands. But arguably the single most direct measure of the planet's health is the status of its biological diversity—usually expressed as the vast complex of species that make up the living world. Measuring biodiversity is an extremely complicated and subtle task, but four basic questions usually dominate the inquiry: How many species are there? What are they? Where are they? And what is happening to them?

The biodiversity around us today is the result of more than 3 billion years of evolution. Species declines and extinctions have always been a natural part of that process, but there is something disturbingly different about the current extinction patterns. Examinations of the fossil record of marine invertebrates suggest that the natural or "background" rate of extinctions—the rate that has prevailed over millions of years of evolutionary time—claims something on the order of one to three species per year. In stark contrast, most estimates of the current situation are that at least 1,000 species are lost a year—an extinction rate 1,000 times the background rate even with the most conservative assumptions. Like the dinosaurs 65 million years ago, humanity now finds itself in the midst of a mass extinction: a global evolutionary convulsion with few parallels in the entire history of life. But unlike the dinosaurs, we are not simply the contemporaries of a mass extinction—we are the reason for it.[1]

The loss of species touches everyone, for no matter where or how we live, biodiversity is the basis for our existence. Earth's endowment of species provides humanity with food, fiber, and many other products and "natural services" for which there simply is no substitute. Biodiversity underpins our health care systems; some 25 percent of drugs prescribed in the United States include chemical compounds derived from wild organisms, and billions of people worldwide rely on plant- and animal-based traditional medicine for their primary health care. Biodiversity provides a wealth of genes essential for maintaining the vigor of our crops and livestock. It provides pollination services, mostly in the form of insects, without which we could not feed ourselves. Frogs, fish, and birds provide natural pest control; mussels and other aquatic organisms cleanse our water supplies; plants and microorganisms create our soils.[2]

Vertebrates can serve as ecological bellwethers for the multitude of organisms that remain undescribed and unknown.

But these natural goods and services—essential though they are—constitute a minor part of the picture. Most of what we are losing is still a mystery to us. As the noted Harvard University biologist Edward O. Wilson puts it, we live on an unexplored planet. We have barely begun to decipher the intricate ecological mechanisms that keep natural communities running smoothly. We do not know—even to a rough order of magnitude—how many species there are on Earth. To date, scientists have catalogued about 1.8 million species of animals, plants, fungi, bacteria, and other organisms; most estimates of the number yet to be formally described range from 4 million to 40 mil-

lion. (The single most species-rich group of organisms appears to be insects; beetles, in particular, currently account for 25 percent of all described species.)[3]

This situation presents some serious problems for exploring the dimensions of the current mass extinction—and the possible responses to it. If we do not even know how many species there are, how can we be sure about the true scale of current species losses? If we do not understand most species' ecological relationships, how can we tell what their disappearance might mean for our planet's life-support systems? One way to approach these hurdles is to focus on the groups of organisms we already know the most about—birds, mammals, reptiles, amphibians, and fish. These are the vertebrate animals, distinguished from invertebrates by an internal skeleton and a spinal column—a type of anatomy that permits, among other things, complex neural development and high metabolic rates.

Vertebrates combined total about 50,000 species, and can be found in virtually all environments on Earth, from the frozen expanses of Antarctica to scorching deserts and deep ocean abysses. By virtue of the attention they receive from researchers, vertebrates can serve as ecological bellwethers for the multitude of small, obscure organisms that remain undescribed and unknown. Since vertebrates tend to be relatively large and to occupy the top rungs in food chains, habitats healthy enough to maintain a full complement of native vertebrates will have a good chance of retaining the invertebrates, plants, fungi, and other small or more obscure organisms found there. Conversely, ecological degradation can often be read most clearly in native vertebrate population trends.[4]

Perhaps the most celebrated example of this "bellwether effect" was the intense research effort set off by the publication of Rachel Carson's *Silent Spring* in 1962, which described the danger that organochlorine pesticides pose to wild vertebrates, particularly birds. The study of wildlife toxicology is now routine: ecologists often monitor vertebrate populations as a way of checking on the general health of an ecosystem. In the North American Great Lakes, for example, researchers gauge water quality partly by examining the health of the fish. Some vertebrate declines may signal trouble that we cannot clearly see in any other way, as with the mysterious amphibian declines discussed later in this chapter.[5]

Even though vertebrates are a relatively small fraction of total biodiversity, tracking their status is a huge task. The institution leading this effort is the World Conservation Union (known as IUCN, from its original name), an international environmental coalition that since the 1960s has published the *Red Data Book*, a listing of all animal species known to be threatened with extinction around the world. The *Red Data Book* is compiled through extensive consultation with scientists who have in-depth field knowledge of the animals concerned. When combined with various other ways of diagnosing the planet's environmental illnesses, the *Red Data Book* findings on vertebrates offer a critical insight into the biodiversity crisis—and on what we must do to halt it.

BIRDS: THE CLEAREST OF ALL INDICATORS

With their prominent voices, vivid colors, and unparalleled mobility, birds have won a great deal of attention from scientists and laypeople alike. As a result, we know more about the ecology, distribution, and abundance of the nearly 10,000 species of birds than we do about any other class of organisms on Earth. Not surprisingly, birds were the first animals that IUCN comprehensively surveyed, in 1992, followed by

Table 3–1. Conservation Status of Birds, 1996

Status	Total	Share
	(number)	(percent)
Not Currently Threatened	7,633	80
Nearing Threatened Status	875	9
Threatened— Vulnerable to Extinction	704	7
Threatened—In Immediate Danger of Extinction	403	4

SOURCE: Jonathan Baillie and Brian Groombridge, eds., *1996 IUCN Red List of Threatened Animals* (Gland, Switzerland: World Conservation Union, 1996).

full reassessments in 1994 and 1996.[6]

The latest news is not good. Estimates are that at least two out of every three bird species are in decline worldwide, although only about 11 percent of all birds are already officially threatened with extinction. (See Table 3–1.) Four percent—403 species—are "endangered" or "critically endangered." These include species like the crested ibis, a wading bird that has been eliminated from its former range in Japan, the Korean peninsula, and Russia, and is now down to one small population in the remote Qinling mountains of China. Another 7 percent of all birds are in slightly better condition in terms of numbers or range size, but still remain highly vulnerable to extinction.[7]

The red-cockaded woodpecker is one vulnerable species that scientists hope is on the road to recovery. This bird is found only in mature pine forests—especially longleaf pine—in the southeastern United States, a habitat leveled by logging and agricultural clearing over the past two centuries. The woodpecker's recovery depends on the success of efforts to restore longleaf pine habitat throughout this area by prescribed burning, replicating the once common low-intensity forest fires that the pines and the woodpeckers are exquisitely adapted to.[8]

Membership in this pool of threatened species is not spread evenly among different taxonomic orders or groups of birds. The most threatened major groups include rails and cranes (both specialized wading birds), parrots, terrestrial game birds (pheasants, partridges, grouse, and guans), and pelagic seabirds (albatrosses, petrels, and shearwaters). About one quarter of the species in each of these groups is currently threatened. Only 9 percent of songbirds are threatened, but they still contribute the single largest group of threatened species (542) because they are far and away the most species-rich bird order.[9]

The leading culprits in the decline of birds are a familiar set of interrelated factors all linked to human activity: habitat alteration, overhunting, exotic species invasions, and chemical pollution of the environment. Habitat loss is by far the leading factor—at least three quarters of all threatened bird species are in trouble because of the transformation and fragmentation of forests, wetlands, grasslands, and other unique habitats by human activities, including intensive agriculture, heavy livestock grazing, commercial forestry, and suburban sprawl. In some cases, habitat alteration is intensive and large-scale, as when an internationally funded development project converts large areas of native forest to plantation crops, or a large dam drowns a unique river basin. In other instances, habitat is eroded gradually over time, as when a native grassland is fragmented into smaller and smaller patches by farming communities expanding under a growing population.[10]

Whatever the pattern, any given instance of habitat loss usually results from complex interactions between different institutions, organizations, and social groups. For instance, the conversion of tropical forest in Darién province in Panama is linked to the actions and aims of commercial logging companies, small landowners (both long-time residents and recent immigrants), large landowners, government representatives, international consumers, international development agencies, and even conservationists. (For other examples of forest loss, see Chapter 2.)[11]

The birds hit hardest by habitat loss are ecological specialists with small ranges. Such species tend to reside full-time in specific, often very local habitat types, and are most abundant in the tropical and subtropical regions of Latin America, sub-Saharan Africa, and Asia. More than 70 percent of South America's rare and threatened birds do not inhabit lowland evergreen rainforests or the commonly cited hotspot of environmental concern, the Amazon Basin. Instead, they hail from obscure but gravely disturbed habitats such as the cloud-shrouded montane forests and high-altitude wetlands of the northern and central Andes, deciduous and semiarid Pacific woodlands from western Colombia to northern Chile, and the fast-disappearing grasslands and riverine forests of southern and eastern Brazil. The long list of imperiled birds native to these little-noticed habitats signals that what is being lost in South America is not just rainforests but a far more diverse and intricate ecological mosaic, vanishing before most people have even become aware of its existence.[12]

High concentrations of gravely endangered birds are also found on oceanic islands worldwide. Birds endemic to insular habitats—that is, found nowhere else—account for almost one third of all threatened species and an astounding 84 percent of all historically known extinctions. These unfortunate numbers reflect the fact that island birds tend naturally to have smaller ranges and numbers, making them more susceptible to habitat disturbance. And since island birds are often concentrated in just a handful of populations, if one such group is wiped out by a temporary catastrophe such as a drought, the birds often have few population sources from which they can recolonize the formerly occupied habitat. Equally important is that many island birds have evolved in isolation for thousands or even millions of years. Such species are particularly vulnerable to human hunting, as well as predation and competition from nonnative, invasive species. (Invasives are highly adaptable animals and plants that spread outside their native ecological ranges—usually with intentional or inadvertent human help—and thrive in human-disturbed habitats.)[13]

It is likely that island birds have had elevated extinction rates for at least the past two millennia. Archeologists have used bird remains from Pacific islands to document a wave of extinctions as Melanesian human populations—and attendant rats, dogs, and other domestic animals—expanded across the western and central Pacific, colonizing new island chains. Disturbance of island ecosystems also was severe during the European colonial era, and advanced again in our modern age of jet travel and global economic trade. As a result, island birds continue to dwindle.[14]

Among countries with more than 200 native bird species, the highest threatened share—15 percent—is found in two island archipelagos, New Zealand and the Philippines. The tiny island nation of Mauritius in the Indian Ocean has recorded 21 bird extinctions since the arrival of humans in the 1600s. Mauritian species gone forever include several species of flightless herons and the famed dodo, an aberrant flightless pigeon nearly the size of a turkey.[15]

No island birds have been more decimated than those of Hawaii, however. Virtually all of Hawaii's original 90-odd bird species were found nowhere else in the world. Barely one third of these

species remain alive today, the rest having vanished under Polynesian and modern-day impacts, and two thirds of these continue to be threatened with extinction. The degree of ecological disruption in Hawaii is so great that all lowland Hawaiian songbirds are now nonnative species introduced by humans.[16]

While island species and those specific to certain habitats dominate the ranks of the world's most endangered birds, an equally disturbing trend is population declines in more widespread species, particularly those that migrate seasonally between breeding and wintering grounds. In the Americas, more than two thirds of the migratory bird species that breed in North America but winter in Latin America and the Caribbean declined in abundance between 1980 and 1991. Some—including yellow-billed cuckoos, Tennessee warblers, and Cassin's kingbirds—declined by more than 4 percent a year. Two decades of bird surveys in Great Britain and central Europe have also revealed strong declines in long-distance migrants that winter in sub-Saharan Africa.[17]

All lowland Hawaiian songbirds are now nonnative species introduced by humans.

Long-term population declines in migratory birds are tied to a host of contributing hazards. Habitat loss squeezes species on both breeding and wintering grounds, as well as at key stopping points—such as rich tidal estuaries for shorebirds—along their migratory routes. In North America, the loss of almost half of all wetlands has been a major factor behind a 30-percent drop in the populations of the continent's 10 most abundant duck species. Further south, from Mexico to Colombia, many migratory songbirds winter in coffee plantations, where coffee bushes have traditionally been grown under a shady canopy of native forest trees. Unfortunately, this habitat is disappearing as plantations intensify and replant with higher yielding, sun-tolerant coffee varieties that do not require shade. The result is that neotropical migrants must search even harder to find suitable wintering territory.[18]

Excessive hunting also remains a hazard for many migratory species. In a number of Mediterranean nations, there is an enduring tradition of pursuing all birds indiscriminately, regardless of size or status. Local species are hunted intensively for food, and migrants that breed in northern Europe must brave an annual fusillade of guns and snares as they fly south to Africa. In Italy alone, as many as 50 million songbirds are harvested every year as bite-sized delicacies.[19]

Exposure to chemical pollution is another problem that many birds face. The greatest risk of pesticide and pollution exposure occurs in developing countries, where many chemicals banned from use in industrial nations continue to be applied or discharged indiscriminately. In late 1995 and early 1996, about 5 percent of the world's population of Swainson's hawks—some 20,000 birds—died in unintentional mass poisonings on their wintering grounds in Argentina's pampas. Local farmers were applying heavy doses of an internationally manufactured organophosphate pesticide called monocrotophos to control grasshopper outbreaks on their crops. The hawks, which breed in western North America, were exposed to the chemical when they fed on the grasshoppers, one of their main winter food sources. Argentina has since banned the use of monocrotophos on grasshoppers and alfalfa, and no large hawk kills were found during the 1996–97 wintering season, but it is unclear how long it will take the Swainson's hawk population to

recover from these large losses.[20]

Whether reduced by the conversion of key habitats such as wetlands, by overexploitation in the form of hunters' guns, or by chemical contamination of water and food supplies, the decline of migratory birds is sobering because it is a loss not just of individual species but of an entire ecological phenomenon. Present-day migrants must negotiate their way across thousands of kilometers of tattered and frayed ecological landscapes. The fact that many birds continue to make this journey, despite the threats and obstacles, is cause for hope and inspiration. Yet as long as bird diversity and numbers continue to spiral downward, there can be no rest in the effort to protect and restore breeding grounds, wintering areas, and key refueling sites that all birds—migratory and resident—simply cannot live without.

MAMMALS: A DARKER PICTURE

When the conservation status of birds was first comprehensively assessed by IUCN, the degree of endangerment—about 11 percent—was taken as the best available estimate of endangerment for all vertebrates, invertebrates, and other life on Earth. Then in 1996, IUCN comprehensively reviewed the status of all mammal species for the first time, allowing for a full comparison with birds. Unfortunately, the news was not good—about 25 percent of all mammal species are treading a path that, if followed unchecked, is likely to end in their disappearance from Earth. (See Table 3–2.) This suggests that mammals are substantially more threatened than birds, and raises a larger question about which of these groups better represents the level of endangerment faced by other organisms.[21]

Out of almost 4,400 mammal species, about 11 percent are already "endan-

Table 3–2. Conservation Status of Mammals, 1996

Status	Total	Share
	(number)	(percent)
Not Currently Threatened	2,661	61
Nearing Threatened Status	598	14
Threatened— Vulnerable to Extinction	612	14
Threatened—In Immediate Danger of Extinction	484	11

SOURCE: Jonathan Baillie and Brian Groombridge, eds., *1996 IUCN Red List of Threatened Animals* (Gland, Switzerland: World Conservation Union, 1996).

gered" or "critically endangered." Another 14 percent remain vulnerable to extinction, including the Siberian musk deer, whose populations in Russia have fallen 70 percent during this decade due to increased hunting to feed the booming trade in musk, used in perfumes and traditional Asian medicine. An additional 14 percent of mammal species also come very close to qualifying as threatened under the criteria used by IUCN to assess species' status. These "near-threatened" species tend to have larger population sizes or be relatively widespread, but nonetheless face pressures that have them on the fast track to threatened status in the not-too-distant future. One near-threatened species is the African red colobus monkey. Its huge range stretches from Senegal to Kenya, but the red colobus faces hunting pressure and habitat loss everywhere it occurs, and is declining in numbers.[22]

Among major mammalian groups, primates (lemurs, monkeys, and apes) occupy the most unfortunate position, with nearly half of all primate species threatened with extinction. Also under severe pressure are hoofed mammals (deer, antelope, horses, rhinos, camels, and pigs), with 37 percent threatened; insectivores (shrews, hedgehogs, and moles), with 36 percent; and marsupials (opossums, wallabies, and wombats) and cetaceans (whales and porpoises), at 33 percent each. In slightly better shape are bats and carnivores (dogs, cats, weasels, bears, raccoons, hyenas, and mongooses), at 26 percent apiece. Rodents are the least threatened mammalian group, at 17 percent, but also the most diverse. As with songbirds, rodents still contribute the most threatened species—300—of any group.[23]

The biggest culprit in the loss of mammalian diversity in the late twentieth century is the same as that for birds—habitat loss and degradation. As humankind converts forests, grasslands, riverways, wetlands, and deserts for intensive agriculture, tree plantations, industrial development, and transportation networks, we relegate many mammals to precarious existences in fragmented, remnant habitat patches that are but ecological shadows of their former selves.

Habitat loss is a principal factor in the decline of at least three quarters of all mammal species, and is the only significant factor for many small rodents and insectivores that are not directly persecuted. The major reason primates are so threatened is their affinity for tropical forests, a habitat under siege around the globe. In regions where forest degradation and conversion have been most intense, such as South and East Asia, Madagascar, and the Atlantic forest of eastern Brazil, on average 70 percent of the endemic primate species face extinction.[24]

The loss of habitat also afflicts marine mammals, though it usually proceeds as gradual, cumulative declines in habitat quality rather than wholesale conversion of ecosystems (as when a forest is replaced by a housing development). Marine mammals, particularly those that inhabit densely populated coastal areas, now have to contend with polluted water and food, physical hazards from fishing gear, heavy competition from humans for the fish stocks on which they feed, and hazardous, noisy boat traffic. Along the coastline of Western Europe, bottlenose dolphins and harbor porpoises—the only two cetaceans that regularly use near-shore European waters—seem to be steadily declining. Seal populations in the Baltic Sea carry very high chemical pollutant loads in their tissues that appear to decrease their reproductive success.[25]

In addition to habitat loss, at least one in five threatened mammals faces direct overexploitation—excessive hunting for meat, hides, tusks, and medicinal products, and persecution as predators of and competitors with fish and livestock. Overexploitation tends to affect larger mammals disproportionately over smaller ones, and when strong market demand exists for a mammal's meat, hide, horns, tusks, or bones, species can decline on catastrophic scales.[26]

One in every four mammals is in danger of extinction.

While the drastic population crashes of great whales, elephants, and rhinos are well known, the long shadow of overexploitation actually reaches much further. For instance, only the most remote or best-protected forests throughout Latin America have avoided significant loss of tapirs, white-lipped peccaries, jaguars, wooly and spider monkeys, and other large mammals that face heavy hunting pressure from rural residents. Much of this hunting is for home subsistence— wild game meat is an important source of protein in the diets of rural residents, particularly for indigenous people. One estimate pegs the annual mammal take in the

Amazon Basin at more than 14 million individuals.[27]

Yet the real problem occurs when hunting is done to supply markets rather than just for home consumption. In central African forests, there is now intensive, indiscriminate hunting of wildlife for the regional trade in wild game or bushmeat. In parts of Cameroon, the Democratic Republic of Congo (formerly Zaire), and other countries, the sale of bushmeat to traders supplying urban areas is the main income-generating activity available to rural residents. Rural and urban bushmeat consumption in Gabon has been estimated at 3,600 tons annually. The bushmeat trade is closely linked in many areas with logging operations, which is the main activity opening up roads in previously isolated areas, thereby giving hunters access to new, game-rich territory.[28]

Throughout South and East Asia, a major factor fueling excessive wildlife exploitation is the demand for animal parts in traditional medicine. Tigers—the largest of all cats—once ranged from Turkey to Bali and the Russian Far East, and have been the subject of organized conservation projects for more than two decades. At first these projects appeared to be having some success—until the mid-1980s brought a burgeoning demand in East Asia for tiger parts as aphrodisiacs and medicinal products. With the body parts of a single tiger potentially worth as much as $5 million, illegal hunting skyrocketed, particularly in the tiger's stronghold—India. Wild tigers now total barely 3,000–5,000 individuals, many in small, isolated populations that are doomed without more intensive protection.[29]

The loss of a region's top predators or dominant herbivores is particularly damaging because it can trigger a cascade of disruptions in the ecological relationships among species that maintain an ecosystem's diversity and function. Large mammals tend to exert inordinate influence within their ecological communities by consuming and dispersing seeds, creating unique microhabitats, and regulating populations of prey species. In Côte d'Ivoire, Ghana, Liberia, and Uganda, certain trees—including valuable timber species—have shown reduced regeneration after the crash of elephant populations, which the trees depend on for seed dispersal. Similarly, decades of excessive whaling reduced the number of whales that die natural deaths in the open oceans. This may have adversely affected unique deep-sea communities of worms and other invertebrates that decompose the remains of dead whales after they have sunk to the ocean floor.[30]

Mammals in most regions have been less susceptible than birds to invasive species, but there is one big exception—the unique marsupial and rodent fauna of Australia, long isolated from other continents. The introduction of nonnative rabbits, foxes, cats, rats, and other animals has combined with changing land use patterns during the past two centuries to give Australia the world's worst modern record of mammalian extinction. Nineteen mammal species have gone extinct since European settlement in the eighteenth century, and at least one quarter of the remaining native mammalian fauna remains threatened. Most declines and extinctions have occurred among small to medium-sized ground-dwelling mammals, such as bandicoots and mice, from interior Australian drylands. These habitats have been drastically altered by invasive species (particularly rabbits) in conjunction with extensive livestock grazing, land clearance for wheat cultivation, and altered fire patterns following the decline of traditional aboriginal burning of brush and grasslands.[31]

Taken together, the problems bedeviling mammals in today's world—habitat loss, overhunting, invasive species—are not all that more intensive than those faced by birds. So how can we account for the fact that one in every four mammals is in danger of extinction, compared with only one in every 10 birds? The answer, it seems, may be found in how well mammals and birds cope with the pressures placed on them by humankind. Since birds tend to be more mobile and wide-ranging, they may be able to find food and shelter more easily in the fragmented and disjointed landscapes produced by human disturbance. Birds are also smaller on average than mammals, so they require smaller ranges and fewer resources for survival—advantages when habitat and food supply become restricted. But while few other organisms have the resource demands of most mammals, few likewise are as mobile as birds, making it difficult to predict which group is a better guide for assessing the level of endangerment of other organisms.

REPTILES AND AMPHIBIANS: THE HIDDEN FAUNA

Like their furred and feathered vertebrate kin, reptiles and amphibians (known collectively to scientists as herpetofauna) do not possess huge numbers of species—about 6,300 documented for reptiles and 4,000 for amphibians. Both groups share with the world's many invertebrates the fate of being less well known and relatively little studied. As a result, only a fifth of all reptile species and barely one eighth of all amphibian species have been formally assessed by scientists for their conservation status. Among reptiles, the status of turtles, crocodilians, and tuataras (an ancient lineage of two lizard-like species living on scattered islands off New Zealand) has been comprehensively surveyed. But most snakes and lizards remain unassessed, as do the two main orders of amphibians, frogs and salamanders.[32]

The herpetofauna that have been surveyed, however, reveal a level of endangerment closely in line with that of mammals. (See Tables 3–3 and 3–4.) Twenty percent of surveyed reptiles currently rank as endangered or vulnerable, while 25 percent of surveyed amphibians are so designated. The country with the highest number of documented threatened herpetofauna is Australia, at 62 species, followed closely by the United States with 52 species. These are not the most species-rich countries for these creatures—Brazil, for instance, leads in amphibians and Mexico has the most reptiles—but are simply the countries where herpetofauna have been most thoroughly surveyed and monitored.[33]

Among reptiles, species are declining for reasons similar to those affecting birds and mammals. Habitat loss is again the leading factor, contributing to the decline of 68 percent of all threatened reptile species. In island regions, habitat degradation has combined with exotic species to fuel the decline of many unique reptiles. In Ecuador's famed Galápagos archipelago, the largest native herbivores are reptiles—long-isolated giant tortoises and land and marine iguanas found nowhere else in the world. Introduced goats are winning out over the native reptiles, however, and these interlopers have already eliminated unique populations of tortoises on 3 of 14 islands within the Galápagos chain. At least two other tortoise populations are in imminent danger.[34]

In addition, a surprising 31 percent of threatened reptiles are affected directly by hunting and capture by humans. This figure may be somewhat inflated since the reptile groups most thoroughly assessed —turtles and crocodilians—are also among those most pursued by humans. Nevertheless, the high percentage is a clear indication of the heavy exploitation suffered by these species.[35]

The plight of sea turtles has been studied and publicized since at least the 1960s, and all seven species are judged by

Table 3–3. Conservation Status of Reptiles Surveyed, 1996

Status	Total[1]	Share
	(number)	(percent)
Not Currently Threatened	945	74
Nearing Threatened Status	79	6
Threatened— Vulnerable to Extinction	153	12
Threatened—In Immediate Danger of Extinction	100	8

[1]Numbers reflect only the species surveyed for conservation status, not the total number of species known in each group.
SOURCE: Jonathan Baillie and Brian Groombridge, eds., *1996 IUCN Red List of Threatened Animals* (Gland, Switzerland: World Conservation Union, 1996).

IUCN as endangered, with many populations continuing to dwindle. Although there has been progress on protecting sea turtles at some of their best known nesting grounds, illegal poaching of turtles for meat and eggs remains a widespread problem. Where beaches are lit at night with artificial lights, as at tourist resorts, hatchling turtles become disoriented and crawl toward the land rather than the sea. Moreover, sea turtles continue to suffer inadvertent but significant mortality from nets set for fish and shrimp. In one survey of a surface driftnet some two kilometers in length set for sharks off the coast of Panama, observers counted one sea turtle accidentally entangled for every 150 meters of fishing net.[36]

Although less well known than their seagoing relatives, tortoise and river turtle species also are exploited intensively in certain regions, to the point where many populations are greatly depleted. Tortoises and river turtles throughout

Table 3–4. Conservation Status of Amphibians Surveyed, 1996

Status	Total[1]	Share
	(number)	(percent)
Not Currently Threatened	348	70
Nearing Threatened Status	25	5
Threatened— Vulnerable to Extinction	75	15
Threatened—In Immediate Danger of Extinction	49	10

[1]Numbers reflect only the species surveyed for conservation status, not the total number of species known in each group.

SOURCE: Jonathan Baillie and Brian Groombridge, eds., *1996 IUCN Red List of Threatened Animals* (Gland, Switzerland: World Conservation Union, 1996).

Southeast Asia have long been an important source of meat and eggs for local residents. There is now also a burgeoning international trade in these species to China, where they are used in traditional medicine. According to a recent report by TRAFFIC, a group that monitors the international wildlife trade, the annual East Asian trade in tortoises and river turtles involves some 300,000 kilograms of live animals, with a value of at least $1 million. At least five turtle species involved in this trade are now candidates for the most stringent listing available under the Convention on International Trade in Endangered Species of Wild Flora and Fauna (CITES), which attempts to regulate international wildlife trade.[37]

Certain species of crocodilians still suffer from overhunting (such as black caimans in the Amazon Basin) and from pollution (such as the Indian gharial and the Chinese alligator), but this is one of the few taxonomic groups of animals whose overall fate has actually improved over the past two decades. Since 1971, seven alligator and crocodile species have been taken off IUCN's *Red Data* list, including Africa's Nile crocodile and Australia's huge estuarine crocodile. In part, these recoveries are due to the development of crocodile ranching operations, which harvest the animals for their meat and hides; when combined with effective wildlife protection efforts, this can take hunting pressure off wild populations. In Zimbabwe, crocodile ranches have been so successful that domestic crocodiles now outnumber the country's 50,000 wild crocs by three to one. In 1991, crocodile farming worldwide generated more than $1.7 million in international trade.[38]

For amphibians, direct exploitation is less of a problem. With the exception of larger frogs favored for their tasty legs, few amphibians face any substantial hunting pressure. Habitat loss remains a serious problem, however, affecting some 58 percent of threatened amphibians. Much of this is due to the drainage, conversion, and contamination of wetland habitats. In addition, the spread of road networks and vehicular traffic leads to increased amphibian mortality that can decimate local populations.[39]

In recent years, however, amphibians have captured worldwide attention due to the rapid and unexplained decline—and, in some cases, even extinction—of frog species in relatively pristine, intact ecosystems where habitat loss is not a factor. These mysterious decreases have been particularly well documented among frogs in little-disturbed mountain habitats in Central America and the western United States, as well as in 14 species of rainforest-dwelling frogs in eastern Australia.[40]

Researchers have advanced various explanations for these declines, including disease epidemics caused by invasive pathogens; increases in ultraviolet radiation, which inhibit egg development;

introduced predators, particularly game fish like bass and trout; acid rain and other industrial pollutants; and unusual climatic fluctuations, such as extended drought. Most likely, it is not a single factor but rather synergistic combinations that best explain the declines. For instance, the presence of industrial pollutants may stress and weaken frogs, and make them more susceptible to infectious diseases. It may be that frogs, with their highly permeable skins and with lifecycles dependent on both aquatic and terrestrial habitats, are signaling—more clearly than any other group of organisms—the gradual but global decline of our planet's environmental health.[41]

Table 3–5. Conservation Status of Fish Surveyed, 1996

Status	Total[1]	Share
	(number)	(percent)
Not Currently Threatened	1,323	61
Nearing Threatened Status	101	5
Threatened— Vulnerable to Extinction	443	21
Threatened—In Immediate Danger of Extinction	291	13

[1]Numbers reflect only the species surveyed for conservation status, not the total number of species known in each group.

SOURCE: Jonathan Baillie and Brian Groombridge, eds., *1996 IUCN Red List of Threatened Animals* (Gland, Switzerland: World Conservation Union, 1996).

FISH: THE DARKEST PICTURE OF ALL

The world's fish offer the best measure of the state of biological diversity in aquatic ecosystems. Fish occur in nearly all permanent water environments, from the perpetually dark ocean abyss to isolated alpine lakes and alkaline desert springs. Fish are also unique in being far and away the most diverse vertebrate group—nearly 24,000 fish species have been formally described by scientists, about equal to all other vertebrates combined.[42]

As with reptiles and amphibians, less than 10 percent of fish species have been formally assessed for their conservation status, with marine fish (some 14,000 species) being particularly understudied. Yet even this partial assessment brings disturbing news, for the numbers suggest that one third of all fish species are already threatened with extinction. (See Table 3–5.) Moreover, the proportion of critically endangered species (7 percent) among fish is double that of other vertebrates.[43]

The causes of fish endangerment—

habitat alteration, exotic species, and direct exploitation—are no different from those affecting other species, but they appear to be more pervasive in aquatic ecosystems. Freshwater hotspots of fish endangerment tend to be large rivers heavily disturbed by human activity (such as the Missouri, Columbia, and Yangtze rivers), and unique habitats that hold endemic fish faunas, such as tropical peat swamps, semiarid stream systems, and isolated large lakes. Saltwater hotspots include estuaries, heavily disturbed coral reefs, and other shallow, near-shore habitats.[44]

Although degradation of terrestrial habitats such as forests may be more obvious and get the most attention, freshwater aquatic habitats receive an even heavier blow from humanity. More than 40,000 large dams and hundreds of thousands of smaller barriers plug up the world's rivers—altering water temperatures, sediment loads, seasonal flow patterns, and other river characteristics to which native fish are adapted. Levees disconnect rivers from their floodplains, eliminating backwaters and wetlands that are important fish spawning grounds. The effects of river engineering works also surface in distant lakes and estuaries, whose ecologies decline when river inflows are altered. Agricultural and industrial pollution of waterways further reduces habitat for fish and other aquatic life. Agricultural runoff in the Mississippi River basin is now so extensive that when the river enters the Gulf of Mexico, the overfertilized brew of nutrients it carries sparks huge algal blooms, which deplete the water of oxygen and create a "dead zone" of some 17,600 square kilometers—nearly the size of New Jersey.[45]

As a result of all these problems, at least 60 percent of threatened freshwater fish species are in decline because of habitat alteration. This includes 26 species of darters—small, often brightly colored fish that frequented the now heavily dammed rivers of the southern United States—and 59 threatened species of fish in India recently identified by a nationwide survey by the Zoological Survey of India. Alteration of aquatic habitats has been particularly catastrophic for native fish in semiarid and arid regions, where human competition for water resources is high.[46]

In the heavily altered Colorado River system of southwestern North America, 29 of 50 native fish species are either extinct or endangered. This includes the totoaba, a marine fish that used to breed in the Colorado River delta in northwest Mexico. In most years now, the river runs dry well before it reaches the ocean. Elsewhere in semiarid areas of Mexico, river and spring systems have lost an average of 68 percent of their native and endemic fish species because of falling water tables and altered river hydrologies, both due to the water needs of a growing human population.[47]

Introductions of nonnative, often predatory fish can unravel diverse native fish assemblages in just a few years, precipitating a cascade of local extinctions. Some 34 percent of threatened freshwater fish face pressure from introduced species, but none have been more devastated than the native cichlids of East Africa's Lake Victoria, the world's second largest freshwater lake. The cichlid community was extraordinarily diverse, with more than 300 specialized species, 99 percent of which occurred only in this lake. Unfortunately the community began to collapse during the 1980s following a population explosion of the Nile perch, a nonnative predatory fish introduced to boost the lake fisheries. It did its job all too well, feeding indiscriminately on the much smaller cichlids and destroying native food webs. As many as 60 percent of the Lake Victoria cichlids may now be extinct, with only a museum specimen and a scientific name to mark their tenure on the planet.[48]

Many fish species also face a high degree of exploitation from commercial fisheries, particularly marine fish and species like salmon that migrate between salt and fresh water. About 68 percent of all threatened marine species suffer from overexploitation. (See also Chapter 4.) The days when experts thought it impossible to deplete marine fish populations are long gone, and scientists now realize that overexploitation is a serious extinction threat for many ecologically sensitive species.[49]

Take seahorses, for example, which are captured for use in aquariums, as curios, and in traditional Chinese medicine. The global seahorse trade is very lucrative—top-quality dried seahorses have sold for up to $1,200 per kilogram in Hong Kong. Current worldwide seahorse harvests may top 20 million animals annually, and in China alone, demand is rising at almost 10 percent a year. Seahorses are unlikely to support such intensive harvesting for long because of their low reproductive rates, complex social behavior (they are monogamous, with males rearing the young), accessible habitat (shallow, inshore waters), and low mobility. Already, some 36 seahorse species are threatened by this growing, unregulated harvest.[50]

Sharks are a second group of marine fish headed for trouble. Being top ocean predators, sharks tend to be sparsely distributed, and grow and reproduce quite slowly. They are valued for their skin, meat, cartilage (reputed to have anti-cancer properties), liver oil, and especially fins, which are one of the highest-valued seafood commodities due to their popularity in East Asian cuisine. Reported worldwide shark catches have been increasing steadily since the 1940s, and topped 730,000 tons by 1994. Unreported and incidental shark catches likely push that figure much higher, and most harvested shark species are probably already declining.[51]

Other fish have supported commercial fisheries for centuries, but now appear unable to continue doing so in the face of additional threats from habitat alteration and pollution. Sturgeon, one of the most ancient fish lineages, occur in Europe, northern Asia, and North America, and have long been harvested for their eggs, famous as the world's premier caviar. Russia and Central Asia are home to 14 sturgeon species—tops in the world—and produce 90 percent of the world's caviar, mostly from the Black and Caspian Sea regions. The sturgeon fishery was relatively well regulated during the Soviet era, but massive water projects and widespread water pollution led to sturgeon population crashes, so that all 14 species are now highly endangered. To compound the problem, sturgeon poaching is now rampant due to minimal enforcement of fishing regulations in the post-Soviet central Asian nations. Uncontrolled exploitation of the few stocks that remain may be the final nail in the coffin for these magnificent fish.[52]

With the collapse of native fish faunas in many river basins and lake systems, and with growing awareness that many marine fish are in decline, the evidence suggests that biological diversity is faring no better underwater than on land. As noted, one out of every three fish species now looks to be on the path to extinction. If this percentage holds up as the conservation status of more fish species is reviewed, it portends a grim future for other aquatic life on Earth.

HALTING THE DECLINES

Together, the various vertebrate groups provide an unmistakable view of the types of injuries being inflicted upon the Earth's biological systems. Habitat alteration is the single biggest problem for most vertebrates. While we are accustomed to thinking about forests being converted to suburbs or savannas being ploughed into cropland, the extreme freshwater fish declines indicate that freshwater ecosystems may be the most pervasively altered habitat of all. Overexploitation threatens fewer species directly, but it is a major pressure on many of the larger animals, particularly marine vertebrates. And given the important ecological roles typical of large animals, it is reasonable to assume that excessive hunting and fishing are now a significant ingredient in the disruption of many ecosystems. The spread of invasive exotic species is a third major problem, particularly in island ecosystems. Pollution and chemical contamination have been responsible for some spectacular vertebrate die-offs, but do not yet appear to affect as many species as these other problems do.

If the trends evident in vertebrates hold for other organisms, then extinction would appear to be a near-term possibility for about a quarter of the world's entire complement of species. And this could well be an underestimate, since beyond the IUCN numbers looms the specter of global climate change. (See Chapter 7.) If the current scientific consensus on the rate and scale of climate change proves accurate, then over the next century natural communities will face a set of unprecedented pressures. A warmer climate will probably mean changes in seasonal timing, rainfall patterns, ocean currents, and various other parts of the Earth's life-support systems. In the evolutionary past, the ecological effects of abrupt climate shifts were somewhat cushioned by the possibility of movement. One part of a plant's or animal's range might dry out, for example, and become uninhabitable, but another area might grow more moist and become available for colonization. Today, with more and more species confined only to fragmented remnants of their former range, this kind of compensatory migration is less and less likely.[53]

In the face of current and expected declines, the world's governments have clear moral and practical reasons to act. One course of action should involve pursuit of the processes begun at the 1992 Earth Summit in Rio, which resulted in the Convention on Biological Diversity (CBD), now signed by 169 countries. This and other environmental treaties provide important forums for coordinating international responses to biodiversity issues. And to some degree, they can function as a sort of international mechanism for self-policing.[54]

In the struggle to preserve biodiversity, international agreements have probably made their biggest contribution in reducing the overexploitation of species, particularly those that are traded globally. But even here the record is mixed. CITES, for instance, was the mechanism through which countries agreed in 1989 to ban international trade in African elephant ivory, which for two decades had fueled heavy poaching that reduced elephant numbers from several million to 500,000 at most. Immediately following the ban, African elephant poaching appeared to drop substantially in many areas. But international demand for ivory, particularly in East Asia, has remained strong since then, while a number of elephant range countries, such as the Democratic Republic of Congo (formerly Zaire), have experienced political instability and declines in government antipoaching efforts. As a result, poaching intensity has crept gradually back upward, and illegal elephant kills are again being reported regularly.[55]

International agreements have probably made their biggest contribution in reducing the overexploitation of species.

Obviously, treaties are only as effective as the will and competence of signatory countries permit. The CBD requires all participant countries to prepare national strategies for conserving their biodiversity; because of its comprehensiveness, it represents the most thorough test to date of the international community's will to face up to the biodiversity crisis. But the primary cause of that crisis—habitat loss—is likely to escape the CBD in large measure, as it has most other treaties. Habitat loss is an issue that must be solved mainly on a national and local level.

The main approach that countries have taken to safeguard habitat has been to establish systems of national parks, wildlife refuges, forest reserves, marine sanctuaries, and other formally protected areas. Nations have steadily increased the number and extent of their protected areas during this century. At present, about 1 billion hectares of the Earth's surface is officially designated as protected, an area nearly equal in size to Canada.[56]

Protected lands safeguard some of the Earth's greatest natural treasures, and have made a big difference for some "conservation-dependent" vertebrates that would otherwise almost certainly be sliding into extinction. These include about 40 species of the famed "megafauna" of East and Southern Africa, such as giraffes, hyenas, wildebeest, and impala. The populations of these animals are presently out of danger, in large part because of an extensive reserve system in their home countries. Yet despite these notable successes, current networks of protected areas are nowhere near capable of saving most biodiversity.[57]

In most of the world, conserving threatened species is as much a cultural as a biological endeavor.

One reason for this failing is that protected areas do not always target sites of high biological diversity. Icy mountain peaks, for instance, are obvious and easy places for national parks due to their spectacular scenery and lack of development pressure, but they are usually not hotspots of species diversity. Although the world added more protected areas— 1,431 new reserves, totalling 224 million hectares—between 1990 and 1995 than during any previous five-year period, most of the increase was due to a few huge designations in lightly populated desert and high mountain areas, such as the empty quarter of Saudi Arabia and the Qiang Tang plateau in western China. Despite these impressive numbers, many highly diverse ecosystems—from tropical dry forest to temperate river basins—continue to receive little formal protection.[58]

To help ensure that future reserve designations do the most to preserve biodiversity, conservation organizations such as the World Wide Fund for Nature and the World Conservation Union have begun mapping "ecoregions"—geographic areas defined by the unique biodiversity they contain—as a priority for deciding where to locate future protected areas. Ecoregions have recently been mapped on a continent-wide scale for North America, Latin America, and the Caribbean. Conservationists are also mapping the distribution of ecological communities against existing protected area networks in what is called a "gap analysis," looking for communities not represented in existing reserves.[59]

Another shortcoming of the reserve system is a lack of implementation. Many parks exist on paper but are completely unprotected on the ground. These "paper parks" are most common in developing countries, which hold the bulk of the world's biodiversity yet have the least in the way of money or expertise to devote to managing protected areas. As a result, many officially designated reserves are subject to agricultural development, mining, extensive poaching, and other forms of degradation.

Such scant commitment to protected areas also makes it easy to decommission them with a stroke of a pen—an all-too-frequent consequence of the rush toward some short-term bonanza in natural resource exploitation, even at the risk of appalling and permanent loss. In India, for example, politicians reduced the size of the Melghat Tiger Reserve by one third in 1992 to accommodate timber harvesting and dam construction, while more than 40 percent of the Narayan Sarovar Sanctuary was turned over by the Gujarat State Assembly in 1995 to mining companies eager to harvest the coal, bauxite, and limestone deposits found there. Narayan Sarovar was home to a rich assembly of wildlife, including wolves, desert cats, and the largest known population of the Indian gazelle.[60]

The "paper park" syndrome has deep roots; it cannot be cured simply by increased funding for protected areas management. It reflects the lack of a wider social commitment to protect biodiversity and wildlands. Without such a commitment—or a viable plan for generating it—more funding alone is unlikely to improve matters significantly. The tactics for building that commitment will vary from one society to another, but virtually everywhere the effort will require two basic strategies. Environmental education programs must be built into school curricula (preferably beginning at an early age) to help people understand the complexity and intrinsic value of natural communities. And practical, culturally sensitive development initiatives are needed that can help local people make a living from nature without permanently damaging it. Well-planned ecotourism projects can play such a role, for example, as can "biodiversity prospecting"—the search for species that might yield new chemicals, drug precursors, genes, or other beneficial products.[61]

The biggest opportunities from this dual strategy can perhaps be seen where biological diversity meets social diversity. A great deal of the natural wealth that conservationists seek to protect is actually on land and under waters long managed by local people. Long-established communities throughout Asia and Africa, as well as the indigenous cultures of the Americas, have traditionally protected many forests, mountains, and rivers as sacred sites and ceremonial centers. In some areas of Sierra Leone, for example, the best remaining native forest patches are found within sacred groves maintained by local villages. Such peoples often have a great fund of pragmatic knowledge too: they know how the local weather works; they know which organisms produce powerful chemicals; they know what grows where.[62]

Environmental education in such places must work both ways: conservationists can often learn a great deal about biodiversity from those who have lived within it for generations. Cutting such people out of the loop is not a good idea: some of the biggest mistakes in natural areas conservation have involved the forcible removal of long-term residents from newly designated parks. Relocating such individuals or denying them access to traditional plant and animal resources has generated a great deal of ill will toward protected areas worldwide. In some cases, local people have reacted by purposefully neglecting plants and animals that they had previously managed wisely for generations. Even in cases where communities have expressed a willingness to move out of a protected area voluntarily—say, to obtain better schooling for their children or improved medical care—governments have often not kept their promises to provide land and housing equal to what the relocated residents left behind.

In most of the world, therefore, conserving threatened species is as much a cultural as a biological endeavor. The various approaches developed—integrated conservation and development projects, for example, or "biosphere reserves" that use zoning schemes to integrate settlements and wildlands—are all complex undertakings. Their success will require a long-term commitment from conservationists and local residents, as well as national and international institutions.[63]

Yet even under the most optimistic scenarios, a large chunk of biodiversity will probably never receive official protection within reserves. Instead, its fate rests with how well we can create sustainable approaches to forestry, agriculture, livestock husbandry, river management, and other land uses. Developing such approaches will require a deeper understanding of how species, communities, and ecosystems interact, and how human communities traditionally and currently influence biodiversity-rich regions. It will also entail fundamental government policy reform in many areas—for instance, in eliminating subsidies for cattle ranching that clears forests (as Brazil did in the late 1980s), and strengthening land and marine tenure laws to recognize the claims of traditional communities with strong ties to land and resources.[64]

While increased funding for projects to generate sustainable natural resource use is certainly needed, this is more likely to make a difference when coupled with reductions in existing subsidies to activities that damage biodiversity. During its first three years of implementation, for example, the CBD provided $335 million in new funding for conservation through the Global Environment Facility. Yet during that same time period, global subsidies to such exploitative activities as overfishing, road building, and excessive fossil fuel burning totalled an appalling $1.8 trillion—5,373 times as much.[65]

In today's increasingly crowded and interconnected world, the most important steps we can all take to conserve biodiversity may be the least direct ones. The fate of birds, mammals, frogs, fish, and all the rest of biodiversity depends not so much on what happens in parks but what happens where we live, work, and obtain the wherewithal for our daily lives. To give biodiversity and wildlands breathing space, we must find ways to reduce the size of our own imprint on the planet. That means stabilizing and ultimately reducing the human population. It means far greater efficiency in our materials and energy use. It means intelligently planned communities. And it means educational standards that build an awareness of our responsibility in managing 3.2 billion years' worth of biological wealth. Ultimately, it means replacing our consumer culture with a less materialist and far more environmentally literate way of life.[66]

Humans, after all, are not dinosaurs. We can change. Even in the midst of this mass extinction, we still largely control our destiny, but only if we act now. The fate of untold numbers of species depends on it. And so does the fate of our children, in ways we can barely begin to conceive.

4

Promoting Sustainable Fisheries

Anne Platt McGinn

In late July 1997, in Prince Rupert, British Columbia—a port nearly 400 kilometers north of Vancouver—more than 100 commercial fishers blockaded a U.S. ferry bound for Alaska. For three days, some 300 innocent bystanders onboard the ferry witnessed firsthand the increasingly common symptoms of global overfishing: mounting social disruption, economic pressures, and the threat of violence.[1]

The crisis began in spring 1997, when U.S. and Canadian representatives of the Pacific Salmon Commission, following allocation disputes, broke off annual negotiations about the permitted catch. In the absence of limits, Alaskan fishers took matters into their own hands and harvested more than three times as much sockeye salmon as ever allowed under the Pacific Salmon treaty. Canadian fishers were furious. Desperate to hold onto their share of the beleaguered salmon—which migrates south toward Vancouver Island and Seattle during the summer—the Canadians responded by resorting to pub-

lic protests and threats of violence.[2]

Far from an isolated incident, this recent flare-up in British Columbia symbolizes rising tensions worldwide. Fishers across the globe are suffering from both resource depletion and an excess capacity to catch available fish, as measured in terms of boats, nets, and fishers. With fishing jobs at a premium and coastal communities bearing the brunt of social and economic stress, the world's fishers and fisheries are crying out for help. Meanwhile, government agencies and fisheries managers respond with too little, too late. And most of the time, they leave those who do the fishing out of the discussion entirely.

One reason for this is that for centuries freedom of the seas reigned and fisheries were open to all comers, at least in theory. The oceans seemed limitless in their bounty and resilience. But for just as long, fishers have had their own laws of the sea. From ancient maritime codes to traditional systems of cooperative management and communal codes of conduct, fishers have operated within systems of rules that often served as effective deterrents to overfishing. Modern fishing agreements and the Convention on the Law of the Sea, which were established to ensure that the industry was well managed, have failed to reconcile the historic and ongoing conflicts between open access and exclusive rights over fishing. And in the face of declining resources, they have actually aggravated competing claims for catches, as seen in British Columbia.

Conflicts between large- and small-scale fishers and the need for restraint of the impulse to catch all the fish possible have been replicated thousands of times across the globe. But today the stakes are higher, and the profits and risks much greater. Many populations of fish are in exceptional peril. More than ever, there is an urgent need to change the way fisheries are managed. Without reforming the underlying causes of overfishing—namely, overcapacity and open access—fisheries and fishers are doomed to a desperate future.

EXTENT OF THE MARINE BIOLOGICAL CRISIS

From a base of 21 million tons in 1950, the world fish harvest—captured and farmed fish combined—grew steadily to reach 116 million tons in 1996, an all-time record. (See Figure 4–1.) Farmed fish (known as aquaculture), which accounted for most of the growth in the past decade, increased to 23 million tons in 1996, up from 7 million tons in 1984. Worldwide, one out of every five fish eaten today was raised on a farm.[3]

Despite warnings of a crash, fish caught in marine and inland waters have maintained a steady plateau at about

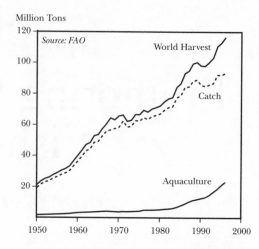

Figure 4–1. World Fish Harvest, Fish Catch, and Aquaculture Production, 1950–96

90–91 million tons in the early 1990s. The growth in world fish catch has slowed since the 1970s, but is not declining—at least not yet. On the surface, this seems to be a healthy picture. But lurking beneath is a completely different story.[4]

Most marine fisheries around the world are in danger of severe depletion. (The word fishery has several different meanings: it can refer to a particular fishing area, such as the South China Sea; to a group of fish species, such as cod or orange roughy; or, more broadly, to the area where fishing occurs and the mix of species captured there. In this chapter, the latter definition is meant unless otherwise specified.) The warning signs are all too clear: 11 of the world's 15 major fishing areas and 69 percent of the world's major fish species are in decline and in need of urgent management, according to the U.N. Food and Agriculture Organization (FAO). Many individual fish populations are on their last gasp. Catches of Atlantic cod, for example, declined by 69 percent between the peak in 1968 and 1992. West Atlantic bluefin tuna stocks dropped by more than 80 percent between 1970 and 1993.

Similarly, shark populations off the southeastern U.S. coast have been cut to 25–50 percent of their original population size in just the past 10–20 years.[5]

Looking at particular fishing grounds reveals a similar picture. Fishers in the Northwest Atlantic have seen their bounty fall by 40 percent since the early 1970s, while Southeast Atlantic fishers off the coast of Namibia and South Africa have experienced more than a 50-percent decline since then. In just the past 10 years, the remote waters of the North Pacific—with seemingly limitless bounty—reached their peak exploitation and the catch since then has fallen by an average of 9 percent throughout the region. Fisheries in the Mediterranean and Black Seas have suffered a similar fate, hitting an all-time peak in 1988, but registering 16-percent fewer returns since then, with catches in the Black Sea falling by more than 80 percent.[6]

In the heavily fished Baltic and North Sea waters, the situation is particularly troubling. The International Council for the Exploration of the Seas, a Denmark-based scientific organization founded in 1902, has warned for years of overfishing in the region. But management efforts have largely failed. Since the 1960s, the North Sea mackerel fishery has declined dramatically, while the herring fishery, which was shut down entirely between 1977 and 1982, has never fully recovered. In March 1997, scientists and environmental ministers from 10 European Union (EU) nations and Norway issued an urgent warning—another in a series of such notices—that the herring-dependent cod fisheries in the North Sea were in danger of collapsing.[7]

In the early 1970s, one of the world's largest fisheries by volume, the Peruvian anchovy, took a dramatic plunge that altered the picture of marine fishing. Increasing from near zero in the 1950s to 13.1 million tons in 1970, the catch of this one species accounted for one fifth of the world's total at the time. A combination of overfishing and natural environmental changes caused the harvest to collapse to less than 2 million tons in 1974, and then to 800,000 tons in 1984, before recovering in 1995 to two thirds of its previous total.[8]

As the most valuable species are overfished, they are quickly replaced by catches of less desirable ones. Fishers are now so efficient that they can wipe out an entire fish species, and then move on either to a replacement that fills the niche once dominated by the depleted species or to another species in some other part of the world. Following the decline of groundfish stocks in the late 1980s and early 1990s, for instance, fishers still working in the Grand Banks region off the Atlantic coast of Canada started catching dogfish (a type of shark), skate, monkfish, and other species once considered trash. Similarly, mid-Atlantic U.S. fishers who targeted bluefin tuna in the 1960s switched to swordfish a decade later, and by the mid-1980s had shifted their efforts to yellowfin tuna as stocks of the more valuable species dwindled.[9]

Indeed, a large share of today's global catch consists of previously underused, less valuable species. The volume of pelagic fish (those that live in the open seas and travel in schools) has increased from an estimated 6 million tons in 1950 to 44 million tons in 1994, from approximately one third to one half of world fish catch. During the 1980s, five low-value pelagic species—the Peruvian anchoveta, South American pilchard, Japanese pilchard, Chilean jack mackerel, and Alaskan pollock (a semi-pelagic fish)—accounted for 73 percent of the increase in total capture production, contributing 13 million tons to world fish output. Between 1970 and 1992, catches of four valuable demersal (bottom-dwelling) species—silver hake, haddock, Cape hake, and Atlantic cod—decreased by 67 percent. (Increases in some high-value species, such as skipjack and yellowfin tuna, have been recorded, however, in the Western Pacific and Indian Oceans.)[10]

Another biological indicator of over-fishing is the size of the captured fish. If a fishery is under stress, fishers tend to haul in smaller fish because the larger ones have already been captured. Catching fish at younger age and smaller size guarantees a declining biological return in the coming years by undermining future breeding populations. The average size of swordfish caught on longlines—those up to several kilometers long, with baited hooks—for example, has decreased from 120 kilograms to 30 kilograms during the past 20 years. As a result, breeding populations of swordfish have declined by half since 1978 and the catch now consists of primarily small, immature fish. Consumers are essentially "eating the babies," according to one marine biologist.[11]

Due to agricultural runoff, the Gulf of Mexico has a biological "dead zone" nearly the size of New Jersey.

At the same time that fish are being overexploited by fishers, marine ecosystems are also under siege from human activities. Threats to the marine environment include land- and air-based pollution; habitat conversion, degradation, and destruction; and even climate change. Underlying these threats is an ever growing human population that increasingly lives in and migrates to coastal areas. Some 3.8 billion people—more than 60 percent of the world—currently live within 100 kilometers of a coastline. Two thirds of the world's largest cities are coastal, including Bangkok, Caracas, Jakarta, Lagos, São Paulo, and Seoul. In the next 30 years, more than 6.3 billion people will make their home in densely populated coastal corridors

worldwide, further stressing the seams between land and sea.[12]

Because coastal and estuarine ecosystems are downstream from farms and cities, they serve as collecting ponds for wastes and runoff. Eutrophication, caused by excessive levels of nutrients, is a growing threat to fish in many urban coastal areas. Seasonal algal blooms grow off the coasts of China, Japan, and South Korea and in the Black and Baltic Seas, sometimes harboring toxic phytoplankton that kill fish and poison shellfish. Nontoxic blooms block sunlight, absorb dissolved oxygen, and disrupt food-web dynamics by literally starving marine organisms of needed nutrients. Due to agricultural runoff in the Mississippi River delta, the Gulf of Mexico has a biological "dead zone" nearly the size of New Jersey that has virtually killed the bottom-dwelling marine organisms and forced fishers further offshore in search of catches.[13]

For many tropical and nearshore fish species, land-based and coastal threats are especially harmful, as these fish depend on coastal areas for spawning, growth, and stock replenishment. An estimated 90 percent of commercial fish in the Bay of Bengal depend on healthy mangroves for survival, while in East Africa and Sri Lanka, 95 percent of shrimp and marine fisheries live in coastal areas. Changes that alter the larvae and juveniles here can greatly affect populations and distribution of adult fish elsewhere. Once abundant along the U.S. Atlantic coast, stocks of menhaden, a fish closely related to pilchard and herring that depends on wetlands for nursery habitat and for food, have declined by 26 percent in 10 years, in part due to the loss of coastal wetlands.[14]

In a 1995 study, researchers from the Manila-based International Center for Living Aquatic Resources Management estimated that humans extract an estimated 8 percent of global marine primary productivity—the sum of energy produced by living organisms in oceans, streams, rivers, and lakes—a share much higher than previously thought. In the vast open ocean, where nutrients are dispersed, the share of human removal is only 2 percent. But for more fertile upwelling areas, continental shelves, and freshwater areas, the proportion is between 25 and 34 percent, on a par with terrestrial ecosystems. This is not surprising, as an estimated 80–90 percent of commercial fish are caught within 320 kilometers of shore.[15]

Humans extract 35 percent of primary productivity from nontropical continental shelves, where a large portion of the catch is from species such as groundfish and tuna. These represent a larger share of biomass, as one predatory fish eats many smaller fish and a large share of marine biological productivity, and so on down the aquatic food chain. Not only are humans eating higher on the food chain of fish, but overfishing these top predators greatly affects the composition of remaining species and redistributes nutrients.[16]

Declines in one species can trigger a cascade of effects throughout the marine ecosystem by altering predator-prey relations, changing the community structure, function, and productivity, and rendering a system vulnerable to invasive species. On the coral reefs of the Caribbean and the northern reaches of the Red Sea, for example, the overharvesting of triggerfish and pufferfish for souvenirs has affected the health of the reef ecology. As these fish declined, populations of their prey— sea urchins—exploded and damaged coral polyps by grazing on the protective layers of algae. Not only were fish being overexploited, but the health of coral reefs suffered and diving businesses for tourists declined.[17]

Adding to the existing pressures on fisheries is climate change, which is likely to exacerbate the effects of pollution, habitat degradation, and ultraviolet radiation. Fish are especially vulnerable to temperature change as they cannot regulate their internal temperature. Some fish stocks may migrate toward the cooler polar areas in response to rising sea temperatures at lower latitudes, while others will grow faster in warmer water. Expected rises in sea level may inundate habitat areas for fish and their prey.[18]

In March 1995, scientists from Scripps Institute of Oceanography reported that the ocean temperature off the coast of San Diego, California, had increased by 0.8 degrees Celsius during the past 40 years. As a result, concentrations of zooplankton, a microscopic animal that forms the base of the marine food chain, declined by 70 percent over the past 20 years. This has severely affected the food supply of several commercial stocks of migratory fish, including sardines, anchovy, hake, jack mackerel, and Pacific mackerel. Indeed, commercial anchovy fishing in the area has completely collapsed and other commercial fish have declined by as much as 40 percent since the early 1970s, in part due to changes in ocean temperature. Similarly, the population of sooty shearwaters, a seabird native to the California Current System, declined by 90 percent between 1987 and 1994 because of its dependence on zooplankton for food. If current predictions by the Intergovernmental Panel on Climate Change prove true, in the next 50–100 years climate change will have a greater impact on the health of world fisheries than overfishing itself.[19]

THE IMPACT OF FISHING GEAR

The type of gear used and the size of fishing vessels both play an important role in the health of fisheries and the marine ecosystem. In the process of fishing, unwanted species are brought onboard and then thrown back to sea dead or dying. Known as discards, these unwanted species are wasted either because they are undersized or a nonmarketable sex or species, or because a fisher does not have a permit to catch them. FAO estimates that discards total 27 million tons, equivalent to one third of annual marine catch—and this figure excludes discards of marine mammals, seabirds, and turtles. Global bycatch, the sum of discards and unintentionally caught species that are retained, is estimated at 28.7 million tons.[20]

To a large extent, bycatch is associated with more industrialized fisheries and is a reflection of current management systems. A concentrated, time-limited window of opportunity forces fishers to rush and catch as much fish as possible, selecting the valuable high-quality ones before the fishery shuts down or the fisher reaches quota, and discarding the unwanted ones. Because fish processors and commercial markets accept only certain types of fish, the nontarget species are less valuable to industrial fishers. Although market incentives encourage fishers to be more selective in what they keep, their gear is by no means selective.[21]

The trawl fishery of the Northwest Pacific—which targets pollock, yellowfin sole, Pacific cod, crab, and mackerel—produces the largest quantity of bycatch in the world. A standard commercial trawl net designed for groundfish can catch high quantities of shrimp, crabs, and even seals. Discards of crabs and their prey from the groundfish fishery caused losses of more than $50 million in the Bering Sea crab fishery in 1991 alone. Losses for all species in the Bering Sea and Gulf of Alaska combined are estimated at more than $250 million annually. Of the 27.2 million tons harvested from the Northwest Pacific region in 1995, some 9.1 million tons of fish were discarded.[22]

Because of small mesh nets and the high species diversity in tropical waters, shrimp trawling also produces high quantities of bycatch. In the Gulf of Mexico shrimp fishery, for example, an estimated 12 million juvenile red snappers and 2,800 tons of sharks are discarded annually. Off the Brazilian coast, discards in the shrimp fishery are comparable to the size of the total landed catch. Worldwide, for every 1 kilogram of shrimp caught, at least 5 kilograms of other species are discarded; in some regions, the ratio is 15 to 1.[23]

In tropical reef fisheries, a growing threat to fisheries and their habitat is the use of cyanide poison. Fishers dive down and squirt enough sodium cyanide on the reef to stun fish (but too little to harm people who eat them). This practice can kill most reef organisms and convert a productive reef community into an "aquatic graveyard." Divers use an estimated 400 kilograms of cyanide a year capturing valuable grouper, humphead wrasse, rock cod, coral trout, and other tropical species to feed a growing demand for live food-fish. Based in Hong Kong, this trade is valued at $1 billion a year, while ornamental fish species for aquariums are worth more than $200 million annually. Live fish can earn fishers 400–800 percent more than the same species dead. Fueled by high profits, cyanide fishing is expected to drive numerous species to collapse in the Philippines, Indonesia, and Maldives within a few years, after which fishers will likely turn to Papua New Guinea and the Pacific Islands. Indeed, cyanide fishing is now reported from Fiji and the Solomon Islands to Tanzania and Eritrea.[24]

Fishing gear and methods can also cause direct harm to the marine environment by reducing cover from predators, harming food supplies, and lowering local biodiversity.

Some areas of the world's oceans are fished more than others, and therefore take a harder hit from gear. A third of the North Sea is intensively harvested each year, for instance, while an 800-square-kilometer bay in northern France is dredged seven times a year for scallops.

The 40,800-square-kilometer area of gravel and marine sediments in the Georges Bank off New England was trawled three to four times a year between 1984 and 1990, making it resemble a "parking lot," according to one researcher. All the ocean's continental shelves are trawled at least once every two years, with some areas scraped several times a season. Trawling has been compared with strip mining on land and clear-cutting in forests. One important difference, however, is that trawling is conducted on a scale about 50 times greater.[25]

How Overcapacity Drives Overfishing

With more than twice the capacity it needs to harvest available fisheries, today's fishing industry is massively overcapitalized. Simply put, too many fishers on too many boats with too many hooks and nets are taking too many fish from the sea. How we got to this point is widely debated, but the contributing factors include the open access nature of fishing, widespread technological change, expansion of national claims to fishing grounds, economic development policies, and growing demand. Together, these powerful forces are driving fishers down the path of self-destruction.[26]

In an open access fishery, resources are owned by no one and the fishery is open to all comers. If one person does not catch the available fish, someone else will. As a result, fishers have little incentive to conserve resources. Without limits in place, they tend to catch as many fish as they possibly can. For large fish populations harvested with relatively low technology and by few fishers, this usually does not cause serious problems. Indeed, in a developing fishery, fishers initially experience high catches. But then strong

earnings usually attract more people to the fishery, which in turn prompts those already there to invest in bigger boats and more effort to sustain or increase their share of the catch.[27]

When fishing effort increases too much or too fast, or the resource itself is declining due to natural causes, the risks of overfishing are higher. These conditions can lead to the classic scenario described by Garrett Hardin in his 1968 *Science* article, "The Tragedy of the Commons," in which natural resources are severely depleted by a growing number of users who harvest a rapidly dwindling share of a resource.[28]

Generally, the harder fishers try, the more fish they will catch—but only up to a certain point, known as maximum sustainable yield. This is the equilibrium between a fish population's biological productivity and the level of fishing effort. Theoretically, it represents the largest amount of fish that can be harvested while still ensuring a productive fishery the following year. Anything beyond this is overfishing. How quickly this happens depends on the health of the fish populations, the quality of data and methods used to determine maximum sustainable yield, and how fishers respond to declining biological returns by reducing their efforts.[29]

The conditions of open access tend to hasten the day of overshooting maximum sustainable yield. By the time multiple users reach this point, it is often too late: most fishers are already too heavily overcapitalized for their average catch rates. Only the most efficient outfits can break even. Some fishers go out of business, and coastal communities suffer economic losses. But with the help of government aid or subsidies, some fishers will remain in an overcapitalized, economically inefficient fishery instead of leaving when it becomes too crowded. And that is just what the world faces today: a heavily subsidized, overcapitalized, economically inefficient industry.[30]

During the past 50 years, uninhibited growth and rapid modernization in the industry have contributed to massive overcapacity. Following technological developments during World War II, fishing underwent dramatic changes. Many nations converted their navy vessels, sonar and electronic navigation systems, and ship-based surveillance technology to benefit commercial fishing. European nations, Japan, and Russia built large fishing vessels that could travel to distant waters, while the World Bank and multilateral aid agencies focused on developing fisheries to reduce poverty, encourage overall economic development, and improve the efficiency of traditional fishers.[31]

In the early 1950s, workers in European shipyards built huge, mechanized vessels that could catch up to 500 tons of fish a day. Known as factory trawlers for the enormous trawl nets that are hauled up the ship's stern and directly to onboard processing and freezing facilities, these floating factories allowed fishers to catch and fully process large quantities of fish in a short period of time. Previously, ships had to return to port before the catch spoiled, thus limiting how long and how far a ship could venture away from home. But once the crew could take care of the processing, freezing, and packaging of fish at sea, these massive industrial trawlers were free to roam the globe in search of profits.[32]

Factory trawlers concentrated on temperate and cold-water offshore fisheries, which typically have high concentrations of single or similar species. With improved reconnaissance and communications systems, fleets of factory trawlers were able to zero in on large schools of fish, harvest the entire concentration, and then locate and converge on the next large congregation of fish, a practice known as pulse fishing. By the mid-1970s, factory trawlers from northern Europe, Russia, and Japan caught a large share of

the world's tuna, squid, and pelagic fish from the high seas, as well as a significant portion of bottom-dwelling species in the North Atlantic and Northwest Pacific Oceans. The trawlers are quite efficient at doing their job: In 1989, factory trawlers represented 1 percent of the world's fishing fleet by number of vessels, but were responsible for 10 percent of the world catch. In the United States, they accounted for only 0.14 percent of the fishing fleet in 1992, yet landed 21 percent of the total catch.[33]

From their first use, factory trawlers changed the picture of world fishing by raising the stakes and the potential for profits and failure. In the highly productive Georges Bank waters off the coast of New England, for example, more than 1,000 factory trawlers from foreign countries captured 2.2 million tons of groundfish in 1974—10 times the amount caught by U.S. fishers that year.[34]

Many coastal states reacted to these developments by unilaterally extending their coastal jurisdiction further offshore in an effort to keep foreign fishers out. In 1945, the United States was the first country to extend its jurisdiction to contiguous high seas areas. Under the Truman Proclamation, U.S. officials justified the move as a way to protect fisheries better, establish conservation zones, and exploit seabed minerals of the continental shelf. Many fishing-dependent countries soon followed suit, triggering a global "sea grab." Within a decade, several Latin American countries, including Argentina, Peru, Chile, and Honduras, extended their jurisdiction to 200 nautical miles to protect their fisheries from outside intrusions.[35]

What began as an isolated trend in the 1950s and 1960s quickly grew into a global phenomenon. By 1973, nearly 35 percent of the ocean's area—an area equal to the Earth's entire land mass—was claimed by coastal states, many of which were developing countries. These claims led to the 1982 U.N. Convention on the Law of the Sea (UNCLOS), which was finally formally ratified in November 1994. Under UNCLOS, coastal nations were granted rights to use and develop fisheries within a 200-nautical-mile exclusive economic zone (EEZ). With the privilege of harvesting the marine resources came an obligation to protect and conserve fish stocks. If all fish were not used, countries could decide to grant harvesting rights to other countries on a case-by-case basis.[36]

At about the same time that nations were extending their claims to fishing grounds, international development agencies were contributing to the problem of overcapacity by increasing lending for fisheries development. The World Bank, the Asian Development Bank, FAO, and the aid agencies of Canada, Japan, Norway, and the United States provided millions of dollars in financial and technical assistance to fishers in coastal developing countries. In the 1980s, lending to this sector emphasized the need for developing countries to improve their own fishing capacity. Specifically, programs were aimed at modernizing fishing technology and vessels, building shore-based support facilities and related infrastructure, and developing market-oriented aquaculture projects. Fishers from Asia to West Africa were encouraged to harvest as much as possible, and then to export a portion of the harvests to industrial countries.[37]

As a result of EEZ claims and outside financial assistance, by the 1980s most of the growth in the world's fishing fleet was occurring in developing countries. Between 1970 and 1989, these countries' share of the world fleet increased from 27 to 58 percent, while vessel tonnage grew in parallel fashion. (See Table 4–1.) With an estimated 43 percent of the world's fishing capacity concentrated in Asia, several newly developed Asian countries now use modern deep-sea fishing fleets of their own, replacing the European and Russian ships of the 1960s.[38]

For the first time, developing countries became major harvesters—and were shouldering a growing responsibility for global overfishing. Claiming EEZs under the Law of the Sea in effect redistributed fishery resources away from distant fishing states to coastal states. Indeed, this reallocation is one of the lasting legacies of UNCLOS. In the early 1950s, about 80 percent of the world's fish catch was taken by industrial countries. Forty years later, 64 percent of the catch was in the hands of developing countries. In 1994, 7 of the top 10 fish producers were developing countries. Unfortunately, these nations have had no better luck managing these resources sustainably than industrial countries did.[39]

Factory trawlers changed the picture of world fishing by raising the stakes and the potential for profits and failure.

Worldwide, gross registered tonnage of the world's fishing fleet—a measure of fishing capacity—grew by 4.6 percent a year between 1970 and 1989. With more boats and fishers on the sea, fish landings increased as well, although at a rate about half as fast, 2.4 percent annually. Even though fleets and catches were both rising during this time, FAO concluded in 1992 that the world's fishing fleet had at least 30 percent more capacity than it needed to catch all the world's commercial stocks. [40]

This growth in marine harvests masks a 25-percent decline in yield of high-value species worldwide. Behind the complicated story of fish prices are the scarcity of some species, growing imports by industrial countries, the increasing share of low-value species in world catch, readily available farmed species, and the substi-

Table 4–1. Size of World's Fishing Fleet, by Region, 1970 and 1992

Region	Gross Register Tonnage		Growth,
	1970	1992	1970–92
	(thousand tons)		(percent)
Asia	4,802	11,013	129
Former Soviet Union	3,997	7,766	94
Europe	3,097	3,018	–3
North America	1,077	2,560	138
South America	362	817	126
Africa	244	699	187
Oceania	37	122	230
World	13,616	25,994	91

SOURCE: U.N. Food and Agriculture Organization, *The State of World Fisheries and Aquaculture* (Rome: 1995); "Water and Fisheries," in World Resources Institute et al., *World Resources 1996–97* (New York: Oxford University Press, 1996).

tutability of fish. As a whole, world seafood prices are rising, while in some industrial countries, the trends are mixed. Worldwide, the cost and effort of catching those fish are increasing.[41]

Price data from the United States illustrate this phenomenon clearly. Although U.S. catches have increased by 60 percent in tonnage since 1982, the total value of that catch has remained stagnant when adjusted for inflation. Between 1982 and 1995, the average of all U.S. seafood prices dropped 15 percent in real terms. Broadly speaking, the average price earned at the dock of individual fish fell from an estimated 41¢ in 1986 to 25¢ in 1995—almost exclusively because cheaper, low-value fish accounted for a much larger share of the total catch. If U.S. fishers had captured the same quantity of fish of each species in 1995 as they did in 1982, they would have earned only two thirds as much (in constant dollars) as 13 years earlier. The bottom line is that U.S. fishers are catching more fish but also losing money.[42]

One key reason that fisheries remain afloat is that governments foot a growing share of the bill. These payments come in the form of tax incentives, low-interest loans, and direct subsidies. Besides being a poor use of public finances, subsidies that encourage fishers to either remain in or enter an overcapitalized fishery mask the true costs of overcapacity and postpone the day of reckoning.[43]

The world's fishers currently operate under a huge deficit. Francis Christy, a fisheries economist, joined forces with FAO statisticians to calculate that economic losses from overfishing amounted to roughly $54 billion in 1989, of which about half was covered by government subsidies. (The figure for total losses in 1989 is based on estimated global fishing costs of $124 billion and fishing revenues of $70 billion.) In other words, for every $1 earned from fishing in the late 1980s, governments, taxpayers, and fishers spent $1.77, a debt that quickly translated into shrinking profits and job layoffs.[44]

Despite the evidence of massive overcapacity and significant economic losses, several governments continue to subsidize fisheries. Matteo Milazzo, a researcher with the U.S. National Marine Fisheries Service, estimated that global fishing subsidies in 1995 totalled $11–16 billion. Data from China, the EU, Japan, Norway, Russia, and the United States show that $3.5–4 billion were budgeted specifically for fishing subsidies, while an additional $3 billion in tax breaks and lending acted as subsidies for fleet capitalization. The remaining money came in the form of low-interest loans and tax preferences for shipbuilding, harbor development and related infrastructure projects, and unbudgeted subsidies. Milazzo concluded that between one fourth and one third of global fishing revenues comes from subsidies.[45]

Primarily bestowed by industrial countries on their failing fleets, subsidies encourage the tragic phenomenon of fishers participating in the downfall of their own industry. While they may help to cushion the economic impact of declining fisheries in the short term, over the long run subsidies encourage fishers to remain in a dying industry and to continue to overextend themselves and the marine resources. Because of this, fisheries subsidies "may be the most environmentally destructive natural resource subsidies of all," according to Gareth Porter, author of a paper on the subject and now a consultant with the Global Environment Facility.[46]

One of the most obvious policies that acts as a subsidy is providing access to national fishing areas at little or no cost. Most governments do not charge their own nation's fleets to harvest from their EEZs, and many charge foreign fleets as little as 5 percent of the value of the catch. Matteo Milazzo estimates that governments forgo $3–7 billion in uncollected user fees from domestic and foreign fishers—in addition to the estimated $11–16 billion they formally budget for subsidies. In contrast, subsidies that encourage fleets to reduce their capacity total only about $500 million. In fact, only 5 percent of government subsidies are targeted at solving the problem of overcapacity.[47]

The lesson from all this is that overexpansion of the world's fishing fleet and production levels comes at a price. Although supported by global fishing sub-sidies, cheap loans, and economic development programs, global deficits in the fishing sector are a massive debt that will soon come due.

SOCIAL AND ECONOMIC RIPPLE EFFECTS

The dilemma of conserving and protecting the marine and coastal commons contributes to a second, less appreciated tragedy: that of the commoners. Overfishing has contributed to a vicious cycle of economic hardship and social disruption.[48]

In strictly economic terms, local consumers, small-scale fishers, and households dependent on fishing for their food and livelihoods cannot compete with big factory trawlers, foreign-owned companies, and distant export markets. About 40,000 of the world's largest fishing vessels can catch the same amount of fish as the more than 3.4 million smaller vessels that ply coastal waters worldwide. Yet more than half the fish eaten in the world today come from inshore and coastal areas that are dominated by small- and medium-scale fishers. As biological limits are hit, frequently it has come down to who can afford to buy fish—and who can afford to go fishing.[49]

Severe overfishing in northern waters has forced fishers to transfer their capacity south, in essence exporting the overcapacity problem. Through joint agreements and other tools of legal exploitation, the North's redundant fleets are making a beeline for southern waters. Waters in the South are for the most part already fished at or near their limits by these nations' increasingly mechanized fleets and by local small-scale inshore fishers.

Since the 1970s, European fleet owners—with the help of the EU—have signed access agreements with individual

West African nations to fish in their EEZ waters. In 1982, distant-water fleets from Europe as well as Russia, South Korea, Japan, and Taiwan claimed about half of African marine fisheries through joint access agreements. Since then, nearly 1,000 European vessels have been redeployed in African waters. In 1996, the EU paid $229 million—or 43 percent of the annual fisheries restructuring budget— for access agreements with Africa. And the vessel owners themselves pay only a small fraction of the cost.[50]

The terms of these agreements are questionable. With few enforceable limits in place and minimal reduction in capacity, this transfer represents an international environmental justice issue. Local fishers are rarely consulted, those using seine nets to catch tuna regularly under-report catches (which are the basis for future agreements), and enforcement of the few environmental provisions is altogether lacking. For the 16 African countries that do benefit financially from these agreements, the rent they receive averages less than 10 percent of the value of the catch.[51]

From the point of view of African nations, generating foreign exchange for debt service and other purposes is the key motivation for annual renewal for these agreements. But the results have been profoundly negative, according to a study by the U.S. Agency for International Development. African pelagic fish are harvested at minimal prices by European fishing companies, and Africans are left with nothing but "overfishing, under-nourishment, and undercompensation."[52]

While boats head south, the catch and production of both foreign fleets and local economies increasingly flow north. (See Table 4–2.) The value of fish traded has increased more than 12-fold, from $2.5 billion in 1970 to $35.8 billion in 1990. During that time, fish trade grew from about 5 percent to 11 percent of global trade in agricultural products. By

1994, world fish trade totalled $47 billion. Nearly half the fish caught today are now traded between nations, compared with an estimated 32 percent in 1980. With diverse markets and varied demand worldwide, "fish trade has virtually no boundaries and few rules," according to environmental reporter John McQuaid.[53]

Consumers in industrial countries account for 85 percent of world fish imports by value. Japan's share of world imports more than tripled, from 8 to 28 percent, between 1969 and 1990. In 1995, Japan imported $18 billion worth of fresh fish, shrimp, surimi, and other fish products from across the globe in order to maintain its per capita intake of 70 kilograms—the highest in the world. By comparison, per capita fish supplies stood at 14.4 kilograms worldwide in 1995, and only at 10.1 kilograms on average in developing countries.[54]

To feed industrial countries' growing appetite for seafood, developing countries are now solid net exporters. Chile, China, and Thailand are responsible for the lion's share of the net trade balance. And their profits come from a fairly narrow product range. Thailand's rapid growth in the past decade, for example, has been achieved through the development of a canned tuna industry and a 1,000-fold increase in giant tiger prawn culture. In Bangladesh, China, India, Indonesia, and Thailand, farmed shrimp are one of the leading food exports. Developing countries trade more than 65 percent of the world's fresh and frozen tuna, 85 percent of the canned tuna, and 84 percent of the world's frozen shrimp and prawns.[55]

In many ways, growth in fish trade is a double-edged sword for developing countries. Exporting high-end fish brings in foreign exchange for countries that desperately need cash. And increased income can certainly contribute to better nutrition, if combined with education, family planning, and a whole range of

Table 4–2. Value of Imports and Exports, Top 10 Countries, 1995

Imports		Exports	
Country	Value[1]	Country	Value[1]
	(billion dollars)		(billion dollars)
Japan	17.85	Thailand	4.45
United States	7.14	United States	3.38
France	3.22	Norway	3.12
Spain	3.11	China	2.85
Germany	2.48	Denmark	2.46
Italy	2.28	Taiwan	2.33
United Kingdom	1.91	Canada	2.31
Hong Kong	1.83	Chile	1.70
Denmark	1.57	Indonesia	1.67
Netherlands	1.19	Russia	1.63

[1]Value includes all types of fish, crustaceans, mollusks, oils, and meals.
SOURCE: U.N. Food and Agriculture Organization, *Yearbook of Fisheries Statistics: Commodities* (Rome: 1997).

social development programs. But trade also poses a conflict with the growing need for food security. As a larger share of fish is exported for foreign exchange and profits, inevitably the net supply for domestic consumption declines. Nearly 1 billion people, predominantly in Asia and coastal developing countries, rely on fish for a majority of their protein needs. Over the long term, exporting a growing share of fish may result in decreasing per capita supplies of food. To satisfy growing human demand, fish supplies for food will rely to an increasing degree on aquaculture output.[56]

Currently, about a third of the world fish harvest is dedicated to nonfood uses, primarily animal feed, fish meal, and oils. This leaves about 82 million tons for direct human consumption. If per capita food supplies are to remain the same in the years ahead, at least 91 million tons will be needed for direct human consumption by 2010. Sustaining this level will require substituting other sources of protein, such as soymeal, for fish in animal feed, as well as better management of marine stocks.[57]

These trends certainly have profound social implications for fishing communities worldwide. In many areas fishers are out of work and families are on the edge of survival. In Newfoundland, for example, more than 30,000 fishers and fish plant workers are unemployed, and many are plagued with gambling problems and with alcohol and drug abuse. As local businesses fail, an average 7,500 people have moved out of the province each year since 1992, leaving a region with more than $700 million in annual economic losses. As Dr. Jon Lien, professor at St. John's Memorial University in Newfoundland, says, "We gave ourselves this crisis."[58]

MANAGING THE FISHERS

The theory of limited access argues that if the oceans and coastal areas were under some degree of local control, and not open to all comers, then fishers would have more incentive to preserve their share of the resource. They would act as stewards of the resource, rather than as plunderers. But perhaps having control of one's future is not the key ingredient here, but rather a feeling of being listened to, a feeling that expertise—whether gained from years at a university or on a particular fishing vessel—is respected and trusted by those in authority. And often it is both.

In response to current policy failures, fishers and policymakers are stitching together a growing patchwork of systems designed to fill the management gap. The pieces of this quilt range from local fishing cooperatives and community-based management schemes to quotas and limited access regimes. Each has certain attributes that can help protect fisheries and fishers and promote sustainable fishing.

Inevitably, the issue of overcapacity comes down to what happens to people who rely on fishing for their livelihoods.

Traditional sea tenure systems have sustained island peoples in the Pacific for thousands of years, while marine tenure systems have evolved over centuries in inshore fisheries. Many of these systems have detailed, site-specific boundaries that define fishing grounds and strict limitations on how fishing is conducted. Most are community-based; some are exclusive to a particular group of fishers by gear or family, designed not just to restrict access and effort, but also to manage people. They serve as effective deterrents to overfishing, for they often encompass a broader belief system that values the sea for its role in social history and cultural identity, as well as food and sustenance.[59]

Many of the principles of community-based management are still used successfully today. A self-governing common-property arrangement exists in Alanya, Turkey, for example. Created in the 1970s after years of trial and error, the system is based on rotating fishing sites from east to west during different seasons. Fishers have an incentive to follow this system of access as it equalizes the opportunities for fishing, and they monitor and enforce their own rules. The Turkish government has given cooperatives such as this one jurisdiction over local arrangements, lending credibility to the participants and helping to legitimize traditional management systems.[60]

Similarly, in 1991 the government of the Philippines devolved management of nearshore fisheries to municipalities and local fishing communities. Although problems of financing, jurisdiction, and enforcement still persist, transferring authority to fishers and fishers' associations has helped keep fisheries management within the context of local development needs. Cooperatives have focused on providing fishers with supplemental income projects and with credit, lending, and marketing services in an effort to diversify income sources.[61]

At the other end of the management spectrum is the movement toward market-based solutions, which essentially privatize the right to fish. Among these schemes, the most publicized has been individual transferable quotas (ITQs). An ITQ confers the right to harvest a certain fixed volume or share of fish in a particular area and time. Quotas can be bought and sold on the market, which in theory will encourage inefficient fishers to leave by selling their right to fish to someone else. Traditionally, ITQs have tended to concentrate quotas (and therefore access rights) in the hands of the few who can afford them and those who extracted a large share of the resource before the system was introduced. Although ITQs do address the issues of overcapacity and economic efficiency, often the results have been devastating for small-scale fishers.[62]

ITQs have been implemented in Australia, Canada, Iceland, the Netherlands, New Zealand, and the

United States. The first national program was implemented in 1986 in 32 commercial fisheries in New Zealand. Just one year later, the three largest fishing companies held title to 43 percent of the ITQs. Within five years, these three companies held half of all ITQs in the system. Many small vessel owners and fishers either subcontracted to larger companies or went out of business completely.[63]

This same scenario is being played out to varying degrees in fisheries across the globe—from the mid-Atlantic surf clam and ocean quahog fishery in the United States to the Icelandic herring and capelin fisheries, among others. ITQs have helped solve economic inefficiencies in fisheries, thanks to compensation for removal and withdrawal of vessels from industry.[64]

But biologically, the verdict is still out on whether the quotas help or hurt the resource. Of 31 ITQ fisheries reviewed by the Committee for Fisheries of the Organisation for Economic Co-operation and Development, 24 have maintained catches below the total allowable level. But for several of these, what was allowed was deemed too high for sustainable production. Most fisheries studied used other regulations as well, including catch size limits, gear restrictions, and closed seasons, which helped mitigate problems of declining productivity but tended to increase discards and monitoring costs. Ultimately, the success of ITQs and other management tools relies to a large extent on accurate fish population data and conservative catch limits, which allow for ecological complexity and interactions, as well as consistent enforcement and management.[65]

Inevitably, the issue of overcapacity comes down to what happens to people who rely on fishing for their livelihoods. In overcapitalized industrial fisheries, a combination of a short-term economic bandage, long-term economic restructuring, and overall downsizing in the industry is necessary. Governments can provide economic aid to fishers who are struggling to make a living. Retraining programs, education, and incentives for people to shift to other sectors and to supplement declining income from fisheries are important to avoid massive social disruption.[66]

When this issue has been confronted in industrial countries, governments have paid to retrain fishers for other jobs or to buy back vessels, often with little success. A nearly $2-billion five-year social adjustment program in Atlantic Canada known as the Atlantic Groundfish Strategy is helping fishers stay out of debt for the time being, but critics argue that it amounts to nothing more than a massive social welfare program. And in 1996, the U.S. government pledged $25 million to buy out part of the commercial groundfish fleet in New England. But without efforts to manage resources for the long term, this reduction in capacity could be overwhelmed in just nine years, based on historical catches. Similarly, the European Union set aside $2.2 billion to fund restructuring and economic transition programs for fishers. But intense pressure from industry officials, politicians, and fishers prompted EU ministers to backslide on fleet reductions and to postpone needed reforms.[67]

In developing countries, alternatives to fishing are more limited and jobs are desperately needed. Seaweed culture is being advanced as a secondary activity for fishers in Lombak and Bali, Indonesia. The growing enterprise involves the labor- and time-intensive process of tying seaweed in clusters on ropes, attaching them to bamboo frames, and harvesting and trading the seaweed. Likewise, low-input aquaculture systems with noncarnivorous species such as tilapia, milkfish, and mullet have proved economically and ecologically beneficial in Bangladesh, China, India, and several Southeast Asian countries. In the long run, societies may decide that it is worth sacrificing economic efficiency in order to reap the social benefits of small-er-scale fishing and preserve fish for food and jobs.[68]

Another issue needing attention is the lack of enforcement and monitoring. Without these, any management plan is almost certain to fail. One innovative solution comes from the South Pacific Forum Fisheries Agency, a regional body with jurisdiction over island nations of the South Pacific. The group recently adopt-ed a plan to develop and implement a satellite-based regional vessel monitoring system. Based on experience in Australia and New Zealand, initially the system will monitor the position of up to 1,000 vessels in South Pacific waters. With technical improvements, it can also provide a means of transmitting catch reports to authorities. The first plan of its kind, this effort has received support from some industrial fishers who feel that monitor-ing will prove they are in compliance with fishing agreements. Several distant-water fishing nations, however, including Japan, have objections about data security, cost, and the implementation time frame.[69]

Reducing high levels of bycatch and waste is critical to improving fisheries. This can be accomplished with more selective gear, broader markets for fish products, and a market orientation away from an intensive focus on one particular species to a more balanced approach of using the entire catch for human con-sumption as well as substituting other sources of protein, meal, and oil for non-food uses of fish. Turtle excluder devices required on shrimp trawl nets by the U.S. Endangered Species Act, for example, have helped preserve the last Kemp's rid-ley turtles in the Gulf of Mexico, as well as numerous finfish. Worldwide, invest-ments in more selective gear types could pay off with reductions in discards of nearly 60 percent, according to FAO.[70]

One critical area for immediate gov-ernment action is a marine equivalent of the "polluter pays principle," to hold ves-sel owners accountable for the destruc-tion they cause to fisheries and the marine environment. Governments would do well to set up a full-cost account-ing system of industrial fishing practices to prevent further ruin of the resource and to pay for the damages, as well as to guarantee that foreign access agreements restrain fishing effort and get a fairer compensation price. Until such destruc-tive practices as cyanide poisoning and dynamite blasting can be phased out, consumers who enjoy shark fin soup, live fish prepared before their eyes, and other aquatic delicacies should be charged the full ecological price for their meals.[71]

Another key ingredient is protecting fisheries habitat areas and juvenile popu-lations through the use of marine reserves. (See Table 4–3.) On the Yucatan Peninsula in Mexico, the Sian Ka'an Biosphere reserve is home to the spiny lobster fishery, which is closely controlled by "an intricate and judicious limited entry system," according to geographer David Miller of the State University of New York in Cortland, that is similar to government leasing out tracts of offshore areas for oil and gas exploration. Through a cooperative, fishers are grant-ed a tract to fish any way they want. If they overfish or damage their tract, they can-not receive an additional one. Fishers can trade, but the entire area has been allo-cated to one fisher or another, so there is little danger of overfishing. For conserva-tion purposes, fishers have constructed artificial reefs to shelter lobsters. These fishers are among Mexico's most outspo-ken advocates for conservation and sus-tainable development.[72]

"No-take" fishing areas, seasonal fish-eries closures, and limited-use agree-ments can help depleted stocks rebound—and profits return. A 1982 study of the offshore shrimp fishery in Texas waters documented an increase of $9.4 million in shrimp harvest value fol-lowing closure of the fishery, which allowed juvenile shrimp to grow to more marketable sizes. A group of international marine biologists, oceanographers, and scientists recently called for governments to increase protected marine reserves from the current 0.25 percent of the ocean's surface area to 20 percent by 2020. Such a move would provide needed respite for commercially depleted fisheries and, combined with effective management, could allow stocks to regain an estimated 10 million tons in production.[73]

Recently, a number of promising international fisheries and marine biodiversity agreements have emerged to fill the void in international fisheries policy. Chapter 17 of *Agenda 21*, the plan of action endorsed by most of the world's governments at the 1992 Earth Summit, addresses the sustainable use and conservation of marine living resources and highlights the importance of integrated management and sustainable development of coastal and marine areas, including EEZs. Although the language of Chapter 17 is weak at best, there is an opportunity to formalize tougher agreements in 1999, when the U.N. Commission on Sustainable Development is scheduled to address oceans and seas.[74]

In 1991, the United Nations passed a moratorium on high-seas driftnets. One year later, more than 60 fishing countries agreed to a voluntary international Code of Conduct for Responsible Fishing proposed by FAO, which calls for nations to adopt selective and environmentally safe fishing methods to protect subsistence fishers, maintain biodiversity, and safeguard aquatic ecosystems. And in 1995, governments signed onto the Convention on Highly Migratory and Straddling Stocks. This addresses fish stocks that travel across EEZ boundaries, especially highly valued tuna, swordfish, and shark; it marked the first time that an international fisheries treaty or agreement accepted the precautionary principle—the idea that even without firm scientific proof,

society should take action when there is the potential of irreversible consequences or severe limits on the options for the next generation. The Convention on Biological Diversity also addresses marine biodiversity and extends a broader framework to the protection of marine fisheries.[75]

SETTING A NEW COURSE

With 1998 designated by the United Nations as "Year of the Ocean," media attention on the condition of the world's oceans and on marine conservation issues offers a chance to build political momentum and public support for rehauling fisheries management worldwide. Some leading scientists advocate establishing an intergovernmental panel focused on oceans and fisheries, formed along the lines of the influential panel on climate change, with input from nongovernmental organizations, FAO, and national governments could help forge new coalitions to reform fisheries management, build support for marine conservation research and outreach, and further protect marine life.[76]

Rather than trying to resolve the tensions between open and closed access, between conservation and growth, sustainable fisheries management can best be achieved when it embraces the inherent balancing act between these approaches. What is needed is management based on the precautionary principle.[77]

Truly sustainable fisheries management requires conservative limits on fisheries to be set well below the biological level of maximum sustainable yield. Decisions are based on local conditions and needs, with stakeholders involved and represented. Some form of property rights is also needed to guarantee sustainable fisheries. But the means of dividing up the waters should be based on equity, fairness, and need as determined by

Table 4–3. Selected Marine Protected Areas and National Legislation

Problem	Management Program	Results

Apo Island Reef Sanctuary, Philippines

Island in danger of losing corals because of destructive fishing methods used; fishing economy devastated by overfishing and ecosystem degradation. Fishers travel 30 kilometers to find fish.	Marine Conservation and Development Program, initiated in 1985, included livelihood projects, environmental education, community development training, and programs in agroforestry and water development. In 1986, 8 percent of the reefs were set aside as marine reserve; use restricted to scuba diving and snorkeling.	By 1988, edible fish and shellfish populations recovered; fishers could fish in surrounding waters After 10 years, reefs are intact, fish are bountiful, and rare species such as the giant clam (which have great economic value) thrive.

Saba Island Marine Park, Lesser Antilles

Islanders want to control ecological impacts of the thriving tourist trade, including coral reef damage from boat anchors and high extraction of marine organisms. Lack of funds for enforcement and monitoring.	Established in 1987, marine park includes entire coastal zone, and is locally designed, self-managed, and internally financed. The park divides the reefs into four zones: multiple use, allowing fishing and diving; anchor zones, where free anchoring and mooring are permitted; recreational diving only; and recreational zones, which accommodate swimming, boating, snorkeling, diving, and fishing. Island residents raise funds to enforce conservation measures and manage the marine ecosystem.	Increase in marine park supports industries such as patrols, buoy maintenance, and visitor services, providing jobs and income to local residents. Increase in tourism revenue without having to pay for a new management scheme. Divers charged user fee. Sustainable use of the island's marine resources.

Mafia Island Marine Park, Tanzania

Fear by islanders that overfished and degraded coastal regions north of the island would attract increased exploitation of their waters.	In 1988, islanders, government representatives, and members of conservation organizations decide to create a multiple use marine park. Islanders and technical experts develop a plan with large non-extractive zone, area of limited fishing, and general-use area with minimal control.	Residents trained and engaged in enforcement patrols, resource monitoring, information collection, conservation programs, and evaluation. Marine habitat gains legal protection.

Table 4–3. *(Continued)*

Passage of Marine Parks & Reserves Act in 1994 and land legislation creating the park in July 1995 establish national law and policy in support of the park.

Destructive fishing practices banned throughout the park.

Sustainable socio-economic benefits, including fishing and tourism, are preserved.

National Legislation, Sri Lanka

Coral reef destruction by coral mining; under-mining of coral reef ecosystem and functions contributing to severe erosion along beach areas.

High level of illegal coral mining due to lack of jobs and alternatives.

Coral mining and related activities banned.

Existing legal mandates strengthened.

Funding for alternative livelihood schemes made available for coral miners.

Public education programs for miners, police officers, and members of the community to raise awareness of the damages from mining and to improve enforcement and compliance.

48 percent decrease in coral illegally mined between 1984 and 1993.

Special Area Management Plan enacted in Rekawa to incorporate sustainable use strategies for shrimp fisheries, agricultural land use, and beach habitat for sea turtles.

Integrated Coastal Zone Management Program, Belize

Uncontrolled tourism damaging fragile reef areas. High boat traffic, sport fishing, and diving.

Declining catches for several fish; frequent illegal fishing of under-sized conch and lobster; overfishing a threat.

Land-based activities causing severe runoff, erosion, and pollution.

Institutional support created through Technical and Steering Committees; monitoring, research, education, and training centers.

Legislative support embodied in the Coastal Zone Management Act; no-fishing zones established.

Community support; fishers, dive operators, and tour guides trained in conservation; land use planning emphasized.

Seven areas of protected reef throughout the country are declared UNESCO World Heritage Sites.

Belize's fishing and tourism industries are becoming self-sufficient through user fees.

Mooring buoys set up to prevent damage to reefs; fishers help with stock monitoring and assessment.

SOURCE: See endnote 72.

dependence on the resource and the best available scientific knowledge, not simply economic might and political pressure. At a minimum, local control, a high degree of enforcement and accountability, resource users involved in management, and a precautionary approach can form the basis of a broad revolution in global fisheries management. The way this is implemented can take many forms, none of which will be easy.[78]

Whatever course is followed, the current state of reacting to crises rather than preventing biological declines cannot continue indefinitely. With fewer and fewer commercially viable species available, fishers will soon face catastrophic losses. Following the same patterns of repeated mistakes will guarantee that fishing is no longer an employer of millions and a source of bounty. In many ways, the form that fishing will take in the future begins at home—in supermarkets and high-end restaurants, in corporate headquarters and parliaments, and on shrimp trawlers and the ferries blockaded from leaving port—far from the high seas and underwater habitats that are desperately under siege. Unfortunately, indifference has been the response to date.

Market forces that support environmentally safe production practices need to be harnessed on behalf of fisheries. A U.S. consumer boycott of canned tuna in the late 1980s successfully forced changes in the way fishers caught tuna and helped protect dolphins from being ensnared in the nets. In April 1996, the World Wide Fund for Nature teamed up with one of the world's largest manufacturers of seafood products, Anglo-Dutch Unilever, to create economic incentives for sustainable fishing. Implemented through an independent Marine Stewardship Council, fisheries products that are harvested in a sustainable manner will qualify for an eco-label. More efforts like this are needed to convince manufacturers to replace fish oils and meals with other products and to stop wasteful fishing practices.[79]

Indeed, what is needed now is the same scale of public outcry that helped save the whales and ban trade in elephant ivory. Ultimately, the future of global fisheries may rest with consumers who buy fish products that have been produced sustainably, ask where a fish came from and how it was raised, and demand that policymakers support the recommendations of scientists to close fisheries and reduce fishing effort. Tough choices are required of fishery managers, who are often swayed by politicians and industry leaders. Public input into the process and agency accountability for decisions will help make fisheries management more true to its purpose.[80]

Promoting sustainable fisheries will also depend, to a large extent, on a renewed commitment to the protection of marine biological diversity and a long-term, ecologically based perspective in fisheries management. To this end, integrated coastal management programs that promote sustainable fishing and the health of marine ecosystems are useful tools that can be incorporated into fisheries management. Finally, there is a great need for direct political action to support new management schemes based on equity and need and to encourage greater participation by fishers in management, decisionmaking, and enforcement.

With timely action, fisheries can continue to provide food, jobs, and enjoyment for millions of people worldwide. But ultimately this means changing our focus from what is done to a fish to what can be done for the fish. And the time for that change is now.

5

Struggling to Raise Cropland Productivity

Lester R. Brown

The world's population is fast approaching 6 billion and, despite a slowdown in the rate of growth, it continues to expand by 80 million a year. Feeding this addition to our ranks requires 26 million tons of additional grain annually. Two hundred years after the famous piece by Thomas Malthus, *An Essay on the Principle of Population*, the race between food and people is still a matter of concern in many national capitals.[1]

While Malthus focused on the effect of population growth on the demand for food, he did not anticipate the effect of rising affluence, of people eating higher on the food chain as incomes rise. In Asia, where more than half the world's people live, incomes are rising at a record rate. As they do, so does the consumption of pork, poultry, beef, eggs, and milk—all grain-intensive products. In China, the world's fastest growing economy during the

An expanded version of this chapter appeared as Worldwatch Paper 136, *The Agricultural Link: How Environmental Deterioration Could Disrupt Economic Progress.*

1990s, easily two thirds of the growth in demand for grain is for feeding livestock and poultry.[2]

This extraordinarily robust world growth in demand comes at a time when the growth in grain production is losing momentum. As a result, during the late 1990s carryover stocks of grain have dropped to the lowest levels on record. And grain prices, after declining for half a century, have been rising since 1993. If this trend cannot be checked, it could lead to unprecedented political unrest in Third World cities.[3]

ONLY TWO OPTIONS

Farmers expand food production either by expanding cultivated area or by raising land productivity. From the beginning of agriculture until the middle of this century, they relied primarily on the former; rises in land productivity were so slow as to be scarcely perceptible within a given generation. But by 1950 the frontiers of agricultural settlement had largely disappeared.

Almost overnight, farmers made the transition to raising yields. For four decades, they lifted land productivity at a rate that easily kept up with the record growth in demand. In fact, they were so successful that the United States was forced to idle a share of its cropland to prevent a precipitous decline in prices. Since 1990, however, the rise in land productivity has slowed rather dramatically, raising questions as to whether farmers will be able to keep up with future growth in demand.

As this rise has slowed, the United States returned to use the cropland that was idled under commodity programs for much of the last half-century. The only remaining land held out now is that in the Conservation Reserve Program (CRP), which is designed to convert highly erodible cropland to grassland or some other sustainable use. Perhaps half of the 14 million hectares in the CRP in 1997 could be farmed sustainably if properly managed. This would expand world grain output enough to cover nine months of world population growth. Similarly, Europe also temporarily idled some cropland during the mid-1990s, but most of that land is also now back in use.[4]

In this chapter, we use grainland as a surrogate for total cropland, simply because total cropland data are neither consistent nor reliable. Most of the world's cropland is used to produce grain, which when consumed directly supplies roughly half of human caloric intake and when consumed indirectly, in the form of livestock products, accounts for a large share of the remainder.[5]

As the world makes the transition into the next century, some countries will be losing cropland while other areas will be gaining it. On balance, the cropland area is not likely to change much. The losses include those to residential, industrial, and recreational uses and those to soil erosion. Whether it is housing developments invading California's vast fruit- and vegetable-growing Central Valley, housing construction in India, or the building of factories in China, farmers are losing cropland.

In India, for example, assuming a density of 8 people per dwelling, the projected growth from 936 million people in 1995 to 1,403 million people in 2030 means building another 58 million residential units, either in single-family units in villages and cities or in urban high rises. Since India's villages and cities are located in the heart of fertile agricultural regions, this projected growth will lead to heavy cropland losses.[6]

China also is facing a heavy loss of cropland from both residential and industrial construction as it adds some 247 million people by 2030 and as it tries to provide jobs for the more than 100 million or so workers who have left rural villages, migrating to cities and construction sites in search of work. The plan is eventually to employ these workers in the industrial sector. Assuming roughly 100 workers per factory, the average in the private sector, China will need to build a staggering 1 million factories. With most of China's population and industry concentrated in a 1,500-kilometer strip on the eastern and southern coast of the country, where most of the cropland is found, this too will inevitably lead to heavy losses of cropland.[7]

Recreational land uses are also beginning to compete with food production. One of the most land-intensive leisure-time activities is golfing. As incomes rise in Asia, the number of golfers is rising at an extraordinary rate. This has led to the construction of thousands of golf courses in Japan, the Philippines, Indonesia, Viet Nam, Malaysia, and China. Sensing the threat this poses, Viet Nam has banned the construction of golf courses on riceland. Similarly, Guangdong Province, the southern coastal province of China, which has been the fastest-growing province in China, also had to ban golf course construction to protect its cropland.[8]

Losses to soil erosion are common, especially in developing countries. Kazakhstan, the largest wheat producer in Central Asia, has lost one third of its cropland to erosion since 1980. On balance, the world's cropland area is not likely to expand much at all over the next few decades. If this happens, the grainland area per person, which has shrunk from 0.23 hectares per person in 1950 to 0.12 hectares in 1997, will decline further, dropping to 0.08 hectares in the year 2030. (See Figure 5–1.) Given this likely development, can scientists restore a rapid rise in grainland productivity, one that will more than offset the shrinkage in cropland area per person?[9]

Assessments of the potential for doing this vary widely. In a recent World Bank report, researchers indicated that they expect grain yields to increase at 1.5 to 1.7 percent per year, or "at rates comparable to those in recent years." With this rosy outlook, the Bank projects surplus capacity in world agriculture as a whole, accompanied by declining food prices. Our analysis comes to a very different conclusion.[10]

World Bank economists base their projections on simple extrapolation, arguing that "historically, yields have grown along a linear path from 1960 to 1990, and they are projected to continue along the path of past growth." Although extrapolating past yield trends worked well enough in previous decades, it will not work in a world where biological and hydrological constraints are emerging. In contrast to the robust rise of 2.1 percent a year between 1950 and 1990, yields rose only 1 percent a year between 1990 and 1995. Although this period is too short to establish a clear trend, it does suggest that raising land productivity fast enough to offset the future shrinkage in cropland area per person may now be one of humanity's greatest challenges.[11]

SOURCES OF HIGHER PRODUCTIVITY

The first recorded case in which farmers achieved a steady, sustained increase in output per unit of land—a "yield take-off"—began more than a century ago in Japan. In 1878, Japanese rice farmers got an average of 1.4 tons per hectare. By 1984, the average yield had more than tripled, to 4.7 tons. Since then, it has plateaued—typically fluctuating between 4.3 and 4.6 tons. (See Figure 5–2.) Japan has been unable to improve average rice yields for more than a decade, even though the government supports the price paid to its farmers for rice at six times the world level, thereby offering a powerful financial incentive to raise yields higher, and despite the government's ability to provide the best technology available.[12]

In the United States, the first yield

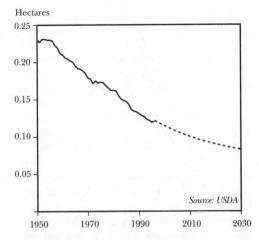

Hectares

Figure 5–1. Grain Area Per Person Worldwide, 1950–97, With Projections to 2030

Source: USDA

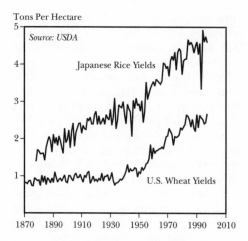

Tons Per Hectare

Source: USDA

Japanese Rice Yields

U.S. Wheat Yields

1870 1890 1910 1930 1950 1970 1990 2010

Figure 5–2. Rice Yields for Japan, 1878–1997, and Wheat Yields for United States, 1866–1997

takeoff came more than a half-century later, with wheat. During the nearly 80 years between the Civil War and World War II, U.S. wheat yields had fluctuated around 0.9 tons per hectare. As the war got under way and demand for U.S. grain rose when production was disrupted abroad, farmers began investing in higher-yielding seeds and in fertilizer. By 1983, wheat yields had climbed to 2.65 tons per hectare, nearly tripling the traditional level. Since then, however, there has been no further rise.[13]

Although the wheat yield takeoff in the United States began decades after that of rice in Japan, farmers in the two countries appear to have "hit the wall" at about the same time. Is this plateauing in two of the most agriculturally advanced countries temporary? Or does it signal a future leveling off in other countries, as farmers exhaust the known means of profitably increasing yields?

The 2.5-fold increase in world grainland productivity since mid-century has come from three sources: genetic advances, agronomic improvements, and synergies between the two. On the genetic front, the principal growth has come

from redistributing the share of the plant's photosynthetic product (photosynthate) going to each of the various plant parts (leaves, stems, roots, and seeds), so that a much larger share goes to the seed—the part used for food. Scientists estimate that the originally domesticated wheats devoted roughly 20 percent of their photosynthate to the development of seeds; they were stalk-heavy and harvest-light. Through plant breeding, scientists have raised the share of photosynthate going into seed—the "harvest index"—in today's wheat, rice, and corn to more than 50 percent. Given the plant's basic requirements of an adequate root system, a strong stem, and sufficient leaves for photosynthesis, scientists believe the physiological limit is around 60 percent.[14]

One of the earliest gains in this area came when Japanese scientists incorporated a dwarf gene into wheat plants during the late nineteenth century. Traditional varieties of these grasses were tall and thin because their ancestors growing in the wild needed to compete with other plants for sunlight. But once farmers began controlling weeds among the domesticated plants, there was no longer a need for tall varieties. As plant breeders shortened both wheat and rice plants, reducing the length of their straw, they also lowered the share of photosynthate going into straw and increased that going into seed. L.T. Evans, a prominent Australian soil scientist and plant physiologist who has long studied cereal yield gains and potentials, notes that in the high-yielding dwarf wheats, "the gain in grain yield approximately equals the loss in straw weight."[15]

With corn, varieties grown in the tropics were reduced in height from an average of nearly three meters to less than two. But Don Duvick, for many years the director of research at the Pioneer Hybrid seed company, observes that with the hybrids used in the U.S. Corn Belt, the key to higher yields is the ability of varieties to "withstand the stress of higher plant densities while still making the same amount of grain per plant." One of the keys to growing more plants per hectare is to reorient the horizontally inclined leaves of traditional strains that droop somewhat, making them more upright and thereby reducing the amount of self-shading.[16]

Although plant breeders have greatly increased the share of the photosynthate going to the seed of various grains, they have not been able to fundamentally alter the basic process of photosynthesis itself. The amount produced by a given leaf area remains unchanged from that of the plant's wild ancestors.

On the agronomic front, the principal means of increasing land productivity have been to use more fertilizer, expand irrigation, and control diseases, insects, and weeds. All these inputs and practices help ensure that plants can reach more of their full genetic yield potential.

Fertilizer helps to ensure that plant growth will not be inhibited by any lack of nutrients. The tenfold rise in fertilizer use, from 14 million tons in 1950 to some 140 million in 1990, has been the engine driving the worldwide rise in land productivity. But in the 1990s, usage of fertilizer—like that of irrigation water—has leveled off in many countries. U.S. farmers, after discovering that there are optimal levels beyond which further applications are not cost-effective, are using less fertilizer in the mid-1990s than they were in the early 1980s. This trend has been followed by similar developments in Western Europe and Japan.[17]

In the former Soviet Union, fertilizer use fell precipitously after subsidies were removed in 1988 and prices climbed to world market levels. After 1990, a combination of the breakup of the Soviet Union and the effort to convert from a planned to a market economy led to a severe economic depression, one that reduced fertilizer use even more. After dropping during the early 1990s as a result of the pronounced drop in the former Soviet Union, the recently restored trend of rising world fertilizer use is likely to continue for some time, with increases concentrated in countries such as India and Argentina that have adequate soil moisture but are using rather modest amounts of fertilizer.[18]

Other agronomic contributions to higher cropland productivity include the more timely planting of crops made possible by mechanization and higher plant populations per hectare, the latter applying particularly to corn. In temperate zones, there is typically a brief window of opportunity for seeding, usually measured in days, when optimum yields can be obtained. After that, yields decline with each day of delay.

Plant breeders have not been able to fundamentally alter the basic process of photosynthesis.

Advances in plant breeding and agronomy often reinforce each other. The dwarfing of wheat and rice plants not only reduced the amount of photosynthate needed for straw, it increased the benefit of adding more fertilizer. For example, the traditional tall, thin-strawed wheat varieties grown in India could effectively use only about 40 kilograms of nitrogen per hectare. More than that made the plants grow heavier heads of grain, but these would often "lodge," or fall over (especially in storms), leading to crop losses. With the dwarf varieties, farmers could boost nitrogen applications to 120 kilograms per hectare or more, thus greatly increasing the yield but with little fear of lodging. This synergy between genetics and agronomics helps explain the doubling or tripling of yields achieved with the first generation of high-yielding wheats and rices—the heart of the Green Revolution.[19]

With corn, a greater tolerance for crowding enabled growers to increase significantly the plant population—and hence the number of ears harvested—per hectare. At the same time, herbicides were being developed that would control weeds, eliminating the traditional need to plant corn rows far enough apart to permit mechanical cultivators to pass through the field early in the growing season. As a result of these two advances, plant populations have climbed. In Iowa, for example, corn plant densities have nearly tripled since 1930.[20]

For each of the three major grains—wheat, rice, and corn—the major worldwide gains in productivity took place between 1950 and 1990. Since 1990, gains have been much smaller, and the question now facing planners is just how much more can be expected.[21]

RAISING GRAIN YIELDS

Yields of wheat, now humanity's principal food staple, vary enormously from one country to another. Kazakhstan, the largest producer among the central Asian republics, produced only 0.6 tons per hectare in 1995, for example; France, the largest producer in Europe, produced more than 10 times as much that year—6.8 tons per hectare. It may be tempting to cite such disparities as evidence of potential for improvement in the lower-yielding countries, but this would be highly misleading. In fact, the prospect for raising yields further may actually be better in France than in Kazakhstan. Rainfall is marginal for agriculture in Kazakhstan, and with wind erosion of soil now widespread, Kazakh soil scientists report that cropland fertility is falling.[22]

A look at the historical trends in such key wheat-producing countries as France, China, and the United States helps explain the potential for raising wheat yields throughout the world. In France, wheat yields have quadrupled since mid-century, climbing from 1.8 tons per hectare in 1950 to 7.2 tons in 1996. (See Figure 5–3.) The United States, with a yield of just over 1 ton per hectare, ranked second after France in 1950. By 1983, farmers had pushed this above 2.6 tons per hectare. But, as noted earlier, since then yields have been flat.[23]

The fallacy of thinking that low yields are a measure of the potential for improvement is further illustrated by a comparison of India and Australia. In 1950, both countries were getting the same yields from their wheat: about 0.9 tons per hectare. By 1995, India had nearly tripled its take, to 2.5 tons. Australia had increased to only 1.7 tons. But the difference is not a reflection of the superior capabilities of Indian farmers. In fact, the Australians had to use great ingenuity and effort to achieve even these modest gains. The difference is that farmers in India, who irrigate much of their wheat, have good soil moisture, whereas those

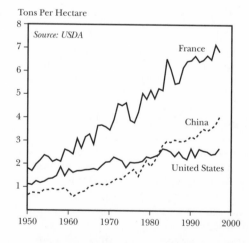

Figure 5–3. Wheat Yields in France, China, and United States, 1950–97

in Australia, who have to rely on sparse rainfall, do not. This also explains why Africa, a largely arid and semiarid continent, has not matched the yield gains of Asia. Lacking either abundant rainfall or irrigation to provide sufficient soil moisture, farmers cannot effectively use much fertilizer—and therefore cannot fully exploit the genetic potential of their crops.[24]

Grainland productivity is directly affected by soil moisture levels, latitude or day length, and solar intensity. The two countries with the highest wheat yields are in Western Europe. (See Table 5–1.) Both have good soil moisture and sufficiently mild climates that they can grow the higher-yielding winter wheats that benefit so much from the long summer days. The next two on the list—Egypt and Mexico—rely heavily on irrigation to achieve relatively high wheat yields. Indeed in Egypt, where it rarely ever rains, wheat would not grow without irrigation. China, next on the list, relies on supplemental irrigation for much of its wheat crop.

Now that developing countries are collectively using more fertilizer than industrial countries and, with few exceptions, are using high-yielding varieties and other advanced technologies, ranking on the yield chart is determined largely by the environmental factors just mentioned—rainfall, day length, and solar intensity. When a country's wheat-growing practices do fall short of their potential, the yield can be improved rapidly until environmental limits are reached—and then no amount of money, ingenuity, or fertilizer can take it much further. The United States nearly tripled its wheat yield by 1983, for example, but even with all its access to technology, fertilizer, and agronomic knowledge, it has not been able to raise yields since then.[25]

Raising wheat yields in China is becoming more difficult as aquifers are depleted, as the response to additional fertilizer

Table 5–1. Annual Wheat Yield Per Hectare in Key Producing Countries, 1994–96

Country	Yield
	(tons)
United Kingdom	7.7
France	6.8
Egypt	5.6
Mexico	4.1
China	3.6
Poland	3.4
Ukraine	2.7
India	2.5
United States	2.5
Canada	2.3
Argentina	2.1
Pakistan	2.0
Australia	1.6
Russia	1.4
Kazakhstan	0.6

SOURCE: U.S. Department of Agriculture, Foreign Agricultural Service, *World Agricultural Production* (Washington, DC: April 1997).

diminishes, and as the country's fast-growing cities pull irrigation water away from agriculture. With the Huang He (Yellow River) now running dry for several weeks each spring, and for progressively longer periods each year, some wheat farmers downstream will face shrinking irrigation water supplies.

In France and other major wheat-producing countries such as Germany and the United Kingdom, it took less than five years for yields to go from 5 to 6 tons per hectare, but more than a decade to go from 6 to 7 tons per hectare. Almost everywhere that wheat is produced, in developing countries as well as highly mechanized ones, the historic rise in yields is slowing. Mexico, the site of the breeding program that produced the high-yielding dwarf wheats that came to be widely used in the Third World, has become the first developing country to "hit the wall" in efforts to raise wheat land productivity. Like the United States, Mexico has not seen any improvement in the past 13 years.[26]

Rice, to achieve its full yield potential, requires large quantities of water, either from the natural flooding that occurs in monsoonal climates or from irrigation. When farmers are forced to rely on monsoon flooding, they lack the water control needed to use fertilizer and pesticides effectively. Japan, which has the highest yield among the major rice producers (see Table 5–2), irrigates 99 percent of its riceland—as does South Korea, which ranks a close second. In Bangladesh, where farmers harvest less than half as much rice per hectare as the Japanese or Koreans do, the irrigated share falls to 24 percent. Three fourths of the riceland in Bangladesh is subject to the whims of the monsoon.[27]

Rice is also affected by latitude, with yields rising as distance from the equator increases. In Japan, the northernmost of the major rice-producing countries, days during the summer growing season can be several hours longer than in a country like Indonesia, which lies astride the equator.[28]

A third factor affecting rice yields is solar intensity. Asia, which produces 90 percent of the world's rice, is actually handicapped because the bulk of this crop is grown during the summer monsoon season, when extensive cloud cover reduces the amount of sunlight reaching fields. Although Japan's latitudinal advantage and full use of irrigation give it the highest yield per hectare in Asia, yields are still one third below those in California, where there is an abundance of sunshine.[29]

The historical trends in rice yields in Japan, China, and India (see Figure 5–4) provide some insight into the longer-term potential for raising world rice yields. As noted earlier, Japan tripled its per-hectare output over a century of genetic and agronomic improvements, plateauing in 1984.[30]

China made its improvements later, but it too appears to have tripled its rice yields. If the area planted to rice in China is underestimated by up to 30 percent, as Chinese officials now believe is likely, then the yield per hectare of rice is overstated and the actual yield may be closer to 3 tons per hectare rather than the official 4.4. Nonetheless, if China's rice yield is adjusted for the latitudinal handicap it suffers relative to Japan, then its farmers may be approaching the same constraints as those in Japan. That conclusion is consistent with the observation that China is already using most of the yield-enhancing techniques: high-yielding varieties, nearly full irrigation, and heavy doses of fertilizer.[31]

In India, rice yields have doubled since mid-century, from roughly 1 ton per hectare to 2 tons. Production in India suffers from a lack of irrigation, and because days are shorter during the summer than in Japan, India cannot realistically be expected to raise yields to anywhere near the same level. Along with whatever potential for higher yields that may remain in India, the greatest promise appears to lie in Bangladesh, Viet Nam, and Myanmar (formerly Burma). But for the world as a whole, the unrealized opportunity to raise rice yields is shrink-

Table 5–2. Annual Rice Yield Per Hectare in Key Producing Countries, 1994–96

Country	Yield
	(tons)
Japan	4.8
South Korea	4.7
China	4.2
Taiwan	4.1
Indonesia	2.9
Viet Nam	2.4
Philippines	1.9
India	1.9
Pakistan	1.8
Bangladesh	1.8

SOURCE: U.S. Department of Agriculture, Foreign Agricultural Service, *World Agricultural Production* (Washington, DC: April 1997).

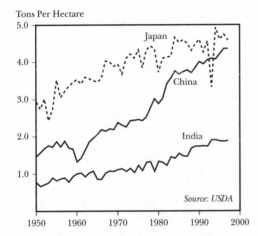

Tons Per Hectare

Figure 5–4. Rice Yields in Japan, China, and India, 1950–97

Source: USDA

ing, suggesting that future gains will be much slower.[32]

Perhaps the most promising source of higher rice yields is the new rice prototype being developed in the Philippines, which is expected to be available for commercial use sometime after the turn of the century. Dr. Gurdev Khush, the Indian scientist who heads the rice breeding project, believes it could raise rice yields in the tropical and subtropical regions, for which it is designed, by up to 20 percent. If it were to succeed in raising yields on two thirds of the world's riceland, this would boost the current world rice harvest of 350 million tons by 50 million tons, enough to cover world population growth for two years. Vitally important though this would be, it is a far cry from the doubling or tripling of yields that came with the first generation of high-yielding varieties.[33]

Corn yield, at just over 4 tons per hectare in 1995, is the highest of all the cereals—well above the 2.5 tons for wheat and rice. The prospect for raising that any further rests largely with the United States and China, the countries that account for two fifths and one fifth, respectively, of the world corn harvest.

Both have been remarkably successful to date (see Table 5–3), more than quadrupling traditional levels.[34]

The U.S. corn yield of 7.9 tons per hectare in 1995 is the highest of any cereal in a major producing country. The rise in yields started there around 1940, the same time as for wheat and for essentially the same reasons: as grain prices rose, improved varieties became available and more fertilizer was applied. After fluctuating between 1.5 and 2 tons per hectare from the Civil War until the early 1940s, corn yields crossed the 2-ton threshold in 1942 for the first time. In 1957, just 15 years later, they passed 3 tons per hectare. Then things really happened quickly. Five years later another ton was added. Another five years and another ton. And again. So from 1957 to 1972, U.S. farmers doubled corn yields from 3 tons per hectare to 6 tons. (See Figure 5–5.)[35]

Then the rate of growth began to slow substantially. Going from 6 tons to 7 tons took 10 years. More recently, rising from 7 to 8 tons between 1982 and 1992, the rate of gain was only 1.6 percent a year. Despite these enormous gains, corn yields do not yet appear to be leveling off as wheat yields have.[36]

China, as a relative newcomer to modern corn production, has seen its yields

Table 5–3. Annual Corn Yield Per Hectare in Key Producing Countries, 1994–96

Country	Yield
	(tons)
United States	7.9
China	4.9
Argentina	4.3
Brazil	2.5
South Africa	2.4
Mexico	2.2
Nigeria	1.8

SOURCE: U.S. Department of Agriculture, Foreign Agricultural Service, *World Agricultural Production* (Washington, DC: April 1997).

rise rapidly. But they are not likely to reach U.S. levels because, unlike the United States, China does not reserve its best cropland for corn.

Argentina, where the 1995 corn yield was 4.3 tons per hectare, may have the largest unrealized potential for raising yields. Despite the high inherent fertility of the pampas, the country's policy of taxing farm exports discouraged investment in agriculture, and little fertilizer was used. The recent elimination of these taxes has set the stage for heavy investment in this sector. That, along with high world corn prices, has already helped double fertilizer use in Argentina between 1994 and 1996.[37]

In Brazil, where the corn yield per hectare is only one third that of the United States, farmers are handicapped by a lack of the highly fertile, deep, well-drained soils on which corn thrives. A similar situation prevails in Mexico, where corn is grown largely by smallholders on marginal land in mountainous regions. These are typically hillside plots where low rainfall and thin soils—often heavily eroded—severely limit the yield potential.

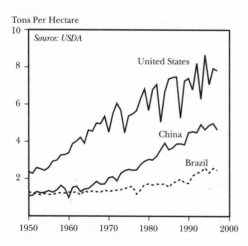

Figure 5–5. Corn Yields in United States, China, and Brazil, 1950–97

FACING BIOLOGICAL REALITY

For individual grains in individual countries, these historic trends show a sobering pattern. In every farming environment where yields have risen dramatically, there comes a time when the increase slows and either levels off or shows signs of doing so. It is equally revealing to look at the global trends. (Three-year averages are used here in order to minimize the effects of weather variations; for example, the yield shown for 1990 is an average of the yield from 1989–91.)

From 1950 to 1990, the world's grain farmers raised the productivity of their land by an unprecedented 2.1 percent a year, but since 1990 the rise has slowed markedly. (See Table 5–4.) Even if the former Soviet Union is excluded from the global data for 1990 to 1995 because of the uncharacteristic drop in yields associated with economic reforms and the breakup of the country, the rate of yield gain rises from 0.7 percent a year to just 1.1 percent—roughly half that of the preceding 40 years. While the first half of the 1990s is too short a period to determine a new trend, the much slower rise in yield is roughly in line with what this analysis would predict. In addition to the plateauing of wheat yields in the United States and Mexico cited earlier, yields in Canada and Egypt have shown no improvement so far in the 1990s.[38]

Global trends for the three major individual grains follow the pattern seen for grain as a whole. Rice production, which was modernized later than that of wheat and corn, achieved an annual increase in productivity of 2.1 percent between 1960 and 1990 but has dropped to 1.0 percent since 1990. Wheat yields grew between 1960 and 1990 at an average of 2.6 percent a year, then slowed to 0.1 percent during the 1990s. (If the former Soviet Union, a major wheat producer, is excluded from the global trend after 1990, the

Table 5–4. Annual Change in World Grain Yields by Decade, 1950–95

Year[1]	Total Grain	Rice	Wheat	Corn	Other Grains
			(percent)		
1950–60	2.0	1.4	1.7	2.6	
1960–70	2.5	2.1	2.9	2.4	2.3
1970–80	1.9	1.7	2.1	2.7	0.4
1980–90	2.2	2.4	2.9	1.3	1.7
1990–95	0.7	1.0	0.1	1.7	–0.8

[1]Each decennial or mid-decennial year is a three-year average centered on that year so as to reduce the effects of weather variability.

SOURCE: U.S. Department of Agriculture (USDA), "World Grain Database," unpublished printout, Washington, DC, 1996; USDA, *Production, Supply, and Distribution,* electronic database, updated February 1997; USDA, Foreign Agricultural Service, *World Agricultural Production* (Washington, DC: April 1997).

figure is 1.0 percent.) Corn productivity rose on average 2.6 percent from 1950 to 1980, then fell to 1.3 percent in the 1980s. The rise in corn yields accelerated slightly during the first half of the 1990s, reaching 1.7 percent a year, largely because of a belated surge in yields in China and Brazil.[39]

With the slower rise in grainland productivity thus far during the 1990s, the obvious next question is whether the momentum can be regained through biotechnology. Yet progress is not promising there either. After 20 years of research, biotechnologists have not yet produced a single high-yielding variety of wheat, rice, or corn. Why haven't some of the leading seed companies put biotechnologists to work developing a second generation of varieties that would again double or triple yields?

The answer is that plant breeders using traditional techniques have largely exploited the genetic potential for increasing the share of photosynthate that goes into seed. Once this is pushed close to its limit, the remaining options tend to be relatively small, clustering around efforts to raise the plant's tolerance of various stresses, such as drought or soil salinity. The one major option left to scientists is to increase the efficiency of the process of photosynthesis itself—

something that has thus far remained beyond their reach.

When genetic yield potential is close to the physiological limit, further advances rely on the expanded use of basic inputs such as the fertilizer and irrigation needed to realize the plant's full genetic potential, or on the fine-tuning of other agronomic practices, such as the use of optimum planting densities or more effective pest controls. Beyond this, there will eventually come a point in each country, with each grain, when farmers will not be able to sustain the rise in yields.

There will eventually come a point in each country, with each grain, when farmers will not be able to sustain the rise in yields.

U.S. Department of Agriculture plant scientist Thomas R. Sinclair observes that advances in plant physiology now let scientists quantify crop yield potentials quite precisely. He notes that "except for a few options, which allow small increases in the yield ceiling, the physiological limit to crop yields may well have been reached under experimental conditions." This means that for farmers who are using the highest yielding varieties that plant breeders can provide, along with the agronomic inputs and practices needed to realize their genetic potential, there may be few options left to raise land productivity.[40]

Viewed broadly, an S-shaped growth curve begins to emerge for the historical rise in world grainland productivity. Throughout most of human history, land productivity was essentially static. Then beginning around 1880, Japan began to raise its rice yield per hectare in a steady, sustained fashion. By the mid-1950s, nearly all the industrial countries were expanding their grain harvest by raising grainland productivity. And by 1970, they had been joined by nearly all the leading grain producers in the developing world.[41]

From 1970 to 1985, yields rose steadily in virtually all the grain-producing countries of any size. Then this unique period came to an end, as wheat yields in the United States and Mexico and rice yields in Japan leveled off. Eventually the rise in grain yields will level off everywhere, but exactly when this will occur in each country is difficult to anticipate. If more countries "hit the wall" in the years immediately ahead, as now seems likely, it probably will further slow the rise in world grainland productivity, dropping it well below growth in the world demand for grain.[42]

Except for the general warning by biologists that grain yields would eventually plateau, no specific warnings were heard in the early 1980s that the long rise of rice yields in Japan or of wheat yields in the United States or Mexico were about to level off. Nor is anyone likely to anticipate precisely when, for example, wheat yields will level off in China, though this could occur at any time. A review of the last half-century's experience in raising yields does, however, offer certain generalizations.

One, the slower rise in grain yields since 1990 is not the result of something peculiar to individual grains or individual countries. It reflects a systemic difficulty in sustaining the gains that characterized the preceding four decades.

Two, every country that initiated a yield takeoff was able to sustain it for at least a few decades.

Three, most countries that have achieved a yield takeoff have managed at least to double if not triple or even quadruple traditional grain yields. Among those that have quadrupled such levels are the United States and China with corn; France, the United Kingdom, and Mexico with wheat; and China with rice.

Four, once plant breeders have essentially exhausted the possibilities for raising the genetic yield potential and once farmers are using the most advanced agronomic practices, including irrigation, the yield potential for any particular grain in a given country is determined largely by the physical environment of the country—by soil moisture, temperature, day length, and solar intensity—factors that are not easily altered.

Five, all countries are drawing on a common backlog of unused agricultural technology that is gradually diminishing and, for some crops in some countries—such as wheat in the United States and rice in Japan—that has largely disappeared, at least for the time being.

Six, as a general matter, the more recently a country launched a yield takeoff, the faster its yields rise and the shorter the interval between yield takeoff and leveling off.

Seven, despite the slower rise in yields worldwide in recent years and the plateauing of yields in a few countries, many opportunities still exist for raising grainland productivity in most countries. These are most promising in countries where there is room for improvement in economic policies affecting agriculture. Although most governments subsidize agriculture, some still have economic policies that discourage investment in this sector. In these cases, the key to realizing the full genetic yield potential of crops is the restructuring of economic policies, as is happening now in Argentina.

Even with a concerted worldwide effort to increase grain yields, the rise during the last half of this decade could slow still further, dropping below 1 percent a year—far below the 2.1 percent that sustained the world from 1950 to 1990.[43]

THE EMERGING POLITICS OF SCARCITY

The slower rise in world grainland productivity during the 1990s may mark the transition from a half-century dominated by food surpluses to a future that will be dominated by food scarcity, a time when growth in supply will lag behind the growth in market demand. In addition to the constraints on food consumption imposed by low incomes, rising prices could further restrict food intake among the poor, expanding the number of those who are hungry.

If the politics of surpluses is replaced by a politics of scarcity, the issue will not be access to markets by a small handful of exporting countries but access to supplies by the more than 100 countries that import grain. Will exporting countries be willing to guarantee access to their supplies even in times of soaring grain prices?

With this loss of momentum in the growth in the world grain harvest, it comes as no surprise that world grain stocks during the 1990s have dropped to their lowest level ever. The bumper harvests of the mid-1980s boosted carryover stocks for 1987 to more than 100 days of consumption. But since then they have dropped below 60 days of consumption.[44]

In response, the United States dismantled the commodity programs designed to support prices by holding land out of production, returning all the set-aside land to use in 1996. Yet even with this additional land and with unusually favorable weather worldwide, there was little rebuilding of stocks from the 1996 harvest. Nor are stocks likely to be rebuilt from the 1997 harvest, adding still more evidence that the era of surpluses may be over.[45]

Stocks that will provide at least 70 days of world consumption are needed for even a minimal level of food security. Without this, one poor harvest can lead to a sharp rise in grain prices. Whenever stocks fall below 60 days' worth, prices become highly volatile. With the margin of security so thin, grain prices fluctuate with each weather report. When carryover stocks of grain dropped to 56 days of consumption in 1973, for example, world grain prices doubled. When they reached the new low of 52 days of consumption in 1996, the world price of wheat and corn— the two leading grains in terms of quantity produced—again more than doubled.[46]

With the world consuming 5 million tons of grain daily, rebuilding stocks from the 57 days of carryover for 1997 to 70 days would require an excess in production over that of consumption of 65 million tons—a gain that would have been easy to achieve during the 1980s, when large parts of U.S. cropland were held out of production, but one that is now much more difficult.[47]

The long-term decline in the real price of wheat, the world's leading food staple, that has been under way since mid-century may have bottomed out during the 1990s. (See Figure 5–6.) After dropping to a recent low of $3.97 per bushel in 1993, the price increased in each of the next three years, reaching $5.54 per bushel in 1996, a rise of 39 percent. While future year-to-year price changes will sometimes be down, as may be the case in 1997, this analysis indicates that the long-term trend is likely to be up. In some countries that are not completely integrated into the global food economy, prices have risen even faster. For example, the price of wheat at the beginning of

Dollars Per Bushel

Figure 5–6. World Wheat Prices, 1950–96

1997 within China was 49 percent above the world market price. In the *National Conditions Report No. 5*, published by the Chinese Academy of Sciences, this higher price for wheat and, to a lesser extent, for other grains, was acknowledged with obvious concern.[48]

As the demand for grain outruns supply, importing countries are more vulnerable than ever because they depend for nearly half their imports on one supplier—the United States—which controls a larger share of grain exports than Saudi Arabia does of oil. This is inherently risky because the U.S. grain harvest, largely rainfed, varies widely from year to year, highly vulnerable to drought and crop-withering heat waves.[49]

Farmers in exporting and importing countries alike who have always had to cope with the vagaries of weather may now have to deal with climate change. The 13 warmest years since recordkeeping began in 1866 have all occurred since 1979. The four warmest years have come during the 1990s, with 1995 topping the list. Unfortunately for farmers and consumers, heat waves like those that shrank harvests in 1995 across the United States, Canada, several European countries, the

Ukraine, and Russia could become even more frequent if atmospheric carbon dioxide levels continue to build.[50]

Three times in the last nine years, the U.S. grain harvest has been reduced by roughly one fifth from the preceding year by weather. When the grain yield per hectare was lowered in 1988 by 22 percent from the year before (see Figure 5–7), grain production dropped below consumption. Fortunately, the United States had vast grain stocks at the time and could satisfy the needs of importing countries by drawing them down. In the event of a similar shortfall in the late 1990s, when grain stocks are at near-record lows, this would not be possible. Knowledge that the U.S. grain harvest can drop below consumption should be of concern to food-importing countries everywhere.[51]

In 1994, grain prices started to rise in China, climbing by nearly 60 percent as demand expanded faster than production. Fearing political unrest, China turned to the outside world for massive imports of grain, which in turn triggered an increase in world grain prices. As this happened, exporting countries were tempted to impose restrictions or even outright embargoes in order to control food prices at home.[52]

In the spring of 1995, for example, Viet Nam embargoed rice exports for some months simply because so much of this staple had moved across its northern border into China, where rice prices were much higher, that it created potentially unmanageable inflationary pressures. In December 1995, the European Union (EU), which ranks third as a grain exporter after the United States and Canada, imposed an export tax on wheat of $32 a ton in order to discourage exports and dampen the rise in bread prices within Europe. In January 1996 it did the same thing for barley, its principal feedgrain, because barley prices had nearly doubled, driving up the prices of livestock products.[53]

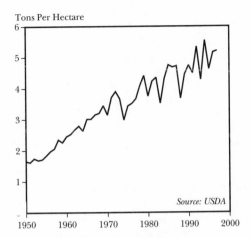

Tons Per Hectare

Source: USDA

Figure 5–7. U.S. Grain Yield Per Hectare, 1950–97

Only when an exceptional 1997 world grain harvest was in prospect and grain prices dropped did the EU remove the export tax. But in April 1997, when wheat prices were again on the rise, officials in Brussels once more levied an export tax. Whenever this happens, the EU in effect creates a two-price system for grain in the world: one within Europe and another, much higher, outside it, where the world's low-income populations live. This is an early example of how rising grain prices can lead governments to restrict exports, putting importing countries at risk.[54]

Over much of the last half-century, food aid provided a safety net for needy countries, whether it was the war-torn nations of Europe in the late 1940s or Africa in the mid-1990s. But from fiscal year 1993 to fiscal year 1996, the international budget for food aid was cut in half—dropping the amount of grain available from roughly 15.2 million tons to 7.6 million. With donor countries facing fiscal stringencies, political support for food aid is weakening. In a world of surpluses, the opportunity to simultaneously reduce excessive supplies and provide food assistance had a strong political appeal in donor countries. But in a world of scarcity, where providing food aid could raise domestic food prices, it will become more difficult to garner political support for such assistance. And this is occurring at a time when the U.S. Department of Agriculture estimates that food aid needs in 2005 will rise to 27 million tons—four times the amount available in 1996.[55]

In this new world of scarcity, countries that depend on imports for a large share of grain, mostly for food, are at risk. The countries of East Asia, such as Japan, South Korea, and Taiwan, that import at least 70 percent of their grain supplies are particularly vulnerable, though each is essentially self-sufficient in rice, the principal food staple. Also at risk are countries such as Algeria, Egypt, Iran, and Saudi Arabia, which import one third to two thirds of their grain.[56]

In 1994, grain prices started to rise in China, climbing 60 percent as demand expanded faster than production.

The assumptions underlying population, agricultural, and trade policies during an age of surpluses need to be reassessed as the world moves into an age of scarcity. National security in this new era dictates that governments devise agricultural and population policies that enable them to avoid excessive dependence on imported food. Despite the fashionable trend toward globalization, there are no global institutions that will assure adequate food supplies for individual countries. Only the government of a country can assume responsibility for the food security of its people.

At the root of these difficult problems is population growth. Many grain-deficit countries are expected to have far larger deficits in the future. In the Middle East, for example, the 1995 population of 215 million is projected to reach 443 million by 2030, forcing this water-limited region to import most of its grain. The population of the northern tier of countries in Africa from Morocco through Egypt—an area already facing acute water scarcity—is projected to grow from 137 million in 1995 to 234 million by 2030. Countries within these two regions that already import half or more of their grain include Algeria, Israel, Jordan, Kuwait, Lebanon, Libya, Saudi Arabia, and Tunisia.[57]

A doubling of grain prices would impoverish more people in a shorter period of time than any event in history.

The projected growth in population in sub-Saharan Africa is even more staggering, going from 588 million in 1995 to 1.37 billion in 2030. With thin soils and a limited potential for irrigation development, Africa seems destined to become a massive importer of grain—assuming that countries in the region can compete for what are likely to be scarce supplies.[58]

To the east, Asia's imports, growing by leaps and bounds, will continue to increase. China, already turning to the outside world for massive quantities of grain, may need to import some 200 million tons by 2030, an amount equal to current world exports.[59]

India's population, likely to pass 1 billion in late 1999, is projected to hit 1.4 billion in 2030. Already facing widespread groundwater depletion, it will likely be importing heavily. Pakistan, also now pushing against the limits of its water resources, is projected to increase its population from 126 million in 1995 to 224 million in 2030.[60]

As Mexico, with a 1995 population of 94 million, moves to 150 million in the year 2030, its current grain deficit is projected to be much larger—again because it is running into the limits of water supplies. Brazil, a country with one of the poorest agricultural land endowments and already the largest grain importer in the western hemisphere, is facing an increase from 161 million people in 1995 to 202 million in 2030.[61]

Many countries sense that they will need to import more grain, and all seem to assume that the United States will be able to cover their needs. But with little new land left to plow, with aquifer depletion continuing in key farm states, and with the rise in land productivity slowing, possibly dropping below population growth, any major expansion of exports will be difficult. At the same time, the export potential of both Canada and Australia is severely limited by rainfall. Argentina might be able to double its annual exports of 12 million tons of grain if it plows enough of its grassland, but cropping has already expanded onto highly erodible land. Even a doubling of Argentinean exports would add only 6 percent to world grain exports.[62]

With the global demand for grain beginning to outrun supplies, this analysis indicates that real grain prices (after adjusting for inflation) will rise in the years ahead—reversing the historical trend of declining real prices that was so strong through the early 1990s. This challenges projections done by the World Bank and the U.N. Food and Agriculture Organization of continuing surpluses and declining real grain prices through the year 2010. The government of Japan, on the other hand, has done a set of global projections indicating that wheat and rice prices could double by 2010—an assessment much more consistent with the prospect outlined here.[63]

A doubling of grain prices, were it to occur, would impoverish more people in a shorter period of time than any event in history. Instead of reducing the number of malnourished people from 800 million to 400 million by 2010, the goal adopted at the World Food Summit in Rome in late 1996, the ranks of the hungry would mushroom, dashing confidence in the capacity of governments to deal with this most pressing issue.[64]

As the world moves into an era of food scarcity, the international safety net that has existed during the half-century since World War II is disappearing. As noted earlier, there is no longer any U.S. cropland idled under commodity programs. World grain carryover stocks, meanwhile, have dropped below 60 days of consumption—little more than pipeline supplies. At this level, they are well below the 70-day minimum needed to cushion even one poor harvest.[65]

If prices rise in the future, how will they affect production? Historically, when grain prices climbed, production responded strongly. Farmers could bring more land under the plow. But now there is little land left to plow. In the past, farmers responded by investing more in developing water resources. When grain prices doubled in the 1970s, investment in irrigation wells climbed, helping to expand production. But in the late 1990s, investment in more irrigation wells in most food-producing regions will simply accelerate the depletion of aquifers. In this situation, it is not the investment in irrigation wells but the sustainable yield of aquifers that determines the availability of irrigation water. Simply stated, the traditional economic determinant of irriga-

tion water supplies is being replaced by an environmental determinant.

Similarly, in the 1970s farmers could substantially expand fertilizer use as grain prices rose. But in much of the world, applying additional fertilizer during the 1990s will have little effect on yields. Again, an environmental constraint—the physiological capacity of existing crop varieties to absorb fertilizer—is replacing an economic constraint, the availability of credit with which farmers could buy fertilizer.

This is not to say there will be no production response to higher grain prices in the 1990s. There will be. But it will be muted compared with earlier responses simply because some key economic determinants of production levels are being eclipsed by environmental determinants.

One of the obvious conclusions of this analysis is that there is a pressing need for a much greater investment in the agricultural sector—in agricultural research, agricultural extension, soil conservation, and irrigation efficiency. But the principal conclusion is that securing food supplies for the next generation goes far beyond agriculture. Achieving an acceptable balance between food and people may now depend at least as much on population policy and family planners as on agricultural policy and farmers. Energy policies that affect climate stability may have a greater effect on future food security than agricultural policy. And in a world of land and water scarcity, policies that govern the allocation of land and water between agriculture and other uses will directly affect future food security.

6

Recycling Organic Wastes

Gary Gardner

In 1876, a German chemist studying the agricultural history of North Africa was troubled about the fate of that region and its implications for his day. In the first century AD, North Africa's fertile fields had supplied two thirds of the grain consumed in Rome. But the nutrients and organic matter in that food were not returned to North Africa; instead, they were flushed into the Mediterranean. By the middle of the third century, the one-way flow of nutrients out of North Africa's grainland soils, along with declining levels of organic matter, had contributed to the region's tumble into environmental and economic decline.[1]

The chemist, Justus von Liebig, worried that Europe's rapidly expanding cities also depended too heavily on one-way nutrient flows, with consequences that would eventually undermine both urban and agricultural areas. His solution was chemical fertilizer, a package of con-

densed and easily transportable nutrients that made it possible to escape dependence on recycling organic matter. This new technology revived the fertility of nutrient-depleted farmland. And because a ton of this plant food could pack as many nutrients as dozens of tons of organic matter, it could be shipped cheaply over great distances. Cities could now expand, and food could be imported from far away, without concern for returning urban garbage and sewage to farmlands. As a result, garbage and sewage became waste products to be discarded rather than soil builders to be reused.

Today, 2.5 billion of us—nearly half of the human family—live in cities, more dependent than ever on long, one-way flows of nutrients and organic matter. But reliance on linear flows instead of the traditional organic "loop" comes at a price. To start with, many regions of the globe are now overfertilized, a trend with consequences well beyond the farm. Drinking water in several European countries is contaminated with fertilizer runoff. Species

An expanded version of this chapter appeared as Worldwatch Paper 135, *Recycling Organic Waste: From Urban Pollutant to Farm Resource.*

diversity is reduced in terrestrial and aquatic ecosystems by excess applications of nitrogen and phosphorus. And plant diseases become more prevalent in soils dependent on manufactured fertilizer.[2]

At the back end of organic flows, disposal of garbage and human excreta is increasingly difficult. Landfills are nearly full in many countries, and they leak toxic chemicals into groundwater and methane into the atmosphere. Sewage systems are expensive and water-intensive, and often mix industrial chemicals with human waste, making safe reuse of that waste more difficult. And on farms, the trend toward concentrated livestock-raising has led to surpluses of manure, which quickly becomes a pollutant rather than the natural resource it has been on farms for millennia.

Many regions of the globe are now overfertilized.

Returning nutrients in organic matter to farm soils—"closing the organic loop"—can help alleviate all these problems. Composting and reusing food scraps and yard clippings would improve soil structure, supply nutrients, and suppress disease, in addition to easing the pressure on waste facilities. Opting for a "dry" system of human waste management—through the use of composting toilets, for example—would free up clean water for more vital uses, and would avoid costly construction of sewer lines and treatment plants. And limiting livestock facilities to a size that does not generate unusable surpluses of manure would help ensure that the material is recycled rather than dumped or washed into rivers and streams. As policymakers grapple with the problems of today's burgeoning cities, they would do well to consider these multiple advantages of reusing organic matter.

ORGANIC MATERIAL FLOWS

A map of nutrient flows from farm soils would resemble a tree, with a major trunk line branching out to smaller flows as nutrients travel farther from the farm. Nutrients might, for example, be taken up by corn, which is harvested and marketed as food or livestock feed. These products, in turn, branch out to one or more waste flows—sewage, garbage, or manure. The nutrient-laden wastes then make their way to hundreds of landfills, incinerators, rivers, or bays, which may be hundreds or even thousands of kilometers from the original soils. As nutrient flows multiply and extend, so do the challenges of recycling them.[3]

Nutrients that leave farm soils must be replaced if crop production is to remain abundant. (Nutrients assist photosynthesis—the plant's use of light energy to transform carbon dioxide and water into organic compounds that give the plant its energy.) Organic wastes, many of which are rich in nutrients and organic matter, can be used to replenish soils. But the common practice in conventional agriculture is to rely primarily on manufactured fertilizer—a package of one or more major nutrients (nitrogen, phosphorus, and potassium), each of which is extracted from its host environment. Nitrogen, for example, is taken from the atmosphere and "fixed," or converted to a form that plants can use. Phosphorus and potassium are mined, then processed for use with crops.[4]

In most countries, nutrients flow predominantly from farms to the nation's own people, rather than to animals or other countries. This is especially true for grain, the source of more than half the calories consumed in most areas. In developing countries, more than three quarters of the grain produced is consumed domestically as food, and the share is even higher in the least complex economies. (See Table 6–1.) Sub-Saharan Africa, for example, uses 97 percent of its grain for food, compared with 28 percent in the United States. The poorest nations produce little exportable surplus, and their animals are largely pasture-fed, leaving nearly all the grain harvest for domestic human consumption. Thus, in most developing countries the recycling challenge is to return human and municipal wastes from cities to agricultural lands.[5]

With greater prosperity, meat consumption tends to rise, and nutrient flows become more complex as grain is diverted to animals. Sub-Saharan Africa, for example, feeds only 2 percent of its grain to animals, but in the United States, 41 percent of grain nutrients are consumed this way. Indeed, more U.S. grain nutrients are fed to animals than are consumed by Americans, by people in other countries, or by industry. Thus in wealthy nations nutrient recycling involves not only human and industrial wastes, but large volumes of animal wastes as well.[6]

Finally, some countries export a considerable share of their nutrient outflow, which complicates recycling possibilities still further. The world's top seven grain exporters, which includes nations as different as Canada and Viet Nam, sell from 12 percent to 67 percent of their domestic grain production to other countries. (See Table 6–2.) Unlike flows to the domestic populace or to animals, exported nutrients can rarely be recovered by the exporting nation, although reuse in the recipient country is possible.[7]

Overall, 10 percent of the world's grain nutrients flow across borders in grain; the figure would be somewhat higher if the grain content of exported meat were included in the analysis. As economies become increasingly integrated and import dependence grows, the volume of crop nutrients crossing national borders will rise. For net food exporters, the nutrient deficit is covered by using fertilizer. But even importers—although they are accumulating nutrients from natural sources—often resort to heavier than necessary fertilizer use because they do not recycle organic wastes, or because getting organics back to farms is too expensive or difficult. Africa takes in six times more nutrients in food than it sends out, but the soils of many African farms are steadily losing nutrients, thus exacerbating their need for imported fertilizer.[8]

Table 6–1. Domestic Consumption of Domestically Grown Grain Nutrients by Humans and Animals, by Continent, Mid-1990s

Region	Share of Nutrients Consumed	
	By Humans	By Animals
	(percent)	
Africa	83	15
Asia	80	16
Latin America	49	39
Eur. Union	28	41
North America	22	48

SOURCE: U.S. Department of Agriculture, *Production, Supply, and Distribution*, electronic database, Washington, DC, updated October 1996.

Table 6–2. Grain Exports from Seven Largest Exporters, 1995

Country	Share of Grain Exported (percent)
Australia	67
Argentina	46
Canada	45
France	44
United States	37
Thailand	31
Viet Nam	12

SOURCE: U.S. Department of Agriculture, *Production, Supply, and Distribution*, electronic database, Washington, DC, updated October 1996.

Research from the mid-1980s that focused on a larger set of commodities gives an idea of the net regional flows of nutrients. Tracking nutrients in 15 sets of foods, including grains, researcher G.W. Cooke found a large net shift out of the Americas and Oceania toward Africa, Europe, Asia, and the former Soviet Union. Perhaps more remarkable was the imbalance (inflows compared to outflows) for each region. The smallest imbalance was found in Asia, which nevertheless imported four times as many nutrients in food as it exported. North and Central America, by contrast, exported 76 tons of nutrients for every ton imported. Cooke's data demonstrate that nutrients in food flow across regions in highly skewed quantities.[9]

The use of manufactured fertilizer is what allows these large imbalances in food nutrient flows to be ignored. But fertilizer is often applied more liberally than necessary for plant growth (sub-Saharan Africa is a notable exception), usually to ensure that crops are not underfed. Indeed, in the United States 56 percent more fertilizer was applied to grainland soils between 1991 and 1995 than left those soils in crops. In China, overapplication appears to be even higher, with nearly three quarters of the fertilizer applied unaccounted for in harvested grain. Although some of the excess is building up in farmland in the short run, a large share is leached or eroded away, polluting waterways and degrading ecosystems.[10]

Overuse of manufactured fertilizer could be reduced and soil quality raised if nutrient outflows were reused on farmland. The "waste" flows from food, feed, or exports are all potentially circular. And these reused nutrients can be augmented using other wastes that did not originate on the farm, such as leaves and grass clippings.

Reuse of organic matter would supply only a fraction of the nutrients needed in agriculture. Nutrient losses are inevitable—as much as 50 percent of the nitrogen content of manure or sewage, for example, returns to the atmosphere through volatilization (a process akin to evaporation), although proper management can reduce these losses. And today's high-yielding crop varieties require more nutrients than native varieties do. Still, reuse of organic matter can reduce the need for manufactured fertilizer while building soil fertility and health—and reducing the waste disposal needs of urban areas.[11]

THE COST OF BREAKING THE LOOP

When the circular flow of organic material is broken, two challenges immediately arise: the new, linear flow must be fed at one end, and emptied at the other. The pump at the front end of the organic pipeline is fertilizer, whose overuse has spawned a panoply of problems. Fertilizer production and other human activities have doubled the global rate of nitrogen fixing, essentially boosting our planet's fertility. (See Figure 6–1.) Indeed, fertilizer production has grown more than ninefold since 1950. And because half of the manufactured fertilizer ever used has been applied only since 1982, the greatest surge in nitrogen, phosphorus, and potassium levels is quite recent, with its full effects yet to be understood.[12]

Many of the consequences of the planet's overfertilization are more pernicious than might be expected. Excessive levels of nutrients, for example, can reduce species diversity in both aquatic and terrestrial ecosystems. Eroded or leached phosphorus and nitrogen promote overgrowth of algae in rivers, lakes, and bays at the expense of other species, including various fish. In fact, leached and eroded nutrients help make agriculture the

Million Tons of
Nitrogen Fixed per Year

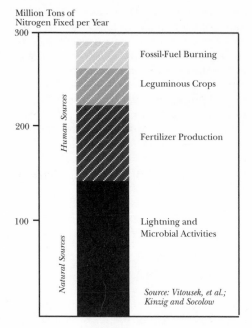

**Figure 6–1. Natural and Human Sources
of Nitrogen Fixing**

largest diffuse source of water pollution
in the United States. So extensive is the
agricultural pollution of the Mississippi
River—the main drainage conduit for the
U.S. Corn Belt—that a "dead zone" the
size of New Jersey forms each summer in
the Gulf of Mexico, the river's terminus.
Rich in fertilizer nutrients that feed algae,
the once productive area now has far
fewer fish and shrimp, which cannot compete with the decomposing algae for oxygen. The phenomenon is repeated on a
smaller scale around the world in countless rivers and lakes that receive agricultural pollutants.[13]

Similarly, excessive levels of nitrogen
have been shown to reduce plant diversity
in prairie ecosystems. In a recent 12-year
study, scientists found that nitrogen
applied to Minnesota grasslands spurred
the growth of some grasses—but at the
expense of others that were less well
adapted, leading to a 50-percent reduc-

tion in species diversity. This is consistent
with the experience in parts of northern
Europe, where high levels of nitrogen
deposition have converted species-rich
heathlands into species-poor grasslands.[14]

The loss of diversity, lamentable in
itself, also made the ecosystem "leakier,"
and therefore more polluting. Because
the invasive species were less able to store
nitrogen than the native grasses they
replaced, nitrogen leaching—an important source of water pollution—increased
over the study period as the ecosystem
became biologically impoverished.[15]

This leakiness can be especially high
on a farm, particularly when manufactured fertilizer is used. A 15-year study by
the Rodale Institute found that conventionally fertilized fields leached 270 kilograms of nitrogen per hectare, compared
with 180 kilos on manure-fed plots, and
only 110 kilos on legume-cropped land.
Indeed, the conventional fields saw soil
nitrogen decrease by 11 percent over 15
years, while manure-fed fields gained
nitrogen (which the soils retained for
future use by crops), and the legume-fed
soils kept it roughly in balance.[16]

Overuse of nitrogen and phosphorus
can also be harmful to human health.
Nitrates in drinking water can become
carcinogens when digested by humans,
and can cause brain damage or even
death in infants by affecting the oxygen-
carrying capacity of the blood. The
Organisation for Economic Co-operation
and Development (OECD) lists nitrate
pollution as one of the most serious water
quality problems in Europe and North
America. Indeed, every member of the
European Union has areas that regularly
exceed maximum allowable levels of
nitrates in drinking water. The problem is
expected to worsen in developing countries where fertilizer use is accelerating,
such as India and Brazil.[17]

In some regions, however, a shortage
rather than a surplus of nutrients is the
problem. Many African farmers, unable

to afford enough fertilizer, essentially mine their soils of nutrients. In the worst cases, nutrients leave agricultural soils three to four times faster than they are replaced. In sub-Saharan Africa overall, fertilizer replaces only 28 percent of the nitrogen, 36 percent of the phosphate, and 15 percent of the potash absorbed by crops. Recycling organic material could help replenish these soils, and, in the long run, keep fertilizer use from reaching the excessive levels found in many industrial countries.[18]

At the back end of the organic pipeline is a different set of problems, mainly related to waste disposal. Landfills in many industrial countries, for example, are closing at a record clip. In the United States, the 8,000 landfills in operation in 1988 had dwindled to 3,091 by 1996, as many sites could not comply with federal environmental regulations, and others simply filled up. While total capacity has increased in this decade (because landfills are now bigger), some areas are feeling a waste capacity squeeze. For example, New York City's Fresh Kills dump—the city's last remaining landfill, and the largest in the world, covering 1,200 hectares—is set to close in 2001. City officials are drawing up plans to export some 13,000 tons of garbage per day to other states, perhaps hundreds of kilometers away.[19]

Organic material forms the bulk of the growing mountains of municipal waste: 36 percent of the waste flow in OECD member states is food or garden wastes. And in developing countries, organic matter typically accounts for more than half, and often more than two thirds, of the total waste stream. In addition to taking up space, rotting organic material emits methane, a greenhouse gas that traps atmospheric heat at 20 times the rate of carbon dioxide. Indeed, the U.S. Environmental Protection Agency (EPA) estimates that decomposing organic material in landfills releases some 10 percent of the world's human-caused methane emis-

sions. New York's Fresh Kills dump alone emits more than 5 tons of methane—nearly 2 percent of the global total from human activities. Landfills also pollute land and water as they leach acidic liquids produced by rotting organic matter.[20]

The environmental costs and space needs of organic waste have raised official interest in reducing the tidal wave of garbage. Several states in the United States have ordered inflows to dumps cut in half by 2000. In the United Kingdom, authorities are working to reach a 25-percent recycling level for household refuse by then. And packed landfills in the Tokyo area have led the city to ponder a garbage collection fee to discourage waste generation. California sees composting as the natural solution to these burgeoning dumps. But the state would have to compost some 70 percent of its urban organic wastes by the end of the decade to meet its waste reduction goals—a hefty boost from the current rate of 40 percent (which already represents an enormous increase from recycling levels of a decade ago).[21]

Human excrement is another resource-turned-waste-product whose disposal is increasingly problematic as urban-rural organic loops are broken. For millennia, many cultures returned human waste to soils, and a few still do today. But increasingly the material is buried, incinerated, or flushed into rivers, bays, or oceans. The human toll from improper disposal (and from an unclean water supply, often a related problem) is intolerably high: some 2 million children die each year and billions of people become sick because of inadequate water and sanitation facilities.[22]

The financial and environmental toll can also be high, especially where sewers are used. Sewers and treatment plants can cost several times as much as a system of on-site sanitation. And sewers are water-intensive, a distinct disadvantage in regions of water scarcity. The United Nations Comprehensive Freshwater

Assessment, released in April 1997, notes that a third of the world's people live in countries with moderate to high water stress; that share could reach two thirds by 2025. As levels of stress increase, the water needs of farmers, businesses, and households are unlikely to be met fully. Dry methods of human waste disposal, such as composting toilets, could save a meaningful share of domestic water. And local containment of human waste would increase the prospects for returning nutrients and organic matter to farm soils, not to mention improving the health of the rivers and bays where they formerly ended up.[23]

COMPOSTING URBAN GARBAGE

The world's cities dump tons of natural wealth daily into landfills, incinerators, bays, and oceans. Rich in organic matter, and with a modest supply of nutrients, the organic share of municipal waste flows—more than a third in industrial countries and well over half in many developing nations—is typically treated as valueless. Indeed, industrial countries reuse only 11 percent of their organic garbage. But increasingly cities recognize the value of this material, and are turning to the ancient practice of composting as a natural way to prepare it for reuse.[24]

Composting is a several-months-long process in which bacteria, worms, or other organisms feast on piles of carbon-rich matter and digest it, leaving behind humus—a rich, stable medium in which roots thrive. Because it is riddled with pores, humus shelters nutrients and provides extensive surface area to which nutrients can bond; indeed, humus traps three to five times more nutrients, water, and air than other soil matter does. These characteristics also help soils retain nutrients that would otherwise be leached or

eroded away. Thus, adding organic matter to soils further reduces the need for additional nutrient applications.[25]

Compost also helps suppress plant diseases. Since the 1970s, horticulturalists have found that compost limits the spread of root rot as effectively as many fungicides. Harry Hoitink, a plant pathologist at Ohio State University and a pioneer in disease suppression research, asserts that compost use by nurseries in Ohio has eliminated the use of methyl bromide—a potent fungicide highly poisonous to humans, and an ozone-depleting substance whose use is soon to be banned. Because chemical alternatives to methyl bromide are less effective or unsafe, the disease-suppression capacity of compost is welcome news.[26]

Compared with its advantages for soil building, water retention, and disease suppression, the nutrient contribution of composted urban organic material is modest, but nonetheless significant. Nutrients in municipal solid waste (not including paper) in OECD countries totaled the equivalent of an average 7 percent of the commercial fertilizer used in those countries in the early 1990s. (See Table 6–3.) Because fertilizer is commonly overapplied, however, the potential contribution of urban nutrients is actually larger than the figure of 7 percent indicates. Coupled with nutrients from recycled human waste, composted organic garbage has the potential to cut the pollution of water caused by fertilizer overuse.[27]

Compost can reduce fertilizer use because of its own nutrient content, but also because it reduces leaching, which allows a greater share of applied fertilizer to be used by plants. At the same time, compost releases its nutrient supply very gradually (unlike fertilizer, whose nutrients are immediately available to plants), so the full nutrient contribution of compost is realized over time. The extent of fertilizer reductions made possible by using compost depends on the makeup of

Table 6–3. Nutrients in Organic Municipal Solid Waste[1] Compared with Nutrients in Fertilizer, Selected Countries, Early 1990s

Country/ Region	Nutrient Equivalent in Commercial Fertilizer Applied (percent)
Mexico	17
Turkey	15
Japan	14
Netherlands	12
Belgium-Luxembourg	11
Italy	9
Portugal	9
Switzerland	9
Australia	8
Spain	7
Austria	6
Canada	6
Sweden	6
Finland	5
Greece	5
United States	5
Norway	4
Denmark	3
France	3
Average	7

[1]Excluding paper.
SOURCE: Worldwatch calculation based on data from OECD, EPA, and FAO.

the compost, the amount applied, soil and climate conditions, and the crops being cultivated. Still, compost use has already led to reductions in fertilizer applications in some areas. According to a World Bank official who has studied composting in India, farmers there who use a commercial compost called Celrich cut chemical fertilizer consumption by some 25 percent.[28]

Finally, composting is accessible to people who are poor. Because it is a decentralized and natural source of wealth—every household produces the needed ingredients—composting can promote better nutrition among the urban poor who cultivate their own food. An estimated 200 million city dwellers worldwide now practice urban agriculture, supplying part of the food needs of some 800 million people. In Kampala, Uganda, for example, 35 percent of households produce their own food. And in Accra, Ghana, urban residents supply the city with 90 percent of the vegetables consumed there. For the urban poor, compost is a virtually free fertilizer and soil builder, whose production requires little space, virtually no equipment, and a modest amount of labor. Such a valuable and affordable resource, available without reliance on outside suppliers, can make an economic and nutritional difference to people living on the economic margins.[29]

Industrial countries reuse only 11 percent of their organic garbage.

For all its wonders, compost presents some important managerial challenges. Composts vary from place to place—and even from batch to batch—because the combination of inputs can vary so widely. Yard clippings are more available in summer than in winter, for instance, and their nutrient makeup changes with the seasons. Paper availability may depend on the ups and downs of the economy. This complexity requires that compost makers know their customers and respond to their diverse needs, and that users understand how the product works in soils. Creating the right compost for a particular job and using it optimally will require more research and outreach than is typically available today.[30]

As the many advantages of composting become apparent, its use is taking off. In the United States, composting facilities multiplied more than fourfold between 1989 and 1996, from some 700 to more than 3,200. Many cities and counties now make organic matter available to the public for use as mulch, or as the feedstock for making compost. In San Jose, California, a recently completed three-year pilot program to promote the use of compost led to a 54-percent increase in its production by local processors, and demand for the product was brisk. Meanwhile, the Flanders region of Belgium saw the level of organics recycling double between 1995 and 1996.[31]

Composting is surging in part because it is good business. Evidence of this is the experience of Community Recycling of Southern California, which saw gold in the spoiled fruits and vegetables of area supermarkets. In 1994, the company began to compost the perishables of 28 stores. Three years later, the program had expanded to include more than 750 supermarkets. The practice benefits all parties. The supermarkets credit recycling for reducing their waste flows by 85 percent. Community Recycling profits by composting the waste and selling it— 125,000 tons worth a year so far—to area farmers. And farmers, who apply the compost to some 12,000 hectares of farmland, save on fertilizer purchases and build their soils back up.[32]

Composting is surging because it is good business.

Such mutual advantages, however, are not automatic or guaranteed. The Indian government has promoted composting of municipal wastes in recent decades, but the schemes have largely failed. Inclusion of nonorganic material lowered the quality of the resulting compost. Poor equipment maintenance led to breakdowns and inconsistent production. City governments were seldom committed to the federal government's vision of widespread composting. And subsidies on fertilizer made compost economically uncompeti-

tive. While the potential benefits of composting are manifold, the Indian experience demonstrates that attention to fundamentals is essential for success.[33]

REROUTING HUMAN WASTE

Most of the world's cultivated food passes through human beings, so it is no surprise that human waste is a trove of nutrients and organic matter. Harvesting this material for agriculture is a natural way to close an important organic loop. Indeed, Chinese farming thrived on recycled excreta for thousands of years. But as more cities process these wastes using technologies designed to dispose of them rather than reuse them, safe recycling of human waste becomes much more difficult. Safe reuse is best ensured by shifting away from disposal technologies—such as conventional treatment plants, or sewers that mix industrial and domestic waste—and toward technologies engineered to produce a clean fertilizer. For countries not yet committed to expensive disposal systems, this shift can occur more quickly. Until it takes place, the reuse of human excreta can be safely practiced only by observing the strictest standards.[34]

Most excreta is not reused, although reuse—often unsafely practiced—is growing. In developing countries, sewers, septic systems, and pit latrines are the dominant disposal systems. Sewers and septic tanks predominate in Latin America and the Middle East, while Africans and Asians rely at least as heavily on pit latrines. Most sewers flow to the nearest river, bay, or ocean; only 10 percent of this sewage receives treatment. Where pit latrines are used, waste material typically remains buried. Except for parts of Asia, which has a long history of excreta reuse, and some arid regions, where sewage water (often untreated) is commonly used for irrigation, human waste is widely regarded as unwanted debris.[35]

Industrial countries have long had the same perspective, but this is changing. Many now encourage reuse of sewage sludge on farmland, and the practice is growing. Europe as a whole applied roughly one third of its sewage to agricultural land in the early 1990s, while the United States applied 28 percent. But the growing interest in reuse may reflect dwindling options for cheap disposal rather than a strong interest in building farm soils. Traditional dumping sites—landfills, incinerators, and oceans—are less available, more costly to use, or legally off-limits today, while farmland is often an inexpensive alternative disposal site. But just as sewers and treatment facilities are not designed for recycling, farmland is not suited to absorb the chemicals and heavy metals often contained in a sewage stream that mixes human and industrial wastes.[36]

If human wastes are made safe for use on farmland, however, their reuse can help reduce applications of chemical fertilizer. In many developing countries, the nutrient content of human waste is the equivalent of a substantial share of the nutrients applied from fertilizer, even after losses of nitrogen to volatilization are taken into account. (See Table 6–4.) In OECD countries, nutrients in human waste that is not already spread on land are the equivalent of roughly 8 percent of the nutrients applied as fertilizer. As with municipal organic waste, this figure understates the potential contribution of nutrients in human waste. If fertilizer use in OECD countries were reduced by a third, nutrients in human waste could amount to 12 percent of nutrients applied as fertilizer.[37]

Recycling human waste safely and effectively will require different technologies, or different ways of using existing ones. Sewers, for example, often contaminate human waste with heavy metals or toxic chemicals from industry or

Table 6–4. Nutrients in Human Waste Compared with Nutrients in Fertilizer, Selected Countries, Mid-1990s

Country	Nutrient Equivalent in Commercial Fertilizer Applied[1]
	(percent)
Kenya	136
Tunisia	52
Indonesia	49
Zimbabwe	38
Colombia	31
Mexico	31
South Africa	29
Egypt	28
India	26

[1]Assumes loss of 50 percent of nitrogen content to volatilization.

SOURCE: Worldwatch calculation based on data from FAO, USAID, and U.S. Department of Commerce, and on E. Witter and J.M. Lopez-Real, "The Potential of Sewage Sludge and Composting in a Nitrogen Recycling Strategy for Agriculture," *Biological Agriculture and Horticulture,* vol. 5 (1987).

households. Conventional treatment plants remove nutrients (and other matter) from wastewater, which lowers the enrichment level of effluent used for irrigation. And conventional treatment methods (with the exception of disinfection, which is rarely practiced in developing countries) reduce pathogens by too little for safe reuse in agriculture. Thus, many of today's disposal technologies are not well suited to producing fertilizing products.[38]

Where sewers and treatment plants are used to recycle waste, the results are mixed, at best. Even in countries considered successful with reuse—Israel, for example, which diverts treated wastewater to irrigation—caution is warranted. The country began large-scale reuse of sewage effluent in 1972, and today recycles 65 percent of its wastewater to crops. No excessive rates of illness have been linked to its use. Nevertheless, cadmium levels have been shown to increase by 5–10 percent annually in Israeli effluent-fed soils, and heavy metals were found to have accumulated in an aquifer below land that was irrigated with effluent for 30 years. If industrial wastes were not dumped in sewers, the country could more safely apply sewage effluent to crops. Better yet, if human wastes were managed using dry (nonsewered) methods such as composting toilets, the water currently used to carry sewage would be available to agriculture as clean water.[39]

Sometimes sewers are little more than feeder lines to irrigation canals; in these cases, risks to human health are much greater. Raw sewage used to irrigate vegetables and salad crops is blamed for the spread of worm-related diseases in Berlin in 1949, typhoid fever in Santiago in the early 1980s, and cholera in Jerusalem in 1970 and in western South America in 1991. Even so, the risky use of wastewater continues in many developing countries. In the Mexican state of Hidalgo, wastewater from Mexico City is used in the world's largest wastewater irrigation scheme, covering some 80,000 hectares. The effluent, which is 55–80 percent raw sewage (the balance is storm water), is barred from use on some salad crops, but other foods—including corn, wheat, beans, and some vegetables—are irrigated with sewage water.[40]

In contrast to effluent reuse, application of sludge (the concentrate that results from sewage treatment) to farmland carries a different set of risks, especially where industrial wastes or household chemicals are part of the sewage flow. Tens of thousands of toxic substances and chemical compounds used in industrial economies, including PCBs, pesticides, dioxins, heavy metals, asbestos, petroleum products, and industrial solvents, are potentially part of sewage flows. Many of these have been linked in the larger environment to ailments ranging from cancer to reproductive abnormalities. They are also a threat to soils: once introduced to cropland, for example,

heavy metals persist for decades (in the case of cadmium) or even centuries (in the case of lead). While the quantities of these substances are typically low on average, the contents of a given load of sewage sludge are unpredictable and their effects on human and environmental health are understudied.[41]

Although industrial nations maintain standards for sludge reuse, these may be lax. U.S. standards are the least stringent of any in the industrial world, with allowable levels of heavy metals on average eight times higher than in Canada and most of Europe (although actual metals levels in U.S. sludge are much lower than allowable levels). Indeed, Cornell University researchers have recommended that U.S. farmers apply sludge at no more than one tenth the levels permitted by EPA. Moreover, testing in the United States is required infrequently—as seldom as once a year for the smallest applied amounts—even though the contents of sludge can vary greatly from load to load.[42]

One simple and ancient alternative to sewage treatment plants is waste stabilization ponds, a series of holding areas in which sewage is retained for 10 days to a few weeks. Bacteria and algae convert the effluent to a stable form as it passes from pond to pond. Stabilization ponds require more land than conventional treatment plants do, but they are much cheaper, simpler to build and maintain, and, best of all from a recycling perspective, more effective at producing safe irrigation water. A conventional treatment plant can reduce the number of fecal coliforms in a milliliter of water from 100 million to 1 million—a 99-percent reduction, but not enough for safe use on crops. For unrestricted irrigation use, the World Health Organization recommends a fecal coliform level a thousand times lower—no greater than 1,000 per milliliter—and waste stabilization ponds can achieve this.[43]

One variant of the waste stabilization pond is a wetland modified to process wastes, the showcase example being one in Calcutta. For more than half a century, sewage has been channeled to a wetland east of the city, where multiple ponds are used not only to process waste, but also to raise fish and provide nutrient-rich irrigation water for farmers. Nutrients in the waste feed fish, plants, and organisms in the ponds. The fish, in turn, greatly reduce or eliminate algal blooms, making the final wastewater product more useful for agriculture. Water hyacinth cultivated at the ponds' edges further purify the water and protect the banks from erosion. And the hyacinth are either harvested for animal feed or composted. These multiple benefits, combined with a cost less than a quarter that of a conventional sewage treatment plant, have made the area a valuable municipal resource.[44]

A constructed micro-version of the Calcutta wetlands system could provide waste-processing capacity for some industries, thereby preventing their wastes from entering the sewer system. Complete with plants, microorganisms, and even fish, these facilities consist of a series of pools and constructed wetlands, often built in a garden-like setting, which progressively treat industrial wastes. One U.S. firm has found a robust market for these facilities, with 20 projects built or under construction since 1992 at businesses and institutions as diverse as the M&M/Mars Company in Brazil and Oberlin College in Ohio.[45]

For all their advantages, these natural filtering systems are land-intensive. Stabilization ponds, for example, require some 30 hectares for every 100,000 people served. Where land is tight, other choices are available, some of which can avoid the expense of sewage infrastructure.[46]

One promising alternative is a series of simple technologies from Mexico known collectively by their Spanish acronym, SIRDO. These systems build on the "dou-ble-vault" waste treatment concept developed in Viet Nam, in which one chamber collects current deposits of waste while the other is closed for several months as previously deposited material composts. Solar heating and bacteria transform wastes and other carbonaceous matter into a safe and odorless "biofertilizer" that is sold to nearby farms.[47]

Some SIRDO designs are "dry," requiring no water—and no sewage infrastructure—for their operation. Dry units serve one or two families, and compost household organic garbage together with human waste, reducing the need for landfills and sewage treatment plants. "Wet" SIRDO units are neighborhood-level mini-plants that biologically process the wastes of up to 1,000 people, operating in conjunction with existing flush toilets and local sewer lines. Even these "wet" systems save water, because they purify it—by percolation through a bed of sand and gravel—enough for reuse on gardens, or for irrigating nonfood crops.[48]

U.S. standards for sludge reuse are the least stringent in the industrial world.

As an effective sanitation technology, SIRDO reduces illnesses caused by pathogen-tainted water supplies. In the warm climates where SIRDOs are currently used, the units' solar-heated waste chambers generate higher temperatures, over longer periods, than are needed to ensure that pathogens are killed. In the town of Tres Marias, Mexico, introduction of SIRDO technology and a new potable water system are credited with cutting the rate of gastrointestinal illness from 25 cases per person in 1986 to less than one case per person in 1990. Since contaminated water is a major cause of sickness and death among children in developing countries, the technology's success in sterilizing wastes is a welcome advance.[49]

Moreover, the SIRDO systems are affordable, and even generate modest flows of revenue. A cost-benefit analysis done by the U.S.-based National Wildlife Federation found that all five SIRDO models studied—three wet and two dry—offered net financial gains under Mexican market conditions for water, labor, and biofertilizer. The simplest dry design, for example, costs $607 over 15 years—but earns the owner $2,088 in fertilizer revenues in the same period. The net income for user families is modest—on the order of $30–60 a year—but nonetheless meaningful for people living on the economic margin. Add to this the social benefits of the technology—the reduced need for sewage treatment, boosted levels of public health, and improved soil structure and fertility on farms that use the biofertilizer—and SIRDO's potential is apparent. Indeed, the technology is now used in Guatemala, Chile, and nine states in Mexico.[50]

Another nonsewer approach to waste processing doubles as a source of energy. Since the 1970s, China has installed more than 5 million anaerobic digesters—large chambers, sitting mostly underground, that break down a rural family's organic waste, including manure, human excreta, and crop residues, producing gas in the process. The units yield enough biogas to meet 60 percent of a family's energy needs, mostly for cooking and for fueling gas lamps. The digesters also produce an odorless dark slurry, used primarily for fertilizer, but also viable as feed for livestock or fish. The digesters are inexpensive—$80 covers the cost of materials and the help of a technician in construction.[51]

In cities with sewers, and where people are accustomed to flush toilets, separation of human and industrial wastes will be more challenging, and may need to be viewed as a medium to long-term goal. Nevertheless, current technologies suggest several possible approaches. Dry composting toilets, for example, can be installed in the bathrooms of many suburban homes. They look like standard flush models—without the water tank—and can hold up to several years' worth of excreta. They require some maintenance, including periodic inspection of the equipment and the compost itself. Service contracts, however, can minimize the burden on homeowners. Other non-sewer technologies include micro-flush toilets, which use as little as one pint of water per flush, and vacuum-powered toilets similar to those in aircraft lavatories. All these systems create a fertilizing product that can be applied to home gardens or, where economically feasible, collected and sold to farmers. And because the excreta are segregated from the flow of detergents, cleaning products, solvents, and other chemicals used in many households, the composted material is clean. The systems are not cheap, however, ranging in price from $1,000 to $6,000 per unit.[52]

Large buildings, such as multistory apartment complexes, would require different technologies. (Composting toilets usually require that the holding chamber be located directly below the toilet, which makes their use in multistory buildings impractical.) Constructed wetlands are one possibility for buildings that have plenty of land. Another option is the use of biogas digesters, similar in concept to those used by some Chinese peasants, but on a larger scale. Located in a building's basement, the digester would collect wastes from standard low-flush toilets and produce two products: methane, which could provide part of the building's power, and uncontaminated sludge, which could be collected and applied to farmland. Digesters offer a glimpse of the multiple benefits possible from full exploitation of human "waste."[53]

RESCALING MANURE PRODUCTION

Fertilizer and cheap transportation were the original scissors that snipped open organic loops, thereby unleashing the pollution and waste problems described earlier. Today, the globalization of agriculture compounds these problems by further stretching nutrient flows. And the concentration of agriculture fattens these flows, especially where livestock raising is concerned, with nutrients and organic matter accumulating to such an extent that they cannot be safely absorbed. The emerging lesson is that scale matters, and that too large a scale can lead to distortion and mishandling of nutrient flows. Prospects for restoring circularity to organic flows may require shortening and unplugging today's linear nutrient flows.

International trade in grain, which tripled between 1960 and 1995, generates nutrient losses in some areas and gains in others. In Europe, for example, an extensive livestock industry purchases feed from as far away as Brazil, Thailand, and the United States. But the industry has outgrown the capacity of nearby lands to absorb its wastes, so manure has steadily accumulated. Indeed, earlier this decade the Netherlands could boast the world's largest "manure mountain"—some 40 million tons' worth. Coupled with heavy fertilizer use, these accumulations are responsible for serious pollution problems in the Netherlands. Nitrate levels in the country's groundwater were more than double the recommended maximum level in the early 1990s. So saturated was the country in nitrogen and phosphorus at mid-decade that farmers could have met their crops' nutrient requirements from manure alone—without a single application of nitrogen or phosphorus fertilizer—and still ended up with a nutrient surplus in their soils.[54]

Taiwan has similar problems, after building a substantial but import-dependent hog-raising industry. The country buys more than 90 percent of its corn feed from farmers in the midwestern United States, half a world away. But the oversized hog-raising industry produces more manure than the country can absorb. As in the Netherlands, the result is serious pollution: officials estimate that two thirds of Taiwan's water pollution comes from manure discharges from hog farms. As a result, the government has been struggling since 1991 to reduce the number of hogs by one third.[55]

Lengthened nutrient supply lines are also found within the United States, where feed is shipped ever greater distances as cattle-, hog-, and chicken-raising facilities move away from feed production regions. Cattle feedlots, for example, were once located in the Corn Belt states that supplied them with feed, but they began to move hundreds of kilometers west to the Great Plains in the 1950s and 1960s. More recently, hog production has shifted hundreds of kilometers east, from the Midwest to Virginia and North and South Carolina. The nutrient supply line for livestock, which once extended a few hundred meters from field to barnyard, has now been stretched across state lines, essentially precluding the return of nutrients to feedcrop fields.[56]

Extended feed lines in the United States often end in excessive accumulations of nutrients because of the growing size of livestock-raising operations. (See Table 6–5.) As these operations centralize, manure piles up, creating a waste disposal dilemma where farmers once saw only a resource. Indeed, facilities with tens of thousands of animals generate hundreds of tons of manure or thousands of cubic meters of slurry, much of which is dumped or runs off into nearby waterways. EPA estimates that effluent from centralized livestock facilities accounts for more than a quarter of the water pollution caused by agriculture in the United

Table 6–5. United States: Concentration of Livestock Production, Mid-1990s

Livestock	Degree of Concentration
Beef	More than a third of marketed cattle come from just 70 of the nation's 45,000 feedlots. The number of feedlots in the top beef-producing states has fallen by 75 percent over the past two decades. The largest facilities are found in Kansas, Nebraska, and Texas.
Poultry	97 percent of U.S. sales are now controlled by operations that each produce more than 100,000 broilers a year.
Pork	U.S. hog and pig inventory has climbed some 18 percent in the past decade, while the number of operations has decreased by 72 percent. In North and South Carolina and Virginia, where the industry is increasingly located, nearly 80 percent of hogs come from facilities with 5,000 or more head. In traditional hog-raising states, only 6 percent of hogs come from facilities of this size.
Dairy	The number of dairies has fallen from 250,000 a decade ago to 150,000 today, and average herd size has increased by more than 50 percent.

SOURCE: Teresa Glover, "Livestock Manure: Foe or Fertilizer?" *Agricultural Outlook,* June 1996.

States. In North Carolina alone, over half a dozen major lagoon spills were reported in 1995, including one involving some 95,000 cubic meters of lagoon effluent—enough to fill more than 60 Olympic-size swimming pools.[57]

The buildup of nutrients from large animal-raising facilities has been documented in several states. In Delaware, for example, farmers were applying 72 percent more nitrogen and phosphorus than their crops needed in the early 1990s, thanks in large part to heavy use of manure from the state's extensive poultry-producing operations. Without enough cropland to absorb the mountains of manure generated each year, the material is applied wherever possible, at a rate of overapplication that averages some 50 kilograms per hectare. The manure generated by poultry could meet well over half of the state's crop nutrient needs if it could be easily and economically distributed, but large, centralized operations make this difficult.[58]

The question of scale is often treated solely as an economic issue. From this limited perspective, bigger is better, because economies of scale typically make large operations more competitive than small ones. But equally relevant are "ecologies of scale," under which larger operations may be more environmentally damaging because they reduce the possibilities for successful recycling. A complete picture of the costs and benefits of large, centralized operations requires careful evaluation of their environmental consequences.

RETURNING TO OUR ORGANIC ROOTS

As the drawbacks of today's linear organic flows become evident, interest in recycling organic material is growing. Commitment to a series of principles of organic matter management can help make this recycling as ordinary as that of aluminum or newspaper.

The baseline precept is this: in a fully sustainable world, all organic flows must cycle. By this principle, any instance of organic dumping—whether of garbage sent to a landfill or incinerator, sewage flowing to a bay, or manure overapplied to farmland—represents unacceptable waste of a natural resource. Taxes or legal restrictions can be used to prevent organic material from entering traditional disposal sites. The United Kingdom, for example, has instituted a landfill tax to discourage landfill use, while several states in the United States have mandated cuts in organic inflows to landfills, or bans on particular kinds of organic matter, such as grass clippings. The United States has also banned ocean dumping of sewage, and Europe is set to do so as well. Just as most countries today do not deliberately trash their forests, fisheries, or other natural resources, neither should their organic matter be wantonly discarded.[59]

Outlawing dumping, however, is only half the battle. Viable recycling options are necessary to ensure that material is actually reused. Such options are best governed by a second principle—that organic wastes should be segregated from other wastes. It is generally simpler and cheaper to prevent contamination of organic material than to try to clean up dirty material, and segregation of wastes is the best way to achieve this.

Segregating organic matter from garbage can be handled in several ways. Separate collection of organic and nonorganic garbage is one option for city governments, with the city assuming responsibility for composting the organic waste. A more innovative and decentralized approach is city sponsorship of educational programs that equip residents to compost their own food and garden wastes. Sonoma County in California sponsors a citizen training program for composting that has reduced participants' landfilled wastes by an average of 18 percent. Best of all, the program is economical, costing $12 for every ton of waste diverted—60 percent less than a landfill would charge to take the material. Institutions such as hospitals, schools, or prisons can also be educated regarding the environmental and financial incentives for composting rather than dumping food wastes.[60]

Separation of human wastes from the chemicals and heavy metals in industrial and some household waste flows may be a long-term process, especially where cities are already committed to disposal technologies. In the meantime, "pretreatment" of wastes by industry to reduce the levels of heavy metals and toxic chemicals in sewage is a good first step for cities that rely on sewers and sewage treatment. To wean these cities of this dependence, however, plumbing codes that prohibit or discriminate against alternative systems such as composting toilets will have to be revised. Then the use of composting toilets or other on-site waste management systems can be promoted through regulations on new housing construction or through tax breaks to residents who replace flush systems with dry ones.

In developing countries—many of which need to invest in construction or maintenance of sanitation systems anyway—a reassessment of sanitation represents an opportunity to leapfrog past the costly problems of systems used in industrial countries. Funding limitations are cited as the chief obstacle to construction of sanitation infrastructure in low-income countries. Yet a system of composting toilets—an option that most cities do not consider—costs less than one seventh as much as sewage systems.[61]

Converting organic wastes to a clean and useful product, however, does not ensure that organic matter will be recycled; farmers have to want to use it. Synthetic fertilizer is easy to use, with the amount of nitrogen, phosphorus, and potassium marked on the package label. But compost, sludge, and manure are highly variable products made from equally variable inputs. Farmers are often unsure about how much to apply and at what rate nutrients will become available to plants. Markets for organic matter will not mature until farmers can be confident about the product they are buying and suppliers can respond to the diverse needs of different soils and different crops.

This level of sophistication will require greater research into the nature and properties of organic matter, especially compost, and how these function in different soils and climates and with different crops. Unfortunately, research in organic agriculture receives little official support. The California-based Organic Farming Research Foundation determined in 1997 that just 34 of the 30,000 research projects—one tenth of 1 percent—funded by the U.S. Department of Agriculture between 1991 and 1996 focused on organic agriculture. Moreover, no provision was made for dissemination to farmers of the results of these few projects. Such institutional indifference will need to be reversed if organic recycling is to make the maximum possible contribution to agriculture.[62]

Markets for organic matter will not mature until farmers can be confident about the product they are buying.

Even if organic dumping were proscribed and farmers were eager to apply organic matter, nutrients might still accumulate in one area and be unnecessarily depleted in another. Here, a third principle emerges: nutrient budgets should be established to keep nutrient flows in rough balance. Nutrient budgets are most meaningful at the farm level, and can be as useful to farmers as they are helpful to the environment. A simple tool known as the Nutrient Management Yardstick has been developed by the Center for Agriculture and the Environment in the Netherlands to track farm-level nutrient flows. The tool is a workbook that helps farmers account for all nutrients brought onto the farm—whether in fertilizer, feed, manure, or other materials—and all nutrients that leave the farm in crops, livestock products, or other materials. Dutch farmers using the yardstick have registered reductions in nutrient surpluses in each of its six years of use, and its adoption is likely to be widespread as farmers develop mandated nutrient management plans starting in 1998. Dissemination of this simple tool through agricultural extension programs could be an inexpensive way to get a handle on nutrient flows at the source.[63]

Because nutrient flows can be measured, agricultural operations can be held accountable for safely maintaining nutrient balances. Indeed, any operation likely to have large on-site nutrient imbalances—like the massive nutrient inflows common to centralized livestock facilities—should have a plan for disposing of nutrient surpluses in a way that is environmentally healthy. Until a facility can demonstrate, for example, that nearby landowners are willing to receive its excess manure and that the manure will be applied at rates that can be safely absorbed by those soils, it should not be allowed to expand.

Once they internalize these principles, citizens and policymakers essentially achieve a major shift in thinking and in worldview. Organic matter is no longer seen as disposable garbage, but as a soil-building natural resource. And nutrients are no longer viewed as wholly benign, to be scattered wantonly throughout the environment, but are understood to serve economies and ecosystems best when kept in balance. This acceptance of the ancient appreciation of organic material will be an important step toward building sustainable cities and farms.

7

Responding to the Threat of Climate Change

Christopher Flavin
Seth Dunn

In December 1997, representatives of more than 160 nations assembled in Kyoto, Japan, to sign a historic protocol to the 1992 Framework Convention on Climate Change. Like the Buddhist monks trying to attain harmony with the cosmos in the temples of this ancient city, environment ministers hoped to help reestablish harmony between humanity and the Earth's atmosphere. Over the last 10 millennia, the relative stability of the climate has nurtured the evolution of human society and the natural environment. Today, however, human activities are rapidly disrupting this stability, placing both in peril.[1]

The challenge laid down at the Kyoto summit was to spur a steady, gradual descent from this last century's precipitous climb up a greenhouse-gas mountain. Global emissions of carbon—which in the atmosphere form carbon dioxide (CO_2), the most important greenhouse

gas released by human activities—from the burning of fossil fuels reached a record 6.2 billion tons in 1996, having increased nearly fourfold since 1950. (See Figure 7–1.) The postwar emissions binge is a planetary experiment unlike anything we have ever tried, overwhelming the natural cycling of carbon by oceans and forests and bringing the atmospheric CO_2 concentration to 29 percent above its preindustrial level—higher than at any time in the last 160,000 years. The Intergovernmental Panel on Climate Change (IPCC), which in 1995 confirmed a "discernible human influence on global climate," estimates that a doubling of CO_2 concentrations—likely to occur late next century if we stay on the current path—will increase global temperature by 1–3.5 degrees Celsius.[2]

This rate of change, the fastest in the last 10,000 years, poses substantial risks to the natural world and human society in coming decades. While the complexity of the Earth's climate system makes it impossible to know precisely the effects of rapid

An expanded version of this chapter appeared as Worldwatch Paper 138, *Rising Sun, Gathering Winds: Policies to Stabilize the Climate and Strengthen Economies.*

Million Tons

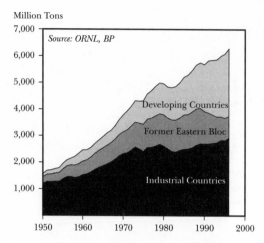

Figure 7–1. World Carbon Emissions from Fossil Fuel Burning, by Economic Region, 1950–96

changes in the composition of the atmosphere, scientists around the world have concluded that flooded cities, diminished food production, and increased storm damage all seem likely—and could well produce catastrophic economic consequences. Whatever the outcomes are, they could take centuries to reverse, and could affect the lives of billions of people.[3]

Just as homeowners buy insurance to cope with uncertain but real dangers, governments face the challenge of minimizing the risks of climate change by investing in affordable means of limiting greenhouse gas emissions. Luckily, the premium for climate protection has dropped dramatically during the 1990s, as many promising new technologies have moved quietly but decisively from experimental curiosity to commercial reality. These new inventions allow rapid improvement in the efficiency of energy use, and can economically turn sunlight, wind, and plant matter into electricity and other useful forms of energy. The cost of solar cells, for example, has fallen 95 percent since the 1970s and is expected to drop another 75 percent in the next

decade. Advances like this open up an intriguing possibility: just as the economic miracles of the twentieth century were powered by fossil fuels, the twenty-first century may be marked by an equally dramatic move away from fossil fuels, and from the global environmental threats they carry.[4]

Such a sweeping change in the world's energy system will unfold rapidly enough only if government policies—many of which support the status quo and retard the development of alternatives—are transformed. In the past few years, a number of governments have demonstrated that bold, innovative policies can spur rapid adoption of new technologies, leading to sharp declines in the combustion of fossil fuels. Efforts to cut fuel subsidies, improve energy efficiency standards, and support the accelerated use of renewable energy are among the initiatives that have proved effective in reducing emissions. This experience shows clearly that greenhouse gas trends can be turned around with surprisingly modest shifts in policy—and that these new policies can actually spur economic development. Indeed, if all nations had by now adopted the most effective policies already taken up piecemeal by one or more countries, global greenhouse gas emissions might now be headed down.

UP THE EMISSIONS MOUNTAIN—AND DOWN AGAIN?

Industrial countries are responsible for 76 percent of the world's cumulative carbon emissions since 1950. Recognizing this disproportionate burden, signatories to the 1992 climate change treaty agreed that these countries should take the lead by voluntarily holding emissions to 1990 levels by the year 2000. But this goal has disappeared in the cloud of greenhouse gases belching from the automobiles and smokestacks of industrial countries. Farthest off track among leading emitters are the United States, Australia, and Japan, whose carbon emissions in 1996 were 8.8, 9.6, and 12.5 percent above 1990 levels. (See Figure 7–2.)[5]

A chief culprit in recent emissions growth is the transportation sector, the fastest-growing source during the past two decades. Much of this is due to the automobile fleet, which has surged from 50 million to 500 million since 1950 and is projected to double over the next quarter-century as millions of people in developing countries purchase cars for the first time. In industrial countries, meanwhile, cars are also being sold in larger sizes and being driven greater distances with each passing year. At the same time, the popularity of larger homes with ever more electrical appliances is also increasing energy use and carbon emissions. These trends, supported by low fuel prices, have overwhelmed the energy efficiency improvements of the last decade.[6]

The record in industrial countries is not universally bleak, however. The collapse of energy-intensive industries in Eastern Europe and the former Soviet Union lowered Russia's carbon emissions 33 percent between 1990 and 1996. Emissions have dropped 7.6 percent in Germany as a result of energy policy reforms and the forced shutdown of inefficient, coal-based industries and power plants in its new eastern states. The United Kingdom and France also kept their carbon emissions below their 1990 levels through 1996.[7]

The fastest growth in greenhouse gas emissions in recent years has been in the developing world, where industrialization is still gathering speed. (See Figure 7–3.) By 1996, carbon emissions in developing countries were 44 percent over 1990 levels, and 71 percent over 1986 levels. Rapid economic growth, particularly in East Asia and Latin America, is driving emissions up as growing numbers of people are able to afford home appliances, motorcycles, cars, and other energy-intensive amenities of a "modern" lifestyle. The International Energy Agency projects that without additional policy initiatives, global carbon emissions from fossil fuels will exceed 1990 levels by 17 percent in 2000 and by 40 percent in 2010, reaching 9 billion tons per year.[8]

The lead-up to Kyoto saw angry finger-pointing between industrial and developing countries over the division of responsibilities agreed to under the climate convention. But such conflicts pale in comparison to the common interests—and benefits—of cooperating to slow global warming. John Holdren of Harvard University likens the energy economy to a supertanker headed at full speed for a reef, asserting that: "We all need to steer cooperatively, not argue who's at the wheel."[9]

Indeed, industrial countries are well positioned to pioneer a new generation of energy and transportation technologies that can be used to slow emissions growth.

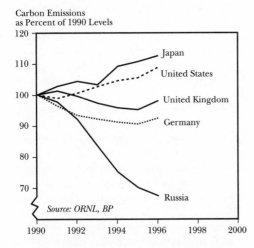

Carbon Emissions
as Percent of 1990 Levels

Source: ORNL, BP

Figure 7–2. Carbon Emissions Trends, Selected Industrial and Former Eastern Bloc Countries, 1990–96

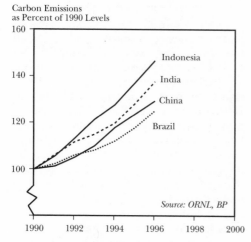

Carbon Emissions
as Percent of 1990 Levels

Indonesia

India

China

Brazil

Source: ORNL, BP

Figure 7–3. Carbon Emissions Trends, Selected Developing Countries, 1990–96

But developing countries need not lag far behind; with the right policies, they could end up with cleaner, more economical energy systems, stay at the cutting edge of innovation, and avoid having to make two energy transitions in just a few decades.[10]

Thanks to a powerful combination of government incentives and private investment, technologies such as synthetic materials, advanced electronics, and biotechnology are now trickling into the energy industry. These technical advances allow quantum leaps in automobile, building, and appliance efficiency, and have made it possible to convert wind and solar energy into electricity at prices that are competitive with fossil fuels.[11]

If combined with improved public transportation, more compact cities, and new industrial processes, these technologies can reduce carbon emissions significantly while strengthening the global economy and creating millions of jobs. Just as automobiles followed horses and computers supplanted typewriters and slide rules, so can the advance of technology make today's energy systems look primitive, inefficient, and uneconomical. The first automobiles and computers

were difficult to use and expensive, but they soon became practical and affordable; the new energy technologies are now moving rapidly down the same engineering cost curves. Although their current role in world energy supply is small (less than 1 percent), their potential contribution is enormous.[12]

Among the recent studies confirming the plausibility of profound change in the energy system, one of the most striking was carried out by the Group Planning Unit of the Royal Dutch Shell oil company. In a 1996 report, it envisioned a "Sustained Growth" scenario in which fossil fuels dominate energy markets in the short run but renewable energy technologies "steadily progress along their learning curves, first capturing niche markets and by 2020 becoming fully competitive with conventional energy sources."[13]

Most studies of the economics of addressing climate change ignore the vast potential for new policies to induce technological change, however, and consequently estimate a high cost of reducing emissions. The reality is different, as demonstrated by the phaseout of ozone-depleting substances in the early 1990s, when low-cost alternatives were found far more quickly and easily than economic projections had predicted. These models also overestimate climate protection costs by assuming a simple, solitary policy tool—putting a price tag on emissions in the form of a tax on fossil fuels. This approach overstates costs by neglecting the potential to lower market barriers, and often assuming the revenue will not be recycled to reduce other taxes.[14]

According to economist Robert Repetto, adjusting models to account for such assumptions suggests that a well-designed effort to deal with the climate problem could actually increase economic output. The challenge for policymakers is to devise and carry out such a strategy—one that simultaneously helps stabilize climate and strengthens economies. In moving forward to implement the Kyoto Protocol, there is much to be learned by looking back at government experiences over the last decade in three key areas: reforming fossil fuel prices, boosting energy efficiency standards, and supporting the use of renewable energy.[15]

FINDING THE RIGHT PRICE FOR CARBON

In building a fossil-fuel-based energy system over the past century, most nations have developed a complex web of policies aimed at accelerating the extraction and use of coal, oil, and natural gas. Special subsidies and tax breaks for fossil fuels encourage heavier use than otherwise would occur; at a time when the goal should be to reduce fossil fuel use, not increase it, these are badly in need of change. Direct supports for conventional energy sources are estimated at $200 billion worldwide—more than half the value of all the crude oil produced each year. According to the IPCC, by phasing out these supports industrial countries could cut their projected carbon emissions for 2050 by 18 percent while increasing overall incomes in the long run.[16]

The most dramatic fossil fuel price reforms so far have taken place in former Eastern bloc countries, which under communist rule had the highest subsidies and which began to phase them out after their revolutions. Poland cut energy subsidies by $3 billion annually, and coal use declined more than 30 percent between 1987 and 1994. Russia has slashed fossil fuel subsidies by more than half since 1990, contributing to the drop in carbon emissions of more than 30 percent. But further reductions are possible.[17]

Energy price reform has been uneven in Western Europe, where fossil fuel subsidies stand at more than $10 billion

annually. The United Kingdom has witnessed dramatic cuts, reducing coal supports from more than $7 billion in 1989 to virtually nil in 1995; the resulting dash to natural gas lowered U.K. carbon emissions steadily between 1990 and 1995. But German coal subsidies have increased by more than half during the last 15 years, and despite a planned phaseout are projected to reach a record high in 1998. Other industrial countries have done less to get rid of subsidies. Australia, the world's leading coal exporter, has left untouched its elaborate system of price supports. The United States is gradually reducing its own, but the subsidies remain as high as $18 billion a year and include tax breaks for the oil and gas industry. Canada also gives large handouts to oil and gas producers: $6 billion in tax incentives each year.[18]

At the same time, fossil fuel subsidy reform is accelerating in developing countries. (See Table 7–1.) China's supports have been reduced from $24 billion annually to $10 billion just in the last five years, slowing carbon emissions growth by 20 percent, according to World Bank estimates. India has also made steep cuts, and Brazil has eliminated subsidies for fossil fuels completely.[19]

Removing subsidies for road building and use can also reduce carbon emissions. Since the 1950s, numerous industrial countries have to varying degrees shifted their transportation emphasis from moving people—through rail, bus, and other mass transit—to moving cars—through the building and expansion of roads and road-related services. While these supports have yet to be fully tabulated, there is little doubt as to their large role in encouraging private car use. The United States is "king of the road," spending as much as $121 billion annually to support road use. In Japan, total road subsidies are estimated at $66 billion. In Europe, the supports are far lower and in some cases negative, ranging from a net

**Table 7-1. Fossil Fuel Subsidies in Selected Developing Countries and
Countries in Transition, 1990–96**

Country or Region	Subsidy Rate		Total Subsidies, 1995–96
	1990–91	1995–96	
	(percent of market price)		(percent of gross domestic product)
Egypt	49	40	3.4
Eastern Europe	42	23	3.2
China	42	20	2.4
Russia	48	25	1.5
India	25	19	1.1
Indonesia	26	21	0.9
Mexico	28	16	0.7
Thailand	9	9	0.4
South Africa	11	4	0.3
Brazil	23	0	0.0

SOURCE: World Bank, *Expanding the Measure of Wealth* (Washington, DC: World Bank, June 1997).

yearly road use subsidy of some $13 billion in Germany to a net road tax of about $5 billion annually in France.[20]

Countries with the largest car populations—and problems—generally have made meager efforts to redirect road subsidies to rail and public transportation, where they could go a long way toward reducing oil dependence, smog, and congestion. Germany, the United Kingdom, and the United States, for example, maintain a heavy bias toward road building—in the United States, the car receives $7 of federal funds for every dollar given to public transport. But even countries with reputations for supporting public transport, such as Denmark, France, and the Netherlands, are also yielding to road building pressure and failing to fend off rising car use. Japan includes road building in its climate change plan, even though such efforts are known to increase driving.[21]

One key to reining in transport emissions is more integrated decisionmaking in transportation and land-use planning, an approach France, the United Kingdom, and the United States now mandate. Another key is combining public transit improvements with charges for road use. Several governments have begun to explore "road pricing" and other restrictions on car use: examples of local initiatives to actively restrain road use can be seen in a variety of cities in Germany, Sweden, and the United States, as well as in Brazil, Poland, and Singapore.[22]

Going a step further, taxes on fossil fuels or on carbon emissions can make their prices better reflect their effect on climate. By internalizing the environmental costs of these fuels, such taxes actively discourage their use. According to the Organisation for Economic Co-operation and Development, adjusting existing energy taxes in proportion to the carbon content of the fuels used could cut emissions by 12 percent. The IPCC estimates that higher gas taxes could cut carbon emissions by up to 25 percent by 2020 in most countries, and by as much as 60 percent where prices are currently very low. The levies can be returned to taxpayers through cuts in other taxes, thereby increasing national income levels.[23]

Five industrial countries have adopted carbon and energy taxes that, though weakened by exemptions and deductions, are showing some results. (See Table

Table 7–2. Carbon/Energy Taxes, Industrial Countries, 1997

Country	Date Introduced	Current Rate	Exemptions
		(price per ton of carbon)	
Denmark	1996	$2.10–24.30 $1–3.70 for industry	Electricity use
Finland	1990	$1.90	Industrial raw materials and overseas transport fuels
Netherlands	1992	$1.20–1.60	Large-scale natural gas use and renewable energy
Norway	1991	$4.60–15.30	Onshore natural gas use and fuels for fishing, air and freight transport
Sweden	1991	$13.10 $6.50 for industry	Electricity and some biomass use

SOURCE: Richard Baron, *Economic Fiscal Instruments: Taxation*, Working Paper 3, Annex 1, Expert Group on the UN Framework Convention on Climate Change (Paris: July 1996).

7–2.) The Dutch tax, which exempts renewable energy, is cutting carbon emissions 2 percent annually. Sweden's levy has increased biomass use, mainly for cogeneration (the combined production of heat and electricity in factories and buildings), by 71 percent. The Danish tax revenue supports industrial energy efficiency, and is also reportedly reducing carbon emissions. All three revenues are recycled to reduce income and wage taxes. In other industrial countries, carbon taxes have been stalled by industry opposition, although in 1997 the European Commission tabled a new proposal. Poland and Costa Rica have in the meantime enacted small carbon taxes, with Poland devoting part of the revenues to energy efficiency and reforestation and Costa Rica setting aside a portion for reforestation as well.[24]

The lion's share of energy taxes are levied on gasoline. Taxes as high as 60¢ per liter ($2.50 per gallon)—more than $1,000 per ton of carbon—are found in a number of European countries. Some, including Germany, Italy, and the Netherlands, have recently increased fuel taxes. Others have had less success: the United Kingdom's annual fuel levy was

removed in August 1997 by the new British government, and the United States—with one of the world's lowest figures, averaging 36¢ per gallon—has been unable to increase fuel taxes.[25]

Just as carbon tax funds can be channeled to clean energy, gas tax revenues can be steered to public transportation rather than road-related services, as they currently are. One nation doing this is Austria, where the fuel tax is partly earmarked for local rail systems and has halted the country's trend to larger cars. If used more widely, this policy could help industrial countries tackle their most problematic—and least addressed—source of emissions.[26]

BOOSTING EFFICIENCY

Another major "market failure" slowing the revolution needed to stabilize climate is the tendency of purchasers of energy-using equipment to focus on the initial price of the devices and ignore the lifetime fuel bills, which are often substantial. One widely accepted and time-tested way to overcome this barrier is to set minimum efficiency standards that manufacturers must follow. If supported by higher energy prices and combined with incentives that motivate manufacturers and inform consumers, standards can be steadily ratcheted up, leading to continuous efficiency improvements and emissions cuts. The sooner they are strengthened, the greater their impact on the large number of cars, buildings, and appliances due to be manufactured and installed in the next decade.[27]

Automobiles, which dominate the transportation sector's 21-percent share of energy-related carbon emissions, demonstrate the potential of and need for efficiency standards. Standards established in the 1970s improved efficiency markedly during the 1980s but have leveled off, leading to a decline in fuel economy. In the absence of standards, emissions from road transport are projected to double by 2020, with much of the increase in developing countries. With higher car fuel economy, however, the emissions forecast could be cut by as much as a quarter. This potential is demonstrated by Toyota's new Prius, a hybrid-electric model with twice the efficiency and half the carbon emissions of other cars on the road. The Prius went on the market at the end of 1997.[28]

Little progress has been made in strengthening automobile efficiency standards so far in the 1990s, and the only legally binding rules in place, in the United States, have become nearly meaningless. Enacted in 1978 and gradually raised to 27.5 miles per gallon (8.6 liters per 100 kilometers) for cars in 1985, the standards nearly doubled the fuel economy of new U.S. cars between 1974 and 1988. But they have remained essentially flat since. Overall, U.S. new-car fuel economy is now declining, due partly to greater use of sport utility vehicles.[29]

In other efforts to increase auto fuel economy, 12 countries have enacted weak voluntary goals that, averaging a 10-percent efficiency improvement over 10 years, are little more than what will occur anyway. To encourage consumers to buy efficient cars, Austria and the Canadian province of Ontario have enacted "feebates," which either offer carbuyers a rebate or require them to pay a fee according to the car's fuel economy. But these will have a limited impact without tougher standards. The European Commission has proposed an ambitious target for 2005 of 47 miles per gallon (5 liters per 100 kilometers) for gasoline-driven cars and 52 miles per gallon (4.5 liters per 100 kilometers) for diesel-powered cars, compared with the current average of 29 miles per gallon (8 liters per 100 kilometers) for gasoline-driven cars— which would require an annual efficiency improvement of 2–3 percent. The status of this proposal is unclear, however. In the developing world, only South Korea has mandatory auto efficiency standards.[30]

Buildings and appliances, responsible for 29 percent of global carbon emissions from energy use, present another large opportunity for cuts. Without further measures, global emissions from these sectors are projected to as much as triple by 2050, mainly due to increases in floor space and in the use of appliances and office equipment—particularly in former Eastern bloc and developing countries, where current buildings are highly inefficient and where most new ones will be built. The IPCC estimates efficiency standards for buildings and equipment could hold 2050 emissions to double the current level while paying consumers back for the higher upfront costs within five years, with the largest opportunities in tightened requirements for thermal insulation, refrigerators, and office equipment. Further reductions are possible if these "sticks" are reinforced with "carrots," such as tax incentives for retrofitting old buildings and purchasing more-efficient equipment. The largest potential savings are in developing countries, where many consumers will soon purchase their first refrigerators and televisions.[31]

Although most industrial countries have building codes in place that they have recently strengthened, in some cases supplementing them with incentives, the toughest are a fraction of what is economically justifiable. Sweden's codes, enacted in 1983, remain the most stringent and have served as an international model, but even they could be significantly tightened to keep up with the latest building technologies. New Dutch codes tap only a quarter of the possible savings. Germany and Japan are offering subsidies for buildings that meet or exceed the standards, but their new codes are relatively weak.[32]

Other industrial countries have struggled to implement weaker systems: a new code in Canada, which if widely used would cut building energy use by one fifth, has been adopted by just one province. Most U.S. building codes at the state level are out-of-date, and the national model code has been adopted by only half the states. This has lessened the impact of complementary efforts, such as an incentive program to build buildings that are 30 percent more efficient than the code and a program to help homeowners handle the high upfront costs of retrofitting buildings by allowing them to finance efficiency improvements through mortgage payments.[33]

Other countries have made limited headway in setting building efficiency rules. Russia has enacted, but is failing to implement, building codes. A handful of mandatory building codes are found in the Third World, most modeled on the U.S. one: Thailand; Singapore, which reports high compliance; and China, which has also introduced tax incentives for the construction of energy-efficient buildings.[34]

While implementation is the greatest challenge for building codes, adopting

new standards and updating existing ones is the key for appliances—the fastest-growing emissions source within buildings, which only a small number of industrial countries have established rules on. The United States has since 1978 established criteria for more than 20 appliances, which have brought significant gains—including a tripling of refrigerator efficiency—and are projected to yield some $56 billion in energy cost savings between 1990 and 2015. Ambitious new U.S. refrigerator and air conditioner standards were enacted in 1997.[35]

Little progress has been made in strengthening automobile efficiency standards in the 1990s.

Recent European Union refrigerator standards, however, have been diluted by industry opposition to below half the proposed levels. Appliance standards in Russia have been set but are not being enforced, while several developing countries have set appliance rules, including China, South Korea, Mexico, and the Philippines—the latter two of which report modest successes in energy savings.[36]

Office equipment—the fastest-growing source of emissions from commercial buildings—lacks standards entirely, though a U.S. computer labeling program has encouraged some efficiency gains, and now covers 60 percent of all personal computers. Voluntary office equipment targets have been set in Switzerland and Japan—where electricity consumption in offices is believed to be one of the largest sources of carbon emissions. The Tokyo-based Global Environment Information Center of the United Nations University recommended in 1997 that Japan take the lead in calling for the establishment of international standards for office equipment and other appliances.[37]

Industry—which accounts for 45 percent of energy-related carbon emissions—incorporates thousands of distinct processes, and demands a more flexible approach to reducing emissions than standards can provide. More effective in this case are targets that companies themselves decide how to meet. If stringent and supported by price reforms and incentives, voluntary covenants between government and industry can tap a carbon savings potential that, despite two decades of efficiency improvements, remains great. The IPCC estimates that industrial countries could bring emissions from industry 25 percent below 1990 levels in the short run, and considerably more in the long run, just by upgrading manufacturing facilities with the most energy-efficient technologies available. If done in step with the normal turnover of equipment, the costs would be negligible. The potential is even greater in developing countries and those in transition, whose industries are 25–50 percent as efficient as those in industrial countries.[38]

Over the past five years, governments and industries have signed some 200 voluntary agreements aimed at reducing greenhouse emissions. (See Table 7–3.) These vary widely in scope, ambitiousness, reporting requirements, and enforceability. The more successful ones resemble formal contracts between government and industry, with specific goals, required reporting, and penalties for noncompliance. Those purely voluntary in nature have been much less effective.[39]

The most ambitious industry covenants to date are found in the Netherlands, whose government has a long tradition of voluntary agreements and has since 1989 established 28 individual "Long-Term Agreements" covering 90 percent of the country's industrial energy use. Calling for 20-percent efficiency improvements between 1989 and 2000, and allowing for mandatory regulations if the targets are not met, they have engendered energy savings greater than origi-

Table 7–3. Industry Covenants, Selected Industrial Countries, 1997

Country	Share of Industrial Energy Use Covered	Targets	Reporting Requirements
	(percent)	(average)	
Netherlands	90	20 percent efficiency improvement from 1989 level by 2000	Govt. agency; required
Germany	80	20 percent emissions reduction from 1990 level by 2005	Independent institute; required
Japan	60	10–20 percent emissions reduction from 1990 level by 2010	Govt. agency; required for noncompliance
United States	7	None	Industry self-monitoring; not required
Canada	70	None	Industry self-monitoring; not required
Australia	30	None	Industry self-monitoring; not required

SOURCE: International Energy Agency, *Voluntary Actions for Energy-Related CO₂ Abatement* (Paris: Organisation for Economic Co-operation and Development, 1997).

nally expected—with government monitoring and complementary tax incentives reportedly playing a crucial role. The energy savings achieved were even greater than expected, and the government is now considering even tougher goals.[40]

Germany's industry covenants, which include 19 sectors (80 percent of industrial energy use), also have specific targets and are independently monitored. Several outside evaluations, however, criticize its lack of regulatory backup and question whether the programs will stimulate improvements beyond "business-as-usual." Tighter targets are being discussed, and the government now claims it will introduce mandatory measures if the current goals are missed.[41]

Japan's voluntary agreements cover about 60 percent of manufacturing and aim for a 10-percent improvement by 2000. Keidanren, Japan's industry association, has further committed its 137 members to reducing emissions 10–20 percent below 1990 levels by 2010. These efforts are supported by a two-decade tradition of tax credits and low-interest loans for industries installing energy-efficient equipment. The country's history of industrial efficiency improvements and the seriousness with which industry has taken previous agreements with government suggest this approach may yield positive results in Japan.[42]

Less likely to succeed are voluntary programs in the United States, which consist of general commitments, optional reporting, and no government authority to decree mandatory measures. A program with industry has attracted a mere 7 percent of the sector's energy use, with few companies having developed action plans. Voluntary agreements with electric utilities include several interesting renewable energy and tree planting programs but suffer from declining participation and are achieving a fraction of the carbon savings originally projected. Funding cutbacks for a modestly effective lighting efficiency program have limited its ability to generate wider interest (though the program's structure is being replicated in Poland and China).[43]

The industry covenants of other carbon-intensive economies suffer as well from vague commitments, optional monitoring and enforcement, and limited public access to information. The majority of companies taking part in Canada's program have submitted only letters of intent, with just a few companies detailing extensive action plans. The Australian program with industry, meanwhile, assumes that the companies will achieve no business-as-usual efficiency improvements—thereby inflating the projected results. Neither are currently expected to have a demonstrable effect on emissions.[44]

Voluntary programs for industry, as well as buildings and appliances, are meanwhile under way in at least eight developing and transitional countries. The most innovative in encouraging industrial efficiency has been China, which bases worker bonuses on achieving standards in several sectors, monitors energy use through a network of energy conservation centers, and sets quotas on energy use. This has stimulated $6 billion in energy efficiency investments.[45]

SUPPORTING NEW ENERGY SUPPLIES

Avoiding dangerous climate change will depend in large part on our ability to develop new energy supply systems quickly. New technologies are now becoming available to combine the use of heat and power, providing energy services far more efficiently and cutting carbon emissions by 60–80 percent. Converting sunlight, wind, and other renewable resources into energy, meanwhile, could in the next century meet most of the world's needs. The

IPCC estimates that the aggressive development of economically competitive alternatives to fossil fuels could reduce by two thirds the cost of cutting carbon emissions 20 percent below 1990 levels. While appropriately pricing fossil fuels will help pull these technologies into the market, a push is also needed to overcome the many barriers currently impeding the adoption of new energy systems.[46]

In Denmark, cogeneration supplies 40 percent of the electricity used.

One of these barriers is the relatively high initial cost of the new technologies. The costs of solar photovoltaic (PV), wind, geothermal, and biomass energy technologies have begun to fall as a result of two decades of public research and development, although this still stands at less than 9 percent of energy R&D budgets in industrial countries. Even more important than raising R&D, however, is to surmount the obstacles to deploying these technologies: the "uneven playing field" of low electricity purchase prices and utility monopolies that has kept them on the sidelines of today's energy market. Fortunately, the 1990s has given birth to a new generation of renewable energy policies that appear to be overcoming these problems—with the initiative shifting from the United States to Europe and Asia. (See Table 7–4.)[47]

Two policies in particular are proving their worth at quickly bringing renewable energy and cogeneration to market. Tax incentives—subsidies for installing equipment and generating electricity—prime the pump for these technologies, and can be phased out once they gain a foothold. Access to power markets at fixed or special prices is the second mechanism that has helped new technologies get off the

ground in several countries. These two tools—alone or, more dynamically, in tandem—can have a demonstrable effect on carbon emissions while creating considerably more jobs and exports than the conventional technologies they replace.[48]

The effective use of tax incentives to stimulate the use of new generating technologies dates back to the 1970s, and is perhaps best seen in Denmark, which in 1979 began to offer wind generators a 30-percent tax deduction for installing new turbines. These incentives, which covered only turbines certified by the Riso National Laboratory, allowed Denmark to become the world's leading manufacturer and exporter of this technology. Over the last decade, the incentives have been shifted from investment to production, and small-scale wind generators now receive a subsidy of 4.2¢ per kilowatt-hour, as well as rebates on the national energy tax, value-added tax, and CO_2 tax. Wind power now accounts for 6 percent of the nation's electricity supply. Since 1992, the Danish government has also subsidized up to half the cost of new cogeneration equipment. Partly as a result, cogeneration supplies 40 percent of the electricity used, and the government is aiming for a 65-percent share by 2005. An independent review of the Danish climate plan projects that by 2010, all of the country's power not provided by wind energy may come from cogeneration.[49]

In the United States, renewable energy tax credits have had a more erratic history. In California in the early 1980s, renewable power generators received generous credits that stimulated some 12,000 megawatts in renewable energy use before being abruptly cut back beginning in 1986. New incentives were introduced in the early 1990s, but their effect has been weakened by low fuel prices, overcapacity in power markets, and the uncertainties of electric industry restructuring. As a result, wind power capacity has actually declined in California during the 1990s.[50]

**Table 7–4. Policies to Promote Renewable Energy,
Selected Industrial Countries, 1997**

Country	Tax Incentives	Purchase Prices
Australia	None	10 percent premium from some utilities
Austria	Production tax credit for PV	Premiums in some regions
Canada	Accelerated capital tax depreciation	Premiums in some provinces
Denmark	15 percent capital credit for wind 4.2¢ per kilowatt-hour production credit for wind Energy, CO_2, value-added tax rebates	85 percent of retail price for wind
France	Tax credits for PV, wind	4.8¢ per kilowatt-hour premium for wind
Germany	50–67 percent capital credit for PV	65–90 percent of retail price for PV, wind (at 10¢ per kilowatt-hour)
Japan	50–67 percent capital credit for PV	100 percent of retail price for PV, wind (at 18¢ per kilowatt hour)
Netherlands	8¢ per kilowatt-hour production credit for wind 11.5 percent energy tax deduction CO_2 tax exemption Tax exemption for green fund investors	None
Sweden	35 percent capital credit for wind 1.2¢ per kilowatt-hour production credit	None
United Kingdom	None	6.3–8.4¢ per kilowatt-hour premium
United States	1.5¢ per kilowatt-hour production credit for wind, biomass 1.4¢ per kilowatt-hour for state and municipal wind, "closed-loop" biomass 10 percent investment credit for PV, geothermal Federal and state accelerated tax depreciation	None

SOURCE: International Energy Agency, *Renewable Energy Policy in IEA Countries* (Paris: Organisation for Economic Co-operation and Development, 1997).

Tax incentives in the Netherlands have helped boost the use of cogeneration to 30 percent of the total power supply, and are also being used in a recent push to promote renewables. From 1986 to 1995, the Dutch government provided capital subsidies of up to 35 percent for new projects. The grant was replaced in 1996 by a generation subsidy of 8¢ per kilowatt-hour for wind projects of 2 megawatts or less. It provides an environmental tax credit of 2.6¢ per kilowatt-hour and a fossil fuel tax refund of 1.5¢ to the market price of 3.9¢, effectively doubling the price paid to wind generators. Developers are also given an accelerated depreciation allowance for the wind turbines and other tax incentives.[51]

Many countries are shifting their tax incentives for renewables from investment to generation, though some—such as Sweden—offer both. The former supports 35 percent of the capital cost of turbines above 60 kilowatts, and the latter pays 1.2¢ per kilowatt-hour. Italian law provides capital subsidies for renewable systems, but the government has yet to disburse any funds owing to budget shortfalls. Canada allows the accelerated depreciation of capital for renewables equipment, and is considering additional tax deductions. Spain has a purchase price of more than 7¢ per kilowatt-hour, and has committed $105 million to a third-party financing scheme. A number of countries are using tax incentives to promote building-integrated solar electric systems. Switzerland subsidizes the installation of such systems on school buildings as part of its strategy to have at least one solar electric system in each of its 3,000 villages by 2000.[52]

The ambitious solar rooftop program in Japan subsidizes half the installation cost to consumers.

One of the most effective policies supporting new generating technologies in the 1990s is the so-called electricity feed law, which sets a fixed price at which small renewable energy generators are provided access to the electricity grid—the second key tool for bringing renewables to market. The most successful example of this so far is Germany's law, which in 1991 obligated utilities to buy renewable electricity at up to 90 percent of the average purchase price for end users. Guaranteeing a premium of 17 pfennigs (10¢) per kilowatt-hour for wind generators, the act spurred the addition of nearly 1,500 megawatts of wind power capacity between 1991 and 1996. Germany surpassed the United States as the leading wind power generator in 1997, and reports the industry has created at least 10,000 new jobs.[53]

Similar laws have taken hold in a half-dozen other European countries and, according to German energy analyst Andreas Wagner, "have become the decisive criteria for renewable energy development in Europe." They vary widely in the technologies covered and the prices paid—and therefore in effectiveness—but they have a proven ability to overcome the biggest single obstacle to new technologies: the tendency of monopoly electric companies to block them from the power market. They have worked best when combined with tax incentives in the early years, as in Spain, which provides more than 7¢ per kilowatt-hour for wind, solar, biomass, and small-hydro electricity, helping make Spain register the fourth largest increase in wind power in 1996.[54]

In another type of market access policy, the United Kingdom's Non-Fossil Fuel Obligation requires distribution utility companies to purchase small but steadily growing portions of renewable power for their electricity portfolios. Independent power suppliers compete for contracts to supply power from wind turbines and other renewable energy sources, supported by a 10-percent levy on fossil-fuel-based electricity. These contracts guarantee a price above that paid to fossil-fuel generators and last for a period of eight or more years while the price support steadily drops. The program, initially designed to prop up the nuclear industry, encouraged a modest rise in wind power installations of some 87 megawatts between 1992 and 1996, and the prices that had to be paid for the new energy sources fell during the course of the first four orders. But an additional 323 megawatts under contract have been held up because of local opposition to the siting of wind farms and financial constraints resulting from a highly competitive bidding process. [55]

Another powerful combination of market guarantees and tax incentives can be seen in the ambitious solar rooftop program launched by the government of Japan in 1993. Aiming to install 70,000 solar power systems on the rooftops and facades of buildings by 2000, the program subsidizes half the installation cost to consumers and two thirds of the cost to commercial building owners. It also requires electric utilities to buy electricity generated by these systems at the full retail price of power.[56]

An estimated 9,400 solar-powered homes were installed in Japan by 1997, most of them with silicon solar tiles integrated directly into their rooftops. This allowed Japan to claim 30 percent of the world PV market in 1997, and the government has made continued PV market dominance a national goal. Japan recently announced a quintupling of its subsidies for renewable energy, although it is unclear what form these will take.[57]

The Japanese rooftop program has a number of rivals, including Germany's "1,000 roofs and façade program," which provides a capital subsidy of 65 percent and a guaranteed power purchase price, spawning 5,000 systems since 1990. The United States is the world's leading manufacturer of solar cells, but so far it has had limited success in boosting domestic use, although this may change in light of the "Million Roofs Program" announced by President Bill Clinton at the United Nations in June 1997. The plan is to offer tax incentives and loans for solar installations, but it remains to be seen whether they will be large enough to be effective. States in both Germany and the United States are also experimenting with net metering laws, which allow consumers to sell surplus solar electricity back to local utility companies.[58]

Some developing countries have moved aggressively to increase their use of renewables and cogeneration. Brazil's 20-year-old price support program for sugarcane-derived ethanol has allowed it to displace half the gasoline used in the country's cars. While lowering carbon emissions 20 percent, the program also helps support its sugarcane industry. In India, a package of new policies, dominated by generous tax breaks and guaranteed purchase prices, has led to explosive growth in the domestic wind industry: wind generating capacity leapt from 39 megawatts in 1992 to 820 megawatts in 1996, making India the fourth-leading user of wind power.[59]

China's government has successfully promoted biogas and small hydropower for decades, but has just begun serious efforts to promote solar and wind energy. It is also stepping up use of cogeneration, which supplied 12 percent of the nation's electricity in 1994; in 1997 the government announced that all large industrial boilers must be converted to cogeneration—a policy that could serve as a model for the rest of the world.[60]

THE CHALLENGE OF KYOTO

The climate protocol agreed to in Kyoto at the end of 1997 may mark an important turning point in the long-term effort to protect the world from the most overarching environmental threat it faces. But the agreement provides only the broadest framework—the targets, timetables, reporting requirements, and trading mechanisms needed to deal with climate change—and leaves to national governments the responsibility for enacting new policies that will enable them to meet the goals. The success of this endeavor will therefore hinge largely on the measures undertaken by individual countries to reduce their emissions of greenhouse gases.

Many valuable policy lessons have been

learned over the past few years, and may pave the way for more solid progress in the post-Kyoto era. Only by learning from those who have gone before can we hope to stabilize the climate in the years ahead. Indeed, the climate itself may serve as a guide on how best to respond to the challenge. Just as the climate is determined by the collective interaction of major components—the atmosphere, oceans, and biosphere—only the interplay of mutually reinforcing policy measures is up to the task of stabilizing it.[61]

Among the policies adopted so far, it is clear that the removal of energy subsidies has had the greatest short-term impact, in some cases contributing to sharp emissions reductions. This is largely a one-time effort, however, and some countries no longer have sizable energy subsidies that can be eliminated. Still, in many nations further subsidy reductions could have a great effect. Experience shows that energy and emissions taxes can have a big impact as well, but so far—with the partial exception of gasoline taxes—few countries have shown the political courage to introduce new energy taxes that really bite. International coordination could make this more politically feasible, overcoming the arguments on competitiveness that have stalled unilateral efforts. Fiscal reform will not by itself solve the climate problem, but it does set the stage for a range of other climate policies to do their work.[62]

Energy efficiency standards have also proved their effectiveness, though the slow turnover of devices such as automobiles and home appliances means that it will take time for standards to have their full impact. Governments have so far been most aggressive in pushing standards for buildings and appliances, but reluctant to adopt auto fuel economy standards in the face of strident industry opposition. Meanwhile, the Netherlands has demonstrated the effectiveness of "voluntary" industry covenants, but only if they are backed by a direct or implied enforcement mechanism. It is unclear whether this approach can work in different cultures and legal systems, however.[63]

Some of the most innovative experience in climate change mitigation has come in the form of new incentive mechanisms used to encourage reliance on renewable energy and cogeneration. Countries such as Denmark, Germany, and India have shown that the right combination of incentives—tax breaks and generous purchase prices—can spur industry to invest large sums, even when the country has limited experience with those technologies. These new systems are not yet in use on a sufficiently large scale to cause major reductions in carbon emissions. But the rapid growth now under way in cogeneration and renewable energy may allow them to make a major contribution in the next few years.[64]

One of the most important lessons of efforts taken so far to slow climate change is that no magic bullet policy will by itself solve the problem. Adjusting energy prices to reflect the environmental consequences of fossil fuel use accurately is arguably the most important policy, but that alone will not suffice. Many market barriers—from lack of information to the anti-competitive practices of some industries—impede the implementation of new technologies and practices.

Only a diverse portfolio of policies can ultimately reverse the growth of emissions. What should this portfolio look like? Based on experience to date, it should probably include fiscal, regulatory, voluntary, and market-based approaches—components that interact synergistically. Government policies that traditionally exist in isolated chambers must instead be combined into complex and harmonious orchestras.[65]

For 10 of the industrial countries voluntarily trying to stabilize greenhouse emissions at their 1990 levels, a clear hierarchy of the relative strengths and weaknesses of their climate policies emerges—allowing a ranking of their performance. At the head of the list are Denmark, the Netherlands, and Germany, each of which has developed a strong policy portfolio, though all have some gaps remaining. In this group, only Germany has actually cut its emissions, but the increases in Denmark and the Netherlands appear to be temporary anomalies. All three countries are likely to reduce their emissions during the next decade.[66]

France, Japan, Sweden, and the United Kingdom form a middle group of countries that are making some progress but still have major holes in their policy mix. Japan, for example, now has a strong solar incentive program, but weak efficiency standards. The United Kingdom has made good progress in reducing subsidies, but has a weak renewables policy. But with further advances, these four nations have a good chance of reducing their already modest per capita emissions.[67]

On the next rung of the climate policy ladder is the United States. The low U.S. energy taxes have not yet been raised, and auto efficiency standards have in effect been permitted to lapse. Renewables incentives are too weak to overcome the negative effects of electric utility restructuring, and voluntary industry programs have been largely weak and ineffectual. The United States does stand out for its strong appliance efficiency standards, however, and a number of state and local governments are experimenting with promising policies in support of renewable energy and public transit. But overall, U.S. policy is weaker today than it was a decade ago—before the need to limit greenhouse gases was officially acknowledged.[68]

The weakest climate policies in this group of industrial nations are found in Australia and Canada, countries built on extractive industries with low fossil fuel prices. Neither has done much to reduce its substantial producer subsidies for fossil fuels, and both continue to have low fuel taxes. Despite having huge renewable resources, both countries have allowed their monopoly power companies to almost completely block renewables from the power grids. Some states and provinces have taken creative steps to promote energy-efficient cars and renewable energy, but these have so far worked at cross-purposes with signals from the capitals. Without major policy changes, carbon emissions from Australia and Canada are likely to continue upward for the indefinite future.[69]

Among the policies adopted so far, the removal of energy subsidies has had the greatest short-term impact.

Given some politicians' criticism of the climate treaty for excluding developing countries from commitments to reduce emissions, it is interesting to assess the actual record of such large nations as China, India, and Brazil. By comparison with the industrial countries examined here, these nations are not doing so badly. Each has implemented meaningful policy reforms in the past decade, with noticeable results in increased renewables use in Brazil and India, and improved efficiency in China.[70]

This short history of climate policy, with its small but instructive success stories, makes it clear that it is far too early to despair. So, too, does experience with past international environmental agreements, which shows that governments are often slow to implement new treaties, but also that they can then move into high gear and make rapid progress. The Vienna Convention to protect the ozone layer was originally passed in 1985, but it took two years to achieve a legally binding protocol, and several more years before steep declines in production of damaging chlorofluorocarbons occurred as the protocol was strengthened by subsequent amendments. The climate convention is on a slower track, but that is hardly surprising, given the central role that fossil fuels play in today's economies and the power of the industries that supply and use them.[71]

The next test in the long struggle toward a more stable climate is how national governments will respond to the challenge laid down in Kyoto. They have much to learn from the successes and failures of the past five years, but the most difficult hurdle remains overcoming short-term economic and political barriers in order to cope with a long-term problem. Action at all levels—state and local governments, private businesses, and concerned citizens—will be needed to make the protocol meaningful. Indeed, some of the most promising climate policy initiatives have been taken not by national governments but by state and local decisionmakers.[72]

These hopeful opportunities are symbolized by Kyoto itself, which was spared from nuclear annihilation in 1945 when U.S. military planners were alerted to its unique cultural heritage as the capital of the ancient Japanese empire. In today's warming world, as former empires come to terms with perhaps the most serious environmental side effect of the Industrial Revolution, Kyoto has the potential to earn another, more peaceful place in history as the city that helped spare the world from devastating climate change.

8

Curbing the Proliferation of Small Arms

Michael Renner

A March 1997 news photograph showed a group of five casually dressed young men gathered for a game of pool in the southern Albanian town of Memaliaj. Engrossed in choosing the best angle for shooting the next ball, they seemed oblivious to a detail that would have captured any outsider's attention: one of them was using an assault rifle as a pool cue. Assault rifles and other so-called small arms and light weapons are now easily available not only in Albania, in the grip of widespread anarchy. As arms that can be carried by an individual have spread, a habitual recourse to violence has been encouraged that threatens the cohesion and well-being of many societies.[1]

Less than a decade ago, newspaper articles and television programs dealing with conflict and security were dominated by images of gleaming nuclear-tipped missiles that the two superpowers deployed in their deadly confrontation, or by the daz-

zling high-tech jet fighters and "smart" bombs used by the United States against Iraq. Although the firepower, reach, and precision-targeting of such major weapons systems dwarf the capacities of assault rifles and other small arms, hundreds of millions of low-tech, inexpensive, sturdy, easy-to-use weapons are the tools for most of the killing in contemporary conflicts—causing as much as 90 percent of the deaths. These weapons may be small in caliber, but they are big—indeed devastating—in their impact.[2]

Fed by essentially unrestrained production of millions or perhaps tens of millions of small arms annually, arsenals continue to swell. Although governments may profess concern about private arms smugglers and "rogue" suppliers such as insurgent groups or drug traffickers, they themselves are by far the most important source of those weapons.

Because small arms are long-lived, they may stay in circulation for decades. Indeed, trade in secondhand arms flourishes. Now that the cold war is over,

An expanded version of this chapter appeared as Worldwatch Paper 137, *Small Arms, Big Impact: The Next Challenge of Disarmament.*

armies in North America, Europe, and the former Soviet Union are shrinking; much of their excess equipment is given away or sold cheaply to other countries. In addition, weapons left over at the end of civil wars often enter the black market and frequently resurface in new hotspots as large parts of government armies and insurgent forces are demobilized.

Possession of a variety of small arms is widespread in many countries, filtering far beyond armies and police forces to opposition groups, criminal organizations, private security forces, vigilante squads, and individual citizens. Although the armaments per se do not necessarily trigger violence, their easy availability has made recourse to violence more likely. And where violence breaks out, a surfeit of arms helps intensify and prolong the fighting.

Perhaps $3 billion worth of small arms and light weapons are shipped across borders each year.

The spread of small arms within society poses a particular challenge for countries emerging from long years of debilitating warfare, including several in Central America and southern Africa. They are striving to escape a culture of violence and consolidate a hard-won peace that still rests on shaky foundations.

Small arms have long been considered insignificant, and arms control efforts have focused instead on major weapons. Now, thanks largely to the efforts of grassroots groups, the full costs of small arms proliferation are beginning to attract the attention of policymakers: the loss of life and property, the climate of fear and pervasive instability, the disruption of economic development, and the threat to democratic governance that result from

the violence made possible by wide availability of small arms.

WARS AND PRIVATIZED VIOLENCE

Small arms are the weapons of choice in today's typical conflict—fighting that rages within rather than between countries. The wide availability of these easily carried and concealed weapons contributes to both the intensity and the duration of conflicts. Indeed, the protagonists in these conflicts are usually able to procure and stockpile enough weapons to sustain the fighting even when the international community adopts an embargo on arms deliveries, as it did in Bosnia and Rwanda, for example.[3]

"Small arms and light weapons" are not easily defined, but the term usually includes weapons that can be carried by an individual. This encompasses such items as pistols and revolvers, rifles and assault rifles, hand grenades, machine guns, light mortars, and light antitank weapons such as grenade launchers and recoilless rifles. Shoulder-fired surface-to-air missiles are also included because they are portable, even though they are far more high-tech and complex than most other small arms. (Another category often included is anti-personnel landmines, but space constraints preclude discussion here of these long-lasting threats to civilians and to development.) The term therefore covers a broad spectrum—from weapons with exclusive military application, to firearms used by police forces, to handguns or hunting rifles in the legitimate possession of civilians.[4]

For a variety of reasons, small weapons are both much harder to track and control and more worrying than the major weapons systems that so far have received the bulk of policymakers' attention. First, small weapons do not carry nearly as large a price tag as big-ticket military items, so their importance is all too easily underestimated. Worldwide, a rough estimate suggests that perhaps $3 billion worth of small arms and light weapons are being shipped across international borders each year; that would be equivalent to about one eighth of all international arms sales.[5]

Second, the relatively low cost of most small arms also means that many substate groups can afford them. For just $50 million—roughly the cost of a single modern jet fighter—a small army can be equipped with some 200,000 assault rifles at today's "fire sale" prices.[6]

Third, unlike major weapons, maintaining and operating small arms does not require any complex organizational, logistical, or training capacities. Hence these are the preferred equipment of the armed forces of many poor countries and of guerrilla and other armed substate groups.[7]

Fourth, many small weapons are so lightweight and can be assembled and reassembled with such ease that children as young as 10 years old can use them. Although the phenomenon of child soldiers is not a new one, the easy availability of lightweight small arms in the contemporary era has boosted the ability of children to participate in armed conflicts.[8]

Fifth, their light weight and small size make small arms easy to conceal and smuggle. Unlike major military equipment, small arms are readily available on a burgeoning black market, and therefore easy for guerrilla groups, criminal organizations, and other interested buyers to obtain.[9]

Finally, major weapons become obsolete relatively quickly and are in constant need of new spare parts and maintenance. By contrast, small arms are sturdy enough to have a long "life," allowing them to be circulated from one conflict to another. For example, an F-5 jet fighter requires an inventory of about 60,000 spare parts, but an AK-47 assault rifle has

only 16 moving parts. Small arms of World War II vintage and—amazingly—some even of World War I vintage are still used in today's conflicts.[10]

As the primary tools of warfare, small weapons have been put to increasing use: the number of conflicts active in any given year worldwide rose steadily from 1946 to 1992. (See Figure 8–1.) According to the Wars, Armaments, and Development Research Unit at the University of Hamburg, the number peaked at 51 in 1992. Only with the resolution of several long-standing wars in Central America and southern Africa was the trend reversed: the number of armed conflicts declined to 37 in 1995.[11]

According to a detailed analysis by researchers at the University of Uppsala in Sweden, only 6 out of 101 conflicts in the period 1989–96 were international, involving the forces or territory of more than one state. Overall, combatants typically are not only uniformed soldiers but also guerrilla groups of various stripes, paramilitary forces, drug and organized crime bands, warlords, and vigilante hit squads. An estimated quarter of a million children are soldiers, and children under 18 years of age were among the combat-

Figure 8–1. Number of Armed Conflicts, 1946–95

ants in 33 current or recent conflicts. Child combatants younger than 15 fought in 26 of these conflicts.[12]

While the number of armed conflicts is still high, few of them are high-intensity wars. Rather, most are what the Uppsala researchers call "minor" and "intermediate" armed conflicts—those that kill fewer than 1,000 persons in a single year and that involve the use of mostly small armaments. But such violence disrupts societies in many ways. Both low- and high-intensity warfare continue to kill large numbers of people. During the first half of the 1990s, at least 3.2 million people died of war-related causes, bringing the cumulative toll since 1945 to at least 25 million. (See Figure 8–2.) This is probably a conservative figure. Civilians have accounted for a large share of the victims: perhaps 70 percent of all war victims since World War II, but more than 90 percent in the 1990s.[13]

Many other countries experience near-war—what Dan Smith, director of the International Peace Research Institute in Oslo, describes as "widespread and even endemic" political violence "without quite meriting the name war." And societies that have emerged from long years of war often still experience considerable levels of violence. Though formally at peace now, South Africa and El Salvador, for instance, have in recent years endured slayings that rival in number the people killed in earlier fighting.[14]

Such near-war violence may stem from a broad variety of causal factors, but it is sustained primarily by one: the easy availability of large amounts of weapons, especially small weapons. Michael Klare, director of the Five College Program in Peace and World Security Studies in Amherst, Massachusetts, argues that "the abundance of arms *at every level of society* means that any increase in inter-communal tensions and hostility will entail an increased likelihood of armed violence and bloodshed."[15]

The dispersal of arms to private armies

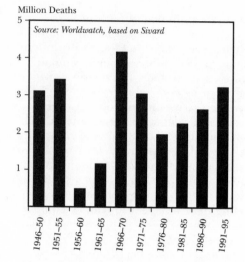

Million Deaths

Source: Worldwatch, based on Sivard

Figure 8–2. Deaths in Armed Conflicts, by Five-Year Period, 1946–95

and militias, insurgent groups, criminal organizations, and other nonstate actors feeds a cycle of violence in many societies that in turn causes even greater demand for guns. A variety of motivations spawn different kinds of violence: political violence, which pits governments against insurgent forces fighting to overthrow the government or to achieve a separate state; communal violence involving different ethnic, religious, or other identity-based groups; and criminal violence involving drug traffickers, organized crime groups, or petty individual crime. And ordinary citizens in many countries are increasingly arming themselves in self-defense.

Southern Africa and several Central American countries, among others, have experienced a seamless transition from politically motivated to criminal violence in the early 1990s. They have only begun to recover from years of fighting and must contend with conditions highly conducive to crime: warfare has destroyed a large portion of the infrastructure and crippled the economy; national treasuries are depleted.[16]

Recently demobilized soldiers and former guerrilla fighters in particular find themselves often poorly equipped to make a living as civilians; not surprisingly, many tend to fall back on the tools and skills they acquired during years of conflict, leading to rising banditry in several countries. And weak or corrupt judiciary systems and ineffective police forces have given rise to vigilante squads intent on what they call "social cleansing"—killing individuals suspected of crimes or otherwise perceived as unwanted. The pervasive reliance on violence threatens the consolidation of still-weak democracies in several countries and compromises the reconstruction and social and economic development that war-torn societies need to get back on their feet.

These are among the factors that feed what Michael Klare calls the privatization of security and violence—"a growing tendency of individuals, groups, and organizations to rely on private security forces rather than on the state's police and paramilitary formations."[17]

Indeed, private security formations are on the rise just as national armies are shrinking in size. After climbing to a peak of 28.7 million persons in the world's regular, uniformed armed forces in 1988, the number declined to 23 million in 1995, or by about 20 percent. A range of factors contributed to this decline, including the end of the cold war and the termination of several long-lasting conflicts in the Third World, as well as the budgetary difficulties of many governments. Without cold war–motivated sponsorship propping them up, many Third World armies and some insurgent forces could no longer be maintained at their previous size. Tales of soldiers going unpaid or underpaid for months on end abound. Large numbers of them turn to commercial ventures to supplement their incomes or resort to looting and extortion, to petty crime, or even to mercenary activity.[18]

In several countries, private security forces rival or outstrip the size of the public police, and in some—among them Australia, South Africa, and the United Kingdom—they outnumber even the

Table 8–1. Private Security and Public Police, Late 1980s, and Military Armed Forces, 1995, Selected Countries

Country	Private Security Forces[1]	Public Police Forces[2]	Military Armed Forces[3]	All Forces, Relative to Citizenry
	(thousand)	(thousand)	(thousand)	(per thousand population)
United States	1,500	600	1,620	14
United Kingdom	250[4]	190	233	11
South Africa	180	146	100	10
Colombia	100	n.a.	146	7
France	96	110	504	12
Australia	90[4]	47	58	11
Israel	40	15	185	41
Spain	25[5]	119	210	9
Netherlands	13[6]	38	67	8
Belgium	7	15	47	7
New Zealand	5	n.a.	10	4
Finland	3	12	32	9

[1]Data for late 1980s. [2]Data for late 1980s and 1990. [3]Data for 1995. [4]High end of range of estimates. [5]Includes personnel of registered companies only. [6]Could reach 30,000, according to government estimates.
SOURCE: See endnote 19.

national army. (See Table 8–1.) In the United States, there are now almost three times as many private security guards as there are police officers. Although the number of private security personnel that are armed (legally or illegally) is uncertain, one report contends that gun-toting private guards in the United States today "have more firepower than the combined police forces of the nation's 30 largest urban centers."[19]

LIKE BUYING FISH IN THE MARKET

Small arms are so ubiquitous that many regions of the world find themselves awash in them. A recent remark by a local political leader in the Philippines captures the essence of the situation in many nations: firearms are so easily available, he said, that acquiring them is "as easy as buying fish in the market."[20]

Reliable data are very hard to obtain. Nevertheless, the numbers that are available are staggering. The most notorious assault rifle is the AK-47, also known by its inventor's name, Kalashnikov. Manufactured in the former Soviet Union and in nine other countries, more than 70 million Kalashnikovs have been produced in some 100 different versions since 1947; most of these are still in service in the armies of 78 countries and in countless guerrilla groups the world over. In Mozambique, one of the countries with the largest number of these rifles, an AK-47 is emblazoned on the national flag.[21]

Still, this symbol of massive if low-tech violence shares its claim to fame with some other assault rifles that are in use by a large number of national armed forces. Among them are the Israeli Uzi machine pistol (10 million produced), the U.S.-made M-16 (8 million), the German G-3 (7 million), and the Belgian-designed FN-FAL (5–7 million). In addition to licensed production of these and other small weapons, several countries are apparently flooding the world market with counterfeit versions. All in all, more than 100 million military-style assault rifles are thought to exist worldwide.[22]

Beyond the small arms found in military arsenals—which some estimates put at 500 million in all—there are, of course, many "civilian" firearms. These are generally weapons with less firepower or less-rapid firing capacity. But the military-civilian dividing line is not always clear-cut. First, some civilian firearms can be converted to automatic or semiautomatic weapons, hence more closely resembling military-style arms. Second, an unknown number of assault rifles and other military-style weapons are in the possession of civilians, albeit often illegally.[23]

No one really knows how many weapons are in circulation among the general population of most countries. The first international effort to gain some insight into the problem was a recent study by the U.N. Commission on Crime Prevention and Criminal Justice. It surveyed member states to collect and compare data on the manufacturing, trade, and private possession of firearms, on national regulations of firearms, and on homicides, suicides, and accidents involving firearms. Forty-six nations responded, covering 68 percent of the world's population, although some provided only part of the information requested.[24]

The survey shows just how far the world community is from having even a rough idea of the order of magnitude of private firearm ownership. The combined official figure of 34 million firearms in private possession for 35 countries that provided data probably represents little more than the tip of the arsenal iceberg. Russia, for instance, reported a figure of 3.6 million, but is generally thought to have a huge number of illegal guns in circulation, with the black market being fed by profuse leaks from the military's arsenal. And in Canada, compared with the figure of 7 million legitimate owners submitted to the United Nations, some think there may be as many as 21–25 million firearms in private possession.[25]

The United States is without doubt one of the countries with the largest private firearms arsenals, and very likely the leading one worldwide. There are a quarter of a million federally licensed firearms dealers in the country—20 times the number of McDonald's restaurants. Estimates of private firearms there run from 192 million in a recent Justice Department study, to 230 million according to the U.S. National Rifle Association, to a figure of 250 million put forward by the Federal Bureau of Investigation. At the high end of this range, this would mean one firearm for every American, from infant to senior citizen.[26]

Aside from illegal transactions, legitimate domestic production adds some 3–6 million firearms annually to the stockpile, and imports, another 1 million. (See Figure 8–3.) About half a million firearms are reported stolen in noncommercial thefts alone each year. The United States is now the only industrial country that allows its citizens to own military-style assault rifles—weapons that account for an estimated 1 percent of all U.S. firearms but, according to the Urban Institute, for at least 8 percent of gun-related crimes.[27]

High levels of gun ownership and a laissez-faire attitude toward guns translate into broad-scale violence. More people are killed with guns in the United States in a typical week than in all of Western Europe in a year. And there are more U.S. firearm homicides in a single day than in a year in Japan. A recent study by the U.S. Centers for Disease Control and Prevention found that American adolescents are 12 times more likely than youngsters in all other industrial countries to be killed by gunfire.[28]

Although high levels of gun ownership

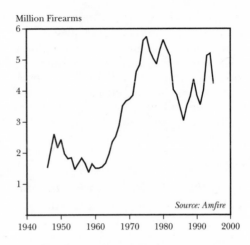

Million Firearms

Figure 8–3. U.S. Firearms Production, 1946–95

do not automatically translate into rampant violence, the easy availability of guns does make a difference, particularly in societies where significant economic inequality holds forth, where poverty and unemployment lead people to commit crimes as a survival tactic, where the social fabric is under severe strain, where strong ethnic or class animosities persist, or where the legitimacy of political institutions is being questioned.

According to the U.N. survey, Brazil has by far the highest number of firearm homicides—41,000 per year—and is a close second to South Africa in the rate of killings per total population. The murder rate in São Paulo has reached one per hour, and 90 percent of all killings are committed with firearms. Of an estimated 18.5 million firearms in Brazil, only one third are registered.[29]

The difficult economic and political transition in Russia has spawned rising crime there and Mafia-like organizations that stage spectacular gangland-style killings to eliminate business rivals. There were almost 1,000 contract murders there in 1996 alone. The resulting sense of insecurity has in turn encouraged ordinary citizens to arm themselves; 14 percent of

Russians carry weapons daily for self-defense. Ownership of mostly illegal arms in Russia is exploding. The burgeoning black market is apparently being fed by a constant stream of assault rifles, submachine guns, pistols, grenades, and explosives from military depots even though the private ownership of military-style weapons is illegal.[30]

In southern Africa, decades of warfare and violent political struggle have given rise to a pervasive gun culture.

As indicated earlier, the danger that easy weapons availability may translate into impulsive recourse to violence is probably greatest in societies struggling to rebuild themselves after long years of warfare and to shake off the legacy of a culture of violence. Among the regions of particular concern are Central America and southern Africa. Emerging from a devastating civil war during the 1980s, El Salvador has formally been at peace since 1992. Yet the number of violent deaths there since then—some 20,000—comes close, on an annual basis, to rivaling the number of people killed during the war.[31]

The postwar violence stems from several factors. With unemployment running at an estimated 50 percent and roughly two thirds of the Salvadoran population living in extreme poverty, crime is rampant. "Military weapons and poverty are proving to be a deadly combination," comments Edward Laurance of the Monterey Institute of International Studies in California.[32]

Most of the 40,000 demobilized soldiers and guerrillas have been unable to establish themselves in civilian society. Some have taken up arms left over from the war. Heavily armed Salvadoran criminal groups formed by former soldiers and by disoriented youth are responsible for murders, kidnappings, and robberies throughout the country. Gang members are buying and smuggling leftover weapons into neighboring countries and the United States, and there is evidence that some of them have formed alliances with Mexican and Colombian drug traffickers.[33]

Southern Africa confronts similar challenges. Some 9 million small arms are thought to be in the arsenals of the armies of Angola, Mozambique, South Africa, and Zimbabwe, but substantial additional numbers of weapons are in private hands, in hidden caches, or flowing in secret arms-trading channels that cross borders with impunity. Although no one knows for sure just how many firearms are in circulation, the region is clearly flooded with weapons. Decades of warfare and violent political struggle have given rise to a pervasive gun culture. "Light weapons have become a form of currency throughout the region," writes Jacklyn Cock of the University of Witwatersrand.[34]

In South Africa, the political violence of the years of transition from apartheid (1990–93), during which some 10,000 people were killed, has declined dramatically. But according to Cock, there has been a parallel, equally dramatic increase in criminal violence fueled by high unemployment and economic hardship. Military-style weapons such as the AK-47 and the G-3 are increasingly used in robberies and in "taxi wars"—clashes between competing taxi owners who employ professional assassins to kill their rivals' passengers and drivers.[35]

A top official of the Mozambique Defense Force, Lazaro Mathe, has said that Mozambique, with a population of 15 million, has more weapons than people. Others have estimated the number at 10 million. There are at least 1.5 million AK-47s, and perhaps as many as 6 million. During that country's civil war, both the government and the rebels were supplied with large amounts of small weapons by South Africa and the Soviet Union. The protagonists, in turn, "passed out weapons almost indiscriminately, arming not just soldiers but everyone they could find," as Suzanne Daley, a *New York Times* reporter, put it. Today poorly paid soldiers, police officers, and others are selling weapons—the one commodity that seems boundless—to what appears to be an insatiable market in South Africa.[36]

The Mozambican experience seems bound to repeat itself in Angola, another country that apartheid-era South Africa sought to destabilize, which was at war from 1975 to 1994. Perhaps as many as 90 percent of Angolans possess firearms. The government's campaign to recover arms from civilians—as required under the country's peace accord—has so far made little more than a dent.[37]

The picture that emerges globally is one of individual countries and entire regions inundated with both military-style small weapons and civilian firearms. Current controls—to the extent they exist at all—appear hopelessly inadequate for dealing with the unencumbered flow of arms. Many countries are just beginning to recognize the potential for large-scale violence and instability that this massive availability of firepower implies.

FEEDING THE HABIT

That small weapons are so ubiquitous should come as no surprise: a multitude of seemingly inexhaustible sources feed the market. Some of the weapons produced each year never cross any borders. But international transfers also play a crucial role. These run the gamut from direct government-to-government sales and government-approved exports by private arms manufacturers to covert deliveries by government agencies, a variety of black market deals involving private arms merchants, the capture of arms by insurgent forces, theft from government arsenals, and the often illicit passing of weapons from one area of conflict to another. But government sales are by far the most important source of arms proliferation.

Whereas the ability to manufacture major weapons is limited to a fairly small number of advanced industrial countries, the capacity to produce small arms is far more widespread. Russia, China, and the United States, along with several European nations, are major producers of small arms, but the United Nations Institute for Disarmament Research (UNIDIR) in Geneva has identified close to 300 companies in 52 countries that were manufacturing small arms and related equipment in 1994. This represents a 25-percent increase in the number of countries since the mid-1980s. In addition, insurgent and opposition groups in several nations are able to produce simple small-caliber weapons. Among them are the Irish Republican Army, the Palestine Liberation Organization, and groups in Mexico, India, Pakistan, and some African countries. Although no statistics are available, it would appear that worldwide production of small arms easily runs to several million, if not tens of million, units each year.[38]

Most international transfers take place either as direct government-to-government transfers (vast quantities were provided by the two superpowers during the cold war, either at heavily discounted prices or for free) or as commercial sales involving private companies, which is the most important source of transfers since the cold war. Unfortunately, available statistics for such transactions do not distinguish between major and small arms. Michael Klare of the Five College Program in Peace and World Security Studies estimates that of $25.9 billion worth of arms that U.S. firms were authorized to sell abroad in 1989–93, small arms accounted for perhaps one third—$8.6 billion. He further maintains that anywhere from 10 to 20 percent of U.S. grant transfers of arms and ammunition (worth $55.2 billion in 1950–94) involved small arms.[39]

Beyond these sales authorized and acknowledged by governments, there are a multitude of secret and illegal deals by governments and others about which, due to their very nature, next to nothing is known. According to Klare, black market sales have greatly expanded in recent years. Illicit transactions appear to be much more significant with regard to light weapons than major ones.[40]

Among such transfers are covert arms deliveries by governments to insurgent and separatist groups in other countries. During the cold war, this was a frequent tool of the United States and the Soviet Union, and it helped spread a massive amount of weaponry that continues to fuel violent conflict and bedevil peacemaking efforts in many locales around the globe. Although less important to Washington and Moscow now, covert supplies are a practice that other governments have resorted to as well. For instance, Pakistan is delivering arms to Kashmiri insurgents, and Iran is supplying Kurdish rebels in Turkey.[41]

In addition to clandestine supplies by government agencies, the international black market is being fed by legions of private arms merchants and criminal organizations. Often, black market deals involve the barter of weapons for natural resources, animal products, drugs, and other commodities, or at least an arrangement to buy arms through the sale of such commodities. (See Table 8–2.) R.T. Naylor, an economics professor at McGill University in Montreal, observes that "much of the world's contraband traffic in diamonds, precious gems, jade, ivory, teakwood, and 'recreational drugs,' along with part of the traffic in looted antiquities, is either controlled at the source by an insurgent group or at least taxed by them."[42]

Other important sources of weapons

flows are the capture of arms by insurgent forces, the looting of military depots, and leaks from government arsenals (that is, the theft and sell-off of weapons by soldiers). The seizure of weapons from government armies has long been essential to Latin American guerrilla forces' acquisition of arms. But in recent years, it has also proved important for the embryonic armies of Bosnia, Croatia, Georgia, and Slovenia, for example, and for armed opposition groups in places as different as Algeria, Cambodia, and Sierra Leone. In South Africa, large quantities of small arms stolen from military bases and armories by white right-wing organizations or supplied to them by sympathetic police forces, along with leaks of weapons from guerrilla armies' depots, fueled the severe political violence that gripped the country in the first half of the 1990s.[43]

One of the most spectacular recent examples is found in Albania. Triggered by the collapse of fraudulent investment schemes that cost many citizens their entire savings, large numbers of Albanians revolted against the economic and political conditions in their country; within a few weeks, most police and military depots were ransacked. The number of weapons seized has variously been estimated at 500,000 to 800,000, and the Defense Ministry reported that a staggering 10.5 billion bullets had been stolen. Within a few weeks, virtually everyone in this country of 3.5 million was armed, including women and children. Though the situation in Albania is calmer now, it remains unstable. Armed gangs still terrorize large areas of the country. And some of the seized weapons may have been sold to Albanians in neighboring Macedonia and in the Kosovo area of Serbia—territories in which tensions run high—and to Greece.[44]

A different leakage problem is found in Russia. Researchers Ksenia Gonchar and Peter Lock cite a long list of factors that facilitate the rise of illicit arms pro-

Table 8–2. Selected Examples of Commodities-for-Arms Transactions, 1980s and 1990s

Country or Region	Observation
Liberia/ Sierra Leone	Charles Taylor and other Liberian warlords trading timber, iron ore, and agricultural products for small arms and military training since 1990; Taylor earned up to $100 million a year.[1] In early 1990s, government and rebel soldiers in neighboring Sierra Leone plundered diamond mines. Rebels exchanged diamonds for rocket launchers and Kalashnikovs from Taylor's forces.
Rwanda	In 1992, Egypt accepted future Rwandan tea harvests as collateral for $6 million worth of artillery, mortars, landmines, and assault rifles sent to the government; Egypt took delivery of $1 million in Rwandan tea before fighting in Rwanda's civil war damaged the tea bushes.
Southern Africa	Many ivory and rhino horn poachers in Zimbabwe and Mozambique are ex-soldiers involved in both buying and selling small arms on the black market. UNITA rebel forces in Angola earn $450–500 million a year in diamond sales. Also, UNITA paid for South African military support with ivory, slaughtering tens of thousands of elephants. RENAMO rebels in Mozambique bartered game (meat, hides, ivory) for guns.
Cambodia	Khmer Rouge financing their military effort by trading timber and gems to "renegades" in the Thai military who control the Cambodian-Thai border, earning $100–250 million a year. Other Cambodian factions also finance their armies with timber sales.
China	Pingyuan in Yunnan province is a major drug and arms trafficking center. Most of the weapons used in criminal activities in 24 of China's 31 provinces come from Myanmar and Viet Nam via Pingyuan.
Mexico/ Central America	Black market arms sales are linked to the illicit drug trade. Traffickers of guns and drugs often combine their operations and use the same routes and transportation systems.

[1]For comparative purposes, $100 million might purchase up to 400,000 assault rifles at typical discounted prices.
SOURCE: See endnote 42.

duction and trade. Among them are ineffective governmental oversight of the arms industry and the armed forces, weak law enforcement, porous borders, and general social disorder. In addition, the desperate state of affairs in the armed forces virtually invites soldiers to sell off portions of the immense arsenal accumulated during Soviet times. During the Chechen war, for instance, poorly equipped and starving Russian soldiers were trading their Kalashnikovs for food. "The Chechens bought all their supplies and weapons from us; otherwise," one conscript explained, "we wouldn't have

had money to eat."[45]

Unstable countries are not the only places where thefts from military arsenals occur. In China, where the central government retains far more authority than its Russian counterpart, criminal gangs apparently have little trouble gaining access to weaponry, due to inadequate controls in the arms industry, the army, and the police force. Even in the United States, a General Accounting Office report found in 1993 that small arms parts (including parts for the M-16 military rifle) are systematically stolen from the Pentagon's repair shops and warehouses, and then sold to gun dealers.[46]

One source of growing importance for both legal and illegal arms sales is surplus stocks. Casting off excess weapons is not a new phenomenon: since the 1950s, the U.S. government has given away or sold cheaply almost 3 million military-style firearms. And this practice is of particular significance now that the end of the cold war has left many members of the North Atlantic Treaty Organization and the former Warsaw Pact with far more military hardware than they need. Narrow cost-benefit considerations have led several governments to sell off surplus equipment, often at bargain rates, instead of dismantling or destroying it. Cheap secondhand arms are particularly attractive to buyers who cannot afford state-of-the-art weaponry.[47]

It is in the world's best interest to help Russia dismantle excess arms.

Researchers at the Bonn International Center for Conversion reckon that the trade in surplus arms reached new records during the 1990s. Much of it involves major weapons such as tanks and ships. Although there are no reliable data on surplus small arms, anecdotal evidence suggests that the numbers are substantial. For instance, Turkey received 304,000 formerly East German Kalashnikovs and 83 million rounds of ammunition from Germany.[48]

Other surplus arms get transferred—illicitly—from one hotspot of the world to another. Often when a conflict in one country comes to an end, the weapons—particularly the small ones—are sold or donated by former protagonists to belligerents in other countries. Indeed, Natalie Goldring of the nongovernmental organization (NGO) British American

Security Information Council points out that light weapons can last for decades, so a single weapon may be transferred many times.[49]

The U.S. supply of arms to the Afghan Mujahideen during the 1980s provides one of the most striking examples of weapons flows from one recipient to another. In response to the 1979 Soviet invasion, millions of tons of military materiel—precise amounts are unknown due to secrecy and poor recordkeeping—were pumped into the region through Pakistan by the U.S. Central Intelligence Agency. Estimates of the value of the weapons (which included arms originally made in China, Egypt, India, Turkey, the Soviet Union, and the United Kingdom) run to $6–9 billion.[50]

U.S.-supplied weapons sustained the resistance to the Soviet occupation, and later fueled a ferocious, ongoing civil war among competing Afghan factions after the Soviet withdrawal in 1989. But the arms "pipeline" had massive leaks from the very beginning and fed violence and instability in large portions of South and Central Asia. Some Afghan rebel leaders and officers of Pakistani Inter-Services Intelligence diverted large amounts of military equipment for resale, with the proceeds subsequently invested primarily in the drug trade. The Mujahideen fighters may have received as little as 30–40 percent of total deliveries intended for them.[51]

Weapons from the Afghan pipeline turned Pakistan's North West Frontier Province into a massive arms bazaar in which "virtually any type of small arm or light weapon [is] available for purchase," according to Chris Smith, Senior Research Fellow at the Centre for Defence Studies at King's College in London. "Ownership of an AK-47 is now *de rigeur*," he reports, and "land disputes now involve the use of mortars and rocket-propelled grenades." Weapons from Afghanistan have also aggravated violence in Pakistan's Sindh province and particularly its capital, Karachi. And they have been smuggled into civil war–plagued Tajikistan, into India's Punjab region, into northern India to Muslims who feel increasingly threatened by Hindu extremists, and into Kashmir, where they raised the severity of the violence between Indian forces and pro-independence militants. Furthermore, there are reports of some of these weapons turning up in Algeria, Myanmar, and Sri Lanka.[52]

The story of the leaky Afghanistan arms pipeline is far from an aberration. Important regional secondhand arms markets have emerged in Bangkok, Beirut, Peshawar, and Prague. In these and other places, embargoed states, guerrilla and separatist forces, private militias, and criminal organizations are stocking their arsenals.[53]

TAKING WEAPONS OUT OF CIRCULATION

The most immediate challenge in coping with small arms proliferation is to reduce the number of weapons already in circulation. We have seen only the beginnings of a large-scale sell-off of surplus weapons among industrial countries. If governments want to prevent the recirculation of even more massive amounts of used weaponry—and the resulting increase in violence likely to ensue—they will need to change their priorities, dismantling surplus stocks instead of selling them off or risk having them stolen and smuggled.

In principle, this should not be a problem for western countries, which are offering these arms at substantial discounts and can afford to forgo the revenue earned. Russia and other former Soviet republics, in contrast, have inadequate financial resources to destroy surplus arms, and their soldiers have every incentive to sell off weapons. It is in the

West's and the world's best interest to help Russia dismantle excess arms. It would also be sensible to incorporate into any future disarmament agreements an explicit stipulation that surplus arms be dismantled rather than just withdrawn from active deployment.

An equally important task is to deal with the arms that have become surplus with the end of civil wars in Central America, southern Africa, and other regions. Because the transition to peace has in many cases been accomplished with the assistance of peacekeeping operations, the United Nations has since 1989 become increasingly involved in the post-conflict disarmament of former combatants. UNIDIR has conducted a Disarmament and Conflict Resolution project to evaluate the experience of 11 U.N. peacekeeping operations; the findings were published in nine separate volumes in 1995–97.[54]

UNIDIR found several recurring problems handicapping operations. Typically, at the end of a conflict there is no firm or reliable inventory of the total number of weapons held by combatants, so it is difficult to assess how much disarmament is actually taking place. A substantial portion of the weapons handed in by ex-combatants tends to be of inferior quality—by implication, then, the best armaments are retained or hidden. Another difficulty arises from the fact that in countries with civil wars, government and insurgent forces alike often pass out large amounts of small arms to civilians. Yet peacekeeping operations either have no mandate to disarm civilians, or they do not have the resources and political backup to do so.

In all the U.N. operations, only some of the arms in circulation were collected. In some cases, the collected weapons were destroyed, but in others, many were actually passed on to the new army (integrating government and rebel soldiers) that emerged after a country's peace accord. The volume of arms is often several times larger than needed to outfit these smaller-sized forces. Weak controls over these arms and the fact that many soldiers subsist on low salaries are a virtual invitation to steal and sell arms.

There are thus many lessons to be learned from the peacekeeping experience. One is that disarmament needs to be given higher priority among the array of tasks these missions are expected to carry out. But improving the disarmament performance also requires a general strengthening of the capacity of peacekeeping missions. This means clearly formulated mandates, properly prepared personnel, sufficient funding, and consistent political support. If disarmament of ex-combatants is to be accomplished satisfactorily, it will sometimes take a lengthy commitment of people, equipment, and resources.[55]

Buy-back schemes will be more successful if they are embedded in broader community programs.

In addition, a greater effort needs to be made to ascertain the quality and quantity of weapons present. More than before, peace accords will need to encompass detailed inventories of the arsenals of the different parties. Once the disarmament and demobilization of ex-combatants gets under way, no faction should perceive an advantage or disadvantage. And once the weapons are collected, a greater effort must be made to place them in secure storage until they can be dismantled, or at least to render them unusable as quickly as possible.

Experience shows that the longer the wait before disarmament is implemented, the more likely it is that the parties to the conflict will begin to renege on their commitment to disarm. This points to the need to proceed swiftly with any disarmament operations. Otherwise, if the pro-

tagonists fail to live up to their promises, the vexing question arises of whether disarmament should be pursued in a coercive rather than a consensual manner. As experience demonstrates, both choices have their pitfalls.[56]

In addition to disarmament efforts in the context of peacekeeping operations, several countries have tried so-called gun buy-back programs. Even some nations that have not had recent wars on their soil have gone this route in an effort to reduce the number of weapons in circulation. Under these schemes, individuals are encouraged to turn arms in voluntarily in return for monetary or in-kind compensation. (See Table 8–3.)[57]

The experience has been quite varied, teaching important lessons that will help to improve and fine-tune future programs. Several observers agree that one possible pitfall of buy-backs is that monetary compensation may provide an incentive to steal guns in order to turn them in for cash. Edward Laurance of the Monterey Institute warns that "without stringent requirements on the quality...and quantity of guns, funds can soon be depleted by exploitative private gun owners and dealers who use the exchange of outdated and poor quality weapons to purchase newer and higher quality firearms."[58]

Pricing can be the crucial factor: at compensation levels too far below the black market value, few firearms will be turned in, but at levels that are too high, the black market will be stimulated. Particularly in developing countries, where many ex-fighters are expected to return to homes in rural areas, buy-back programs that provide food or agricultural implements are more appropriate than those that offer cash. Generally speaking, buy-back schemes will tend to be more successful if they are embedded in broader community programs.[59]

Firearm owners need to feel secure that turning in an illegally held weapon will not expose them to retribution. A "no-questions-asked" policy may work best. The governments of the Dominican Republic, Lesotho, and Sri Lanka, among others, have instituted "amnesty" programs in recent years, permitting unlicensed or otherwise illegal firearms to be turned in during a certain period without fear of prosecution. The United Kingdom has used the amnesty approach on four different occasions—in 1965, 1968, 1988, and 1996—yielding a total of more than 130,000 firearms.[60]

The tools to reduce the number of weapons in circulation are not in much question. What needs attention and improvement, however, is the ways they are wielded. The experience of the last few years has shown that programs to collect arms will need considerable refine-

Table 8–3. Selected Examples of Gun Buy-Back Programs, 1990s

Country	Observation
Colombia	Nationwide food-for-guns program established (those with legally owned weapons receive a check for the value of the weapon). Bogotá cash-for-weapons program helped cause a sharp drop in 1997 homicides.
El Salvador	Goods-for-guns program run by Patriotic Movement Against Crime collected close to 5,000 weapons during 1996 and early 1997. Yet the acquisition of new weapons—1,500 registered arms a month—far outpaces this effort. Another program, sponsored by New York–based Guns for Goods, exchanges vouchers to buy food and clothes for guns in three cities. In both cases, lack of funding limits effectiveness.
Nicaragua	Buy-back program incorporated cash and food incentives and an Italian-sponsored microenterprise program. During 1992–93, about 64,000 weapons were bought back and 78,000 confiscated, and all were destroyed; 250,000 pieces of ammunition were also collected. Total cost $6 million.
Haiti	A U.S. Army gun buy-back program paid cash for functional weapons and confiscated nonfunctional ones. By March 1995, more than 33,000 weapons taken in, at a cost of $1.9 million. The weapons in good condition were passed on to the Haitian police; the remainder were melted down.
Mozambique	A program sponsored by the Christian Council of Mozambique allows people to exchange weapons for cows, sewing machines, plows, and other goods. Program began in 1996 with a $1.2-million grant from Germany and Japan.
United Kingdom	A 1996 law requires that all handguns larger than .22 caliber must be turned in to police stations or taken out of the country, affecting some 200,000 legally held guns. New legislation being passed will ban private ownership of handguns. Cost of compensating owners estimated at $250–850 million.
Australia	The massacre of 35 people by a gunman in April 1996 prompted the government to enact a broadly supported ban on automatic and semiautomatic weapons. More than 600,000 of perhaps 2 million arms were handed in. The government paid $217 million in compensation.
United States	More than 80 local programs with widely differing incentives. A Seattle effort in 1992 took in 1,772 guns—less than 1 percent of the guns in Seattle homes; a St. Louis, Missouri, program collected more than 7,500 weapons in 1991. In both cases the impact on gun-related violence was minimal.

SOURCE: See endnote 57.

ment and more substantial financial and political support if they are to succeed.

REGISTERS, CODES, AND CONTROLS

There are no internationally agreed norms or standards regarding small arms; their production, trade, and possession still remain essentially unmonitored and unregulated. To tackle this challenge, a multitude of approaches can be pursued. These include creating greater transparency, restricting both legal and illegal international transfers, establishing restrictions on new production, and banning particular types of weapons.[61]

Better access to data is clearly the most immediate need if policymakers are not to proceed blindly. One way to move forward is to establish a register of small arms, on a global or regional basis. This could be modeled on the existing U.N. Register of Conventional Arms. Since 1993, the United Nations has published this annual register of imports and exports of seven types of major weapons systems, based on voluntary submissions of data by member states. Over the years, it has found increasing acceptance as a growing number of governments participate. Unlike the existing register, a small arms register (or set of regional registers) might also encompass information on national production and stockpiles and provide prenotification of pending transfers rather than after-the-fact information. The idea of a regional register has been discussed by the Organization of American States (OAS) and by the Association of South East Asian Nations.[62]

Greater transparency would allow improved restrictions on questionable arms transfers. One key recommendation in this regard is the adoption of a "code of conduct" by national governments.

Former Costa Rican President and Nobel Peace Prize recipient Oscar Arias has initiated a campaign for a global code. Under his proposal, official arms transfers would not be made to countries that fail to meet the following criteria: compliance with international human rights standards and humanitarian law, respect for democratic norms, adherence to international arms embargoes and military sanctions, and participation in the existing U.N. arms register. Nor could weapons be sold to countries that engage in armed aggression. With the support of several other Nobel Peace laureates, Dr. Arias published his code in May 1997, and he plans to present it to the U.N. General Assembly as the first step in a process that is aimed at concluding an international treaty embodying the code's principles.[63]

In the United States, a coalition of grassroots groups has waged a campaign for a similar code for several years. In June 1997, a watered-down version was passed in the House of Representatives. Instead of an airtight prohibition against arms sales to countries that fail to live up to the code's provisions, the President could seek a waiver and Congress would have eight months to block or condition the request. Unfortunately, opposition in the Senate may prevent even this moderate version of the code from becoming law.[64]

But support for a code is growing elsewhere. Some 15 former and current Latin American heads of state endorsed the idea in 1997, and it is under discussion in southern Africa. In Europe, a growing number of national governments, parliaments, individual parliamentarians, and grassroots groups have called for a code of conduct. Institutions such as the European Parliament, the European Council of Ministers, and the Organization on Security and Co-operation in Europe have endorsed sets of criteria to govern arms exports of member states. Yet their members still differ widely on how the criteria should be interpreted, and governments are still not legally bound by them. In the United Kingdom, the new Labour government has shown greater willingness than its predecessor to bar sales to governments with poor human rights records and to support a common European approach.[65]

In addition to restricting governmentally approved sales, a greater effort must also be made to clamp down on illegal transfers. Although it may appear futile to try to restrict clandestine flows of small arms, it may be sufficient to block the biggest transfers and interrupt the most important transfer routes. And such efforts might particularly focus on flows of ammunition: not only is the capacity to manufacture ammunition less widespread than that to produce the small weapons themselves (making transfers a potential choke point), but ammunition is less easy to transfer secretly because it is heavy and bulky.[66]

Restricting illicit transfers of weapons and ammunition alike would involve enhancing national customs controls and other measures to improve the monitoring of cross-border flows of goods. But arms traffickers will always be able to circumvent strict regulations in one country as long as others have weak laws. Hence, there is a need to harmonize export regulations and to step up international cooperation, for instance by establishing shared databases on known or suspected traffickers and illicit end users.[67]

Several regional efforts to counter gun-smuggling are under way. In fall 1996, Mexico proposed a regional convention against illicit firearms trafficking; the OAS is now preparing a draft of such an agreement. Central American governments, meanwhile, are expected to ratify an agreement to enhance exchange of information and inspections of exports. And a tripartite agreement was signed between South Africa, Swaziland, and Mozambique in June 1993 to deal with the problem of illegal arms flows into South Africa. In January 1995, South Africa and Mozambique agreed to facilitate cross-border police cooperation to track down illegal weaponry; three successful joint operations are likely to pave the way for similar missions between South Africa and other neighbors. Finally, in Europe, the Council of Ministers of the European Union launched an initiative in June 1997 to develop a common database on illicit arms trafficking, to strengthen collective efforts to prevent and combat such transfers, and to assist other countries in similar efforts.[68]

Restricting the flow of weaponry without addressing the issue of continued production, however, is like stopping the flow of water from a hose by holding the nozzle closed; before too long, the water pressure will cause leaks. The longer that large-scale production continues, the greater the future supply of weapons and ammunition whose whereabouts and use will be of concern. Yet reining in production is as difficult politically as its need is obvious.

Arms traffickers will always be able to circumvent strict regulations in one country as long as others have weak laws.

One obstacle is the "addiction to war industries," as R.T. Naylor of McGill University puts it. Although small weapons do not figure prominently in the corporate drive for profits and the governmental interest in boosting export revenues, this addiction will be an impediment as long as no effective programs provide economic alternatives to work forces and communities dependent on arms production.[69]

Skeptics will argue that there are simply too many small arms manufacturers to make a ban, or sharp reductions in production, possible. It is true that the number of factories, small workshops, or even individual gunsmiths fabricating crude homemade weapons is large and diverse enough to defy any attempt at totally controlling output. But the success of restricting production rests on reaching those factories that are capable of churning out large volumes of more advanced types of small arms and ammunition.

On the demand side, another problem is that a considerable portion of small arms production is destined for such legitimate users as national police and—because of weak domestic gun control laws—ordinary citizens. The belief that police forces have to have sufficient firepower to deter criminals (and therefore have to engage in a domestic "arms race" of sorts) or that the right to bear arms is a hallmark of personal freedom is deeply entrenched in many societies.

Initially, attempts to restrict small arms production may best be focused on the most "objectionable" types of weapons—those least likely to be found in the hands of the general population. Domestic gun control efforts in many countries have zeroed in on possession of assault rifles and other automatic and semiautomatic firearms. Australia, Canada, and the United Kingdom are among the countries that have recently tightened their laws. But the lack of effective regulation in other countries, and the ease with which weapons are smuggled across borders, can undermine these efforts. Laws addressing firearms possession may be condemned to ineffectiveness unless production and trade are confronted as well.[70]

The challenge of small arms knows no borders. Whether it be assault rifles, landmines, or other small weapons that are spreading, countermeasures can only hope to be effective if they are taken in a context of international—and preferably global—cooperation. The efforts of a single country or small group of nations are too easily circumvented by far-flung networks to produce and trade small arms.

Out of political and military-strategic considerations, governments tend to place weak constraints on arms. The actions of human rights groups and other NGOs, on the other hand, tend to be motivated by social, environmental, or humanitarian concerns. To the extent that policymaking in response to the proliferation of small arms is strongly influenced by NGOs, it is more likely that far-reaching measures are adopted. This is particularly the case when NGOs are able to form a working coalition with like-minded governments, as happened in the anti-personnel landmines campaign. This brought together more than 1,000 NGOs around the world and several "small" powers—Canada, South Africa, and a number of European states. The coalition was able to place landmines on the international agenda against the express desires of the more status quo–oriented big powers and to establish a new norm against such weapons in a relatively short stretch of time.[71]

But key to changing current policies is public awareness. A strong constituency for alternative policies can be brought to life—and pressure on governments to act be brought to bear—by making clear the horrendous effects of the virtually unlimited availability of small arms: the suffering of victims, the endless cycle of violence, the persistent insecurity, the severe economic and political costs. Once people understand the repercussions, the political dynamic changes. What was previously unthinkable begins to come within reach.

For a long time, small arms and light weapons have escaped thorough scrutiny; their ubiquitous presence has been accepted as a necessary evil or even welcomed as a guarantor of security and a symbol of freedom. But this is beginning to change as growing numbers of people realize that excessive quantities of small arms can have devastating consequences.

9

Assessing Private Capital Flows to Developing Countries

Hilary F. French

One of the goals of the June 1992 Earth Summit in Rio de Janeiro was to forge a historic North-South partnership to help the world's poorer countries make the transition to sustainable development. A key element of this new partnership was a pledge by industrial countries to step up their aid spending. Yet five years later, little of the promised funding has materialized. Indeed, overall aid levels have declined rather than risen in real terms since Rio, falling by nearly a quarter between 1995 and 1996 alone. This reflects efforts to cut back government deficits in major donor countries, as well as weaker public support for aid in some donor countries.[1]

At the same time, a dramatic and unanticipated shift has occurred since Rio that is powerfully influencing prospects for sustainable development: international private investment in and lending to developing countries has exploded, rising from $44 billion at the beginning of this decade to $244 billion in 1996, according

to the World Bank. In 1990, less than half the international capital moving into the developing world came from private sources, but by 1996 the private share had risen to 86 percent. (See Figure 9–1.) Preliminary estimates by the Washington-based Institute of International Finance (IIF) indicate that private flows declined slightly in 1997 in response to the economic crisis in Southeast Asia, but IIF analysts expect them to rebound in 1998.[2]

A primary reason for this seismic financing shift is that many developing countries are now welcoming foreign capital with open arms—a dramatic reversal of the prevailing development fashion of earlier decades. They have thus repealed policies that discouraged foreign investment, such as ownership restrictions, and promulgated others that encourage it, such as property rights protections. The wave of privatization sweeping the developing world has also played a role. Governments in many countries are selling off enterprises such as utilities and telecommunica-

Billion Dollars

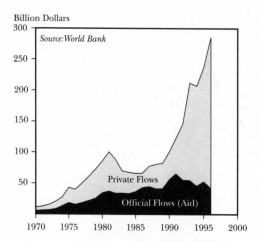

Figure 9–1. International Capital Flows to Developing Countries, 1970–96

tions networks to private bidders, opening up big opportunities for both domestic and international investors.[3]

Changes in the major industrial countries that supply most of the international capital—mainly Japan, the United States, and West European nations—have been important as well. For instance, interest rates have been low in many countries, providing an incentive to look for stronger returns overseas. And some countries have loosened controls on their capital markets. Moreover, this new legal latitude is matched by growing technological powers: computerized financial networks now allow investors to shift vast sums of money from one part of the globe to another.[4]

The resulting inflows of foreign capital have helped fuel a record-breaking economic boom in the countries receiving them. This is perhaps the strongest magnet for international money, as investors gamble on achieving higher returns than they can find at home. China, for instance, with far and away the largest overall inflow of funds, expanded its economy at double-digit annual rates during the first half of the 1990s. Indeed, eco-

nomic growth in the developing world as a whole has far outpaced that of industrial countries in recent years; their economies expanded three times as fast in 1996—at 6 percent. Measured in conventional economic terms, the new openness to international investment has thus had generally impressive results.[5]

A better yardstick of long-term success, however, is whether the large influxes of international capital are contributing to the goals of environmentally sustainable development—meeting human needs today in a manner that does not jeopardize prospects for future generations by damaging the health of the natural resource base. This is a far more difficult question to answer, as the impact of growing private capital movements on the well-being of people and the health of the natural world are at once enormous, complex, and somewhat contradictory.[6]

For one thing, most private funds go to a relatively small group of recipient countries, and, with the exception of China, they are generally middle-income countries rather than the poorest of the poor. Just 10 countries accounted for some three quarters of all private flows to the developing world in 1995. Notably, not one of them is African. Yet when measured as a percentage of gross domestic product (GDP), the list looks rather different, with many small countries ranking high. (See Table 9–1.) In countries receiving private funds, the richer segments of society often benefit disproportionately. Nonetheless, some of the money does appear to be trickling down, with many of the recipient countries registering declining national poverty rates.[7]

For the environment, perhaps the most worrisome implication of the surging inflows of foreign capital is the fact that they help export western consumerism. Given the profligate rates of resource consumption in industrial countries, this spread of the consumer culture is ominous. The newfound mobility of international capital also

Table 9–1. International Private Capital Flows, Top 10 Developing-Country Recipients, 1995[1]

Country	Total Amount	Share of Gross Domestic Product
	(million dollars)	(percent)
Ranked by Absolute Value		
China	46,276	7
Brazil	19,096	3
Mexico	13,069	5
Malaysia	11,924	14
Indonesia	11,649	6
Thailand	9,143	5
Hungary	7,841	18
Argentina	7,204	3
Czech Republic	5,595	13
Poland	5,058	4
Ranked by Share of GDP		
Hungary	7,841	18
Angola	523	14
Malaysia	11,924	14
Czech Republic	5,595	13
St. Vincent and Grenadines	31	12
Papua New Guinea	578	12
St. Lucia	63	11
Lebanon	1,152	10
St. Kitts and Nevis	19	8
Ghana	526	8

[1]The World Bank defines developing countries as "all low and middle-income countries." This includes all of Africa and Latin America, and selected countries in Asia and the Pacific, the Caribbean, Eastern Europe, and the Middle East.
SOURCE: World Bank, *World Development Indicators on CD-ROM* (Washington, DC: 1997).

allows it to seek out the most hospitable home—which may well be a place with weak or unenforced environmental laws. Many people and communities are seriously harmed as the environment that sustains them is damaged or destroyed, such as villagers who are displaced by large construction projects or indigenous peoples whose homelands disappear as forests are felled by timber companies.[8]

Yet on the positive side, international investment often brings with it cutting-edge environmental technologies that may help developing countries leapfrog over the dirtiest and most damaging phases of the development path pioneered by the industrial world. Furthermore, private investors as well as national governments and international organizations have begun to devise a growing array of deliberately "green" international investment strategies. These programs aim to promote the transition to enterprises that nurture rather than decimate the natural world.

Although international capital flows may appear to be beyond the reach of effective regulation, a range of policy tools exist that could help point today's burgeoning private capital flows in a more environmentally sound direction. There is no time to lose in launching these much-needed initiatives on the large scale and in the quick time frame that will be needed to keep up with the relentless pace of global ecological decline.

FOLLOWING THE MONEY

The first step in reorienting private capital flows is to track them better. At the moment, the available statistics tell us little about what, exactly, is being financed. This contrasts with official development assistance, such as that provided by the World Bank, for which detailed reports spell out what is being funded. Yet despite the data gaps, we can construct a general picture of private flows. (See Table 9–2.)[9]

During the 1970s, most of the funds came in the form of loans from commercial banks, as the petrodollars piling up in the North allowed these institutions to extend more and more credit to developing-country governments. Much of this money unfortunately was squandered on uneconomical projects, paving the way

Table 9–2. Private Capital Flows to Developing Countries, 1996[1]

Source	Amount	Share
	(billion dollars)	(percent)
Foreign Direct Investment	110	45
Portfolio Equity (Stocks)	46	19
Portfolio Debt (Bonds)	46	19
Commercial Bank Loans	34	14
Other[2]	8	3
Total	244	100

[1]Preliminary numbers.   [2]Principally export credits from companies and official export credit agencies.
SOURCE: World Bank, *Global Development Finance 1997: Volume 1* (Washington, DC: 1997).

for the debt crisis of the 1980s and the consequent stagnation in lending. The last few years have seen a resurgence of commercial bank loans, but this time the recipients are more likely to be private enterprises than governments. Often the money is used to help finance large infrastructure projects such as highways or power plants. In 1996, commercial bank lending accounted for 14 percent of total private flows, or $34 billion. However, early estimates indicate that these loans declined substantially in volume in 1997 during the Southeast Asian economic meltdown.[10]

The other traditional route for private capital moving into the developing world is as foreign direct investment (FDI) by transnational corporations setting up local plants, often through joint ventures with local companies. In recent years, FDI inflows into the developing world have expanded rapidly, climbing more than threefold between 1990 and 1996—from $25 billion to $110 billion, accounting for 45 percent of total private flows in 1996. In comparison, gross domestic investment from public and private sources in developing countries added up to $905 billion

in 1990 and to $1.2 trillion in 1995. Thus though domestic sources of investment continue to overwhelm foreign ones, the foreign share of total investment is growing. FDI is the international capital flow of greatest significance for development, as it is long-term and it brings with it technology, know-how, and management skill. It has the added advantage of not contributing to a country's debt burden.[11]

Companies based in industrial countries—principally France, Germany, Japan, the United Kingdom, and the United States—are the source of most FDI outflows, accounting for some 85 percent of the global total in recent years. Ranked by the size of their foreign assets, the five largest transnationals as of 1995 were Royal Dutch Shell, Ford Motor Company, General Electric, Exxon, and General Motors, with combined foreign assets of $339 billion and overseas work forces of some 553,000 people. Developing countries represent a significant and increasing share of these totals.[12]

Yet transnational corporations are no longer headquartered only in the industrial world. In recent years, several developing countries and their enterprises have become significant sources of capital as well as recipients of it. Companies based in Brazil, Chile, China, Hong Kong, Kuwait, Malaysia, Singapore, South Korea, Taiwan, and Thailand are all investing abroad, increasingly as far afield as Africa, Europe, and North and South America. Outflows of direct investment from the developing world as a whole have risen rapidly in recent years. According to estimates by the U.N. Conference on Trade and Development, they reached $51 billion in 1996—15 percent of total world outflows.[13]

The quest for natural resources has traditionally drawn international investors into distant ventures in the developing world. Oil has been a particularly strong pull since the dawn of the petroleum age, with oil-producing countries accounting for fully half of all FDI flows to developing countries between 1979 and 1981. But this picture has changed rapidly in recent decades. First, investment in manufacturing began to climb. Now the services sector, which includes diverse activities such as construction, electricity distribution, finance, and telecommunications, is poised for takeoff. Oil-producing countries, meanwhile, accounted for only one fifth of FDI flows into the developing world in 1995 and 1996. The World Bank estimates that the services sector now accounts for more than a third of overall FDI flows to these countries, while manufacturing has declined to less than half of the total. The primary sector, which includes agriculture, forestry, and mining, makes up the remainder—roughly 20 percent.[14]

These broad overall trends mask considerable regional variation, however. The general pattern is found clearly in most of the "emerging market" countries of Asia and Latin America. In Indonesia, for example, some 53 percent of FDI went to manufacturing in 1996, 35 percent to services, and the remaining 13 percent to commodities. Yet many developing countries remain highly dependent on direct natural resource extraction—farming, logging, mining, and drilling for oil. Consequently, most of their foreign investment remains focused on the commodity sector. In Chile, for instance, commodities receive nearly 60 percent of incoming FDI, most of which goes to the mining industry. Diamond mining attracts most of the FDI that flows to Botswana, while in Tunisia, the oil and gas industry is the big draw.[15]

Nearly all the remaining private flows—just under 40 percent of the total—are moving through a category that barely existed less than a decade ago. This is "portfolio" investment, in which developing-country stocks and bonds are purchased abroad—increasingly by large institutional investors, such as insurance companies, mutual funds, or pension plans. Popular sectors for investment include manufacturing, mining, telecommunications, transportation, and utilities. These investments are the most volatile ingredient in the mix of private flows. Investors may withdraw their funds quickly if they lose confidence in a country's economic prospects, as happened in Mexico during the peso crisis of 1994 and in Southeast Asia in 1997.[16]

Portfolio equity investments rose from just 7 percent of total private flows in 1990 to 29 percent in 1993. The Mexican crisis triggered a sharp decline worldwide over the next two years, but by 1996 portfolio equity investments had bounced back. By the end of the year, they reached an all-time annual high in absolute terms of $46 billion, or 19 percent of total private flows. Preliminary estimates suggest that they reached another new high in 1997, despite projected declines in flows into the battered Southeast Asian markets. Bond issues, in which private investors make long-term loans to governments or businesses at fixed interest rates, largely mirror the portfolio equity trend. Bond purchases increased from 5 percent of private flows in 1990 to 23 percent in 1993. After a two-year decline, they too rebounded to $46 billion in 1996, and likely increased again in 1997.[17]

NATURAL WEALTH

Although primary commodities are receiving a declining share of total international investment in the developing world, these investments continue to increase in absolute terms in many countries. Indeed, international investment in resource extraction is now flowing rapidly into the developing world, with its rich endowments of natural assets, including primary forests, mineral and petroleum reserves, and biological diversity. Among other things, this trend reflects degraded environmental conditions in the countries that are a source of the capital, as well as the growing impact of environmental legislation in these countries aimed at minimizing further destruction.

Countries rich in natural resources have on average performed worse economically than resource-poor countries in recent decades.

The flow of funds into natural resources is particularly pronounced within the mining industry. From 1994 to 1997, spending on exploration of nonferrous minerals doubled in Latin America, almost tripled in the Pacific region, and more than tripled in Africa, while leveling off in the traditional mining countries of Australia, Canada, and the United States. Spending on exploration for gold has been growing particularly fast, accounting for more than half of total spending on minerals exploration in recent years. In what *Business Week* calls a "great global gold rush," prospectors are increasingly shifting from their traditional locales in Canada, South Africa, and the United States in search of gold mines abroad.[18]

The U.S. mining industry blames environmentalists for the migration. More to the point, perhaps, is the fact that host countries are inviting international investors in with open arms; some 70 countries have rewritten their national mining codes in recent years with the aim of encouraging investment. Yet few are devoting similar energy to strengthening environmental laws and enforcement. And no matter how good the laws are, mining takes a heavy environmental toll. Even in the United States, a country with relatively strong environmental controls, for every kilogram of gold produced, some 3 million kilograms of waste rock are removed from the Earth. The social costs are also high: one out of every five gold prospecting sites over 1995–96 was on land owned or claimed by indigenous peoples.[19]

Multinational oil and gas companies are also continually looking for new horizons, as the most accessible fields in industrial countries have already been tapped. Indeed, more than 90 percent of known oil and gas reserves are now in the developing world. The major oil and gas companies are thus increasingly striking deals—and oil—in the Central Asian republics, deep in the South American rainforest, and off Asian and West African shores. As with minerals, the environmental and social costs are high as previously remote and pristine areas are opened up to development.[20]

Uncontrolled logging by international companies poses yet another threat to the world's rapidly dwindling tropical forests and those who inhabit them. Companies from countries with largely liquidated primary forests are now moving overseas in search of easier pickings. U.S. firms, for instance, say they are going abroad to escape what Luke Popovich of the American Forest and Paper Association calls the "constant green harassment" they feel they are subjected to at home. But the forests elsewhere have grown increasingly crowded with competing firms from other countries with decimated forests, such as Malaysia and Indonesia. In recent years, companies from there as well as from China, France, Germany, Japan, South Korea, the United States, and elsewhere have won timber concessions that threaten to deforest large swaths of the globe. Among the countries offering the concessions are those with some of the world's last remaining untouched forests. They include Brazil, Cambodia, Cameroon, Chile, Gabon, Guyana, Nicaragua, Nigeria, Papua New Guinea, the Solomon

Islands, and Suriname. (See Chapter 2.)[21]

As the pace of natural resource exploitation picks up in many countries, intriguing research is raising questions about whether this is a sound economic strategy—let alone a wise environmental one. Research by Jeffrey Sachs and Andrew Warner of Harvard University demonstrates that countries rich in natural resources have on average actually performed worse economically than resource-poor countries in recent decades. One reason may be that resource extraction often leads to only marginal spin-off benefits when it involves few linkages with other segments of economies. Furthermore, natural resource extraction creates relatively few jobs. The mining and petroleum sectors in Papua New Guinea, for example, employ less than 2 percent of the population, although the sectors' exports provide 25 percent of the country's GDP. A wiser strategy for both the environment and the economy would be to funnel international capital into activities that sustain rather than destroy natural endowments. This is what a number of innovative experiments now under way aim to do.[22]

"Bioprospecting" is one example. Drug and seed companies have long used the genetic diversity of the developing world to create new products. Yet even when a traditional crop variety proves essential for breeding a new line of seeds, or when a wild plant yields some valuable new drug, corporations have rarely paid anything for access to the genetic resource. The Convention on Biological Diversity signed at the Earth Summit in 1992 gives nations the right to charge for access to genetic resources, and it allows them to pass national legislation setting the terms of any bioprospecting agreements. The intent of the treaty is to provide a strong conservation incentive by encouraging countries to view genetic diversity as a source of potential profits. And the growing power of biotechnology, which allows

for much more direct manipulation of genes than was previously possible, virtually guarantees that the profit potential will continue to rise in the years ahead.[23]

A number of bioprospecting programs are now taking shape that build upon the pioneering agreement in 1991 between Merck and Company and Costa Rica's Instituto Nacional de Biodiversidad. A bioprospecting initiative in Suriname, for instance, involves a number of different partners, including indigenous healers, a Surinamese pharmaceutical company, the U.S.-based Bristol Myers Squibb company, the environmental group Conservation International, and the Missouri Botanical Gardens. Royalties from any drugs developed will be channeled into a range of local institutions, including nongovernmental organizations (NGOs), the national pharmaceutical company, and the forest service. In addition, a Forest Peoples Fund has been established to support small-scale development projects to benefit local indigenous peoples.[24]

Ecotourism also shows promise as a strategy for channeling international investment capital into the preservation of threatened ecosystems, if it is pursued in an ecologically sensitive way. Costa Rica is leading the way. The country's sandy beaches, dry deciduous forests, and moist cloud forests have made tourism the top foreign exchange earner, surpassing traditional export mainstays such as bananas and coffee. Since ecotourism is not generally capital-intensive, domestic investment may often be sufficient for underwriting much of the industry. But even ecotourism has its infrastructure: international investment may find a role in upgrading airports and building the kind of carefully conceived, small-scale, low-impact hotels that fit with the industry's aims.[25]

Finally, although the vast majority of international investment in forestry continues to support destructive practices, there is nonetheless an opportunity offered by a growing demand for timber that has been independently certified as being sustainably produced. (See Chapter 2.) A few international investors are setting themselves up to tap into this market. Precious Woods Management Ltd., for instance, a Swiss-owned firm, has established a subsidiary in the Brazilian Amazon that is now harvesting timber from an operation certified by SmartWood as well managed. This is a certification program sponsored by the New York–based Rainforest Alliance and accredited by the Forest Stewardship Council, an independent body established in 1993 to set standards for sustainable forest production.[26]

MANUFACTURING ABROAD

The conventional economic wisdom of recent years has been that the rapidly growing East Asian countries are showing the path to the future. Poor in natural resources, these countries owe much of their current economic success to a take-off in manufacturing—much of it destined for export markets and financed by large infusions of foreign capital. Many countries around the world are now trying to replicate this. Yet from an environmental point of view, the manufacturing takeoff is a double-edged sword.[27]

The category of manufacturing covers a vast array of products and processes. It includes relatively low-tech yet labor-intensive enterprises such as textiles, sawmilling, and food processing, as well as higher-tech industries such as chemicals, electronics, and pharmaceuticals. Although it is difficult to generalize, labor-intensive activities tend to be less environmentally damaging than capital-intensive ones, because by definition they use less energy and less machinery, and therefore tend to produce fewer damaging by-products.[28]

In part because of the low cost of their labor, developing countries moved first into the lower-tech industries as they diversified their economies. Their share of world production of textiles, for instance, increased from 23 to 39 percent between 1975 and 1996, while their share of iron and steel smelting rose from 12 to 36 percent. In recent years, however, many developing countries have moved into higher-tech activities as well, such as chemicals, electronics, and pharmaceuticals—industries that carry substantial environmental risks. For instance, their share of world production of industrial chemicals increased from 17 percent in 1975 to 25 percent in 1996, and that of electrical machinery rose from 11 to 20 percent.[29]

Foreign direct investments largely mirror these broader changes, with the World Bank reporting in 1997 that higher-tech industries such as chemicals and electronics were accounting for a growing share of FDI manufacturing flows to the developing world. For example, almost 45 percent of U.S. capital outflows to Argentina in 1996 were for chemicals, and in Malaysia that year more than half of U.S. funds went into electronics.[30]

The current surge of international investment in manufacturing thus brings with it environmental dangers. Hazardous industries, such as battery manufacturers, chemical companies, and toxin-laden computer chip assembly facilities, are becoming increasingly concentrated in countries ill equipped to handle the pollution. Indeed, a recent review by the Silicon Valley Toxics Coalition in San Jose, California, of 22 high-tech companies based in industrial countries found that more than half of their collective manufacturing and assembly operations—processes intensive in their use of acids, solvents, and toxic gases—are now located in developing countries.[31]

Studies suggest that industries are generally drawn to the developing world by the low cost of labor, the availability of natural resources, or the strategic access to new markets. In most cases, environmental control costs alone are not high enough to be a determining factor in location decisions. But even if companies move to the developing world for other reasons, they may well take advantage of lax environmental laws and enforcement once there.[32]

In a few cases, moreover, relaxed enforcement does appear to have been a motivating factor in companies' location decisions. The debate over the 1993 North American Free Trade Agreement (NAFTA) put the spotlight on one region where this seems to have been the case for some firms—the border between northern Mexico and the United States. That area is the site of nearly 2,000 mostly foreign-owned manufacturing plants known as *maquiladoras*. In the city of Mexicali, near the California border, more than a quarter of the factory operators surveyed in the late 1980s said that Mexico's lax environmental enforcement influenced their decision to be there.[33]

The *maquiladoras* region is but one of some 230 export or special processing zones that span 70 countries and collectively employ some 44 million workers. These zones normally permit goods to be imported duty-free, on the condition that they are then used to produce exports. A range of other inducements may be used to encourage companies to locate production in these zones. There is considerable evidence that one of them is often a look-the-other-way attitude toward substandard labor practices such as dangerous working conditions and restrictions on the right to organize. Although no comprehensive data on the question have been gathered, it is likely that environmental abuses are equally common. In the coastal Cavite province near Manila, for instance, local fishers accuse Taiwanese, Korean, and other factories in special economic zones of dumping into Manila Bay pollutants that are responsible for killing off thousands of fish. And the Chinese National Environmental Protection Agency has accused firms from these same countries of setting up shop in China in order to flee tougher environmental regulations at home.[34]

Beyond spreading hazardous manufacturing processes, international investment is also implicated in spurring growth in the production of environmentally problematic products. The major multinational automobile companies, for example, plagued by saturated markets in the industrial world, are salivating over the "emerging markets" of Asia, Eastern Europe, and Latin America. Some three quarters of the auto factories projected to be built over the next three years are expected to be in emerging markets. European, Japanese, U.S., and South Korean companies are competing aggressively to build these plants. General Motors recently sank some $2.2 billion into a "four-plant strategy" to build nearly identical plants simultaneously in Argentina, China, Poland, and Thailand. And nine of the world's major automakers—including Ford, General Motors, and Mercedes-Benz—have set up shop in India in just the last few years. If these countries develop auto-centric transportation systems along the lines of the U.S. model, the consequences for local air pollution, climate change, and food security will be serious indeed.[35]

Despite the environmental risks, international investment in manufacturing also offers environmental opportunities for developing countries. One of them is access to cutting-edge production technologies, which are usually cleaner and more efficient in their use of energy and materials than older equipment. A 1992 World Bank study compared the rates at which 60 countries were adopting a cleaner wood pulping process, and concluded that countries open to foreign investment acquired the new technology far more rapidly than did those that were closed to it. Furthermore, privatizing state-owned factories by selling them to domestic or foreign private investors can lead to environmental improvements by eliminating the conflict of interest that can arise when the government is being both a producer and a regulator. Limited evidence also suggests that the pressure to turn a profit can introduce an incentive to adopt manufacturing techniques that reduce energy and materials use and thus pollution.[36]

Foreign investment can also help disseminate new, more environmentally sound products worldwide. For example, efficient compact fluorescent light bulbs, first produced in the United States, are increasingly manufactured in the developing world. In 1995, China made some 80–100 million of these bulbs—more than any other country. The funding and technology came in part through joint ventures with lighting firms based in Hong Kong, Japan, the Netherlands, and Taiwan. Compact fluorescents produced by joint ventures consistently outperform those of domestic companies in performance standards such as efficiency levels.[37]

Renewable energy components are also now often being manufactured in the developing world. For instance, India has become a major manufacturer of advanced wind turbines with the help of technology obtained through joint ventures and licensing agreements with Danish, Dutch, and German firms. This has helped India become the world's second largest wind power producer, with an installed wind capacity of more than 800 megawatts.[38]

THE INFRASTRUCTURE BOOM

The third major category into which international capital flows is the services sector, which according to the World Bank now accounts for more than a third of all foreign direct investment in the developing world. The definition of this sector depends on who is keeping the statistics. In general terms, it includes knowledge-based enterprises such as consulting, health care, and legal advice. It also covers investment-oriented businesses, such as banking and real estate. The services label is also often applied to activities such as communications, construction, electricity and water distribution, and transportation—otherwise known as infrastructure. It is this last category that poses some of the most direct and daunting environmental challenges.[39]

People in developing countries lack access to many services crucial to a high quality of life. For instance, 1.2 billion people—more than one fifth of humanity—have no access to clean drinking water, some 2 billion have no electricity, and nearly 3 billion do not have adequate sanitation services. It is thus an important goal of developing-country governments to provide these services to their citizens. But supplying services such as electricity, transportation, and sewage treatment often involves large construction projects that are costly both to national treasuries and to the health of the natural world. The challenge is to find ways to provide these crucial services to people in ways that are environmentally sound, socially equitable, and economically affordable.[40]

One of the most dramatic trends of the 1990s has been the rapid rate at which developing-country governments have turned many traditionally public activities over to the private sector. Private companies are building power plants, telecommunications networks, water treatment plants, dams, and toll roads in many corners of the globe. And in two thirds of the cases, the private investor hails from abroad. Foreign funds devoted to infrastructure construction climbed from $2.6 billion at the beginning of the 1990s to $22.3 billion by 1995 (although these World Bank figures exclude FDI due to methodological complications). Notably, 70 percent of these funds went to private companies rather than governments, who have traditionally owned and managed most large infrastructure. Over this period, power projects accounted for 44 percent of the total, telecommunications for 30 percent, transport for 13 percent, and other types of projects for the remaining 13 percent.[41]

This burst of private infrastructure activity will in theory have the benefit of providing hundreds of millions of people with much-needed services that are beyond the financial reach of cash-starved governments. The projected price tags are indeed staggering. According to the Asian Development Bank, Asia alone needs infrastructure investment of some $10 trillion over the next 30 years. The bulk of this is in the power, transport, and telecommunications sectors. Yet the privatization of services that have traditionally been within the public domain raises complicated questions of accountability, equity, and environmental sustainability. It is also important that the construction of new infrastructure not take precedence over more cost-effective strategies on the demand side, such as plugging leaky pipes to save water or caulking windows to cut down on energy use.[42]

The numerous power sector projects now in the pipeline have particularly grave implications for the future health of the planet—especially for the quality of the air and the stability of the climate. Over the next several decades, the bulk of new global investment in the power sector is projected to take place in developing countries. The world's ability to avert a catastrophic global warming over the next several decades will depend in no small measure on what kind of power plants are built.[43]

A sizable share of current international investment in the power sector is bankrolling multimillion-dollar coal- and oil-fired power plants that are intensive in their production of both local air pollutants and greenhouse gases. For instance,

international investors are queuing up to participate in the construction of the more than 500 medium-sized power plants that China plans to construct by 2010. Many of these will be fueled by coal. This will add to the country's already staggering burden of air pollution–related disease and death. In addition, current emissions trends suggest that China, already the world's second largest emitter of carbon, could well surpass the United States and top the list by 2010.[44]

The power sector projects now in the pipeline have particularly grave implications for the future health of the planet.

More promising for the health of the environment are the plans of many countries to build cleaner gas-fired plants, often using advanced gas turbines or cogeneration (the combined production of heat and electricity in factories and buildings). El Salvador, India, Indonesia, and Viet Nam are among the countries where foreign-funded gas-fired plants are either under construction or being planned. Yet gas development has its own environmental liabilities, including plans to construct massive pipelines to transport the gas from remote areas. These pipeline projects are generally paralleled by service roads, which bring with them ecological and social disruption as previously remote areas are opened up to settlement and other incursions. "Welcome to the 1990s version of Rudyard Kipling's Great Game," notes the Wall Street Journal. "Instead of imperial powers scrambling for territory in Central Asia, giant energy companies, mainly U.S. ones, are vying to dominate access routes between Latin America's natural-gas fields and its big cities." Similar scrambles are under way in Central and Southeast Asia and in the Middle East.[45]

The private sector is also stepping in to help build large hydro dams that provide electricity, water for irrigation, and flood control—though often at enormous environmental and social cost. In China, international companies are competing fiercely for contracts to help build the Three Gorges Dam on the Yangtze River, which is projected to supply roughly a tenth of China's electricity when completed around 2009. The dam is expected to flood 60,730 hectares of land and 160 towns, and force the resettlement of some 1.3 million people. The Chinese government has announced that it will finance the dam through commercial bank loans, bond offerings, and stock investments. An initial bond offering in February 1997 for 1 billion yuan ($120 million) sold out in five days. The project was listed on the Shanghai stock exchange in July 1997, and preparations have been made to list it in Hong Kong as well if necessary.[46]

Encouragingly, however, developers of power projects fueled by renewable energy are also seeking to enter emerging markets. In one particularly ambitious undertaking, Amoco and Enron are looking for finance for a joint venture to build a 50-megawatt photovoltaic power plant in India. Other investors aim to channel money into smaller-scale, less-centralized approaches to meeting energy needs in the developing world. For instance, the Triodos Bank, a Dutch investment bank, launched a Solar Investment Fund in late 1996 whose purpose is to finance loans in Africa, Asia, and Latin America for household solar systems that provide electricity to rural communities that lack access to grid-supplied power.[47]

Another rapid growth area for international private infrastructure investment is the provision of water, sanitation, and waste management services. With investment needs in these areas in the developing world adding up to at least $600 billion over the next decade, according to World Bank estimates, governments clearly need private help. Over the last few years, a handful of British and French companies have moved aggressively into this market. For example, the French company Lyonnaise des Eaux entered into a concession agreement in 1993 with several partners to invest more than $4 billion in upgrading and expanding water and sanitation services in Buenos Aires. It has also joined forces with Compagnie Générale des Eaux and other partners to provide similar services in Mexico City.[48]

Like all other aspects of privatization, granting concessions for water and waste treatment services to private investors is controversial. Critics worry that the profit motive will provide little incentive to protect vital ecological functions or to expand coverage to the poor. Furthermore, companies whose bottom line depends on selling as much water as possible have little incentive to invest in water conservation programs. Yet proponents argue that governments retain full powers to set the terms of private concession contracts. For instance, the Buenos Aires water concession contract stipulates what share of the population is to be provided with potable water and sewerage services, and by what date. Within the first two years, 400,000 new water and 250,000 new sewerage connections were made, many in low-income neighborhoods. The quality of drinking water also improved, and the city's customary summer water shortages became a thing of the past.[49]

THE POWER OF THE PURSE

The rapid infusion of private capital into emerging markets has led to considerable confusion on the part of those accustomed to the more familiar world of aid-financed development. Somewhat nostalgically, a report by Friends of the Earth notes that "with yesterday's centralized funding, NGOs could lobby particular organizations and stage demonstrations outside meetings. But it is difficult to effectively influence something as nebulous as private capital flows." Difficult, but by no means impossible. In fact, a number of important points of leverage offer considerable promise for helping to shape the developing world's environmental future. One of the most important is the power wielded by investors themselves.[50]

The obvious place to start is with bilateral and multilateral development lending agencies, which by now accept that their lending programs should adhere to an array of environmental and social guidelines. By encouraging these agencies to attach environmental conditions to programs that support private investments, a limited amount of aid money could serve as an environmental "screen" for a far larger pool of private capital.[51]

One application of this strategy came in April 1995, when the U.S. Overseas Private Investment Corporation (OPIC) decided to cancel the $100-million political risk insurance policy it was providing to a New Orleans–based mining company, Freeport McMoRan Copper and Gold, on the grounds that the company was violating the environmental conditions written into its contract as well as OPIC's more general environmental requirements. The policy covered the company's operations at the Grasberg Mine in the Indonesian province of Irian Jaya, on the island of New Guinea. The mine is one of the world's largest; its enormous copper, gold, and silver deposits were reportedly worth more than $60 billion at 1996 market prices. The mine was dumping 100,000 tons of tailings into nearby rivers every day, which local people claimed was contaminating the fish they ate and the water they drank. The clogged rivers were also flooding large swaths of rainforest and threatening a diverse array of forest species. Environ-

mentalists argued that the mine would not have been allowed to operate in the United States, and should therefore not be eligible for OPIC support.[52]

Despite the promise of this strategy, later developments in the Freeport case show how difficult it can be to make a victory stick. A year after its initial decision, OPIC reinstated Freeport's policy after the company agreed to establish a $100-million trust fund to clean up the site at the end of the mine's life. Then just a few months later, Freeport announced that it would not renew its policy with OPIC.[53]

A similar case involves the U.S. Export-Import Bank, which provides government-subsidized loans to other countries for the purchase of U.S. goods and services. In May 1996, the bank announced that its environmental guidelines prohibited it from providing this type of support for China's Three Gorges project—a blow to companies such as the heavy equipment manufacturer Caterpillar, which had hoped to participate in the construction of the dam. The bank said it might reconsider if China improved its plans for protecting water quality and preserving endangered species. But in the meantime the bank's counterparts in Canada, France, Germany, Japan, and Switzerland, which are not constrained by environmental policies, have indicated that they will step into the breach. Stung by the experience, the United States is trying to persuade other donor countries to apply environmental conditions to their export credit loans.[54]

Among international organizations, perhaps the biggest opportunity involves the World Bank and two affiliated agencies, the International Finance Corporation (IFC) and the Multilateral Investment Guarantee Agency (MIGA). Though the World Bank has traditionally made loans only to governments, in the last few years it has begun to use some of its funds to back commercial lending to the private sector. The IFC, which lends directly to private enterprises, is much smaller than the Bank itself. But on average each $1 the IFC lends is attached to $5 of private investment—a ratio that greatly expands this agency's influence. Given the World Bank's growing interest in private-sector lending, the IFC is expected to expand in the years ahead. MIGA also promotes private investment, principally by insuring against political risks, such as expropriation, civil disturbance, and breach of contract. Since it issued its first contract in 1990, MIGA has guaranteed more than 200 contracts involving at least $15 billion of FDI. And MIGA, too, is likely to play an increasingly prominent role in international development.[55]

Environmental NGOs are now looking to private lenders as potential allies.

Both the IFC and MIGA are involved in many large investment projects with heavy environmental impacts. Infrastructure, manufacturing, and mining are among the activities the agencies back. MIGA, for instance, was participating in Freeport's Grasberg Mine project—until the company canceled its MIGA policy as well. (Freeport took that action just before the agency was scheduled to send over a team of investigators to look into charges of environmental and human rights abuse.)[56]

The World Bank has an extensive set of environmental and social policies, which among other things require environmental impact assessments of projects and protection of the rights of indigenous peoples. Theoretically, all Bank agencies including the IFC and MIGA are bound by these policies, although Bank officials acknowledge that actual operating procedures are sometimes different in private-sector operations, in part due to confi-

dentiality concerns. Critics charge that the rules are often violated at the Bank itself, not to mention at the IFC and MIGA.[57]

Since taking office in 1995, Bank President James Wolfensohn has indicated that he agrees with some of the criticism—and that he is interested in stepping up environmental enforcement in all branches of the World Bank, including those that involve the private sector. Yet a recent case involving an IFC loan to a privately owned Chilean electric utility for the construction of a series of dams on the scenic Bíobío River, an area that is home to 8,000 indigenous people and to myriad rare plant and animal species, reveals some of the limits of the Bank's power. The IFC recently commissioned an independent review of the project; it concluded that the utility had repeatedly violated the environmental and social conditions written into the loan agreement. Environmentalists were outraged when the Bank censored parts of this report before releasing it to the public. Meanwhile, the utility has prepaid its IFC loan, thereby untying itself from any of the environmental strings attached to the money.[58]

More encouragingly, however, over the past few years the IFC has collaborated with the Global Environment Facility (GEF—a joint undertaking of the U.N. Development Programme, the U.N. Environment Programme (UNEP), and the World Bank) to develop an explicitly green investment program to complement its standard offerings. The idea is to devise financing mechanisms for projects that are too small or unproven to attract standard IFC support or other sources of international capital; the average IFC loan is $15 million, while many environmentally sound ventures are looking for loans denominated in thousands. The goal of the new initiatives is to demonstrate the viability of these smaller-scale enterprises with a small injection of public funds so that the industries will grow in size and be able to attract private capital on their own.[59]

One particularly promising IFC program channels funds through environmental NGOs, nonprofit venture capital firms, and other intermediaries to a range of small-scale, environmentally sound enterprises. Projects in renewable energy, energy efficiency, sustainable forestry and agriculture, and ecotourism are the funding targets. The program, developed with a GEF grant, was originally capitalized at $4.3 million. It has now been scaled up with an additional $16.5 million and will involve some 100 different projects when fully up and running. Still, the whole program remains smaller than most individual IFC projects. And the IFC has been slow to devote its own resources to the program, preferring to use the GEF's scarce funds instead.[60]

Although environmental NGOs have traditionally focused principally on public lending institutions as possible agents of change, they are now also looking to private lenders and investors as potential allies. Commercial banks, for instance, require exhaustive studies of possible risks before making loans, a process known as "due diligence." Increasingly, banks are viewing environmental issues as an important consideration in this process. The banks have a diverse range of concerns. In the wake of recent U.S. court cases, they worry that a hazardous waste dump will be discovered on a property that they lent money for, and that they will be held liable. They also fear that violations of environmental laws will lead to large financial penalties that will undermine a borrower's creditworthiness. In the most extreme case, a project might be stopped altogether in the face of opposition from environmental groups.[61]

"International commercial banks, whether they intend to be or not, are frequently very effective enforcers of local and international environmental requirements," maintains Bradford Gentry of

Yale University. "The level of scrutiny given to these issues by banks is often well above that of local environmental enforcement." Nonetheless, a recent study by the Washington-based National Wildlife Federation found substantial room for progress: less than half of 51 financial institutions from 13 countries on four continents routinely perform environmental due diligence on transactions other than those secured with real estate.[62]

Stock market investors are also slowly beginning to show more interest in environmental questions. It used to be assumed that it was costly for companies to be good environmental stewards. But this view is giving ground to a new understanding that the reverse may actually be true: studies indicate that environmentally progressive companies may in fact perform better, on average, than companies that are plagued by large environmental liabilities.

For instance, a 1995 report by the Washington-based Investor Responsibility Research Center compared the stock market performance of the 500 companies within the Standard & Poor's index, a group of 500 representative stocks and bonds. They divided the firms into "high" and "low" polluting companies. Overall, the study found no penalty for investing in green-shaded portfolios, and in some cases it concluded that low-pollution portfolios actually demonstrated superior performance. A November 1996 study by the consulting firm ICF Kaiser was more bullish still. Its survey of more than 300 Standard & Poor's companies revealed that adopting a forward-looking environmental stance had a "significant and favorable impact" on a firm's value in the marketplace, as it reduced the company's risk profile and thus its cost of capital.[63]

As studies like this begin to accumulate, environmentally screened investment funds will likely grow in popularity. Some $529 billion worth of investment—

nearly 4 percent of all managed funds—is currently screened with some social criteria, according to the Washington-based Social Investment Forum. An additional $736 billion is controlled by investors who partake in shareholder activism such as proxy votes. In many cases, environmental criteria are one element in a broader social screen; in a few cases, funds are explicitly environmental in nature. The performance of these funds, like all investment funds, varies greatly. Overall, however, the returns have been competitive. For instance, the Domini 400 Social, an index of socially screened firms, has outperformed the Standard & Poor 500 over much of the 1990s. Most screened funds are composed of companies listed on domestic stock exchanges, however, rather than international ones. One reason for this is the difficulty of tracking and monitoring international companies. Nonetheless, a few screened funds are beginning to venture into international markets.[64]

A frontrunner in this arena is the Global Environment Fund, a Washington-based for-profit investment fund manager founded in 1989. Loan guarantee agreements with OPIC have allowed the group to raise $190 million in investment capital from institutional investors for two Global Environment Emerging Markets Funds, which between them now have holdings in 10 countries in Africa, Asia, Eastern Europe, and Latin America. The principal focus of these funds is environmentally related infrastructure, such as renewable energy projects and water and sewage treatment plants. In another effort to promote private-sector environmental initiatives, the IFC and the GEF are spearheading the creation of two venture capital funds: a $20–25 million biodiversity fund for Latin America to be called the Terra Capital Fund that will finance sustainable forestry and agriculture programs and eco-tourism projects, and a $210-million venture capital fund to pro-

mote energy efficiency and renewable energy projects worldwide.[65]

Meanwhile, environmentally risky megaprojects look increasingly like poor investment gambles. For instance, if built as planned, the 2,400-megawatt Bakun hydroelectric project on the island of Borneo will require the clearing of 69,000 hectares of rainforest, the flooding of an area the size of Singapore, and the displacement of 9,500 indigenous people. Yet efforts to sell shares to international investors in the controversial project on the Kuala Lumpur stock exchange have so far met with little success, with one of the project's financial backers recently forced to cancel a planned stock issuance.[66]

THE RULES OF THE GAME

Although public and private investors clearly have an important role to play in shaping the environmental content of private investment flows, it remains the role of governments to set the rules under which markets and investors operate. But it has become fashionable to question whether national governments are still able to play that traditional role, given the growing power and nimbleness of international financial markets.[67]

It is certainly premature to declare the nation-state dead. In fact, countries have a number of tools at their disposal if they choose to use them. For instance, traditional environmental laws and enforcement systems badly need to be strengthened in many developing countries. Major advances could also be achieved by innovations in national fiscal policy, such as reducing subsidies to environmentally harmful activities and taxing them instead. (See Chapter 10.) These sorts of policy reforms would change incentive structures throughout national economies, tipping the balance away from environmentally harmful investments and toward eco-friendlier ones.

But though nations still retain considerable latitude for environmental innovation, it is also true that the global nature of today's economy means that individual countries have less power than they once did to chart their own environmental course. Action on the international front is therefore essential.

Most multinational corporations already claim to adhere to roughly uniform environmental standards throughout their worldwide operations. And a number of international industry groups have now crafted voluntary codes of environmental conduct; many of these call for companies to approximate the standards of their home countries wherever they do business. In part, this is simply more practical than operating with a patchwork quilt of different practices around the world. Meeting international environmental criteria also allows companies to trumpet green credentials, which is of growing value in the international marketplace. An additional impetus for stricter internal corporate environmental policies is a desire to avoid adverse publicity—as well as a growing tendency for costly lawsuits to be filed in home-country courts.[68]

Over the last few years, numerous companies from around the world, many from developing countries, have asked to be certified as in compliance with the voluntary environmental management guidelines forged by the Geneva-based International Organization for Standardization (ISO), a worldwide federation of national standards-setting bodies. The first set of standards in the ISO 14,000 series, as it is known, was finalized in the fall of 1996. They cover internal management and auditing procedures—how, for instance, a company should monitor its pollution. These environmental management guidelines are not to be confused with actual performance standards that would specify, for example, what levels of pollution would be acceptable. But they are nonetheless a useful tool.[69]

It is important to integrate environmental considerations into the official forums where the rules of international commerce are being written.

A major weakness of the ISO process, however, has been its relatively narrow base: industry has been an active player from the beginning, but environmental groups did not participate until the negotiations were well along. More promising in this regard is the precedent provided by the Forest Stewardship Council (FSC). The FSC's criteria for forest management were developed by its diverse members, who represent timber traders and retailers as well as environmental organizations and forest dwellers. A Marine Stewardship Council along the lines of the FSC is now being set up to devise criteria for sustainable fish harvesting. (See Chapter 4.)[70]

Although these independent initiatives have a critical role to play, it is also important to integrate environmental considerations into the official forums where the rules of international commerce are now being written—international trade and investment negotiations. The discussions in 1993 on the North American Free Trade Agreement represented one of the first attempts to put environmental issues high on the economic negotiating agenda. In this case, lobbying by environmental NGOs produced some concrete results, albeit relatively weak ones. For instance, the three NAFTA governments agreed to an environmental "side agreement" that, among other things, was intended to lead to stricter environmental enforcement. NAFTA was also written with a clause that directs the parties not to lower their environmental standards—or their enforcement of them—in order to attract investment. By some accounts, NAFTA's environmental provisions and side agreement have had positive environmental effects. Yet there remains much room for progress. In particular, the pollution problems in the border area continue to be staggering: a 1995 report found that roughly a quarter of *maquiladora* hazardous waste—some 44 tons daily—could not be accounted for, presumably because it is dumped in ditches.[71]

At least one other major trade regime appears to be following NAFTA's lead, although in its own way. The Asia-Pacific Economic Cooperation (APEC) forum is a loose coalition of 18 Pacific Rim states, including the United States, China, and Japan. It has put the cause of sustainable development high on its agenda, focusing in particular on the challenge of creating sustainable cities, cleaner industries, and healthier oceans and fisheries. In addition, APEC's "Non-binding Investment Principles" contain an environmental provision similar to NAFTA's investment clause.[72]

Currently, the Organisation for Economic Co-operation and Development (OECD), a body composed mainly of western industrial countries, is negotiating a Multilateral Agreement on Investment intended to reduce obstacles to the flow of foreign investment. Yet so far, at least, negotiators have paid scant attention to the agreement's worrisome ecological implications, despite the efforts of environmental groups to put this issue on the table. If this agreement goes ahead as planned, it could constrain the ability of countries to put in place policies that would minimize the environmental damage and social disruption of foreign investment projects. Though negotiated by OECD members, membership in the treaty will be open to other countries as well. And developments in the OECD often lay the groundwork for future accords at the World Trade Organization.[73]

The United Nations could also do more to help put global commerce on a sustainable course. Just as the International Labour Organisation drafts standards on matters such as workplace safety and child labor, so might a strengthened U.N. environment agency be charged with developing baseline environmental standards. This effort could expand an existing UNEP initiative in which sectoral task forces produce technical guidelines, case studies, and examples of "best practice" for diverse industries such as textiles, electronics, and pulp and paper. It could also build on the World Bank's environmental policies and guidelines, which are already a common point of reference for private investors.[74]

For any international standards to be effective, they would need to meet three basic principles of their own: they should be minimum standards that companies and countries are free to exceed if they wish; they must be set high enough to have a real impact, rather than at a least-common-denominator level; and they would need to be developed in an open and inclusive process that would build a strong consensus in support of them.

This suggests a final critical governance challenge: democratizing decision-making in a world where remote investors and often-impenetrable international institutions are increasingly calling the shots. Already, a grassroots NGO movement is rapidly gaining strength in many parts of the world as a powerful countervailing force. For instance, in a landmark victory for local environmentalists, the Chilean Supreme Court in March 1997 overturned the national environment agency's approval of a plan to allow the Trillium Corporation (based in Bellingham, Washington) to log an ancient beech forest. Importantly, environmental activists are increasingly well linked internationally, with e-mail communications and sophisticated networks allowing well-coordinated campaigns that span the globe. This international NGO campaign tries to influence and in some cases to halt environmentally damaging projects through multifaceted efforts involving traditional grassroots tactics as well as through direct lobbying of corporations, private investors, and international institutions.[75]

Perhaps the strongest proof of the strength of the growing NGO movement is the seriousness with which the international business community is taking it. A recent report by the Control Risks Group, a London-based firm that advises businesses on political and security risks, describes "the pressure on companies, wherever they operate, to adopt the high-est international environmental, labour and ethical standards." According to the report, "heightened international scrutiny means that perceived transgressors truly have 'no hiding place.'"[76]

As today's rapidly growing private capital flows to the developing world increasingly alter the natural world, they are thus also redefining the international political landscape. New relationships are beginning to be forged between governments, international organizations, businesses, private financial institutions, and NGOs. The active engagement of all these players will be required to redirect private capital flows to the developing world into activities that support rather than undermine environmentally sustainable development.

10

Building a New Economy

Lester R. Brown
Jennifer Mitchell

As the world economy has expanded nearly sixfold since 1950, it has begun to outrun the capacity of the Earth to supply basic goods and services. As noted in Chapter 1, we forget how large our continually expanding global economy has become relative to the Earth's ecosystem. The annual growth of 4 percent in 1997 seems rather modest, but that one year's additional output of $1.1 trillion exceeded the growth in output during the entire seventeenth century.[1]

Despite the many collisions with the Earth's natural limits described in the preceding nine chapters, we continue to expand our numbers and raise our consumption levels as though the Earth's capacities were infinite. If the global economy grows at 3 percent a year, it will expand from an output of $29 trillion in 1997 to $57 trillion in 2020, nearly doubling. It will then more than double again by the year 2050, reaching $138 trillion. Yet even in reaching $29 trillion, the economy has already overrun many of the Earth's natural capacities.[2]

Nearly all forms of environmental deterioration—including soil erosion, aquifer depletion, rangeland deterioration, air pollution, and climate change—adversely affect agriculture. Combined with a shrinking backlog of technology available to farmers to raise land productivity, these are slowing growth in the world grain harvest. Meanwhile, the world demand for grain is expanding at a near-record pace, driven by the addition of 80 million people each year and unprecedented gains in affluence in the developing world, led by China. Despite the recent return to production of idled cropland, world grain stocks have dropped to the lowest level on record, leaving the world just one poor harvest away from potential chaos in world grain markets.[3]

With world water use tripling since mid-century and continuing to expand, water scarcity is threatening economic progress indirectly through its effect on the food supply. Wherever there is irrigation overpumping today there will be irrigation cutbacks tomorrow; cuts in irrigation mean cuts in food production. With nearly half the world's grain produced on irrigated land, this is not good news. If we are facing a future of water scarcity, we are also facing food scarcity. Irrigation water shortages are already raising grain imports in many countries, including Algeria, China, Egypt, India, Iran, Mexico, Pakistan, and Saudi Arabia. In the three years after Saudi Arabia's aquifer began to dry up in 1994, irrigation cutbacks raised the country's net grain imports from 3 million tons to more than 7 million.[4]

As populations outrun their water supplies, there is much talk of conflicts over water. Some analysts note that in regions facing acute water scarcity, such as the Middle East, future wars are more likely to be over water than oil. But the competition for water is moving into world grain markets as countries try to offset irrigation water shortages by expanding grain imports. In this arena, the winners are likely to be those who are financially strongest, not those who are the strongest militarily.[5]

In the absence of a technological breakthrough that can create a quantum jump in output, such as the ones that followed the discovery of fertilizer or the hybridization of corn, the world is likely to be facing higher grain prices. The rise in world grain prices from 1993 to 1997, reversing a long-term trend of decline, may give us a picture of the future. If so, it could lead to instability in Third World cities on a scale that could disrupt global economic progress.[6]

We are already getting some glimpses of what may lie ahead. For example, in the summer of 1996, the government of Jordan—a country suffering from aquifer depletion, higher prices for imported wheat, and a scarcity of foreign exchange—was forced to eliminate its bread subsidy. The resulting bread riots lasted several days and threatened to bring down the government. In 1997, Pakistan—a country of roughly 140 million people—needed to double its wheat imports to 5 million tons but was unable to do so, having exhausted its line of credit. As a result, wheat prices rose and in April long lines formed at bread shops in Karachi, leading to political unrest and sporadic looting in the city.[7]

If the world economy as it is now structured continues to expand, it will eventually destroy its natural support systems and decline. Despite the inescapable logic of this decline-and-collapse scenario, we seem unable to limit our claims on the Earth to a sustainable level. Canadian ecologist William Rees talks about "a world addicted to growth, but in deep denial about the consequences."[8]

The good news is that we know what an environmentally sustainable economy would look like. We have the technologies needed to build such an economy. And we know that the key to getting from here to there lies in restructuring the tax system, decreasing personal and corporate income taxes while increasing taxes on environmentally destructive activities. The challenge is to convince enough people of the need to do this in order to make it happen.

A NEW ECONOMY

While ecologists have long known that the existing economic system is unsustainable, few economists share this knowledge. What kind of system would be ecologically sustainable? The answer is simple—a system whose structure respects the limits, the carrying capacity, of natural systems. A sustainable economy is one powered by renewable energy sources. It is also a reuse/recycle economy. In its structure, it emulates nature, where one organism's waste is another's sustenance.

The ecological principles of sustainability are well established, based on solid science. Just as an aircraft must satisfy the principles of aerodynamics if it is to fly, so must an economy satisfy the principles of ecology if it is to endure. The ecological conditions that need to be satisfied are rather straightforward. Over the long term, carbon emissions cannot exceed carbon dioxide (CO_2) fixation; soil erosion cannot exceed new soil formed through natural processes; the harvest of forest products cannot exceed the sustainable yield of forests; the number of plant and animal species lost cannot exceed the new species formed through evolution; water pumping cannot exceed the sustainable yield of aquifers; the fish catch cannot exceed the sustainable yield of fisheries.

Recognizing the limits of natural systems is often seen as a call for no growth, but the issue is not growth versus no growth. The question is, What kind of growth? And where? Growth based on the use of renewable energy may be able to continue for some time, while that based on fossil fuels is ultimately limited by remaining reserves, but more immediately by potentially unacceptable climate disruption. Similarly, a reuse/recycle economy can grow much larger than a throwaway economy without imposing excessive demands on the Earth's ecosystem. Growth in the information economy puts minimal pressure on the Earth's natural systems, especially compared with heavy industry, a common source of past growth. Within agriculture, huge growth is needed to satisfy future food needs in developing countries but not in industrial ones, where population has stabilized and where diets are already sated with livestock products.

Building such an economy means stabilizing population sooner rather than later and replacing the fossil-fuel-based economy with a solar/hydrogen energy economy. These two key steps—both

extraordinarily difficult undertakings—are discussed later in this chapter. If we can do both, many of the other problems the world faces will become manageable.

In mature industrial economies with stable populations, claims on the planet are leveling off. In the European Union (EU), for example, population has stabilized at 380 million. With high incomes, grain consumption per person has plateaued at around 470 kilograms a year. As a result, EU members, now consuming roughly 180 million tons of grain annually, have essentially stabilized their claims on the Earth's agricultural resources—the first region in the world to do so. (See Figure 10–1.) And, perhaps more important, the region has done this within the limits of its land and water resources, since it is a net exporter of grain.[9]

As noted earlier, one of the keys to an environmentally sustainable future is to convert the existing throwaway economy to a reuse/recycle economy, thus reducing the environmentally disruptive flow of raw materials from mines or forests to smelters and mills, as well as the vast one-way flow of discarded materials to landfills. With a reuse/recycle structure, mature industrial economies with stable

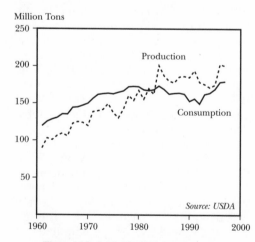

Figure 10–1. Grain Production and Consumption in the European Union, 1961–97

populations, such as those in Europe, can operate largely on the existing stock of steel, aluminum, glass, paper, and other materials already in the economy.

The huge material flows associated with industrialization can be reduced in developing economies if these countries go directly from the preindustrial to the postindustrial stage of development, leapfrogging the intermediate stage. For example, they can invest directly in cellular phones without spending money on millions of miles of telephone lines and poles. Instead of relying on the transportation system to carry a letter to a distant destination, modern technologies can send a facsimile halfway around the world using the global network of satellites. And with computerization, e-mail can replace the fax, eliminating the need even for paper. Similarly, if developing economies bypass the automobile stage of development, going directly to sophisticated public transportation and to bicycles, they can save huge amounts of materials and energy, while providing greater mobility.[10]

The transition from a throwaway economy to a reuse/recycle one is well under way. In the United States, where the steel industry is now dominated by electric-arc steel furnaces that feed on scrap metal, 55 percent of 1996 steel output was from scrap. Abandoned cars are melted down to produce soup cans. When these are discarded, they can be melted down to produce refrigerators. When they wear out, refrigerators can be used to produce automobiles. And so on. A steel industry feeding largely on scrap both minimizes the disruption associated with mining and transporting virgin ore and reduces energy use by some 60 percent.[11]

As industries move from using primarily virgin raw materials to using recycled materials, their geographic distribution changes. The U.S. steel industry, once concentrated in western Pennsylvania, where there was an abundance of both

iron ore and coal, is now spread throughout the states. Modern electric-arc minimills scattered across the country often feed entirely on locally available scrap metal to produce steel, and at the same time create local jobs and revenue flows.[12]

New Jersey has 13 paper mills that use only wastepaper and eight steel minimills that rely almost exclusively on scrap.

Similarly with paper. Instead of cutting trees, paper companies now negotiate long-term contracts with local communities to buy their scrap paper. In the United States, few if any recent paper mills have been built in the heavily forested northwest or in Maine. Instead, they are being built near heavily populated areas where paper use is concentrated. This shift to wastepaper helps bring demands on forests down toward a sustainable level.[13]

The small, densely populated state of New Jersey, for instance, has little forested area and no iron mines. Yet there are 13 paper mills that use only wastepaper and eight steel minimills that rely almost exclusively on scrap. Collectively, these paper plants and steel mills market more than $1 billion worth of products each year, providing both local jobs and hefty tax revenues.[14]

For communities considering whether to dispose of solid waste by recycling, incinerating, or landfilling, the employment advantages are obvious: for every 150,000 tons of waste, recycling creates nine jobs, incinerating creates two, and landfilling, just one. Within Europe, Germany has been a leader in reducing the amount of packaging used and in recycling packaging waste. In 1996, 80 percent of all packaging in Germany—

including glass, paper, plastic, tin plate, and aluminum, totalling some 5.3 million tons—was recycled, greatly reducing pressure on landfills.[15]

Another way to reduce waste is to redesign industrial economies to emulate nature so that one industry's waste becomes another's raw material, a science that is becoming known as industrial ecology. In the industrial zone of Kalundborg in Denmark, a network of materials and energy exchanges among companies has been formed. It involves a wide variety of linkages: the warm water from cooling a power plant is used by a company with fish farms; sludge from the fish farms is sold to a nearby farmer for fertilizer; the fly ash from a power plant is used as a raw material by a cement manufacturer; and surplus yeast from a pharmaceutical plant producing insulin is fed to pigs by local farmers.[16]

The result is a system that emulates nature—a win-win situation. Air pollution is down, water pollution is down, waste is down, and profits are up. A $60-million investment by participating firms in a transport infrastructure to facilitate the exchange of energy and materials has yielded $120 million in revenues and cost savings. At the international level, one effort to assess the potential of such systems is the Zero Emissions Research Initiative at the United Nations University, in Tokyo; it recently expanded into a $12-million research project at the University of Tokyo.[17]

In contrast to the wholesale restructuring of the energy economy needed to make it environmentally sustainable, what is needed in the world food economy is more a change in degree than in kind, partly because the principal transformation required to achieve an acceptable balance between food and people lies outside agriculture. Balancing the food supply/demand equation may now depend more on family planners than on fishers and farmers. Decisions made in ministries of energy about fossil fuel use

may have a greater effect on climate and therefore on the food security of the next generation than those made in ministries of agriculture.

But within agriculture, there are also major challenges. Building a sustainable food economy depends on protecting cropland both from soil erosion and from conversion to nonfarm uses. It also means using land and water more efficiently. On soil erosion, the United States is a leader, with the Conservation Reserve Program (CRP) launched in 1985. Among other things, the CRP promotes the conversion of highly erodible cropland into grassland, thus protecting its only sustainable use. Beyond this, U.S. farmers with excessive erosion on their land are denied the benefits of any government programs if they do not adopt conservation tillage practices that reduce losses of soil from erosion below the amount of new soil formed from natural processes.[18]

In a world of food scarcity, land use emerges as a central issue. Cropland is no longer a surplus commodity. Perhaps the best model of successful cropland protection is Japan, whose determination to protect its riceland with land-use zoning can be seen in the thousands of small rice plots within the city boundaries of Tokyo. By tenaciously protecting its riceland, the nation remains self-sufficient in its staple food. While Japan has relied heavily on zoning to protect cropland, a stiff tax on the conversion of cropland to nonfarm uses can also be highly effective in protecting the global cropland base. China is encouraging cremation of the dead rather than burial as it tries to save cropland. Viet Nam, like Japan, has turned to regulation, banning the construction of golf courses in order to protect its riceland.[19]

With little new land left to plow anywhere and with Asia sustaining heavy cropland losses as it industrializes, the need to raise land productivity is more pressing than ever. As yield per crop moves toward the physiological limits, further gains will come increasingly from raising the number of crops per year. The challenge to scientists is to breed crop varieties that mature earlier, permitting northern hemisphere countries, for example, to expand the double-cropping of a winter crop such as wheat or barley with a summer crop such as soybeans. Other changes, such as transplanting more crops from seedbeds into the field, shorten the field-growing season, as happens with most of Asia's rice, which is produced from transplanted seedlings.[20]

Aside from stabilizing population, the key to reducing the unsustainable demand on aquifers is to convert the existing systems that supply water to farmers, industries, and urban dwellers either at no cost or at a nominal cost into water markets where users pay the market price for water. Combined with special rates that protect minimum supplies for low-income consumers, water markets such as those now operating in California and Chile can help lower water demand to the sustainable yield of aquifers. Shifting to a market economy for water would automatically create a market for more water-efficient technologies, ranging from irrigation equipment to household appliances.[21]

Reducing water use to a sustainable level means boosting the efficiency with which it is used, emulating the achievements of Israel—the pacesetter in this field. Land productivity has long been a part of our vocabulary, something we measure in yield per hectare. But the term "water productivity" is rarely heard. Until it, too, becomes part of our everyday lexicon, water scarcity will cloud our future. In addition to using more-efficient irrigation techniques, cropping patterns can be adjusted, shifting toward more water-efficient crops as Egypt is doing in shifting land from rice to wheat.[22]

The efficiency of converting grain into animal protein—milk, meat, and eggs—can be enhanced by adopting modern feeding practices, including shifting to nutritionally balanced, formulated rations in developing countries and by everywhere shifting to the more grain-efficient livestock products. Most of the world's beef and mutton is produced with forage from rangeland that is not suitable for plowing. But once rangelands are fully used, as is now the case, then additional output can come only from feedlots. At this point, the ability of chickens to add a pound of body weight with only 2.2 pounds of feed gives them an advantage over cattle, which require some 7 pounds of feed per pound of weight gain. The expected shift from beef to poultry is already under way: poultry overtook beef in 1996. (See Figure 10–2.)[23]

If grain prices rise rapidly, the world's affluent will start eating less meat, but they are not likely to do so before prices threaten the survival of the world's urban poor. With little idled cropland remaining and the carryover stocks of grain at near-record lows, the grain fed to livestock is the only reserve that can be tapped in a world food emergency. The most efficient way of doing this is to levy a tax on the consumption of livestock products, offsetting it with an income tax cut. Such a step would not solve the food

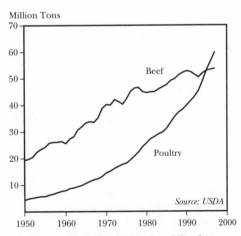

Figure 10–2. World Beef and Poultry Production, 1950–97

problem, but as a temporary measure it could help avoid politically destabilizing grain price rises, buying additional time to stabilize population. Public education programs on the adverse health effects of excessive consumption of fat-rich livestock products can also help people move down the food chain.

STABILIZING POPULATION

A sustainable society is a demographically stable one, but today's population is far from that point. The United Nations projects that over the next 50 years world population will reach 9.4 billion—3.6 billion more people than today. Since the population of the industrial world is expected to decline slightly during this period, these 3.6 billion people will be added to the developing world, where natural resources and social services are already in short supply. Even with only modest gains in nutrition, this addition will require a doubling of the world grain harvest and, for irrigation alone, a quantity of water equal to more than 20 Nile Rivers. It will also require hundreds of millions of new classrooms, homes, and jobs.[24]

Nearly 60 percent of the projected population growth is expected to occur in Asia, which will grow from 3.4 billion people in 1995 to more than 5.4 billion in 2050. By then, China's current population of 1.2 billion is expected to exceed 1.5 billion, while India's is projected to soar from 930 million to 1.53 billion. Over this same time period, the population of the Middle East and North Africa is likely to more than double, while that of sub-Saharan Africa will triple. By 2050, Nigeria alone is expected to have 339 million people—more than the entire continent of Africa had 35 years ago.[25]

Stabilizing population is an essential step in arresting the destruction of natur-

al resources and ensuring that the basic needs of all people are met. Thirty-three countries now have stable populations, including Japan and most of those in Europe. (Those with 10 million or more people are listed in Table 10–1.) These countries—representing 14 percent of world population—provide a solid base for a population stabilization effort. The sooner the remaining countries follow, the better the chance of stabilizing population at a level that the Earth can support.

A comparison of population trends in Bangladesh and Pakistan illustrates the importance of acting now. When Bangladesh was created in a split with Pakistan in 1971, its political leaders made a strong commitment to reduce fertility rates, while the leaders in Islamabad wavered over the need to do so. At that time, the population in each country was roughly 66 million. Today, however, Pakistan has roughly 140 million people, while Bangladesh has some 120 million.

Table 10–1. Sixteen Countries With Zero Population Growth, 1997

Country	Annual Rate of Natural Increase	Midyear Population
	(percent)	(million)
Belarus	-0.1	10.4
Belgium	0.1	10.2
Czech Republic	-0.1	10.3
France	0.2	58.6
Germany	-0.2	82.0
Greece	0.1	10.6
Hungary	-0.4	10.3
Italy	0	56.8
Japan	0.2	125.7
Netherlands	0.4	15.6
Poland	0.2	38.6
Romania	-0.3	22.5
Russia	-0.6	147.3
Spain	-0.1	39.1
Ukraine	-0.4	50.4
United Kingdom	0.2	57.6

SOURCE: U.S. Bureau of the Census, *International Data Base*, electronic database, Suitland, MD, 10 October 1997.

By putting family planning programs in place sooner rather than later, Bangladesh not only avoided the addition of nearly 20 million people during this 25-year period, it is projected to have 50 million fewer people than Pakistan does in 2050. (See Figure 10–3.)[26]

The world now faces a similar choice. The United Nation projects that the number of people on the Earth could reach anywhere from 7.7 billion to 11.1 billion by 2050. Ultimately, the future size of the population will depend on actions that are taken or not taken today.[27]

The first step in stabilizing population is to remove the physical and social barriers that prevent women from using family planning services. Approximately one third of projected world population growth will be due to unwanted pregnancies that occur because couples still do not have access to the family planning services they desire, according to John Bongaarts of the Population Council. Worldwide, more than 120 million married women, and many more unmarried sexually active adults and teens, fall into this category.[28]

There are several reasons why couples are not planning their families despite their desire for fewer children. In many countries such as Saudi Arabia and Argentina, government policies restrict access to contraceptives. Geographic accessibility also affects use; in some rural areas of sub-Saharan Africa, it can take two hours or more to reach the nearest contraceptive provider. Furthermore, family planning services can be expensive, many couples lack health care to cover services, and family planning clinics are often underfunded—leaving them short of supplies or understaffed.[29]

Women who want fewer children may also be constrained from using family planning by a lack of knowledge, prevailing cultural and religious values, or the disapproval of family members. In Pakistan, for example, 43 percent of husbands object to family planning. Moreover, as recently as 1989 some 14 countries required a woman to obtain her husband's consent before she could receive any contraceptive services, while 60 required spousal authorization for permanent methods. Although it has been argued that these practices lessen conflicts between spouses and health care personnel, they are serious impediments to a woman's ability to control her fertility.[30]

Information about contraceptives and family planning for young men and women also facilitates the use of birth control. In Thailand, people of all ages have been educated on the importance of family planning. Mechai Viravidaiya, the charismatic founder of the Thai Population and Community Development Association (PCDA), encouraged familiarity with contraceptives through demonstrations, ads, and witty songs. Math teachers even use population-related examples in their classes. As a result of the efforts of Mechai, the PCDA, and the government, the growth of Thailand's population has slowed from more than 3 percent in 1960 to approximately 1 percent today—the

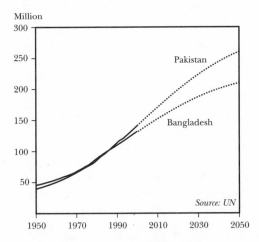

Million

Figure 10–3. Population of Pakistan and Bangladesh, 1950–97, With Projections to 2050

same as in the United States.[31]

Access to family planning services, however, will not by itself stabilize population growth. Even if services were available to all who desired them, the population is still expected to increase by some 2.3 billion over the next 50 years. One reason for this is that many couples choose to have large families. John Bongaarts projects that reducing the demand for large families by addressing the underlying social factors that create it could bring population growth in developing countries down another 18 percent. Changing desired family size is of course more difficult for governments to accomplish.[32]

Rapid economic growth is not a prerequisite for reduced fertility rates.

In many developing countries, having lots of children is a matter of survival: children are a vital part of the family economy and a source of security in old age. Institutions such as the Grameen Bank, which specializes in microenterprise loans, are attempting to change this situation by providing credit to well over a million villagers—mostly impoverished women—throughout Bangladesh and other countries. These loans are empowering women, helping to end the cycle of poverty, and thus reducing the need for large families.[33]

Although alleviating poverty is an important goal, rapid economic growth is not a prerequisite for reduced fertility rates. Bangladesh has reduced fertility rates from nearly 7 children per woman in the early 1970s to 3.3 children per woman today despite incomes averaging only around $200 a year. In the struggle to slow population growth, access to family planning services, solid government leadership, and improvement in social conditions are proving to be more important than the growth of a nation's economy.[34]

Reducing infant and child mortality will give parents the confidence to have fewer children. In situations where many children die young, parents often have more children than they want to ensure that some will survive. Children born less than a year and a half apart are twice as likely to die as those born two or more years apart. Educating couples about birth spacing, increasing child immunizations, and improving health care can reduce child mortality.[35]

Education also reduces family size. The education of women in places like the south Indian state of Kerala has given women options beyond childbearing, as well as an alternative source of future security. Furthermore, requiring school attendance for all children lowers their use as laborers while accelerating cultural change. And finally, publicized studies on local carrying capacities and campaigns to raise awareness can help individuals understand the need for smaller families and make the idea of two-child families familiar and acceptable.[36]

Yet even if each couple were to have only two children, population would continue to grow due to the sheer number of young women reaching reproductive age. This third force—called population momentum—accounts for nearly half of projected population growth. It can be lowered by policies that encourage women to delay childbearing, which stretches the time between generations. Delaying childbearing by 2.5 years would reduce population growth by maybe 10 percent over the next 50 years, while delaying it by 5 years would reduce it by perhaps 21 percent.[37]

Raising the legal age of marriage, as Tunisia and China have done, delays childbearing. But policies that educate and empower women have the same result, and are ultimately more effective.

The longer girls stay in school, the later they marry and the later they start bearing children. In 23 developing countries, for instance, women with a secondary education married on average four years later than those with no education.[38]

Slowly, governments are realizing the value of investing in population stabilization. One study found that the government of Bangladesh spends $62 to prevent a birth, but saves $615 on social services expenditures for each birth averted—a 10-fold return on investment. Based on the study's estimate, the program prevents 890,000 births annually. The net savings to the government totals $547 million each year, leaving more to invest in education and health care.[39]

At the 1994 International Conference on Population and Development in Cairo, the governments of the world agreed to a 20-year population and reproductive health program. The United Nations estimates that $17 billion a year will be needed for this effort by 2000 and $21.7 billion by 2015. (In both cases, this is less than is spent every two weeks on military expenditures.) Developing countries and countries in transition have agreed to cover two thirds of the price tag, while donor countries have promised to pay the rest—$5.7 billion a year by 2000 and $7.2 billion by 2015.[40]

Unfortunately, while developing countries are on track with their part of the expenditures, donor countries are not. A recent U.N. Population Fund study reports that the assistance of bilateral donors, multilateral agencies and banks, and charitable foundations amounted to only $2 billion in 1995. Although donors' contributions in 1995 were 24 percent more than in 1994, preliminary estimates indicate that contributions declined some 18 percent in 1996. And it is likely that funding levels in 1997 declined even further.[41]

As a result of donor shortfalls following the Cairo conference, the United Nations estimates that an additional 122 million unintended pregnancies will occur by 2000. A little over a third of these unwanted pregnancies will be aborted, and more than half will be considered unintended births. Moreover, an additional 65,000 women will die in childbirth and 844,000 million will suffer chronic or permanent injury from their pregnancies.[42]

Yet "global population problems cannot be put on hold while countries reform their health care, rebuild their inner cities, and reduce...budget deficit[s]. Avoiding another world population doubling...requires rapid action," notes Sharon Camp, former Vice President of Population Action International. The difference between acting today and putting it off until tomorrow is the difference between a world in which population stabilizes at a level the Earth might be able to support and one where it expands until environmental deterioration disrupts economic progress.[43]

STABILIZING CLIMATE

Evidence that the Earth is getting warmer is building with each passing year. In the 132 years since recordkeeping began in 1866, the 13 warmest years have occurred since 1979. (See Figure 1–4 in Chapter 1.) Concern about the effects of climate change comes from many quarters. Aside from the reports of environmental scientists, the global insurance industry—faced with a dramatic surge in weather-related insurance claims—is worried about the increasing intensity and destructiveness of storms. Another source of concern comes from the possible effect on food security, since agriculture is keyed to a climate system that has been remarkably stable over the 10,000 years since farming began.[44]

Stabilizing climate depends on reestablishing a balance between carbon emissions and nature's capacity to absorb CO_2. There are two principal ways to do this: use energy more efficiently and replace fossil fuels with noncarbon energy sources. Although impressive gains have been made in raising energy efficiency since the oil price shocks of the 1970s, there is still a vast potential for raising it further.

One way to boost the energy efficiency of the global economy is, as noted earlier, to shift from a throw-away economy to a reuse/recycle economy. Another obvious area that needs improvement is the energy-intensive automobile-centered transportation systems of industrial societies, which are extraordinarily inefficient not only in energy use, but in the congestion they produce, which leads to an inefficient use of labor as well. In congested London today, average automobile speed is similar to that of the horse drawn carriages of a century ago. In Bangkok, the typical motorist now spends the equivalent of 44 working days a year sitting in traffic jams.[45]

Two indicators of the human desire for mobility are the sales of bicycles and cars. In 1969, world manufacture of bicycles totaled 25 million and that of automobiles was 23 million. The production of cars, expanding rapidly, was on the verge of overtaking bicycles. But then rising environmental awareness, as evidenced in the first Earth Day in 1970, and the 1973 oil price shock each boosted bicycle production relative to that of automobiles. By 1980, some 62 million bicycles were manufactured compared with 29 million automobiles, an edge of two to one.[46]

A third surge came following the 1978 economic reforms in China as rapidly rising incomes boosted the number of people who could afford bicycles. As bicycle ownership surged in China, so did their production, pushing world output to 105 million in 1988. In 1995, bicycle manufacturing totaled 109 million, compared with 36 million automobiles, an advantage of

three to one. (See Figure 10–4.) Many cities, from Amsterdam to Lima, are now actively encouraging the use of bicycles. In the United Kingdom, the government hopes to double 1996 bicycle use by 2002 and then double it again by 2012.[47]

The original attraction of the automobile was its promise of unlimited mobility, something it could deliver when societies were largely rural. But in an urbanized world, there is an inherent incompatibility between the automobile and the city—witness the air pollution, traffic congestion, and urban sprawl now facing the world's cities. In addition, the segment of global society that can afford to buy and operate an automobile is likely to remain small.

The only reasonable alternative to the automobile in urban settings is a combination of state-of-the-art rail passenger-transport systems augmented by other forms of public transportation and bicycles. Whether the goal is mobility, breathable air, the protection of cropland, limits on congestion, or stabilization of climate, the automobile is not the answer. Indeed, these criteria suggest that the bicycle is the transport vehicle of the future. The sooner governments realize that the worldwide dream of a car in every garage

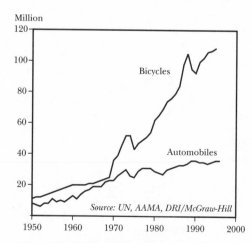

Figure 10–4. World Bicycle and Automobile Production, 1950–96

is not realistic, the sooner they can get on with building transportation systems that will provide the desired mobility and are environmentally sustainable.

There are many new technologies for raising energy efficiency. One of the most effective is the compact fluorescent light bulb, which provides the same illumination as a traditional incandescent bulb but uses only a fourth as much electricity. Compact fluorescent bulbs in use in 1995 saved the electricity equivalent of the output of 28 large, coal-fired power plants. Although the compact fluorescents cost 10 times as much as incandescents, investing in them is highly profitable because they last much longer and use so little electricity. Worldwide manufacture has increased from 45 million in 1988 to 240 million in 1995. (See Figure 10–5.) Encouragingly, China has moved to the forefront in the manufacture of these bulbs, relying on them to reduce the need for building coal-fired power plants.[48]

Historically, the world has relied on two sources of renewable energy, firewood and hydropower. Firewood continues to provide cooking fuel for perhaps 2 billion people, most of whom live in Third World villages and cities, while hydropower supplies one fifth of the world's electricity. Future growth in renewables, however, is likely to come from other sources, notably wind power, photovoltaic cells, and solar thermal power plants. Installed wind electric generating capacity worldwide exceeded 7,600 megawatts by 1997. (See Figure 10–6.) In California, wind farms in Altamont Pass east of San Francisco, in the Tehachapi Pass, and in the desert near Palm Springs now generate enough electricity to satisfy the residential needs of San Francisco.[49]

An inventory of U.S. wind resources by the Department of Energy indicates a vast national potential, with three wind-rich states alone—North Dakota, South Dakota, and Texas—having enough harnessable wind energy to satisfy national electricity needs. A similar inventory in China indicates that the nation could easily double its current electricity generation by harnessing wind energy.[50]

Early leadership in the harnessing of wind energy came from the United States and Denmark. More recently, Germany and India, both rapidly growing wind powers, have forged into the lead. Tomen, a Japanese firm, plans to invest $1.2 billion

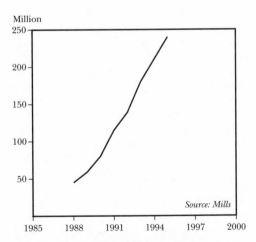

Figure 10–5. Sales of Compact Fluorescent Bulbs Worldwide, 1988–95

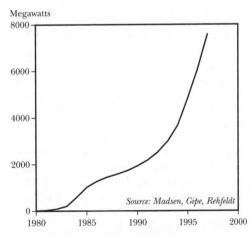

Figure 10–6. World Wind Energy Generating Capacity, 1980–97

in the installation of 1,000 large wind turbines in Europe over the next five years. The world's fastest-growing energy source during the 1990s, wind generation is expanding by 25 percent a year. With the cost continuing to decline as technologies advance and as the scale of turbine manufacturing increases, wind promises to become a major power source.[51]

Taxing environmentally destructive activities both raises revenue and is socially constructive.

A second highly promising source of electricity is the photovoltaic cell. This silicon-based technology, which found its first commercial use as the energy source for satellites and space stations, has since become economical for remote sites, including in secluded vacation homes in industrial countries or in remote Third World villages. In many developing countries faced with the cost of both building a centralized power plant and constructing a grid to deliver the electricity from it, it is now cheaper to install photovoltaic cells for individual households. At the end of 1996, some 400,000 homes, mostly in villages, were getting their electricity from photovoltaic cells.[52]

The latest advance, a photovoltaic roofing material, is becoming competitive in buildings already linked to a grid. Japan, a leader in solar cell manufacturing, has announced plans to install 4,600 megawatts of rooftop generating capacity by 2010, an amount equal to the generating capacity of Chile. The United States and several European countries are expected to follow soon with similarly ambitious programs. With this technology, the roof in effect becomes the power plant for the building. In Germany and Switzerland, new office buildings are incorporating

photovoltaic cells into the windows in their south-facing facades. A two-way metering system with the local utility enables building owners to sell electricity to the utility when generation is excessive and to buy it back when generation is not sufficient.[53]

As the cost of electricity generated from wind and other renewable sources falls, it will become economical to electrolyze water to produce hydrogen, thus providing a way to both store and transport wind and solar energy. Electricity and hydrogen can together provide energy in all the forms needed to operate a modern economy, whether it be powering computers, fueling cars, or manufacturing steel.

As the energy revolution gains momentum, some of the largest gas and oil companies are beginning to support it. Enron, originally a large Texas-based natural gas company, has made a strong move in the renewables field with its acquisition of Zond, the largest wind power company in the United States, and its investment in Solarex, the second largest U.S. manufacturer of photovoltaic cells.[54]

British Petroleum and Royal Dutch Shell are also investing in renewable energy resources. For example, British Petroleum has announced a major commitment to renewable energy, starting with construction of a $20-million solar-cell manufacturing facility in California. Shell plans to invest more than $500 million in solar cells and sustainable forestry plantations in developing countries to fuel local power plants. Bechtel, one of the world's largest construction firms and a traditional builder of hydroelectric dams and nuclear power plants, is now investing in a jointly owned company to develop decentralized energy sources, including solar and wind. Some governments and some corporations continue to resist the energy revolution, but the question is not whether there will be a revolution, only how rapidly it will unfold.[55]

The transition from a fossil-fuel-based

energy economy to a high-efficiency, solar/hydrogen energy economy provides enormous investment and employment opportunities. This energy transition is not something that may happen; it is happening. We can see glimpses of the new climate-stabilizing energy economy in the wind farms in California, the bicycles in Amsterdam, photovoltaic arrays in Third World villages, compact fluorescent light bulbs in China, and photovoltaic rooftops in Japan.

STEERING WITH TAX POLICY

Once we determine what an environmentally sustainable economy would look like, then we have to determine how to build it, how to get from here to there. Staggering though this challenge is, we have a policy instrument, largely unused, for building an environmentally sustainable economy—namely tax policy. Governments now rely heavily on personal and corporate income taxes for revenue, but these discourage constructive activities, such as work and savings. Meanwhile, taxes on environmentally destructive activities are typically negligible or nonexistent. The challenge is to restructure the existing tax system, a relic from an earlier age, decreasing the taxes on such constructive activities as work and savings and increasing the taxes on destructive activities, such as carbon emissions or the generation of toxic waste.

One reason for today's environmental problems is that the market does not tell the truth. The full cost of many economic activities is not borne by the beneficiary. For example, the motorists who pollute the air do not necessarily pay the bills for the resulting health care costs of respiratory illnesses. The countries primarily responsible for the buildup in atmospheric CO_2 levels are not necessarily those that will be most directly affected by climate change. The forest products firms that clear-cut do not bear the costs of the resulting destruction of fisheries associated with the silting of streams.

Among the more environmentally destructive economic activities that deserve to be taxed are carbon and sulfur dioxide emissions, the generation of toxic waste, the use of virgin raw materials, and the use of pesticides. Taxing these destructive activities simultaneously discourages them and indirectly encourages sustainable ways of satisfying our needs. For example, a tax on virgin raw materials encourages the use of recycling.

Governments tax income because it is an easy way to raise revenue, not because it serves any particular social goal other than redistributing income. Taxing environmentally destructive activities both raises revenue and is socially constructive. Shifting part of the tax burden has progressed the furthest in Europe. (See Table 10–2.) The leaders in the use of tax policy to build an environmentally sustainable economy are Denmark, the Netherlands, and Sweden. In most cases, income taxes were reduced as taxes on environmentally destructive activities were increased. Tax data for the Netherlands indicate that by 1993, 5.1 percent of its revenue came from environmental taxes, excluding carbon and gasoline taxes. Denmark was close behind, with 4 percent.[56]

There is little doubt about the effectiveness of environmental taxes. When Malaysia, for example, adjusted its gasoline taxes so that it cost more to use leaded than unleaded fuel, the shift to unleaded gasoline quickly followed. A tax on the generation of toxic waste in Germany reduced it by 15 percent in three years. In the Netherlands, an early leader in the field, a tax on the emissions of heavy metals, such as lead, mercury, and cadmium, was highly successful, reducing emissions of these metals by roughly 90 percent over two decades.[57]

Table 10–2. Tax Shifts from Work and Investment to Environmentally Damaging Activities

Country, Year Initiated	Taxes Cut On	Taxes Raised On	Revenue Shifted[1]
Sweden, 1991	Personal income	Carbon and sulfur emissions	1.9
Denmark, 1994	Personal income	Motor fuel, coal, electricity, and water sales; waste incineration and landfilling; motor vehicle ownership	2.5
Spain, 1995	Wages	Motor fuel sales	0.2
Denmark, 1996	Wages, agricultural property	Carbon emissions; pesticides, chlorinated solvents, and battery sales	0.5
Netherlands, 1996	Personal income and wages	Natural gas and electricity sales	0.8
United Kingdom, 1996–97	Wages	Landfilling	0.2

[1]Expressed relative to tax revenue raised by all levels of government.
SOURCE: See endnote 56.

The Swedish Society for the Conservation of Nature has recommended a new tax plan to the government that includes taxes on carbon emissions, nuclear power generation, electricity generation, diesel fuel, gasoline, nitrogen oxide emissions, and sulfur emissions, while cutting taxes on wages. This shift makes labor less costly and natural resources more costly. Since labor is abundant to the point of being excessive, while natural resources are scarce, the group argues that this win/win situation is the only logical way for Swedish society to proceed. As payroll taxes are reduced, labor becomes less costly, making it cheaper for companies to create jobs, thus favoring the use of labor over capital, an advantage that has elicited the support of organized labor.[58]

Not only are we not taxing many environmentally destructive activities, some of these efforts are actually being subsidized. More than $600 billion a year of taxpayers' money is spent by governments to subsidize deforestation, overfishing, the burning of fossil fuels, the use of virgin raw materials, and other environmentally destructive activities. Governmental subsidies for fishing have boosted the capacity of the world's fishing fleet to twice the sustainable yield of oceanic fisheries. (See Chapter 4.) Eliminating these subsidies would not only reduce income taxes, it would also reduce environmental destruction. As an analysis of subsidies by the Earth Council noted, "There's something unbelievable about the world spending hundreds of billions of dollars annually to subsidize its own destruction."[59]

Using tax policy to steer the economy in an environmentally sustainable direction takes advantage of the inherent efficiency of the market. In addition, taxes can be phased in over time in a systematic, predictable manner, enabling corporations making investment decisions or consumers making purchases to take scheduled tax changes into account.

Polls indicate that 70 percent of Europeans and North Americans support tax shifting. Once explained, this initiative makes sense. It also brings with it the excitement of building an economic system for the next generation that will be environmentally sustainable rather than one that is slowly destroying itself.[60]

CROSSING POLITICAL THRESHOLDS

Now that we know what an environmentally sustainable economy would look like, do we want it badly enough to make the needed changes? Do we have the political will needed to create a sustainable economy? Do we care enough about the next generation to take the steps now to move off the path of environmental deterioration and eventual economic decline and social disintegration?

The gap between what we need to do to reverse the degradation of the planet and what we are doing widens with each passing year. How do we cross the threshold of political change that will shrink this gap, reversing the trends of environmental degradation that are undermining the economy? Most environment ministers understand that we are headed for economic decline, but there is not yet enough political support to overcome the vested interests that oppose changes.

In a landmark 1997 book, Ross Gelbspan, an investigative reporter for the *Boston Globe*, documents the efforts of these vested interests to protect the status quo. He chronicles a disinformation campaign on global warming that is funded by coal and oil interests, ranging from U.S. coal mining firms to the government of Kuwait. He lists grants provided by fossil-fuel interests to a few scientists who regularly issue statements challenging the global warming hypothesis and creating confusion in the public mind. This technique of using "hired guns" is reminiscent of the tobacco industry's earlier use of medical experts to deny the relationship between cigarette smoking and lung can-

cer, a practice they have now abandoned.[61]

Mustering the needed political support is hampered by the difficulty in understanding the complex interactions among three distinct systems: the ecosystem, the economic system, and the political system. Analyzing any one of these is difficult enough, but understanding the ongoing interaction among the three is infinitely more complex, thoroughly challenging our intellectual capacities. Although there are reasonably good computer models for the global economy, there are none that simulate the behavior of the Earth's ecosystem or the global political system. For the ecosystem, modeling just the climate segment taxes our abilities.

The challenge is how to cross political thresholds—how to raise awareness and understanding to a level that will support the needed change. We change our behavior as the result of new information, new experiences, or some combination of the two. If information does not bring about change when it is needed, then suffering the consequences of failing to act may bring change if it is not too late. After World War I, for instance, many people were convinced of the need for the League of Nations. U.S. President Woodrow Wilson was one of the most ardent supporters, but he could not convince the U.S. Congress to support it. It took another war, unprecedented human suffering, and the loss of some 40 million lives to convince the world, including the U.S. Congress, that such an organization was indeed needed.

Public concern about environmental deterioration is reflected in the formation of thousands of environmental groups, many of them small, local, single-issue groups, such as those organized to oppose construction of a nuclear power plant in Niigata Prefecture in Japan or the burning off of the Amazonian rainforest by cattle ranchers. Others operate at the national level on a broad range of environmental issues, such as the Korean Federation for Environmental Movement, a group with a full-time membership of 36,000 and a staff of 60. And some go on to become prominent at the international level, such as Greenpeace, the World Wide Fund for Nature, and Friends of the Earth. Some of the larger U.S. environmental membership groups, including the National Wildlife Federation, have budgets that rival that of the U.N. Environment Programme. Even much of the research that underpins environmental policymaking comes from nongovernmental environmental research institutes. In few areas of public policy do nongovernmental organizations play such a prominent role.[62]

Many countries have crossed key sustainability thresholds on basic environmental issues based on new information. One of the best known is China's effort to stabilize the size of its population before its growing demands overwhelmed the carrying capacity of its life-support systems. When Chinese leaders undertook a series of population and resource projections during the early post-Mao era, they discovered that even if they moved to a two-child family they were faced with the addition to their already huge population of as many people as then lived in India. They realized there simply was not enough land and water to provide adequate diets for such an increase. And they decided to press for a one-child family, an action for which they have been widely criticized. Yet the criticism should not be for adopting this program, but for the delay in facing the population issue until there was no rational alternative but to press for a one-child family, and for the way the program was administered.[63]

Another example of how information can change behavior is found in the United States, where tens of millions of people have quit smoking over the last 35 years. This massive shift in social behavior was the result of a continuous flow of information that was launched in 1963 with the first Surgeon General's report on smoking and health. Every year since then, this report has been updated, triggering literally thousands of research projects on smoking and health, the findings of which are covered regularly by the news media. The result was a steady rise in public understanding of the effect of cigarette smoke, both direct and passive, on health—and a widespread decline in smoking.[64]

With the big steps that are still needed—stabilizing population and stabilizing climate—some countries have crossed the thresholds, others have not. Some have policies to stabilize their populations; others do not even recognize the need to do so. Some countries are pushing for heavy cuts in carbon emissions; others refuse even to consider doing so.

A reduction in carbon emissions is supported by some segments of the global community, but the support is not yet strong enough to bring about a major reorientation of energy policy. (See Chapter 7.) Will we respond to the information on the threat posed by global warming, or will we delay until we are shocked into action by the result of failing to do so—possibly by crop-withering heat waves that abruptly reduce the world grain harvest, creating chaos in world grain markets? The mainstream scientific community, as represented by the 2,500 scientists on the Intergovernmental Panel for Climate Change, is quite clear on the need to reduce carbon emissions. The Alliance of Small Island States, a group of some 36 island countries that feel particularly vulnerable to rising sea levels and more powerful storms, is also actively pressing for a reduction in global carbon emissions.[65]

Another major challenge to the existing industrial development model is coming from the insurance industry. Shaken by an increase in weather-related insurance claims from $17 billion during the

1980s to $66 billion thus far during the 1990s, the insurance industry is urging a reduction in carbon emissions—in effect, a reduction in the use of fossil fuels. Some 60 of the world's leading insurance companies have signed a statement urging governments to move in this direction, marking perhaps the first time in history that one major industry has pressured governments to reduce the output of another major industry.[66]

Within the fossil fuel industry itself, as noted earlier, some companies such as Enron, British Petroleum, and Royal Dutch Shell are already looking to the future, and beginning to invest in alternative energy sources. Enron's chairman, Ken Lay, who publicly discusses the need to reduce carbon emissions and to stabilize climate, sees Enron at the heart of the transition from fossil fuels to renewable energy sources. The infrastructure it has built to store and distribute natural gas can one day be used for hydrogen as the solar/hydrogen economy unfolds.[67]

In an important speech at Stanford University in May 1997, British Petroleum's CEO, John Browne, said, "The time to consider the policy dimensions of climate change is not when the link between greenhouse gases and climate change is conclusively proven, but when the possibility can ⸱ be discounted and is taken seriously ᴅʏ the society of which we are a part. We in BP have reached that point." This was a big jump for big oil.[68]

Realization that the existing fossil-fuel-based industrial development model that evolved in the West and Japan is not viable for the entire world is beginning to emerge in some unexpected quarters. For example, as noted in Chapter 1, a group of eminent scientists in China, many of them in the National Academy of Sciences, challenged the government's decision to develop an automobile-centered transportation system in a white paper, arguing that their country did not have enough land both to accommodate

the automobile and to feed its people. Beyond that, they noted the problems of a growing dependence on imported oil, traffic congestion, and air pollution.[69]

A few other corporate leaders are also beginning to grasp this new reality. Among this new breed of corporate CEOs is Robert Shapiro of Monsanto, who puts it simply: "The whole system has to change." Hiroyuki Fujimura, the head of EBARA, a large Japanese corporation involved in water cleaning and purification, is equally blunt. He argues that the only acceptable way to keep water safe for human use is not to pollute it in the first place. Firms such as his that install end-of-the-pipe cleanup technologies are losing the battle to provide safe water as their efforts to purify water are overwhelmed by countless thousands of dangerous compounds being released into the environment. The only viable alternative, Fujimura says, is redesigning the economy.[70]

Within the fossil fuel industry, some companies are beginning to invest in alternative energy sources.

Shapiro has gone further than perhaps any other CEO in developing a strategic plan by asking, What will an environmentally sustainable economy look like and how can Monsanto use its resources to help get from here to there? In this vein, Monsanto has sold off its pesticides division, choosing to focus on the use of genetic engineering to breed pest-resistant crop varieties. Shapiro sees the encrypting of genetic information in crops to enable them to resist insects and diseases as being part of the information revolution. He believes this is less of a threat than that posed by pesticides as the world tries to double world food output over the next several decades. Further,

Shapiro believes that corporations that do not chart their course by the vision of an environmentally sustainable future will become obsolete and disappear.[71]

Among corporations, there will be winners and there will be losers. Farsighted, well-managed firms will anticipate the opportunities and exploit them. The same is true of countries. Some have crossed the political threshold and are working hard to create an environmentally sustainable economic system. Others actively oppose it. The two extremes can be seen in Denmark and Saudi Arabia. On the big issues of stabilizing population, stabilizing climate, and ensuring future food supplies, Denmark is well positioned. It has stabilized its population at just over 5 million and it has done so within the limits of its food-producing capacity. On the energy front, although it ranks high in carbon emissions per person, it has recently refused to license the construction of coal-fired power plants and is investing heavily in wind power, which now supplies 5 percent of its electricity.[72]

It is time for corporate leaders to recognize that they are responsible for more than just the short-term bottom line.

In contrast, Saudi Arabia still has not recognized the threat posed by its population growth of 3 percent a year, a rate that will ensure a 20-fold increase over the next century. Ideally positioned to benefit from the fossil fuel age, it refuses to recognize global warming as a threat, and at international gatherings the Saudis actively oppose meaningful efforts to reduce carbon emissions. Just as Denmark is well endowed with wind energy, so is Saudi Arabia richly endowed with solar energy, but it is doing little to exploit this envi-ronmentally benign energy source.[73]

If we care about the next generation, then we have little choice but to launch a full-court press to stabilize population as soon as possible everywhere. The difference between an all-out effort now and a continuation of business-as-usual could be the difference between a population that will stabilize around 8 billion and one that will approach 11 billion—the difference, in other words, between adding 2 billion and 5 billion more people. We need to do this not because it is easy or necessarily popular, but because future political stability and economic progress may depend on it.[74]

In a world where the pressures on deteriorating natural support systems continue to build, business-as-usual is not likely to continue much longer. Reversing the trends that are undermining our future depends on a massive mobilization of resources, one comparable to that associated with World War II. The educational effort needed to support change on this scale requires the dissemination of a vast amount of information, which can only be led by national governments.

During the Depression Decade of the 1930s, an earlier time of crisis, U.S. President Franklin Roosevelt launched the "Fireside Chats" over nationwide radio as he worked to restore confidence in the country's future. In September 1997, as the Clinton White House also recognized the need to better inform the American people on climate change and to counter industry's disinformation campaign, it began organizing special media events. One was a White House press conference featuring six of the country's leading scientists addressing the various dimensions of the climate change issue. And in another effort to reach the public, the Clinton White House organized a briefing on climate change for television weather forecasters. The goal was to help them better understand climate change so they could report daily weather events not as isolated matters but in a broader context. In this way, they can help the public better understand the reason for record-high temperatures, more destructive storms, or more intense droughts.[75]

All the major news organizations bear a responsibility for helping people understand that business-as-usual is no longer a viable strategy, that sustaining the technological and social progress that has been a hallmark of human civilization now depends urgently on changes in policies and priorities. One defining characteristic of a civilized society is a sense of responsibility to the next generation. If we do not assume that responsibility, environmental deterioration leading to economic decline and social disintegration could threaten the survival of civilization as we know it.[76]

Although governments must lead this effort, only the global communications media—print and electronic—can disseminate the needed information in the time available. This puts a heavy burden on such electronic giants as the British Broadcasting Corporation, Voice of America, and Cable News Network (CNN) as well as on wire services, such as the Associated Press and Reuters, and the leading weekly news magazines, such as *Time, Newsweek,* and the *Economist.* While heads of the world's major news organizations may not have sought this responsibility, only they have the tools to disseminate the information needed to fuel change on the scale required and in the time available.

The need today is for leadership—and not just for marginal, incremental change, but for a boldness of leadership of the caliber demonstrated by Ted Turner, founder of the Turner Broadcasting System and CNN, when he announced in September 1997 that he would be giving $1 billion to the United Nations over the next 10 years to be spent on population, environment, and humanitarian relief programs. His gift reflected a deep concern with our failure to address the great challenges of our time effectively, the need for a global approach to the key issues facing humanity, and the futility of endlessly accumulating wealth to be passed on to the next generation while leaving them a planet so degraded that their world would be declining economically and disintegrating socially. One of Turner's goals is to encourage other billionaires not merely to be more charitable, but also to respond to the great issues of our day.[77]

If ever there was a need for leadership, it is now. It is time for corporate leaders to step forward, recognizing that they are responsible for more than just the short-term bottom line, that they can help keep the dream of a better life alive. While it is true that "the business of business is business," it is also true that corporations have a stake in building an economy in which economic progress can continue.

In a world of resource scarcity, political leadership is the scarcest of all. History judges political leaders by whether or not they respond to the great issues of their time. For Lincoln, the challenge was to free the slaves. For Churchill, it was to turn the tide of war in Europe. For Nelson Mandela, it was to end apartheid. For Bill Clinton, the challenge is to build a new economy.

Notes

Chapter 1. The Future of Growth

1. International Monetary Fund (IMF), *World Economic Outlook, May 1997* (Washington, DC: 1997); Gerard Baker, "World's Future Is Rosy Says IMF," *Financial Times*, 24 April 1997.

2. Herbert R. Block, *The Planetary Product in 1980: A Creative Pause?* (Washington, DC: U.S. Department of State, 1981); IMF, op. cit. note 1; United Nations, *World Population Prospects: The 1996 Revision* (New York: forthcoming); U.N. Development Programme (UNDP), *Human Development Report 1997* (New York: Oxford University Press, 1997).

3. IMF, *World Economic Outlook, October 1997* (Washington, DC: 1997).

4. U.N. Food and Agriculture Organization (FAO), *Forest Products Yearbook* (Rome: various years); FAO, *Yearbook of Fishery Statistics: Catches and Landings* (Rome: various years); U.S. Department of Agriculture (USDA), *Production, Supply, and Distribution*, electronic database, Washington, DC, updated May 1997; United Nations, *Energy Statistics Yearbook* (New York: various years).

5. James R. Hepworth and Gregory McNamee, eds., *Resist Much, Obey Little—Remembering Ed Abbey* (San Francisco, CA: Sierra Club Books, 1996).

6. FAO, *Forest Products Yearbook*, op. cit. note 4; FAO, *State of the World's Forests 1997* (Oxford, U.K.: 1997).

7. Maurizio Perotti, fishery statistician, Fishery Information, Data and Statistics Unit, FAO, Rome, e-mail message to Anne Platt McGinn, Worldwatch Institute, 14 October 1997; FAO, *Yearbook of Fishery Statistics*, op. cit. note 4.

8. FAO, *Yearbook of Fishery Statistics*, op. cit. note 4; United Nations, op. cit. note 2.

9. Caroline Southey, "EU Puts New Curbs on Fishing," *Financial Times*, 16 April 1997.

10. Sandra Postel, *Last Oasis*, rev. ed. (New York: W.W. Norton & Company, 1997); I.A. Shiklomanov, "Global Water Resources," *Nature & Resources*, vol. 26, no. 3 (1990).

11. USDA, Natural Resources Conservation Service, *Summary Report: 1992 National Resources Inventory*, rev. ed. (Washington, DC: January 1995); Sandra Postel, "Forging a Sustainable Water Strategy," in Lester R. Brown et al., *State of the World 1996* (New York: W.W. Norton & Company, 1996); Postel, op. cit. note 10.

12. United Nations, op. cit. note 2; USDA, op. cit. note 4; Charles J. Hanley, "Saudi Arabia Farming Sucks the Country Dry," Associated Press, 29 March 1997.

13. Figure 1–1 from USDA, op. cit. note 4.

14. USDA, op. cit. note 4; United Nations, op. cit. note 2; Engineering Research Institute quoted in Patralekha Chatterjee, "Water In India," *Development + Cooperation*, March/April 1997; Tata Energy Research Institute (TERI), *Looking Back to Think Ahead: Executive Summary* (New Delhi: undated); Postel, op. cit. note 10.

15. Working Group on Environmental

Scientific Research, *The Role of Sustainable Agriculture in China*, The Fifth Conference of the China Council for International Cooperation on Environment and Development, Shanghai, China, 23–25 September 1996; Professor Chen Yiyu, Chinese Academy of Sciences, Beijing, China, discussion with author, 12 March 1996; United Nations, op. cit. note 2.

16. FAO, *Yield Response to Water* (Rome: 1979).

17. USDA, op. cit. note 4; FAO, *Water Resources of the Near East Region: A Review* (Rome: 1997).

18. Postel, op. cit. note 10; McVean Trading and Investments, Memphis, TN, discussion with author, 29 May 1996.

19. Postel, op. cit. note 10; United Nations, op. cit. note 2; USDA, op. cit. note 4.

20. FAO, *Production Yearbook 1996* (Rome: 1997).

21. Ibid.

22. FAO, *The State of Food and Agriculture 1995*, FAO Agricultural Series No. 28 (Rome: 1995); Figure 1–2 from ibid., and from USDA, op. cit. note 4.

23. Rattan Lal, "Erosion-Crop Productivity Relationships for Soils of Africa," *Soil Science Society of America Journal*, May-June 1995.

24. Ibid.; United Nations, op. cit. note 2.

25. FAO, *Forest Products Yearbook 1994* (Rome: 1996); FAO, op. cit. note 6.

26. Figure 1–3 from FAO, *Forest Products Yearbook*, op. cit. note 4; FAO, op. cit. note 6; TERI, op. cit. note 14; B. Bowonder et al., *Deforestation and Fuelwood Use in Urban Centres* (Hyderabad, India: Centre for Energy, Environment, and Technology and National Remote Sensing Agency, 1985).

27. Dirk Bryant, Daniel Nielsen, and Laura Tangley, *The Last Frontier Forests* (Washington, DC: World Resources Institute, 1997).

28. T.A. Boden, G. Marland, and R.J. Andres, *Estimates of Global, Regional and National Annual CO$_2$ Emissions From Fossil Fuel Burning, Hydraulic Cement Production, and Gas Flaring: 1950–92*, electronic database, Carbon Dioxide Information Analysis Center, Oak Ridge National Laboratory, Oak Ridge, TN, December 1995; British Petroleum (BP), *BP Statistical Review of World Energy 1997* (London: Group Media & Publications, 1997); Timothy Whorf and C.D. Keeling, Scripps Institution of Oceanography, La Jolla, CA, letter to Seth Dunn, Worldwatch Institute, 10 February 1997; Figure 1–4 from James Hansen et al., Goddard Institute for Space Studies Surface Air Temperature Analyses, "Table of Global-Mean Monthly, Annual and Seasonal Land-Ocean Temperature Index, 1950–Present," <http://www.giss.nasa.gov/Data/GISTEMP>, 19 January 1996.

29. Gerhard A. Berz, Muchener Ruckversicherungs-Gesellschaff, press release (Munich, Germany: 23 December 1996); Michael Tucker, "Climate Change and the Insurance Industry: The Cost of Increased Risk and the Impetus for Action," *Ecological Economics*, August 1997.

30. Hansen et al., op. cit. note 28; "Global Climate Change: An East Room Roundtable," proceedings from The White House Roundtable on Climate Change, 24 July 1997; USDA, op. cit. note 4.

31. "Smoke Over Rain Forest Worse Than In Indonesia," *Journal of Commerce*, 1 October 1997; Keith B. Richburg, "Haze Compounds Malaysia's Air Problems," *Washington Post*, 5 October 1997; Peter Pae and Susan Saulny, "Hitting 100 Degrees At Last—But Not For Long," *Washington Post*, 18 July 1997; TERI, op. cit. note 14; Karl Vick, "Sticky, Stifling, Stagnant: No One's Breathing Easy in Bad Air and High Heat," *Washington Post*, 16 July 1997.

32. James E. Nickum, "Issue Paper on Water and Irrigation," for the Project Strategy and Action for Chinese and Global Food

Security (Arlington, VA: Millennium Institute, September 1997).

33. Jonathan Baillie and Brian Groombridge, eds., *1996 IUCN Red List of Threatened Animals* (Gland, Switzerland: World Conservation Union, 1996).

34. Janet N. Abramovitz, *Imperiled Waters, Impoverished Future: The Decline of Freshwater Ecosystems*, Worldwatch Paper 128 (Washington, DC: Worldwatch Institute, March 1996).

35. World Bank, *Global Economic Prospects and the Developing Countries in 1997* (Washington, DC: 1997); "By The Year 2020," *Christian Science Monitor*, 12 September 1997.

36. United Nations, op. cit. note 2; IMF, op. cit. note 1; World Bank, *World Development Report 1997* (New York: Oxford University Press, 1997).

37. Lester R. Brown and Christopher Flavin, "China's Challenge to the United States and to the Earth," *World Watch*, September/October 1996.

38. USDA, Foreign Agricultural Service (FAS), *Livestock and Poultry: World Markets and Trade* (Washington, DC: October 1996 and March 1997); Figure 1–5 from USDA, op. cit. note 4.

39. USDA, op. cit. note 38; United Nations, op. cit. note 2.

40. United Nations, op. cit. note 2; FAO, *State of the World's Fisheries and Aquaculture* (Rome: 1995).

41. Patrick E. Tyler, "China's Transport Gridlock: Cars vs. Mass Transit," *New York Times*, 4 May 1996; BP, op. cit. note 28; see also Christopher Flavin, "Fossil Fuel Use Surges to New High," in Lester R. Brown, Michael Renner, and Christopher Flavin, *Vital Signs 1997* (New York: W.W. Norton & Company, 1997).

42. Brown and Flavin, op. cit. note 37; Boden, Marland, and Andres, op. cit. note 28;

BP, op. cit. note 28.

43. "Authorities Reveal 3 Million Deaths Linked To Illness From Urban Air Pollution," *International Environment Reporter*, 30 October 1996; Weishuang Qu, Millennium Institute, discussion with author, 5 August 1997.

44. United Nations, op. cit. note 2; Institute of Geography of the Chinese Academy of Sciences, State Planning Committee of the State Economic Information Centre, and the Institute of Statistics of the State Statistical Bureau, *The National Economic Atlas of China* (Hong Kong: Oxford University Press, 1994).

45. Tyler, op. cit. note 41.

46. USDA, op. cit. note 4; United Nations, op. cit. note 2; United Nations, *World Population Growth From Year 0 To Stabilization*, mimeograph (New York: 10 January 1996).

47. United Nations, op. cit. note 2; IMF, op. cit. note 1.

48. United Nations, op. cit. note 2; IMF, op. cit. note 1.

49. Figure 1–6 from USDA, op. cit. note 4.

50. FAO, *Fertilizer Yearbooks* (Rome: various years); K.G. Soh and K.F. Isherwood, "Short Term Prospects for World Agriculture and Fertilizer Use," presentation at IFA Enlarged Council Meeting, International Fertilizer Industry Association, Marrakech, Morocco, 19–22 November 1996.

51. Information on idled cropland from K.F. Isherwood and K.G. Soh, "Short Term Prospects for World Agriculture and Fertilizer Use," presented at 21st Enlarged Council Meeting, International Fertilizer Industry Association, Paris, 15–17 November 1995, and from USDA, FAS, *World Agricultural Production* (Washington, DC: October 1995); Figure 1–7 from USDA, op. cit. note 4, and from USDA, FAS, *Grain: World Markets and Trade* (Washington, DC: September 1997).

52. USDA, op. cit. note 4; USDA, *Grain:*

World Markets and Trade, op. cit. note 51.

53. IMF, *International Financial Statistics* (Washington, DC: 1996).

54. IMF, op. cit. note 53.

55. "Grain Prices Continue to Climb; Official Urges Calmer Trading," *New York Times,* 26 April 1996; "Futures Prices," *Wall Street Journal,* various editions.

56. World Bank, *Food Security for the World,* statement prepared for the World Food Summit by the World Bank, 12 November 1996.

57. United Nations, op. cit. note 2.

58. Ibid.

59. Mark Clayton, "Hunt for Jobs Intensifies as Fishing Industry Implodes," *Christian Science Monitor,* 25 August 1994; "Canada's Cod Leaves Science In Hot Water," *Nature,* 13 March 1997.

60. Boden, Marland, and Andres, op. cit. note 28; Ruth Walker, "US Global Warming Plan 'Not Good Enough,'" *Christian Science Monitor,* 24 October 1997.

61. Brad Knickerbocker, "Jane Lubchenco," *Christian Science Monitor,* 15 August 1997.

Chapter 2. Sustaining the World's Forests

1. Wood demand from U.N. Food and Agriculture Organization (FAO), *FAO Forest Products Yearbook* (Rome: various years); FAO, *FAO Forest Products Yearbook 1983–1994* (Rome: 1996); paper demand and projections from International Institute for Environment and Development (IIED), *Towards a Sustainable Paper Cycle* (London: 1996).

2. FAO, *State of the World's Forests 1997* (Oxford, U.K.: 1997).

3. Dirk Bryant, Daniel Nielsen, and Laura Tangley, *The Last Frontier Forests: Ecosystems and Economies on the Edge* (Washington, DC: World Resources Institute (WRI), 1997).

4. Figure 2–1 from ibid.

5. Nigel Dudley, Jean-Paul Jeanrenaud, and Francis Sullivan, *Bad Harvest? The Timber Trade and the Degradation of the World's Forests* (London: Earthscan Publications Ltd., 1995); FAO, op. cit. note 2; WRI et al., *World Resources 1996–97* (New York: Oxford University Press, 1996).

6. Deforestation in 1980s from WRI, *World Resources 1994–95* (New York: Oxford University Press, 1994); tropical dry forests from Anil Agarwal, "Dark Truths and Lost Woods," *Down to Earth* (India), 15 June 1997; mangrove forests from Solon Barraclough and Andrea Finger-Stich, *Some Ecological and Social Implications of Commercial Shrimp Farming in Asia,* Discussion Paper 74 (Geneva: United Nations Research Institute for Social Development, March 1996); temperate rain-forests in North America from Dominick DellaSala et al., "Protection and Independent Certification: A Shared Vision for North America's Diverse Forests," mapping analysis (Washington, DC: World Wildlife Fund–US and World Wildlife Fund–Canada, 1997), and from Conservation International, Ecotrust, and Pacific GIS, "Coastal Temperate Rain Forests of North America," map (Washington, DC, and Portland, OR: 1995).

7. Bryant, Nielsen, and Tangley, op. cit. note 3; Reed Noss, E.T. LaRoe III, and J.M. Scott, *Endangered Systems of the United States: A Preliminary Assessment of Loss and Degradation* (Washington, DC: U.S. Department of the Interior, National Biological Service, 1995); DellaSala et al., op. cit. note 6.

8. FAO, op. cit. note 2; FAO counts palm oil plantations as agricultural area. If they were included under forest plantation extent, the figure would be much higher; Dudley, Jeanrenaud, and Sullivan, op. cit. note 5.

9. U.N. Economic Commission for Europe, International Co-operative Programme on Assessment and Monitoring of Air Pollution Effects on Forests, "Forest Condition Report 1996 (Summary)," <http://www.dainet.de/bfh/icpfor/icpfor.htm>, viewed 23 October 1997.

10. FAO, op. cit. note 2; Dudley, Jeanrenaud, and Sullivan, op. cit. note 5; slash-and-burn farming from Consultative Group on International Agricultural Research (CGIAR), "Poor Farmers Could Destroy Half of Remaining Tropical Forest," press release, < http://www.worldbank.org/html/cgiar/press.forest.html>, viewed 23 October 1997.

11. Agriculture as primary cause of deforestation from FAO, op. cit. note 2, and from CGIAR, op. cit. note 10; other causes from Dudley, Jeanrenaud, and Sullivan, op. cit. note 5.

12. International trade volume and value from FAO, op. cit. note 2; position in global marketplace from Environmental Investigation Agency (EIA), *Corporate Power, Corruption & the Destruction of the World's Forests* (Washington, DC: September 1996); portion of timber from temperate and boreal forests from James McIntire, ed., *The New Eco-Order: Economic and Ecological Linkages of the World's Temperate and Boreal Forest Resources* (Seattle, WA: Northwest Policy Center, University of Washington, 1995).

13. FAO, *Yearbook 1983–1994*, op. cit. note 1.

14. Ibid.; FAO, op. cit. note 2; Emmanuel N. Chidumayo, "Woodfuel and Deforestation in Southern Africa—A Misconceived Association," *Renewable Energy for Development*, July 1997.

15. Historic consumption trends and paper sources from IIED, op. cit. note 1; Nigel Dudley and Sue Stolton, *Pulp Fact: The Environmental and Social Impacts of the Pulp and Paper Industry*, World Wide Fund for Nature (WWF), <http://www.panda.org/tda/forest/contents.htm>, viewed 20 August 1997.

16. Figure 2–2 from FAO, *Yearbook 1983–1994*, op. cit. note 1, and from United Nations, *World Population Prospects: The 1996 Revision* (New York: forthcoming).

17. Janet N. Abramovitz, "Valuing Nature's Services," in Lester R. Brown et al., *State of the World 1997* (New York: W.W. Norton & Company, 1997); Reed Noss and Allen Cooperrider, *Saving Nature's Legacy* (Washington, DC: Island Press, 1994); Norman Myers, "The World's Forests: Problems and Potentials," *Environmental Conservation*, vol. 23, no. 2 (1996).

18. Michael McRae, "Road Kill in Cameroon," *Natural History*, February 1997.

19. Road density and length (reported as 380,000 miles) in U.S. national forests from Carey Goldberg, "Quiet Roads Bringing Thundering Protests; Congress to Battle Over Who Pays to Get to National Forest Trees," *New York Times*, 23 May 1997; length of federal highways from Paul Svercl, Office of Highway Information, Federal Highway Administration, discussion with Ashley Mattoon, Worldwatch Institute, 21 October 1997; L. Potter, "Forest Degradation, Deforestation and Reforestation in Kalimantan: Towards a Sustainable Land Use?" paper presented at the conference on "Interactions of People and Forests in Kalimantan," New York Botanical Garden, 21–23 June 1991, cited in Charles Victor Barber, Nels C. Johnson, and Emmy Hafild, *Breaking the Logjam: Obstacles to Forest Policy Reform in Indonesia and the United States* (Washington, DC: WRI, 1994).

20. Highway to Brasília from Emilio F. Moran, "Deforestation in the Brazilian Amazon," in Leslie E. Sponsel, Thomas N. Headland, and Robert C. Bailey, eds., *Tropical Deforestation: The Human Dimension* (New York: Columbia University Press, 1996); amount of forest cleared for pasture from Dennis Mahar (1988), cited in ibid.; increase in timber production from Friends of the Earth (FOE) International, *Cut and Run: Illegal Logging and Timber Trade in Four Tropical Countries* (Amsterdam: March 1997); deforested area in the

Amazon in 1975–88 from David Skole and Compton Tucker (1993), cited in Moran, op. cit. in this note; current deforestation from Stephan Schwartzman, "Fires in the Amazon— An Analysis of NOAA-12 Satellite Data 1996–1997," factsheet (Washington, DC: Environmental Defense Fund, 23 September 1997); agricultural expansion from Atossa Soltani and Tracey Osborne, *Arteries of Global Trade, Consequences for Amazonia* (Malibu, CA: Amazon Watch, April 1997).

21. Michael Christie, "The Amazon Is Burning Again, Officials Say," Reuters Newswire, 3 October 1997; Schwartzman, op. cit. note 20.

22. Robert G. Kaiser, "Forests of Borneo Going Up in Smoke," *Washington Post*, 7 September 1997; "Rain Forests on Fire: Conservation Consequences," World Wildlife Fund, <http://www.worldwildlife.org>, viewed 26 September 1997; Lewa Pardomuan, "Officials: Indonesian Forest Fires Spreading," Reuters Newswire, 13 October 1997; "Forest Fires Multiply," *Indonesia Times*, 15 October 1997; carbon dioxide estimate from "Government Indifference Fuels Indonesian Forest Fire Disaster," press release (Amsterdam: FOE International, 1 October 1997); 1983 Borneo fires from Dudley, Jeanrenaud, and Sullivan, op. cit. note 5; costs to Indonesia from Robert Repetto, *The Forest for the Trees? Government Policies and the Misuse of Forest Resources* (Washington, DC: WRI, 1988).

23. Watershed services from Myers, op. cit. note 17; deforestation in Ganges river valley from George Ledec and Robert Goodland, *Wildlands: Their Protection and Management in Economic Development* (Washington, DC: World Bank, 1988); William Weaver and Danny K. Hagans, "Aerial Reconnaissance Evaluation of 1996 Storm Effects on Upland Mountainous Watersheds of Oregon and Southern Washington: Wildland Response to the February 1996 Storm and Flood in the Oregon and Washington Cascades and Oregon Coast Range Mountains," prepared for The Pacific Rivers Council, Eugene, OR

(Arcata, CA: Pacific Watershed Associates, May 1996); "A Tale of Two Cities—and Their Drinking Water," in Sierra Club, *Stewardship or Stumps? National Forests at the Crossroads* (Washington, DC: June 1997); Romain Cooper, "Floods in the Forest," *Headwaters' Forest News*, Spring 1997; David Bayles, "Logging and Landslides," *New York Times*, 19 February 1997; William Claiborne, "When a Verdant Forest Turns Ugly: 8 Oregon Deaths Blamed on Mud Sliding Down Clear-Cut Hillsides," *Washington Post*, 18 December 1996.

24. Dudley, Jeanrenaud, and Sullivan, op. cit. note 5.

25. Jonathon Friedland and Raphael Pura, "Log Heaven: Troubled at Home, Asian Timber Firms Set Sights on the Amazon," *Wall Street Journal*, 11 November 1996; Soltani and Osborne, op. cit. note 20.

26. These trade agreements include the General Agreement on Tariffs and Trade, the North American Free Trade Agreement (NAFTA), the European Union, the Southern Cone Common Market (MERCOSUR), and the Association of South East Asian Nations; Nigel Sizer and Richard Rice, *Backs to the Wall in Suriname: Forest Policy in a Country in Crisis* (Washington, DC: WRI, April 1995); Nigel Sizer, *Profit Without Plunder: Reaping Revenue from Guyana's Tropical Forests Without Destroying Them* (Washington, DC: WRI, September 1996); Soltani and Osborne, op. cit. note 20.

27. Solomon Islands from EIA, op. cit. note 12; Suriname from Sizer and Rice, op. cit. note 26.

28. *State of Canada's Forests 1995–1996*, <http://www.nrcan.gc.ca>, viewed 19 August 1997; Barber, Johnson, and Hafild, op. cit. note 19.

29. Repetto, op. cit. note 22.

30. Greenpeace Canada, *Broken Promises*, report produced in consultation with the Sierra Legal Defense Fund (SLDF) (Vancouver, BC: 1997); Indonesia from Barber, Johnson and Hafild, op. cit. note 19.

31. Josh Newell and Emma Wilson, *The Russian Far East, Forests, Biodiversity Hotspots, and Industrial Developments* (Tokyo: FOE–Japan, 1996); World Bank, Agriculture, Industry and Finance Division, *Russian Federation Forest Policy Review, Promoting Sustainable Sector Development During Transition* (Washington, DC: 10 December 1996); Suriname from Sizer and Rice, op. cit. note 26; Guyana from Sizer, op. cit. note 26; Indonesia from Barber, Johnson and Hafild, op. cit. note 19.

32. Jim Jontz, "Forest Service Indictment: A Mountain of Evidence," in Sierra Club, op. cit. note 23; Randal O'Toole, "Reforming a Demoralized Agency: Saving National Forests," *Different Drummer*, vol. 3, no. 4 (1997); "National Forest Timber Sale Receipts and Costs in 1995," *Different Drummer*, vol. 3, no. 4 (1997); Paul Roberts, "The Federal Chain-saw Massacre," *Harper's Magazine*, June 1997.

33. Tax concessions from Repetto, op. cit. note 22; government plans to increase harvest levels from Barber, Johnson, and Hafild, op. cit. note 19.

34. Moran, op. cit. note 20; Repetto, op. cit. note 22; Leslie E. Sponsel, Robert C. Bailey, and Thomas N. Headland, "Anthropological Perspectives on the Causes, Consequences, and Solutions of Deforestation," in Sponsel, Headland, and Bailey, op. cit. note 20; taxes and credits for land in spite of reforms from Congressman Gilney Viana, *Initiatives in the Defense of the Amazon Rainforest* (Brasília: September 1996); infrastructure from Soltani and Osborne, op. cit. note 20; Angus Foster, "Brazil Seeks a 'Sustainable' Amazon," *Financial Times*, 19 April 1995.

35. Costs to government from Repetto, op. cit. note 21; failed resettlements from Nigel Dudley, forest researcher, Equilibrium, letter to author, 18 September 1997.

36. Myers, op. cit. note 17; Owen J. Lynch and Kirk Talbott, *Balancing Acts: Community-Based Forest Management and National Law in Asia and the Pacific* (Washington, DC: WRI, September 1995); Nancy L. Peluso and Christine Padoch, "Changing Resource Rights in Managed Forests of West Kalimantan," in Christine Padoch and Nancy L. Peluso, eds., *Borneo in Transition: People, Forests, Conservation, and Development* (New York: Oxford University Press, 1996); John W. Bruce and Louise Fortmann, "Why Land Tenure and Tree Tenure Matter: Some Fuel for Thought," in Louise Fortmann and John W. Bruce, eds., *Whose Trees? Proprietary Dimensions of Forestry* (Boulder, CO: Westview Press, 1988).

37. FOE International, op. cit. note 20; Mark Poffenberger and Betsy McGean, eds., *Village Voices, Forest Choices, Joint Forest Management in India* (Delhi: Oxford University Press, 1996); Madhav Gadgil, "India's Deforestation: Patterns and Processes," *Society and Natural Resources*, vol. 3, 1990, pp. 131-43; Shelton H. Davis and Alaka Wali, "Indigenous Land Tenure and Tropical Forest Management in Latin America," *Ambio*, December 1994; Daniel Bromley, "Property Relations and Economic Development: The Other Land Reform," *World Development*, vol. 17, 1989; "Whose Common Future?" *The Ecologist* (entire issue), July/August 1992; "Brazil Cuts Funds Used to Demarcate Indian Lands," *Baltimore Sun*, 11 October 1997; Sponsel, Bailey, and Headland, op. cit. note 34; Marcus Colchester and Larry Lohmann, eds., *The Struggle for Land and the Fate of the Forests* (Penang, Malaysia: World Rainforest Movement, 1995).

38. Barber, Johnson, and Hafild, op. cit. note 19; Lynch and Talbott, op. cit. note 36.

39. Robin Broad, "The Political Economy of Natural Resources: Case Studies of the Indonesian and Philippine Forest Sectors," *The Journal of Developing Areas*, April 1995.

40. Global Witness, "Just Deserts for Cambodia? Deforestation & the Co-Prime Ministers' Legacy to the Country," June 1997, <http://www.oneworld.org/globalwitness>, viewed 23 September 1997; Broad, op. cit. note 39.

41. Broad, op. cit. note 39; Schwartzman,

op. cit. note 20; Barber, Johnson, and Hafild, op. cit. note 19.

42. Papua New Guinea from Greenpeace International, *Logging the Planet, Asian Companies Report* (Amsterdam: May 1997); Ghana from FOE International, op. cit. note 20; Brazil from Secretaria de Assuntos Estratégicos. Grupo de Trabalho sobre Política Florestal: A Exploraçào Madeireira na Amazônia. Relatório. Brasília, 8 April 1997, cited in Schwartzman, op. cit. note 20.

43. Global Witness, op. cit. note 40; "Cambodia: King Gives Backing to Report Calling for Overhaul of Government's Logging Policy," *International Environment Reporter*, 26 June 1996; value of exports, money to treasury from Daniel Pruzin, "Loggers Use Loophole to Decimate Cambodia's Disappearing Forests," *Christian Science Monitor*, 2 May 1997; Ted Bardacke, "Cambodia Failing to Curb Illegal Logging," *Financial Times*, 16 September 1997; importance of Tonle Sap from Janet N. Abramovitz, *Imperiled Waters, Impoverished Future: The Decline of Freshwater Ecosystems*, Worldwatch Paper 128 (Washington, DC: Worldwatch Institute, March 1996).

44. Suriname from Sizer and Rice, op. cit. note 26; U.S. forests from Roberts, op. cit. note 32.

45. Marites Danguilan Vitug, "The Politics of Community Forestry in the Philippines," *Journal of Environment & Development*, September 1997; Broad, op. cit. note 39.

46. Indonesia from Broad, op. cit. note 39; "Environmental Group Again Loses Court Case on Alleged Diversion of Forest Funds," *International Environment Reporter*, 23 July 1997; Cambodia from Global Witness, op. cit. note 40. On Cambodia, see also Bardacke, op. cit. note 43.

47. Forest export values and distribution of revenues by province from "National Forestry Database—Summary 1996," <http://nrcan. gc.ca>, rank of Canadian exports from FAO,

op. cit. note 2; Cheri Burda et al., *Forests in Trust: Reforming British Columbia's Forest Tenure System for Ecosystem and Community Health* (Victoria, BC: University of Victoria, Eco-Research Chair of Environmental Law and Policy, July 1997).

48. Greenpeace Canada, *Rainforest Ravagers* (Vancouver, BC: Greenpeace Canada, undated); two thirds and salmon stocks from Greenpeace Canada, op. cit. note 30.

49. SLDF, *Stream Protection Under the Code: The Destruction Continues*, report written on behalf of the Forest Caucus of the British Columbia Environmental Network (Vancouver, BC: February 1997); SLDF, *Wildlife at Risk*, report written on behalf of the Forest Caucus of the British Columbia Environmental Network (Vancouver, BC: April 1997); fines from Province of British Columbia, Ministry of Forests, "Annual Report of Compliance and Enforcement Statistics for the Forest Practices Code: June 15, 1996–June 16, 1997," <http://www.for.gov.bc.ca>, viewed 5 November 1997.

50. SLDF, "British Columbia's Clear Cut Code," factsheet (Vancouver, BC: November 1996); industry complaints and government response from Bernard Simon, "British Columbia Eases Logging Rules," *Financial Times*, 11 June 1997; "B.C. Environmental Regulations Said to Cost Forest Industry Share of U.S. Market," *International Environment Reporter*, 30 April 1997; B.G. Dunsworth and S.M. Northway, "Spatial Assessment of Habitat Supply and Harvest Values as a Means of Evaluating Conservation Strategies: A Case Study" in EFI Proceedings, *Assessment of Biodiversity for Improved Forest Planning* (Cambridge, MA: Kluwer Academic Publishers, 1997); Ministry of Forests, Province of British Columbia, "Important Changes to the Forest Practices Code," < http://www.for.gov.bc.ca/hfp/issues/ amend/june09.htm>, viewed 8 August 1997.

51. Abramovitz, op. cit. note 17; Robert Costanza et al., "The Value of the World's Ecosystem Services and Natural Capital,"

Nature, 15 May 1997; Philip M. Fearnside, "Environmental Services as a Strategy for Sustainable Development in Rural Amazonia," *Ecological Economics*, no. 20, 1997; Norman Myers, "The World's Forests and Their Ecosystem Services," in Gretchen C. Daily, ed., *Nature's Services* (Washington, DC: Island Press, 1997).

52. Fearnside, op. cit. note 51; H.J. Ruitenbeek, *Mangrove Management: An Economic Analysis of Management Options with a Focus on Bintuni Bay, Irian Jaya*, Environmental Reports No. 8 (Gabriola Island, BC: Environmental Management Project, 1992).

53. Share managed for sustained yield from Duncan Poore, "Conclusions," in Duncan Poore et al., *No Timber Without Trees* (London: Earthscan Publications Ltd., 1989); for sustainable forestry initiatives in industry, see, for example, *Sustainable Forestry Initiative, 2nd Annual Progress Report* (Washington, DC: American Forest and Paper Association, 1997), and British Columbia Ministry of Forests, *Providing for the Future, Sustainable Forest Management in British Columbia* (Victoria, BC: March, 1996).

54. Kathryn A. Kohm and Jerry F. Franklin, eds., *Creating a Forestry for the 21st Century: The Science of Ecosystem Management* (Washington, DC: Island Press, 1997); E. Thomas Tuchmann et al., *The Northwest Forest Plan A Report to the President and Congress* (Portland, OR: U.S. Department of Agriculture, December 1996); Gregory H. Aplet et al., eds., *Defining Sustainable Forestry* (Washington, DC: Island Press, 1993); Narendra P. Sharma, ed., *Managing the World's Forests* (Dubuque, IA: Kendall/Hunt Publishing Company, 1992); international criteria and indicators from Richard G. Tarasofsky, *The International Forests Regime: Legal and Policy Issues* (Gland, Switzerland: World Conservation Union (IUCN) and WWF, December 1995).

55. Kohm and Franklin, op. cit. note 54; Herb Hammond, *Seeing the Forest Among the Trees* (Vancouver, BC: Polestar Press Ltd., 1991); Noss and Cooperrider, op. cit. note 17;

Theodore Panayotou and Peter S. Ashton, *Not By Timber Alone, Economics and Ecology for Sustaining Tropical Forests* (Washington, DC: Island Press, 1992); Alan Drengson and Duncan Taylor, eds., *Ecoforestry* (Gabriola Island, BC: New Society Publishers, 1997); Duncan Poore, "The Sustainable Management of Tropical Forest: The Issues," in Simon Rietbergen, ed., *The Earthscan Reader in Tropical Forestry* (London: Earthscan Publications Ltd., 1993); WWF and IUCN, *Forests For Life* (Godalming, Surrey, U.K.: 1996).

56. Kohm and Franklin, op. cit. note 54; Noss and Cooperrider, op. cit. note 17; WWF and IUCN, op. cit. note 55; Panayotou and Ashton, op. cit. note 55.

57. Canadian Standards Association, "Standards for Canada's Forests," <http://www.sfms.com>, viewed on 27 October 1997; Ministry of Forests, op. cit. note 50; Indonesian Ecolabelling Foundation in Jim Della-Giacoma, "Indonesian Forest Pact to Head Off Green Backlash," Reuters, 4 June 1996.

58. Forest Stewardship Council in WWF-UK, *World Wildlife Fund Guide to Forest Certification 1997*, Forests for Life Campaign (Godalming, Surrey, U.K.: 1997).

59. Ibid.; roundwood trade from FAO, *Yearbook 1983–1994*, op. cit. note 1.

60. WWF-UK, op. cit. note 58, reports 2.4 billion pound sterling turnover for UK-1995 Plus groups; statements by Lennart Ahlgren, CEO Assi Domain, by Alan Knight, Environmental Policy Controller, B&Q, and by Nicholas Brett, Publishing Director of Radio Times, BBC Magazine, at WWF Forests for Life Conference, San Francisco, CA, 8–10 May 1997.

61. As of September 1997, there were buyers' groups in Australia, Brazil, Denmark, France, Germany, Ireland, Japan, Spain, Switzerland, the United Kingdom, and the United States; import data from FAO, op. cit.

note 1; Japan certification from Dudley, op. cit. note 35.

62. WWF-UK, op. cit. note 58; Intergovernmental Seminar on Criteria and Indicators for Sustainable Forest Management, *Background Document* (Helsinki, Finland: Ministry of Agriculture and Forestry, June 1996).

63. Hectares certified from Francis Sullivan, Director, WWF Forests for Life Campaign, briefing, Washington, DC, 11 November 1997; "World Bank and WWF Join Forces to Conserve Earth's Forests," press release (Washington, DC: WWF, 26 July 1997).

64. WWF-Netherlands, WWF, and World Conservation Monitoring Centre, "World Forest Map 1996" (Gland, Switzerland: WWF, 1997). Only 8 percent of tropical moist forests, 5 percent each of tropical dry and temperate needleleaf forests, 6 percent of temperate broadleaf forests, and 9 percent of mangroves have some protected status.

65. FAO, op. cit. note 2; collateral damage from Government of Indonesia and FAO in Barber, Johnson, and Hafild, op. cit. note 19.

66. Wood used in making shipping crates from Catherine Mater, Mater Engineering, presentation at WWF Forests for Life Conference, San Francisco, CA, 8–10 May 1997.

67. U.S. sawmill wastes used for pulp and fuel from Maureen Smith, *The U.S. Paper Industry and Sustainable Production* (Cambridge MA: The MIT Press, 1997); FAO, op. cit. note 2; IMAZON from Christopher Uhl et al., "Natural Resource Management in the Brazilian Amazon: An Integrated Research Approach," *Bioscience*, March 1997.

68. Consumption in Europe, United States, and Japan from FAO, *Yearbook 1983–1994*, op. cit. note 1; U.K. paper discarded, German survey, and lumber for crates and pallets from EIA, op. cit. note 12.

69. Paper consumption calculated with data from FAO, *Yearbook 1983–1994*, op. cit. note 1; population figures and projections from United Nations, op. cit. note 16.

70. Barry Polsky, Director of Media Relations, American Forest and Paper Association, discussion with author, 30 September 1997; waste sent to landfills from Smith, op. cit. note 67.

71. Herman E. Daly and John B. Cobb, Jr., *For the Common Good* (Boston: Beacon Press, 1989); Clifford Cobb, Ted Halstead, and Jonathan Rowe, *Redefining Progress: The Genuine Progress Indicator, Summary of Data and Methodology* (San Francisco, CA: Redefining Progress, 1995); Robert Repetto et al., *Wasting Assets: Natural Resources in the National Income Accounts* (Washington, DC: WRI, 1989); Myers, op. cit. note 17.

72. David Malin Roodman, "Reforming Subsidies," in Brown et al., op. cit. note 17.

73. Alternative measures of GDP and other methods of calculating benefits from Herman E. Daly, *Beyond Growth: The Economics of Sustainable Development* (Boston: Beacon Press, 1996); Cobb, Halstead, and Rowe, op. cit. 71; Repetto et al., op. cit. 71; Panayotou and Ashton, op. cit. note 55; Wilfredo Cruz and Robert Repetto, *The Environmental Effects of Stabilization and Structural Adjustment Programs: The Philippines Case* (Washington, DC: WRI, 1992); Tim Jackson and Susanna Stymne, *Sustainable Economic Welfare in Sweden—A Pilot Index 1950–1992* (Stockholm, Sweden: Stockholm Environment Institute, 1996); Costanza et al., op. cit. note 51; conversion to sustainable rural development in the Amazon from Fearnside, op. cit. note 51.

74. Costanza et al., op. cit. note 51; gross world product from International Monetary Fund, *World Economic Outlook, October 1996* (Washington, DC: 1996).

75. Lynch and Talbott, op. cit. note 36.

76. Ibid.; Gadgil, op. cit. note 37; Poffenberger and McGean, op. cit. note 37; Broad, op. cit. note 39; Nicholals K. Menzies

and Nancy L. Peluso, "Rights of Access to Upland Forest Resources in Southwest China," *Journal of World Forest Resource Management*, vol. 6, 1991.

77. Burda et al., op. cit. note 47.

78. Tarasofsky, op. cit. note 54.

79. Treaty signatories from CBD Subsidiary Body for Scientific, Technical, and Technological Advice, <http://www.biodiv.org/sbstta.html>, viewed 20 October 1997.

80. United Nations, *Agenda 21: The United Nations Program of Action From Rio* (New York: U.N. Publications, 1992).

81. Tarasofsky, op. cit. note 54. As of mid-November 1997, the World Commission had not yet published its findings.

82. United Nations, "United Nations Panel Proposes Action to Implement Earth Summit Forest Accords," press release (New York: 21 February 1997); "Plan on Forests Adopted by Ministers Leaves Question Open of Negotiating Treaty," *International Enviroment Reporter*, 9 July 1997; UN Department for Policy Coordination and Sustainable Development, "Report of the Open-ended Ad-hoc Intergovernmental Forum on Forests on its First Session" (advanced unedited text), New York, 1–3 October 1997.

83. "Plan on Forests Adopted," op. cit. note 82; Janet N. Abramovitz, "Another Convention Won't Save the Forests, *World Watch*, May/June 1997; "International Citizen Declaration Against a Global Forest Convention," released by various nongovernmental organizations in New York City at the fourth meeting of the Intergovernmental Panel on Forests, 10 February 1997; Government of Canada, "Canada Supports an International Forests Convention," press release, <http://www.nrcan.gc.ca/cfs/proj/ppiab/for-conv_e.html>, viewed 19 August 1997.

84. Opportunities for international cooperation include MERCOSUR, NAFTA, the World Trade Organization, the Central American Forest Agreement, RAMSAR, and Asia-Pacific Economic Cooperation, under negotiation; Tarasofsky, op. cit. note 54.

85. Bardacke, op. cit. note 43; "World Bank and WWF Join Forces," op. cit. note 63; Cambodia from "Consultative Group Meeting on Cambodia, Paris, 1–2 July 1997," Global Witness, <http://www.oneworld.org/globalwitness>, viewed 23 September 1997.

86. Repetto, op. cit. note 22; Myers, op. cit. note 17.

Chapter 3. Losing Strands in the Web of Life

1. Calculations of background extinction rates from David M. Raup, "A Kill Curve for Phanerozoic Marine Species," *Paleobiology*, vol. 17, no. 1 (1991). Raup's exact estimate is one species extinct every four years, based on a pool of 1 million species; we list a range of one to three species per year based on current conservative estimates of total species worldwide reviewed by Nigel Stork, "Measuring Global Biodiversity and Its Decline," in Marjorie L. Reaka-Kudla, Don E. Wilson, and Edward O. Wilson, eds., *Biodiversity II: Understanding and Protecting Our Biological Resources* (Washington, DC: Joseph Henry Press, 1997). To translate rates from percentages, we have assumed a total pool of 10 million species. For previous mass extinctions, see Michael L. Rosenzweig, *Species Diversity in Space and Time* (Cambridge, U.K.: Cambridge University Press, 1995).

2. Importance of wild organisms in pharmaceutical and health care systems from Norman R. Farnsworth, "Screening Plants for New Medicines," in E.O. Wilson, ed., *Biodiversity* (Washington, DC: National Academy Press, 1988); Janet N. Abramovitz, "Valuing Nature's Services," in Lester R. Brown et al., *State of the World 1997* (New York: W.W. Norton & Company, 1997).

3. Edward O. Wilson, *The Diversity of Life* (Cambridge, MA: Belknap Press, 1992); esti-

mates for total species on Earth are reviewed by Stork, op. cit. note 1; the high percentage of beetles among currently described species is from Terry L. Erwin, "Biodiversity at Its Utmost: Tropical Forest Beetles," in Reaka-Kudla, Wilson, and Wilson, op. cit. note 1.

4. Jonathan Baillie and Brian Groombridge, eds., *1996 IUCN Red List of Threatened Animals* (Gland, Switzerland: World Conservation Union (IUCN), 1996).

5. Rachel Carson, *Silent Spring* (Boston: Houghton Mifflen, 1962); Robert J. Hesselberg and John E. Gannon, "Contaminant Trends in Great Lakes Fish," in Edward T. LaRoe et al., eds., *Our Living Resources: A Report to the Nation on the Distribution, Abundance, and Health of U.S. Plants, Animals, and Ecosystems* (Washington, DC: National Biological Service, 1995).

6. Dates for bird conservation assessment from Baillie and Groombridge, op. cit. note 4; bird species total rounded off from ibid., and from Howard Youth, "Flying Into Trouble," *World Watch*, January/February 1994.

7. Threatened species statistics from Baillie and Groombridge, op. cit. note 4; information on crested ibis from James A. Hancock, James A. Kushlan, and M. Philip Kahl, *Storks, Ibises and Spoonbills of the World* (London: Academic Press, 1992).

8. Ralph Costa and Joan Walker, "Red-Cockaded Woodpeckers," in LaRoe et al., op. cit. note 5.

9. Baillie and Groombridge, op. cit. note 4.

10. Percentage of threatened birds facing habitat loss from Baillie and Groombridge, op. cit. note 4.

11. The situation in Darién province, Panama, from personal observations of author (Tuxill).

12. Numbers calculated by Worldwatch from N.J. Collar et al., *Threatened Birds of the Americas* (Cambridge, U.K.: International Council for Bird Preservation, 1992).

13. Baillie and Groombridge, op. cit. note 4; figure of one third calculated by Worldwatch from IUCN data. Note that certain large islands relatively near mainland areas have bird fauna that are more continental than insular in composition. Thus this estimate excludes the larger islands of Japan, Sumatra, Borneo, New Guinea, and Cuba.

14. Archeological evidence for prehistoric Polynesian bird extinction wave from Richard Cassels, "Faunal Extinction and Prehistoric Man in New Zealand and the Pacific Islands," and Storrs Olson and Helen James, "The Role of Polynesians in the Extinction of the Avifauna of the Hawaiian Islands," both in Paul Martin and Richard Klein, eds., *Quaternary Extinctions: A Prehistoric Revolution* (Tucson, AZ: Academic Press, 1984).

15. Numbers for New Zealand, Philippines, and Mauritius from Baillie and Groombridge, op. cit. note 4.

16. Current bird endangerment rate from Baillie and Groombridge, op. cit. note 4; other numbers on Hawaiian birds from Olson and James, op. cit. note 14, and from Leonard Freed, Sheila Conant, and Robert Fleischer, "Evolutionary Ecology and Radiation of Hawaiian Passerine Birds," *Trends in Ecology and Evolution*, July 1987.

17. North American neotropical migrant figures from Bruce J. Peterjohn, John R. Sauer, and Chandler S. Robbins, "Population Trends from the North American Breeding Bird Survey," in Thomas E. Martin and Deborah M. Finch, eds., *Ecology and Management of Neotropical Migratory Birds* (Oxford, U.K.: Oxford University Press, 1995); European information from Katrin Bohning-Gaese and Hans-Gunther Bauer, "Changes in Species Abundance, Distribution, and Diversity in a Central European Bird Community," *Conservation Biology*, February 1996.

18. Wetlands loss and duck population declines from Youth, op. cit. note 6; coffee

plantation information from Ivette Perfecto et al., "Shade Coffee: A Disappearing Refuge for Biodiversity," *Bioscience*, September 1996.

19. Mediterranean hunting figures from Youth, op. cit. note 6.

20. Information on 1995–96 hawk kills from Les Line, "Lethal Migration," *Audubon*, September-October 1996; update on 1996–97 Swainson's hawk situation from Catherine Baden-Daintree, "Pesticide Withdrawn to Save Hawk," *Oryx*, July 1997.

21. Baillie and Groombridge, op. cit. note 4.

22. Musk deer figure from, "Musk Deer Declining Further," *Oryx*, January 1995; other figures from Baillie and Groombridge, op. cit. note 4; red colobus example from John F. Oates, *African Primates* (Gland, Switzerland: IUCN, 1996).

23. All figures from Baillie and Groombridge, op. cit. note 4.

24. Figure for habitat loss as endangerment cause from Baillie and Groombridge, op. cit. note 4; figure for 70 percent endemic primate endangerment calculated from species totals for Asia from A.A. Eudey, *Action Plan for Asian Primate Conservation 1987–1991* (Gland, Switzerland: IUCN, 1987), for Madagascar from Russell A. Mittermeier et al., *Lemurs of Madagascar: An Action Plan for Their Conservation 1993–1999* (Gland, Switzerland: IUCN, 1993), for Atlantic forest from Anthony B. Rylands, Russell A. Mittermeier, and Ernesto Rodriguez Luna, "A Species List for the New World Primates (Platyrrhini): Distribution by Country, Endemism, and Conservation Status According to the Mace-Land System," *Neotropical Primates*, September 1995, and for threatened primates as per Baillie and Groombridge, op. cit. note 4.

25. European cetacean status from Mark Simmonds, "Saving Europe's Dolphins," *Oryx*, October 1994; Baltic seal information from M. Olsson and A. Bergman, "A New Persistent Contaminant Detected in Baltic Wildlife: Bis(4-Chlorophenyl) Sulfate," *Ambio*, vol. 24, no. 2 (1995); general information from Thomas Jefferson, Stephen Leatherwood, and Marc Webber, *Marine Mammals of the World* (Rome: U.N. Environment Programme/U.N. Food and Agriculture Organization, 1995).

26. Hunting as endangerment figure calculated by Worldwatch from Baillie and Groombridge, op. cit. note 4.

27. Annual Amazon Basin hunting estimate and Latin American fauna loss from Kent H. Redford, "The Empty Forest," *Bioscience*, vol. 42, no. 6 (1992); fauna loss also discussed in E.F. Raez-Luna, "Hunting Large Primates and Conservation of the Neotropical Rain Forests," *Oryx*, January 1995.

28. Bushmeat as main rural income source from David S. Wilkie, John G. Sidle, and Georges C. Boundzanga, "Mechanized Logging, Market Hunting, and a Bank Loan in Congo," *Conservation Biology*, December 1992; figure on Gabonese bushmeat consumption from Michael McRae, "Road Kill in Cameroon," *Natural History*, February 1997.

29. Peter Matthiessen, "The Last Wild Tigers," *Audubon*, March-April 1997.

30. Ecological role of large mammals from John W. Terborgh, "The Big Things That Run the World—A Sequel to E.O. Wilson," *Conservation Biology*, December 1988; elephant-dispersed trees from R.F.W. Barnes, "The Conflict Between Humans and Elephants in the Central African Forests," *Mammal Review*, vol. 26, no. 2/3 (1996); whales and deep-sea biodiversity from Cheryl Butman, James T. Carlton, and Stephen Palumbi, "Whaling Effects on Deep-Sea Biodiversity," *Conservation Biology*, April 1995.

31. Figure for total Australian mammal extinctions from Ross McPhee and Clare Flemming, "Brown-eyed, Milk-giving...and Extinct," *Natural History*, April 1997; percentage of current fauna threatened and other details of Australian mammal declines from Jeff Short and Andrew Smith, "Mammal

Decline and Recovery in Australia," *Journal of Mammalogy*, vol. 75, no. 2 (1994); and from Michael Common and Tony Norton, "Biodiversity: Its Conservation in Australia," *Ambio*, May 1992.

32. Reptile species total from Harold G. Cogger, *Reptiles and Amphibians of Australia* (Ithaca, NY: Reed Books/Cornell University Press, 1992); amphibian species total from Darrel R. Frost, ed., *Amphibian Species of the World: A Taxonomic and Geographic Reference* (Lawrence, KS: Allen Press/Association of Systematics Collections, 1985); assessment percentages and assessment status of reptile groups from Baillie and Groombridge, op. cit. note 4.

33. Baillie and Groombridge, op. cit. note 4.

34. Habitat loss percentage calculated from Baillie and Groombridge, op. cit. note 4; Galapagos Islands information from Stephen Herrero, "Galapagos Tortoises Threatened," *Conservation Biology*, April 1997.

35. Baillie and Groombridge, op. cit. note 4.

36. Status of all seven turtle species as endangered from Baillie and Groombridge, op. cit. note 4; general information on sea turtles' problems from Howard Youth, "Neglected Elders," *World Watch*, September/ October 1997; data from Panamanian waters is from field notes by the author (Tuxill), March 1997.

37. TRAFFIC report on Southeast Asia tortoise and river turtle trade cited in Catherine Baden-Daintree, "Threats to Tortoises and Freshwater Turtles," *Oryx*, April 1996.

38. Information on Amazonian crocodilians from P. Brazaitis et al., "Threats to Brazilian Crocodilian Populations," *Oryx*, October 1996; other information on crocodilians' status from Youth, op. cit. note 36.

39. Habitat loss figure for amphibians from Baillie and Groombridge, op. cit. note 4; loss of wetlands as a problem for amphibians from Andrew R. Blaustein and David B. Wake, "The

Puzzle of Declining Amphibian Populations," *Scientific American*, April 1995; impacts of roads and traffic from "Frogs and Toads Take the Road Less Traveled," *Delta* (Journal of the Canadian Global Change Program), Fall 1994.

40. Western U.S. frog declines from Charles A. Drost and Gary M. Fellers, "Collapse of a Regional Frog Fauna in the Yosemite Area of the California Sierra Nevada, USA," *Conservation Biology*, April 1996; Australian frog declines from William F. Laurance, Keith R. McDonald, and Richard Speare, "Epidemic Disease and the Catastrophic Decline of Australian Rain Forest Frogs," *Conservation Biology*, April 1996.

41. Invasive pathogens as cause from Laurance, McDonald, and Speare, op. cit. note 40; UV radiation or acid rain as causes, and synergistic combinations, from Blaustein and Wake, op. cit. note 39; introduced predators as cause from Robert N. Fisher and H. Bradley Shaffer, "The Decline of Amphibians in California's Great Central Valley," *Conservation Biology*, October 1996; drought as problem from J. Alan Pounds and Martha L. Crump, "Amphibian Declines and Climatic Disturbance: The Case of the Golden Toad and the Harlequin Frog," *Conservation Biology*, March 1994.

42. Baillie and Groombridge, op. cit. note 4.

43. Ibid.

44. Large rivers as hotspots for endangered fish and saltwater hotspots from Peter B. Moyle and Robert A. Leidy, "Loss of Biodiversity in Aquatic Ecosystems: Evidence from Fish Faunas," in P.L. Fiedler and S.K. Jain, eds., *Conservation Biology: The Theory and Practice of Nature Conservation, Preservation, and Management* (New York: Chapman and Hall, 1992); tropical peat swamps as fish diversity hotspots from Peter K.L. Ng, "Peat Swamp Fishes of Southeast Asia: Diversity Under Threat," *Wallaceana*, vol. 73 (1994).

45. Figure for dams worldwide from Sandra

Postel, *Last Oasis*, rev. ed. (New York: W.W. Norton & Company, 1997); Mississippi dead zone from Joby Warrick, "'Dead Zone' Plagues Gulf Fishermen," *Washington Post*, 24 August 1997.

46. Habitat endangerment percentage and darter total from Baillie and Groombridge, op. cit. note 4; Sanjay Kumar, "Indian Dams Will Drive Out Rare Animals...While Fish Fall Prey to Progress," *New Scientist*, 4 February 1995.

47. Wayne C. Starnes, "Colorado River Basin Fishes," in National Biological Service, U.S. Department of Interior, *Our Living Resources 1994* (Washington, DC: 1995); Salvador Contreras and M. Lourdes Lozano, "Water, Endangered Fishes, and Development Perspectives in Arid Lands of Mexico," *Conservation Biology*, June 1994.

48. Percentage of fish threatened by invasives from Baillie and Groombridge, op. cit. note 4; Richard Ogutu-Ohwayo, "Nile Perch in Lake Victoria: Effects on Fish Species Diversity, Ecosystem Functions and Fisheries," in O.T. Sandlund, P.J. Schei, and A. Viken, eds., *Proceedings of the Norway/U.N. Conference on Alien Species* (Trondheim, Norway: Directorate for Nature Management and Norwegian Institute for Native Research, 1996); Les Kaufman and Peter Ochumba, "Evolutionary and Conservation Biology of Cichlid Fishes as Revealed by Faunal Remnants in Northern Lake Victoria," *Conservation Biology*, September 1993.

49. Baillie and Groombridge, op. cit. note 4.

50. Ibid.; Amanda C.J. Vincent, *The International Trade in Seahorses* (Cambridge, U.K.: TRAFFIC International, July 1996).

51. Debra A. Rose, *An Overview of World Trade in Sharks and Other Cartilaginous Fishes* (Cambridge, U.K.: TRAFFIC International, 1996).

52. Vadim Birstein, "Sturgeons and Paddlefishes: Threatened Fishes in Need of Conservation," *Conservation Biology*, December 1993; Alexander Amstislavskii, "Sturgeon and Salmon on the Verge of Extinction," *Environmental Policy Review*, vol. 5, no. 1 (1991); Baillie and Groombridge, op. cit. note 4.

53. Chris Bright, "Tracking the Ecology of Climate Change," in Brown et al., op. cit. note 2.

54. Biodiversity convention requirements from Anatole F. Krattiger et al., eds., *Widening Perspectives on Biodiversity* (Gland, Switzerland: IUCN and International Academy of the Environment, 1994); ratification status from CBD Subsidiary Body for Scientific, Technical, and Technological Advice, <http://www.biodiv.org/sbstta.html>, viewed 20 October 1997.

55. Robin Sharp, "The African Elephant: Conservation and CITES," *Oryx*, April 1997; Susan L. Crowley, "Saving Africa's Elephants: No Easy Answers," *African Wildlife News*, May-June 1997.

56. Global protected area total from Catherine Baden-Daintree, "Protected Area Boom," *Oryx*, April 1997.

57. Total for conservation-dependent East African megafauna from Baillie and Groombridge, op. cit. note 4.

58. Increase in protected areas coverage in 1990–95 from Baden-Daintree, op. cit. note 56; the lack of protection given to tropical wetlands and other freshwater habitats is commented on by Norman Myers, "The Rich Diversity of Biodiversity Issues," in Reaka-Kudla, Wilson, and Wilson, op. cit. note 1.

59. Ecoregion mapping from Eric Dinerstein et al., *Una Evaluación del Estado de Conservación de las Ecoregiones Terrestres de América Latina y El Caribe* (Washington, DC: World Bank, 1995).

60. Degazetting of Indian nature reserves from Sanjay Kumar, "Mining Digs Deep Into India's Wildlife Refuges," *New Scientist*, 26 August 1995.

61. The need to view protected areas as natural resources themselves has been eloquently argued by Daniel H. Janzen, "Wildland Biodiversity Management in the Tropics," in Reaka-Kudla, Wilson, and Wilson, op. cit. note 1.

62. The extent to which protected areas have been overlain on traditionally managed lands is detailed by Marcus Colchester, *Salvaging Nature: Indigenous Peoples, Protected Areas and Biodiversity Conservation* (Geneva, Switzerland: United Nations Research Institute for Social Development, 1994); Aiah R. Lebbie and Raymond P. Guries, "Ethnobotanical Value and Conservation of Sacred Groves of the Kpaa Mende in Sierra Leone," *Economic Botany*, vol. 49, no. 3 (1995).

63. Michel P. Pimbert and Jules N. Pretty, *Parks, People and Professionals: Putting "Participation" Into Protected Area Management* (Geneva Switzerland: United Nations Research Institute for Social Development, 1995).

64. Ronald A. Foresta, *Amazonian Conservation in the Age of Development* (Gainesville, FL: University of Florida Press, 1991).

65. Totals for Global Environment Facility funding and biodiversity-damaging subsidies from Myers, op. cit. note 58; subsidy total from David Malin Roodman, *Paying the Piper: Subsidies, Politics, and the Environment*, Worldwatch Paper 133 (Washington, DC: Worldwatch Institute, December 1996).

66. Niles Eldredge, *The Miner's Canary: Unraveling the Mysteries of Extinction* (New York: Prentice Hall Press, 1991).

Chapter 4. Promoting Sustainable Fisheries

1. Anthony DePalma, "Canadians Block U.S. Ferry in a Salmon-Fishing Fight," *New York Times*, 22 July 1997; "Fishermen Release Alaskan Ferry," *Providence Journal-Bulletin*, 23 July 1997.

2. Ross Howard and Craig McInnes, "Salmon War Declared by B.C.: Alaskan Catch Angers Clark," (Toronto) *Globe and Mail*, 18 July 1997; Carey Goldberg, "Fishing Talks and Fighting Words," *New York Times*, 5 June 1997.

3. In this chapter, the term "catch" refers to wild catch only, although U.N. Food and Agriculture Organization (FAO) "catch" statistics include aquaculture yields as well. Figure 4–1 is based on the following: data for 1984–96 from Maurizio Perotti, fishery statistician, Fishery Information, Data and Statisticus United (FIDI), Fisheries Department, FAO, Rome, e-mail message to author, 11 November 1997; before 1984, catch and culture data are Worldwatch estimates are based on 1950–95 world, marine, and inland catches from FAO, *Yearbook of Fishery Statistics: Catches and Landings* (Rome: 1967–97); growth rates from FAO, *Marine Fisheries and the Law of the Sea: A Decade of Change*, FAO Fisheries Circular No. 853 (Rome: 1993); 1975 aquaculture production estimate from National Research Council, *Aquaculture in the United States: Constraints and Opportunities* (Washington, DC: National Academy of Sciences, 1978), with country estimates in Conner Bailey and Mike Skladeny, "Aquacultural Development in Tropical Asia," *Natural Resources Forum*, February 1991. Figure of one out of five fish today from Bob Holmes, "Blue Revolutionaries," *New Scientist*, 7 December 1996.

4. FAO, *The State of World Fisheries and Aquaculture, 1996* (Rome: 1997).

5. World's major fishing areas excludes inland catches and Antarctic waters; figure of 11 out of 15 is a Worldwatch estimate based on data from Maurizio Perotti, fishery statistician, FIDI, FAO, Rome, e-mail message to author, 14 October 1997; 69 percent and urgent management from FAO, *The State of World Fisheries and Aquaculture, 1994* (Rome: 1995); cod and bluefin tuna from Lisa Speer et al., *Hook, Line and Sinking: The Crisis in Marine Fisheries* (New York: Natural Resources Defense Council, February 1997); sharks from Marjorie L.

Mooney-Seus and Gregory S. Stone, *The Forgotten Giants: Giant Ocean Fishes of the Atlantic and Pacific* (Washington, DC: Ocean Wildlife Campaign, 1997).

6. Based on data in Perotti, op. cit. note 5; Black Sea from World Bank, *Saving the Black Sea: Programme for the Environmental Management and Protection of the Black Sea* (Washington, DC: June 1993).

7. International Council from Michael L. Weber and Judith A. Gradwohl, *The Wealth of Oceans* (New York: W.W. Norton & Company, 1995); mackerel and herring from "Introduction," in "Overfishing: Causes and Consequences," Special Double Issue, *The Ecologist*, March/April, May/June 1995; herring also from David J. Whitmarsh et al., "Natural Resources Exploitation and the Role of New Technology: A Case-History of the UK Herring Industry," *Environmental Conservation*, Summer 1995; R. M. Cook, A. Sinclair, and G. Stefansson, "Potential Collapse of North Sea Cod Stocks," *Nature*, 6 February 1997; "Disaster Is Feared in Fish Population," *International Herald Tribune*, 15–16 March 1997.

8. Simon Fairlie, Mike Hagler, and Brian O'Riordan, "The Politics of Overfishing," *The Ecologist*, March/April, May/June 1995; Peruvian anchovy catch in 1995 from FAO, *Yearbook of Fishery Statistics: Catches and Landings* (Rome: 1997).

9. Speer et al., op. cit. note 5.

10. FAO, op. cit. note 4; five pelagic species from FAO, *Review of the State of World Fishery Resources, Part 1: Marine Resources*, FAO Fisheries Circular No. 710, Revision 8, Part 1 (Rome: 1992); figure of 73 percent is Worldwatch estimate based on FAO data; four demersal species from S.M. Garcia and C. Newton, "Current Situation, Trends, and Prospects in World Capture Fisheries," in E.K. Pikitch, D.D. Huppert, and M.P. Sissenwine, eds., *Global Trends: Fisheries Management*, American Fisheries Society (AFS) Symposium 20 (Bethesda, MD: AFS, in press).

11. Swordfish data from Speer et al., op. cit. note 5; quote from William K. Stevens, "Long-Line Fishing Seen as Damaging to Some Fish and to the Albatross," *New York Times*, 5 November 1996.

12. Share of population near coastline from Peter M. Vitousek et al., "Human Domination of Earth's Ecosystems," *Science*, 25 July 1997; 3.8 billion from Don Hinrichsen, "Humanity and the World's Coasts: a Status Report," *Amicus Journal*, Winter 1997; coastal cities and 6.3 billion from Don Hinrichsen, "Coasts in Crisis," *Issues in Science and Technology*, Summer 1996; Michael H. Glantz, *The Impacts of Climate on Fisheries*, United Nations Environment Programme (UNEP) Environment Library No. 13 (Nairobi: UNEP, 1994).

13. Asia from Don Anderson, "Turning Back the Harmful Red Tide," *Nature*, 7 August 1997; Baltic problems from Jonas Gunnarsson et al., "Interactions Between Eutrophication and Contaminants: Towards a New Research Concept for the European Aquatic Environment," *Ambio*, September 1995; toxic and nontoxic blooms from Donald B. Anderson, "Red Tides," *Scientific American*, August 1994; Mississippi River from Mark Schleifstein, "Fertilizer, Sewage Brew Dead Zone," *New Orleans Times-Picayune*, 25 March 1996; New Jersey reference from Joby Warrick, "'Dead Zone' Plagues Gulf Fishermen: Stagnant Waters Reach 6,800 Square Miles," *Washington Post*, 24 August 1997.

14. Boyce Thorne-Miller and John Catena, *The Living Ocean: Understanding and Protecting Marine Biodiversity* (Washington, DC: Island Press, 1991); Bay of Bengal, East Africa, and Sri Lanka from Martin W. Holdgate, "The Sustainable Use of Tropical Coastal Resources—A Key Conservation Issue," *Ambio*, November 1993; menhaden from Susan-Marie Stedman and Jeanne Hanson, "Wetlands, Fisheries, and Economics in the Gulf of Mexico Coastal States," *Habitat Connections* (Office of Habitat Conservation, National

Marine Fisheries Service (NMFS), National Oceanic and Atmospheric Administration), vol. 1, no. 4 (1997).

15. D. Pauly and V. Christensen, "Primary Production Required to Sustain Global Fisheries," *Nature*, 16 March 1995; 80–90 percent from John Cordell, "Introduction: Sea Tenure," in John Cordell, ed. *A Sea of Small Boats* (Cambridge, MA: Cultural Survival, Inc., 1989).

16. Pauly and Christensen, op. cit. note 15; John Beddington, "The Primary Requirements," *Nature*, 16 March 1995; nutrient redistribution from Ferren MacIntyre, Kenneth W. Estep, and Thomas T. Noji, "Is It Deforestation or Desertification When We Do It to the Ocean?" *NAGA, the ICLARM Quarterly*, July 1995.

17. Caribbean from Callum M. Roberts, "Effects of Fishing on the Ecosystem Structure of Coral Reefs," *Conservation Biology*, October 1995; Julie P. Hawkins and Callum M. Roberts, "The Growth of Coastal Tourism in the Red Sea: Present and Future Effects on Coral Reefs," *Ambio*, December 1994.

18. Robert T. Watson et al., eds., *Climate Change 1995—Impacts, Adaptations, and Mitigation of Climate Change: Scientific-Technical Analyses*, Contribution of Working Group II to the Second Assessment Report of the Intergovernmental Panel on Climate Change (IPCC) (Cambridge, U.K.: Cambridge University Press, 1995); David Schneider, "The Rising Seas," *Scientific American*, March 1997; Glantz, op. cit. note 12.

19. John McGowan and Dean Roemmich, "Climatic Warming and the Decline of Zooplankton in the California Current," *Science*, 3 March 1995; Richard R. Veit et al., "Apex Marine Predator Declines Ninety Percent in Association with Changing Oceanic Climate," *Global Climate Biology*, vol. 3 (1997); IPCC from Watson et al., op. cit. note 18.

20. Dayton L. Alverson et al., *A Global Assessment of Fisheries Bycatch and Discards*, FAO Fisheries Technical Paper 339 (Rome: FAO, 1994).

21. Mike Hagler, "Deforestation of the Deep," *The Ecologist*, March/April, May/June 1995.

22. Alverson et al., op. cit. note 20; data for 1995 from FAO, op. cit. note 8.

23. Gulf of Mexico from Carl Safina, "The World's Imperiled Fish," *Scientific American*, November 1995; Brazil and worldwide from Alverson et al., op. cit. note 20.

24. Charles Victor Barber and Vaughan R. Pratt, *Sullied Seas: Strategies for Combating Cyanide Fishing in Southeast Asia and Beyond* (Washington, DC: World Resources Institute and International Marinelife Alliance, August 1997); Mark V. Erdmann and Lida Pet-Soede, "How Fresh Is Too Fresh? The Live Reef Food Fish Trade in Eastern Indonesia," *NAGA, the ICLARM Quarterly*, January 1996.

25. Janet Raloff, "Fishing for Answers: Deep Trawls Leave Destruction in Their Wake—But for How Long?" *Science News*, 26 October 1996; Dick Russell, "Hitting Bottom," *Amicus Journal*, Winter 1997; North Sea and France from Robert T. Paine, "Coasts in Crisis," *Issues in Science and Technology*, Fall 1996; Georges Bank from Peter J. Auster et al., "The Impacts of Mobile Fishing Gear on Seafloor Habitats in the Gulf of Maine (Northwest Atlantic): Implications for Conservation of Fish Populations," *Reviews in Fisheries Science*, vol 4, no. 2 (1996); "parking lot" comment from Jeremy Collie, University of Rhode Island, Graduate School of Oceanography, Naragansett, RI, presentation at 1997 Annual Meeting of the Society for Conservation Biology, University of Victoria, British Columbia, 7 June 1997; strip mining and clear-cutting analogy from Elliott A. Norse, "Bottom-Trawling: The Unseen Worldwide Plowing of the Seabed," *The NEB Transcript* (Beverly, MA: New England Biolabs, Inc., January 1997); 50 times greater from Peter Auster, National Undersea Research Center, University of Connecticut at Avery

Point, Groton, CT, presentation at 1997 Annual Meeting of the Society for Conservation Biology, University of Victoria, British Columbia, 7 June 1997.

26. Twice capacity from Peter Weber, *Net Loss: Fish, Jobs, and the Marine Environment*, Worldwatch Paper No. 120 (Washington, DC: Worldwatch Institute, July 1994).

27. Rögnvaldur Hannesson, *Fisheries Mismanagement: The Case of the North Atlantic Cod* (Cambridge, MA: Fishing News Books, Blackwell Science, Inc., 1996); Karyn L. Gimbel, ed., *Limiting Access to Marine Fisheries: Keeping the Focus on Conservation* (Washington, DC: Center for Marine Conservation and World Wildlife Fund, 1994).

28. Garrett Hardin, "The Tragedy of the Commons," *Science*, 13 December 1968.

29. Lennox Hinds, "World Marine Fisheries: Management and Development Problems," *Marine Policy*, September 1992. For discussion of biological model of fish populations, see NMFS, *Our Living Oceans: The Economic Status of U.S. Fisheries* (Silver Spring, MD: December 1996). Although precise in description, maximum sustainable yield is difficult to pinpoint for one species, let alone for several interrelated species. The process of determining biological sustainable yield often becomes more of an art than a science.

30. Hannesson, op. cit. note 27; David W. Pearce and Jeremy J. Warford, *World Without End: Economics, Environment, and Sustainable Development* (New York: Oxford University Press, 1993); Thorolfur Matthiasson, *Why Fishing Fleets Tend to Be "Too Big"*, Iceland Economic Papers No. 38 (Réykjavik: Faculty of Economics and Business Administration, University of Iceland, January 1996); today's situation from Rory McLeod, *Seafood Trade Access Study* (Wellington: New Zealand Fishing Industry Board, 1996).

31. Weber and Gradwohl, op. cit. note 7; see also James R. McGoodwin, *Crisis in the World's Fisheries: People, Problems, and Policies*

(Stanford, CA: Stanford University Press, 1990).

32. Weber and Gradwohl, op. cit. note 7; also Ken Stump and Dave Batker, *Sinking Fast: How Factory Trawlers Are Destroying U.S. Fisheries and Marine Ecosystems* (Washington, DC: Greenpeace, August 1996).

33. Stump and Batker, op. cit. note 32.

34. Weber and Gradwohl, op. cit. note 7.

35. R.P. Anand, "Changing Concepts of Freedom of the Seas: A Historical Perspective," in Jon M. Van Dyke, Durwood Zaelke, and Grant Hewison, eds., *Freedom for the Seas in the 21st Century: Ocean Governance and Environmental Harmony* (Washington, DC: Island Press, 1993).

36. Ibid.; UNCLOS from Terry D. Garcia and Jessica A. Wasserman, "The U.N. Convention on the Law of the Sea: Protection and Preservation of the Marine Environment," *Renewable Resources Journal*, Spring 1995; David M. Dzidzornu, "Coastal State Obligations and Powers Respecting EEZ Environmental Protection Under Part XII of the UNCLOS: A Descriptive Analysis," *Colorado Journal of International Environmental Law and Policy*, vol. 8, no. 2 (1997).

37. Claudia Carr, "The Legacy and Challenge of International Aid in Marine Resource Development," in Van Dyke, Zaelke, and Hewison, op. cit. note 35; Asian Development Bank (ADB), *Draft Working Paper on the Bank's Policy on Fishing* (Manila: 1996); U.S. Agency for International Development, *The Status of Fisheries and Aquaculture Development Assistance Programs* (Washington, DC: August 1993).

38. Fleet growth in developing countries from Garcia and Newton, op. cit. note 10; Asia's share from Trish Saywell, "Fishing for Trouble," *Far Eastern Economic Review*, 13 March 1997; modern deep sea fleets from ADB, op. cit. note 37.

39. Sebastian Mathew, "Coastal Communi-

ties and Fishworkers: Factors in Fisheries Laws and Management," presentation at the Law of the Sea Institute, 30th Annual Conference, Al-Ain, United Arab Emirates, 20 May 1996, citing C. Sanger, *Ordering the Oceans: The Making of the Law of the Sea* (London: Zed Books, 1986); producers in 1994 from FAO, op. cit. note 4.

40. Garcia and Newton, op. cit. note 10.

41. Decline of 25 percent from Garcia and Newton, op. cit. note 10.

42. Price data from NMFS, op. cit. note 29.

43. Gareth Porter, "Fisheries Subsidies, Overfishing and Trade," draft paper for UNEP in *Environment and Trade* series, May 1996. For broader discussion of environmental subsidies, see David Malin Roodman, *Paying the Piper: Subsidies, Politics, and the Environment*, Worldwatch Paper 133 (Washington, DC: Worldwatch Institute, December 1996).

44. FAO, *Marine Fisheries and the Law of the Sea*, op. cit. note 3.

45. Matteo J. Milazzo, "Reexamining Subsidies in World Fisheries," unpublished paper (Silver Spring, MD: Office of Sustainable Fisheries, NMFS, May 1997).

46. Porter, op. cit. note 43.

47. "Little or no cost" from Gareth Porter, "Euro-African Fishing Agreements: Subsidizing Overfishing in African Waters," in Scott Burns, ed., *Subsidies and Depletion of World Fisheries: Case Studies* (Washington, DC: World Wildlife Fund's Endangered Seas Campaign, April 1997); Milazzo, op. cit. note 45; McGoodwin op. cit. note 31; 5 percent from "The Catch About Fish," *The Economist*, 19 March 1994.

48. Bonnie J. McCay, "Sea Tenure and the Culture of the Commoners," in Cordell, op. cit. note 15.

49. Vessel data from Stump and Batker, op. cit. note 32; share of fish from inshore and coastal areas from *The Ecologist*, eds., "The Commons: Where Community Has Authority," *Whose Common Future? Reclaiming the Commons* (Philadelphia, PA: New Society Publishers, in conjunction with Earthscan Publications, 1993); "Introduction," op. cit. note 7.

50. Okechukwu C. Iheduru, "The Political Economy of Euro-African Fishing Agreements," *The Journal of Developing Areas*, October 1995; $229 million and portion paid by vessel owners from Porter, op. cit. note 47.

51. Porter, op. cit. note 47.

52. Quote from Iheduru, op. cit. note 50.

53. Growth in fish trade from Garcia and Newton, op. cit. note 10; value in 1990 from FAO, op. cit. note 4; 32 percent from Meryl Williams, *The Transition in the Contribution of Living Aquatic Resources to Food Security*, Food, Agriculture, and the Environment Discussion Paper 13 (Washington, DC: International Food Policy Research Institute, April 1996); John McQuaid, "Fish Markets Going Global," *New Orleans Times-Picayune*, 30 March 1996.

54. Imports from FAO, op. cit. note 4; Japan imports from Garcia and Newton, op. cit. note 10; $16 billion from FAO, *Yearbook of Fishery Statistics: Commodities* (Rome: 1997); 1995 per capita estimates based on catches from FAO, op. cit. note 8, and on population data from U.S. Bureau of Census, *International Data Base*, electronic database, Suitland, MD, updated 15 May 1996.

55. FAO, op. cit. note 4; Biksham Gujja and Andrea Finger-Stich, "What Price Prawn? Shrimp Aquaculture's Impact in Asia," *Environment*, September 1996; percent traded from Garcia and Newton, op. cit. note 10.

56. Williams, op. cit. note 53; Garcia and Newton, op. cit. note 10; 1 billion people from "Water and Fisheries," in World Resources Institute et al., *World Resources 1996–97* (New York: Oxford University Press, 1996).

57. Figure for 2010 from FAO, op. cit. note 5; nonfood uses and fish meal from R.J.R. Grainger and S.M.Garcia, *Chronicles of Marine Fishery Landings (1950–1994): Trend Analysis and Fisheries Potential*, FAO Fisheries Technical Paper No. 359 (Rome: FAO, 1996).

58. Problems and abuse from C.J. Chivers, "Its Seas Barren, A Village Slowly Dies," *Providence Journal-Bulletin*, 18 August 1996; Jon Lien, Ocean Sciences Center, Memorial University of Newfoundland, St. John's, Newfoundland, presentation at 1997 Annual Meeting of the Society for Conservation Biology, University of Victoria, British Columbia, 8 June 1997.

59. Thousands of years from Jeffrey S. Walters, "Coastal Common Property Regimes in Southeast Asia," in Elisabeth Mann Borgese, Norton Ginsburg, and Joseph R. Morgan, eds., *Ocean Yearbook*, Vol. 11 (Chicago: University of Chicago Press, 1994); Cordell, op. cit. note 15; McGoodwin, op. cit. note 31; broad belief system from Moana Jackson, "Indigenous Law and the Sea," in Van Dyke, Zaelke, and Hewison, op. cit. note 35.

60. Elinor Ostrom, *Governing the Commons: The Evolution of Institutions for Collective Action* (New York: Cambridge University Press, 1990).

61. Robert S. Pomeroy and Michael D. Pido, "Initiatives Towards Fisheries Co-management in the Philippines: the Case of San Miguel Bay," *Marine Policy*, vol. 19, no. 3 (1995); problems and lessons from Robert S. Pomeroy et al., "Impact Evaluation of Community-Based Coastal Resource Management Projects in the Philippines," *NAGA, the ICLARM Quarterly*, October 1996.

62. Joshua John, *Managing Redundancy in Overexploited Fisheries*, World Bank Discussion Paper 240, Fisheries Series (Washington, DC: World Bank, 1994).

63. Jed Greer, *The Big Business Takeover of US Fisheries: Privatizing the Oceans Through Individual Transferable Quotas (ITQs)* (Washington, DC: Greenpeace, April 1995); Leith Duncan, "Closed Competition: Fish Quotas in New Zealand," *The Ecologist*, March/April, May/June 1995; Ransom E. Davis, "Individually Transferable Quotas and the Magnuson Act: Creating Economic Efficiency in Our Nation's Fisheries," *Dickinson Journal of Environmental Law and Policy*, Summer 1996; see also McLeod, op. cit. note 30.

64. Overview of ITQ programs in Organisation for Economic Co-operation and Development (OECD), *Toward Sustainable Fisheries: Economic Aspects of the Management of Living Marine Resources* (Paris: 1997), and in John, op. cit. note 62.

65. OECD, op. cit. note 64.

66. John Gates, Dan Holland, and Eyjolfur Gudmundsson, "Theory and Practice of Fishing Vessel Buyback Programs," in Burns, op. cit. note 47.

67. Ibid.; "Trimming the Fleet: Can Wild Fisheries Recover?" *Coastal Heritage*, Fall 1996; Caroline Southey, "Brussels Retreats on Cuts to Fishing Fleets," *Financial Times*, 11 October 1996; Caroline Southey, "Move for Large Cuts in Fish Catches Undermined," *Financial Times*, 11 November 1996.

68. A. M. Hatta and G.M.B.K. Dahoklory, "Seaweed-Based Economic Activities in Lombok and Bali, Indonesia," *NAGA, the ICLARM Quarterly*, April 1996; Imre Casavas, "Aquaculture Development and Environmental Issues in the Developing Countries of Asia," in R.S.V. Pullin, H. Rosenthal, and J.L. Maclean, eds., *Environment and Aquaculture in Developing Countries* (Manila: ICLARM and Deutsche Gesellschaft für Technische Zusammenarbeit, 1993).

69. Chris Carr, Western Pacific Regional Fishery Management Council, Honolulu, Hawaii, report from the South Pacific Forum Fisheries Agency, Sixth Technical Consultation on Vessel Monitoring Systems, 13–15

November 1996, Nadi, Fiji.

70. Turtle devices from Alverson et al., op. cit. note 20; Gulf of Mexico from Ted Williams, "The Turtle Gulf War," *Audubon*, September-October 1995; 60 percent from FAO, op. cit. note 5.

71. Foreign access agreements from Michael L. Weber, "Effects of Japanese Government Subsidies of Distant Water Tuna Fleets," in Burns, op. cit. note 47. For the economic and ecological effects of shark fin trade, see Debra A. Rose, "An Overview of World Trade in Sharks and Other Cartilaginous Fishes," *Species in Danger Series*, TRAFFIC Network and Species Survival Commission (Cambridge, U.K.: World Wide Fund for Nature (WWF) and World Conservation Union (IUCN), 1996).

72. Table 4–3 from the following: Apo Island, Saba Island, and Mafia Islands from A. Charlotte de Fontaubert, David R. Downes, and Tundi Agardy, *Biodiversity in the Seas: Implementing the Convention on Biological Diversity in Marine and Coastal Habitats*, IUCN Environmental Policy and Law Paper No. 32, Marine Conservation and Development Report (Gland, Switzerland: Center for International Environmental Law, IUCN, and WWF, 1996); Apo Island also from Linda Bolido and Alan White, "Reclaiming the Island Reefs," *People & the Planet*, vol. 6, no. 2 (1997); Sri Lanka from Piyasena Ganewatte, "Collaborative Management at Rekawa Lagoon, Sri Lanka," *Intercoast Network: Mangrove Edition*, Special Edition No. 1, March 1997, and from Lynne Zeitlin Hale, "Putting an End to Coral Mining," *People & the Planet*, vol. 6, no. 2 (1997); Belize from Sue Wells, "Protecting a Marine Wonderland," *People & the Planet*, vol. 6, no. 2 (1997). Quote from David L. Miller, "Learning from the Mexican Experience: Area Apportionment as a Potential Strategy for Limiting Access and Promoting Conservation of the Florida Lobster Fishery," in Gimbel, op. cit note 27.

73. Peter J. Auster and Nancy L. Shackell,

"Fishery Reserves," in J.G. Boreman et al., eds., *Northwest Atlantic Groundfish: Perspectives on a Fishery Collapse* (Bethesda, MD: AFS, in press); Texas from Alverson et al., op. cit. note 20; 20 percent from Karen F. Schmidt, "'No-Take' Zones Spark Fisheries Debate," *Science*, 25 July 1997; Jane Lubchenco, "The Blue Report: Launching Marine Conservation Biology," presentation at the 1997 Annual Meeting of the Society for Conservation Biology, University of Victoria, British Columbia, 6 June 1997; 10 million tons from FAO, op. cit. note 4.

74. De Fontaubert, Downes, and Agardy, op. cit. note 72; U.N. Department for Policy Coordination and Sustainable Development, "Programme for the Further Implementation of Agenda 21: Adopted by the Special Session of the General Assembly, 23–27 June 1997," Advanced Unedited Text, New York, 1 July 1997.

75. James Carr and Matthew Gianni, "High Seas Fisheries, Large-Scale Drift Nets, and the Law of the Sea," in Van Dyke, Zaelke, and Hewison, op. cit. note 35; FAO, *Code of Conduct for Responsible Fisheries* (Rome: 1995); United Nations Non-Governmental Liaison Service, "UN Conference on Straddling and Highly Migratory Fish Stocks: Final Negotiating Session," *Environment and Development File* (New York: August 1995); de Fontaubert, Downes, and Agardy, op. cit. note 72.

76. Intergovernmental oceans panel from Ehsan Masood, "Scientists Set Sail in Search of Influence," *Nature*, 13 March 1997.

77. Tensions from John, op. cit. note 62; FAO, *Precautionary Approach to Capture Fisheries and Species Introductions*, FAO Technical Guidelines for Responsible Fisheries No. 2 (Rome: 1996); Louis W. Botsford, Juan Carlos Castilla, and Charles H. Peterson, "The Management of Fisheries and Marine Ecosystems," *Science*, 25 July 1997; Ellen Hey, "The Precautionary Approach: Implications of the Revisions of the Oslo and Paris Conventions," *Marine Policy*, July 1991; Ellen

Hey, "The Precautionary Principle," *Marine Pollution Bulletin*, January 1993.

78. FAO, *Fisheries Management*, FAO Technical Guidelines for Responsible Fisheries No. 4 (Rome: 1997); Callum M. Roberts, "Ecological Advice for the Global Fisheries Crisis," *TREE*, January 1997; difficulty of implementation from Svein Jentoft and Bonnie McCay, "User Participation in Fisheries Management: Lessons Drawn from International Experiences," *Marine Policy*, vol. 19, no. 3 (1995).

79. Michael Sutton, "The Marine Stewardship Council: New Hope for Marine Fisheries," *NAGA, the ICLARM Quarterly*, July 1996; Ehsan Masood, "Fish Industy Backs Seal of Approval," *Nature*, 29 February 1996.

80. Public outcry from Michael Sutton, "Reversing the Crisis in Marine Fisheries: The Role of Non-Governmental Organizations," presentation at the Law of the Sea Institute, 30th Annual Conference, Al-Ain, United Arab Emirates, 20 May 1996.

Chapter 5. Struggling to Raise Cropland Productivity

1. United Nations, *World Population Prospects: The 1996 Revision* (New York: forthcoming); U.S. Department of Agriculture (USDA), *Production, Supply, and Distribution*, electronic database, Washington, DC, updated May 1997.

2. United Nations, op. cit. note 1; International Monetary Fund (IMF), *World Economic Outlook, May 1997* (Washington, DC: 1997); USDA, op. cit. note 1.

3. USDA, op. cit. note 1; IMF, *International Financial Statistics* (Washington, DC: 1996).

4. Information on U.S. idled cropland from Tim Warman, "1996 Farm Bill: A Triumph for Conservation," *American Farmland*, Spring 1996, from USDA, Economic Research Service (ERS), "AREI Updates: 1995 Cropland Use," No. 12, Washington, DC, 1995, and from K.F. Isherwood and K.G. Soh, "Short Term Prospects for World Agriculture and Fertilizer Use," presented at 21st Enlarged Council Meeting, International Fertilizer Industry Association, Paris, 15–17 November 1995; information on set-aside land in the European Union from USDA, Foreign Agricultural Service (FAS), *World Agricultural Production* (Washington, DC: October 1995), and from USDA, FAS, *World Agricultural Production* (Washington, DC: September 1996).

5. Tim Dyson, *Population and Food: Global Trends and Future Prospects* (London: Routledge, 1996).

6. U.S. Bureau of the Census, *International Data Base*, electronic database, Suitland, MD, updated 15 May 1996.

7. Ibid.; Seth Faison, "Chinese Happily Break the 'One Child' Rule," *New York Times*, 17 August 1997.

8. Viet Nam from "South Korean Golf Course Exempted From Decree on Rice Fields," *New Frontiers*, June 1995; Wang Rong, "Food Before Golf on Southern Land," *China Daily*, 25 January 1995.

9. Kazakhstan data from U.N. Food and Agriculture Organization (FAO), *The State of Food and Agriculture 1995*, FAO Agricultural Series No. 28 (Rome: 1995); Figure 5–1 from USDA, op. cit. note 1, and from USDA, FAS, *Grain: World Markets and Trade* (Washington, DC: July 1997), with per capita information based on Bureau of the Census, op. cit. note 6.

10. Quote from Merlinda D. Ingco, Donald O. Mitchell, and Alex F. McCalla, *Global Food Supply Prospects*, World Bank Technical Paper No. 353 (Washington, DC: World Bank 1996).

11. Quote from Donald O. Mitchell and Merlinda D. Ingco, International Economics Department, *The World Food Outlook* (Washington, DC: World Bank, 1993); yield data from USDA, op. cit. note 1.

12. Lester R. Brown, *Increasing World Food Output: Problems and Prospects,* Foreign Agriculture Economic Report No. 25 (Washington, DC: USDA, ERS, April 1965); Figure 5–2 from USDA, op. cit. note 1, with current grain data from USDA, FAS, *World Agricultural Production* (Washington, DC: April 1997); Japanese price supports from Scott Thompson, FAS, USDA, Washington, DC, discussion with author, 8 July 1997.

13. Brown, op. cit. note 12; USDA, op. cit. note 1; USDA, op. cit. note 12.

14. L.T. Evans, "The Natural History of Crop Yields," *American Scientist,* July–August, 1980; L.T. Evans, *Crop Evolution, Adaptation, and Yield* (Cambridge, U.K.: Cambridge University Press, 1993).

15. Evans, "Natural History of Crop Yields," op. cit. note 14; Evans, *Crop Evolution, Adaptation, and Yield,* op. cit. note 14.

16. Donald N. Duvick, Affiliate Professor of Plant Breeding, Iowa State University, letter to author, 14 March 1997.

17. FAO, *Fertilizer Yearbook* (Rome: various years); K.G. Soh and K.F. Isherwood, "Short Term Prospects for World Agriculture and Fertilizer Use," presentation at IFA Enlarged Council Meeting, International Fertilizer Industry Association, Marrakech, Morocco, 19–22 November 1996.

18. FAO, op. cit. note 17; Isherwood and Soh, op. cit. note 4.

19. Lester R. Brown, *Seeds of Change* (New York: Praeger Publishers, 1970); Mitchell and Ingco, op. cit. note 11.

20. Duvick, op. cit. note 16.

21. Grain data for 1950–59 from USDA, "World Grain Database," unpublished printout, Washington, DC, 1991; USDA, op. cit. note 1; USDA, op. cit. note 12.

22. USDA, op. cit. note 12; FAO, op. cit. note 9.

23. Figure 5–3 from USDA, op. cit. note 21, from USDA, op. cit. note 1, and from USDA, op. cit. note 12.

24. USDA, op. cit. note 21; USDA, op. cit. note 1; USDA, op. cit. note 12.

25. USDA, op. cit. note 21; USDA, op. cit. note 1; USDA; op. cit. note 12.

26. USDA, op. cit. note 21; USDA, op. cit. note 1; USDA, op. cit. note 12.

27. Mary Cabrera, International Rice Research Institute, Philippines, letter to Worldwatch, 26 February 1997.

28. Mitchell and Ingco, op. cit. note 11.

29. Brown, op. cit. note 19; USDA, FAS, op. cit. note 9.

30. Figure 5–4 from USDA, op. cit. note 21, from USDA, op. cit. note 1, and from USDA, op. cit. note 12.

31. Fredrick W. Crook and Hunter Colby, *The Future of China's Grain Market,* USDA, ERS, Agriculture Information Bulletin Number 730, October 1996; USDA, op. cit. note 12.

32. USDA, op. cit. note 21; USDA, op. cit. note 1; USDA, op. cit. note 12.

33. Gurdev S. Khush, "Modern Varieties— Their Real Contribution to Food Supply and Equity," *GeoJournal,* March 1995.

34. USDA, op. cit. note 12; USDA, FAS, op. cit. note 9.

35. Brown, op. cit. note 12; Figure 5–5 from USDA, op. cit. note 21, from USDA, op. cit. note 1, and from USDA, op. cit. note 12.

36. USDA, op. cit. note 1; USDA, op. cit. note 12.

37. USDA, op. cit. note 12; Soh and Isherwood, op. cit. note 17.

38. USDA, op. cit. note 21; USDA, op. cit. note 1; USDA, op. cit. note 12.

39. USDA, op. cit. note 21; USDA, op. cit. note 1; USDA, op. cit. note 12.

40. Thomas R. Sinclair, "Limits to Crop Yield?" in American Society of Agronomy, Crop Science Society of America, and Soil Science Society of America, *Physiology and Determination of Crop Yield* (Madison, WI: 1994).

41. Brown, op. cit. note 12; USDA, op. cit. note 1; USDA, op. cit. note 12.

42. USDA, op. cit. note 1.

43. Ibid.; USDA, op. cit. note 21.

44. USDA, op. cit. note 1; USDA, FAS, op. cit. note 9.

45. Warman, op. cit. note 4; USDA, ERS, op. cit. note 4; USDA, FAS, op. cit. note 9.

46. USDA, op. cit. note 1; USDA, FAS, *World Agricultural Production* (Washington, DC: various issues); USDA, FAS, *Grain: World Markets and Trade* (Washington, DC: August 1995); grain price information from IMF, *International Financial Statistics* (Washington, DC: various years).

47. USDA, FAS, op. cit. note 9; USDA, op. cit. note 1.

48. Figure 5–6 from IMF, op. cit. note 3; "Agriculture and Development," *National Conditions Report No. 5*, National Conditions Analysis and Research Group, Chinese Academy of Sciences, received from Wang Yi, Associate Professor, Chinese Academy of Sciences, Washington, DC, 1 July 1997.

49. USDA, FAS, op. cit. note 9.

50. James Hansen et al., Goddard Institute for Space Studies Surface Air Temperature Analyses, "Table of Global-Mean Monthly, Annual and Seasonal Land-Ocean Temperature Index, 1950–Present," <http: //www.giss.nasa,gov/Data/GISTEMP>, 19 January 1996; USDA, op. cit. note 1.

51. Figure 5–7 from USDA, op. cit. note 1.

52. USDA, FAS, *Grain: World Agricultural Production* (Washington, DC: December 1995).

53. "Viet Nam to Limit Exports of Rice for Four Months," *Journal of Commerce*, 19 May 1995; information on China from Christopher Goldthwaite, FAS, USDA, Washington, DC, letter to Worldwatch, 25 April 1995; "Wheat Soars to 15-Year High As Europe Puts Tax on Exports," *New York Times*, 8 December 1995; "EU to Conserve Barley by Curbing Exports," *Journal of Commerce*, 12 January 1996.

54. Laurie Morse and Gary Mead, "EU Tax News Boosts Wheat," *Financial Times*, 25 April 1997.

55. FAO, *Food Outlook*, August/September 1995; Shalha Shipouri and Margaret Missiaen, "Shortfalls in International Food Aid Expected," *FoodReview*, September–December 1995.

56. USDA, FAS, op. cit. note 9.

57. Ibid.; United Nations, op. cit. note 1.

58. United Nations, op. cit. note 1.

59. Lester R. Brown, *Who Will Feed China? Wake-Up Call for a Small Planet* (New York: W.W. Norton & Company, 1995).

60. Bureau of the Census, op. cit. note 6.

61. Ibid.; USDA, FAS, op. cit. note 9.

62. USDA, FAS, op. cit. note 9.

63. Ingco, Mitchell, and McCalla, op. cit. note 10; FAO, *World Agriculture: Towards 2010* (New York: John Wiley & Sons, 1995); "Grain Prices Could Double by 2010," *Kyoto News*, 25 December 1995; "Big Rise in Grain Price Predicted," *China Daily*, 26 December 1995.

64. FAO, *Rome Declaration on World Food Security and World Food Summit Plan of Action*, Rome, 13–17 November 1996.

65. USDA, FAS, op. cit. note 9.

Chapter 6. Recycling Organic Wastes

1. Grain to Rome from "History of North Africa," *Encyclopedia Britannica*, vol.13 (macropaedia), 1976; environmental decline from Herbert Girardet, "Cities and the Biosphere," paper presented to the UNDP-Marmaris Roundtable, Cities for People in a Globalizing World, 19–21 April 1996.

2. Urban population from Population Reference Bureau, "1997 World Population Data Sheet," wallchart (Washington, DC: June 1997); drinking water from Organisation for Economic Cooperation and Development (OECD), *Towards Sustainable Agricultural Production: Cleaner Technologies* (Paris: 1994); species diversity from David Wedin and David Tilman, "Influence of Nitrogen Loading and Species Composition on the Carbon Balance of Grasslands," *Science*, 6 December 1996; quality of organic matter from Harry A.J. Hoitink et al., "Making Compost to Suppress Plant Disease," *Biocycle*, April 1997.

3. Besides leaving soils through harvested crops, nutrients also erode away with wind and water, or leach down to an aquifer or out to a river or lake, or volatilize in a process akin to evaporation, changing to a gaseous form. This chapter focuses on nutrients that leave through harvested crops.

4. "Photosynthesis," *Encyclopedia Britannica*, vol.14 (macropaedia), 1976.

5. Accounting for all nutrient flows of all crops in all countries would be exceedingly complex. By focusing on grain in selected countries and regions, the essential features of nutrient movements become clearer. U.S. Department of Agriculture (USDA), *Production, Supply, and Distribution*, electronic database, Washington, DC, updated October 1996.

6. USDA, op. cit. note 5.

7. Ibid.

8. Figure of 10 percent calculated from data in USDA, op. cit. note 5; African flows from G.W. Cooke, "The Intercontinental Transfer of Plant Nutrients," in *Nutrient Balances and the Need for Potassium*, Proceedings of the 13th International Potash Institute Congress, August 1986, Reims, France (Basel, Switzerland: International Potash Institute, 1986).

9. Cooke, op. cit. note 8.

10. Overapplication based on data in USDA, op. cit. note 5.

11. Volatilization from E. Witter and J.M. Lopez-Real, "The Potential of Sewage Sludge and Composting in a Nitrogen Recycling Strategy for Agriculture," *Biological Agriculture and Horticulture*, vol. 5 (1987); high-yielding varieties from Balu L. Bumb and Carlos A. Baanante, *The Role of Fertilizer in Sustaining Food Security and Protecting the Environment to 2020*, Food, Agriculture, and the Environment Discussion Paper 17 (Washington, DC: International Food Policy Research Institute, September 1996).

12. Nitrogen fixation from Peter M. Vitousek et al., "Human Alteration of the Global Nitrogen Cycle: Causes and Consequences," *Ecological Issues*, February 1997; fossil-fuel burning and cultivation of nitrogen-fixing crops are the other human sources of nitrogen fixation. Still other human activities—the burning of forests, wood fuel, and grasslands; draining of wetlands; and clearing of land for crops—release trapped nitrogen that was already fixed. Figure 6–1 from Vitousek et al., op. cit. in this note, and from Ann P. Kinzig and Robert H. Socolow, "Human Impacts on the Nitrogen Cycle," *Physics Today*, November 1994. Fertilizer application from Lester R. Brown, "Fertilizer Use Rising Again," in Lester R. Brown, Michael Renner, and Christopher Flavin, *Vital Signs 1997* (New York: W. W. Norton & Company, 1997).

13. Gulf of Mexico from Jonathan Tolman,

"Poisonous Runoff from Farm Subsidies," *Wall Street Journal*, 8 September 1995.

14. Wedin and Tilman, op. cit. note 2; northern Europe from Vitousek et al., op. cit. note 12, and from C. Mlot, "Tallying Nitrogen's Increasing Impact," *Science News*, 15 February 1997.

15. Wedin and Tilman, op. cit. note 2.

16. L. Drinkwater et al., "Net Primary Productivity, Nitrogen Balance and Carbon Sequestration in Organic and Conventional Maize/Soybean Cropping Systems," submitted for publication to *Ecological Applications*; Laurie Drinkwater, Rodale Institute Research Center, Kutztown, PA, letter to author, 12 June 1997. Like the conventionally fertilized field, the manure-fed fields received more nitrogen than was taken up by crops. But unlike the conventional field, which had a high rate of leaching, the manure-fed land was effective at storing nitrogen for later use by crops.

17. OECD, op. cit. note 2; India and Brazil from "Comprehensive Assessment of the Freshwater Resources of the World," report to the United Nations, U.N. Commission on Sustainable Development, <http://www.un.org/dpcsd/dsd/freshwat.htm>, viewed 14 March 1997.

18. African fertilizer use from Amitava Roy, "Nutrient Inputs as Critical Variables in the Long-Term Projections for Sustainable Global Food Security," unpublished paper (Muscle Shoals, AL: International Fertilizer Development Center, undated).

19. Landfill closures from Nora Goldstein, "The State of Garbage in America," *Biocycle*, April 1997; capacity increase from Council on Environmental Quality, *Environmental Quality* (Washington, DC: U.S. Government Printing Office, 1997); Fresh Kills from Vivian S. Toy, "Bids for Exporting Trash Are Lower than Expected," *New York Times*, 3 March 1997; Institute for Local Self-Reliance, *Beyond 25 Percent: Materials Recovery Comes of Age* (Washington, DC: 1989).

20. OECD, *OECD Environmental Data: Compendium 1995* (Paris: 1995). Share is an average of member states' reporting rates for the early 1990s; including paper in the organic total boosts the organic share to nearly two thirds. Methane potency from U.S. Environmental Protection Agency (EPA), *Anthropogenic Methane Emissions in the United States, Estimates for 1990* (Washington, DC: Office of Air and Radiation, April 1993); methane share is a Worldwatch calculation based on data in EPA, *International Anthropogenic Methane Emissions: Estimates for 1990* (Washington, DC: January 1994); Fresh Kills from Nancy Reckler, "New Yorkers Near World's Largest Landfill Say City Dumps on Them," *Washington Post*, 7 August 1996.

21. Robert Steuteville, "The State of Garbage in America," *Biocycle*, April 1996; Alastair Guild, "Britain's Landfill Tax Raises Stakes for Compost Makers," *Financial Times*, 10 October 1996; "Tokyo Examines Fees for Collection of Garbage from Households by 1999," *International Environment Reporter*, 5 February 1997; Paul Relis and Howard Levenson, "Using Urban Organics in Agriculture," *Biocycle*, April 1997.

22. John Briscoe and Mike Garn, *Financing Agenda 21: Freshwater*, paper prepared for the U.N. Commission on Sustainable Development (Washington, DC: World Bank, February 1994).

23. Water stress from "Comprehensive Assessment," op. cit. note 17; flush toilets from Peter Gleick, "Basic Water Requirements for Human Activities: Meeting Basic Human Needs," *Water International*, June 1996; cost from Briscoe and Garn, op. cit. note 22.

24. Organic share is an average of member states' reporting rates for the early 1990s, and is calculated from data in OECD, op. cit. note 20; including paper in the organic total boosts the organic share to nearly two thirds; developing countries from Centre de Cooperation

Suisse pour la Technologie et le Management, *Valorisation des Dechets Organiques dans les Quartiers Populaires des Villes Africaines* (St. Gallen, Switzerland, 1996); 11 percent is an average of member states' reporting rates for the early 1990s, and is based on data in OECD, op. cit. note 20.

25. Nyle C. Brady and Ray R. Weil, *The Nature and Property of Soils*, 11th edition (Upper Saddle River, NJ: Prentice Hall, 1996).

26. H.A.J. Hoitink, A.G. Stone, and D.Y. Han, "Suppression of Plant Diseases by Composts," accepted for publication in *HortScience*, 1997; replacement of methyl bromide from William Quarles and Joel Grossman, "Alternatives to Methyl Bromide in Nurseries—Disease Suppressive Media," *IPM Practitioner*, August 1995.

27. In Table 6–3, share of nutrients in municipal waste is a Worldwatch calculation based on data from OECD, op. cit. note 20, on U.S. waste data from EPA, "Characterization of Municipal Solid Waste in the United States: 1995 Update," Executive Summary (Washington, DC: March 1996), on nutrient value of municipal waste from Xin-Tao He, Terry J. Logan, and Samuel J. Traina, "Physical and Chemical Characteristics of Selected U.S. Municipal Solid Waste Composts," *Journal of Environmental Quality*, May-June 1995, and on fertilizer use from U.N. Food and Agriculture Organization (FAO), <http://www.fao.org>. Countries selected were those for which complete data were available. Nutrient overapplication based on Dale Lueck, *Policies to Reduce Nitrate Pollution in the European Community and Possible Effects on Livestock Production* (Washington, DC: ERS, USDA, September 1993), which reports nitrogen overapplication in Europe to be 57 percent greater than crop needs, on U.S. grain data from USDA, op. cit. note 5, and on fertilizer application rates from USDA, Economic Research Service (ERS), "Agricultural Resources," February 1993, which were used to calculate a fertilizer overapplicaton rate in the United States of 36 percent.

28. Slow release from Brady and Weil, op. cit. note 25; India from Panneer Selvam, "A Review of Indian Experiences in Composting of Municipal Solid Wastes and a Case Study on Private Sector Participation," paper presented to the Conference on Recycling Waste for Agriculture: The Rural-Urban Connection, World Bank, Washington, DC, 23–24 September 1996.

29. Toni Nelson, "Closing the Nutrient Loop," *World Watch*, November/December 1996.

30. Yard clippings from Integrated Waste Management Board, *Agriculture in Partnership with San Jose*, Final Report (Sacramento, CA: Integrated Waste Management Board, April 1997); need for customizing from Francis R. Gouin, "Compost Use in the Horticultural Industries," *Green Industry Composting*, undated.

31. Composting facilities from Goldstein, op. cit. note 19; San Jose from Integrated Waste Management Board, op. cit. note 30; Flanders from Flemish Organisation for the Promotion of Marketing of VFG and Green Waste Compost, *VLACO's Activity Report '96* (Mechelen, Belgium: March 1997).

32. Waste reduction from Stephen Grealy, "Supermarket Composting in California," *Biocycle*, July 1997; compost volume and area applied from Dave Baldwin, Community Recycling and Resource Recovery, Inc., Lamont, CA, conversation with author, 21 February 1997; value of compost from Community Recycling and Resource Recovery, Inc., "Community Recycling Compost Typical Analysis," factsheet (Lamont, CA: undated).

33. Selvam, op. cit. note 28.

34. China from Alice B. Outwater, *Reuse of Sludge and Minor Wastewater Residuals* (Boca Raton, FL: Lewis Publishers, 1994). While sludge is already recycled with few problems in many countries, the risk lies in the lack of control over materials that enter sewers, which means that any batch of sludge could contain

materials that are harmful to human or environmental health. Laura Orlando, Resource Institute for Low-Entropy Systems, Boston, MA, conversation with author, 18 June 1997.

35. Regional distinctions from World Resources Institute et al., *World Resources 1996–97* (New York: Oxford University Press, 1996); 10 percent from Witter and Lopez-Real, op. cit. note 11; arid regions from Carl R. Bartone, "International Perspective on Water Resources Management and Wastewater Reuse—Appropriate Technologies," *Water Science Technology*, 23, 1991.

36. Official encouragement from Peter Matthews, ed., *A Global Atlas of Wastewater Sludge and Biosolids Use and Disposal* (London: International Association on Water Quality, 1996); U.S. reuse rates and dumping sites problems from National Research Council, *Use of Reclaimed Water and Sludge in Food Production* (Washington, DC: National Academy Press, 1996); European reuse rates from Matthews, op. cit. in this note, and from Peter Matthews, Director of Innovation, Anglian Water, Cambridgeshire, U.K., letter to author, 24 June 1997. Ocean dumping, once a common method of sewage disposal for some coastal cities, was outlawed in the United States in 1992, and will be illegal in Europe after 1998; see Cecil Lue-Hing et al., "Sludge Management in Highly Urbanized Areas," in Matthews, op. cit. in this note.

37. Share of nutrients in human waste does not include the 33 percent of sludge produced in OECD countries that is already applied to land. Share is a Worldwatch calculation based on nutrient value of human waste from Witter and Lopez-Real, op. cit. note 11, on population from Thomas M. McDevitt, U.S. Bureau of the Census, *World Population Profile: 1996* (Washington, DC: U.S. Government Printing Office, July 1996), and on fertilizer use from FAO, op. cit. note 27.

38. Bartone, op. cit. note 35.

39. Israeli reuse from Sandra Postel,

Dividing the Waters: Food Security, Ecosystem Health, and the New Politics of Scarcity, Worldwatch Paper 132 (Washington, DC: Worldwatch Institute, September 1996); heavy metal levels from Yoram Avnimelech, "Irrigation with Sewage Effluents: The Israeli Experience," *Environmental Science and Technology*, vol. 27, no. 7, 1993.

40. Outbreaks from Hillel I. Shuval, *Wastewater Irrigation in Developing Countries: Health Effects and Technical Solutions*, Summary of World Bank Technical Paper Number 51 (Washington, DC: World Bank, 1990); Mexico from Duncan Mara and Sandy Cairncross, *Guidelines for the Safe Use of Wastewater and Excreta in Agriculture and Aquaculture* (Geneva: World Health Organization, 1989).

41. Substances from Laura Orlando, "The Sewage Scam: Should Sludge Fertilize Your Vegetables?" *Dollars and Sense*, May/June 1997; persistence of metals in soils from "1997 Cornell Recommends for Integrated Crop Management" (Ithaca, NY: Cornell Cooperative Extension, September 1996); understudied risks from Ellen Z. Harrison, Murray McBride, and David R. Bouldin, *The Case for Caution: Recommendations for Land Application of Sewage Sludges and an Appraisal of the US EPA's Part 503 Sludge Rules* (Ithaca, NY: Cornell Waste Management Institute, August 1997).

42. Standards from Harrison, McBride, and Bouldin, op. cit. note 41; testing from Mark Lang, Carolyn E. Jenkins, and W. Dale Albert, "USA: Northeastern States," in Matthews, op. cit. note 36; Witter and Lopez-Real, op. cit. note note 11.

43. Ponds from Bartone, op. cit. note 35; pathogen kill from D.D. Mara et al., *Waste Stabilization Ponds: A Design Manual for Eastern Africa* (Leeds, U.K.: Lagoon Technology International, 1992). Other sources list the rate of pathogen kill in conventional plants as only 90–95 percent; see Shuval, op. cit. note 40.

44. Peter Edwards, *Reuse of Human Wastes in Aquaculture*, Water and Sanitation Report No.2

(Washington, DC: UNDP–World Bank Water and Sanitation Program, 1992); multiple uses from Dhrubajyoti Ghosh, "Wastewater-Fed Aquaculture in the Wetlands of Calcutta—an Overview," in P. Edwards and R.S.V. Pullin, *Wastewater-Fed Aquaculture,* Proceedings of the International Seminar on Wastewater Reclamation and Reuse for Aquaculture, Calcutta, India, 6–9 December 1988.

45. Living Technologies, "What Is a Living Machine?" factsheet (Burlington, VT: 1997).

46. Pond area from Shuval, op. cit. note 40; Calcutta from Bartone, op. cit. note 35.

47. SIRDO's full name is Sistema Integral de Reciclamiento de Desechos Organicos, or Integral System for Recycling Organic Waste.

48. Grupo de Tecnologia Alternativa (GTA), "The SIRDO from Mexico, 1979–1992" (Mexico City: undated); Josefina Mena Abraham, GTA, , Mexico City, e-mail message to author, 16 June 1997; Sidonie Chiapetta, National Wildlife Federation (NWF), Washington, DC, e-mail message to author, 18 June 1997.

49. Sidonie Chiapetta, NWF, Washington, DC, conversation with author, 17 June 1997; Tres Marias from Josefina Mena Abraham, GTA, Mexico City, letter to author, 20 February 1996.

50. Sidonie Chiapetta, "Costs and Benefits of SIRDO Technology," information sheet (Washington, DC: NWF, September 1996). The $607 is $307 for set-up and $20 per year for maintenance. The NWF analysis of net benefits works out to $33 per household per year (assuming 7–8 persons per household). The GTA estimates net household revenues of $30–60 per year; Abraham, op. cit. note 48.

51. J. Paul Henderson, "Anaerobic Digestion in Rural China," *Biocycle,* January 1997.

52. Carol Steinfeld, "Compost Toilets Reconsidered," *Biocycle,* March 1997.

53. Laura Orlando, Resource Institute for Low-Entropy Systems, Boston, MA, conversation with author, 18 June 1997.

54. Manure mountain from Angela Paxton, *The Food Miles Report: The Dangers of Long-Distance Transport* (London: SAFE Alliance, September 1994); nitrate levels from Dale J. Leuck, *Policies to Reduce Nitrate Pollution in the European Community and Possible Effects on Livestock Production* (Washington, DC: ERS, USDA, September 1993).

55. Corn feed from USDA, op. cit. note 5; pollution from USDA, "U.S. Grain Producers Have Big Steak in Taiwan's Market," *Grain: World Markets and Trade,* June 1997.

56. Teresa Glover, "Livestock Manure: Foe or Fertilizer?" *Agricultural Outlook,* June 1996.

57. Ibid.

58. Brady and Weil, op. cit. note 25.

59. Steuteville, op. cit. note 21; Guild, op. cit. note 21.

60. Cut in flows from Paul Vossen and Ellen Rilla, "Trained Home Composters Reduce Solid Waste by 18%," *California Agriculture,* September-October 1996; costs from Ellen Rilla, "CE Offices Facilitate Community Composting Efforts," *California Agriculture,* September-October 1996.

61. Funding limitations and composting toilets from Peter H. Gleick, ed., *Water in Crisis: A Guide to the World's Fresh Water Resources* (New York: Oxford University Press, 1993). A much higher cost differential—28 times—is given in Briscoe and Garn, op. cit. note 22.

62. Bob Scrowcroft, Organic Farming Research Foundation, Santa Cruz, CA, conversation with author, 25 June 1997.

63. Emily Green and Jim Kleinschmidt, "Nutrient Management Yardsticks," information sheet (Minneapolis, MN: Institute for Agriculture and Trade Policy, 1996).

Chapter 7. Responding to the Threat of Climate Change

1. J.T. Houghton et al., eds., *Climate Change 1995: The Science of Climate Change*, Contribution of Working Group I to the Second Assessment Report of the Intergovernmental Panel on Climate Change (Cambridge, U.K.: Cambridge University Press, 1996); R.T. Watson, Marufu C. Zinyowera, and Richard H. Moss, eds., *Climate Change 1995: Impacts, Adaptation, and Mitigation*, Contribution of Working Group II to the Second Assessment Report of the Intergovernmental Panel on Climate Change (Cambridge, U.K.: Cambridge University Press, 1996); Stephen H. Schneider, *Laboratory Earth: The Planetary Gamble We Can't Afford to Lose* (New York: Basic Books, 1997).

2. Figure 7–1 is a Worldwatch estimate based on T.A. Boden, G. Marland, and R.J. Andres, *Estimates of Global, Regional and National Annual CO$_2$ Emissions From Fossil Fuel Burning, Hydraulic Cement Production, and Gas Flaring: 1950–92*, electronic database, Carbon Dioxide Information Analysis Center, Oak Ridge National Laboratory, Oak Ridge, TN, December 1995, and on British Petroleum (BP), *BP Statistical Review of World Energy 1997* (London: Group Media & Publications, 1997); Houghton et al., op. cit. note 1.

3. Watson, Zinyowera, and Moss, op. cit. note 1.

4. James Bruce, Hoesung Lee, and Erik F. Haites, *Climate Change 1995: Economic and Social Dimensions of Climate Change*, Contribution of Working Group III to the Second Assessment Report of the Intergovernmental Panel on Climate Change (Cambridge, U.K.: Cambridge University Press, 1996); Christopher Flavin and Nicholas Lenssen, *Power Surge* (New York: W.W. Norton & Company, 1994); Molly O'Meara, "Solar Cell Shipments Keep Rising," in Lester R. Brown, Michael Renner, and Christopher Flavin, *Vital Signs 1997* (New York: W.W. Norton & Company, 1997).

5. Share of carbon emissions from industrial countries and Figure 7–2 are Worldwatch estimates based on Boden, Marland, and Andreas, op. cit. note 2, and on BP, op. cit. note 2; United Nations, *United Nations Framework Convention on Climate Change, Text* (UN FCCC) (Geneva: U.N. Environment Programme/World Meteorological Organization Information Unit on Climate Change, 1992).

6. Worldwatch estimate based on American Automobile Manufacturers Association, *World Motor Vehicle Data* (Washington, DC: 1997); John Griffiths, "Car Numbers to Double and Threaten the Environment," *Financial Times*, 15 February 1996; International Energy Agency (IEA), *Indicators of Energy Use and Efficiency: Understanding the Link Between Energy and Human Activity* (Paris: Organisation for Economic Co-operation and Development (OECD), 1997); Lee Schipper, "The Rio Carnival Is Over," *Tomorrow*, September/October 1997.

7. Worldwatch estimate based on Boden, Marland, and Andreas, op. cit. note 2, and on BP, op. cit. note 2.

8. Figure 7–3 is Worldwatch estimate based on Boden, Marland, and Andreas, op. cit. note 2, and on BP, op. cit. note 2; IEA, *World Energy Outlook: 1996 Edition* (Paris: OECD, 1996).

9. William K. Stevens, "U.S. and Japan Key to Outcome in Climate Talks," *New York Times*, 12 August 1997; Holdren quote from White House Conference on Climate Change, Georgetown University, Washington, DC, 6 October 1997.

10. Vicky Norberg-Bohm and David Hart, "Technological Cooperation: Lessons from Development Experience," in Henry Lee, ed., *Shaping National Responses to Climate Change* (Washington, DC: Island Press, 1995); Watson, Zinyowera, and Moss, op. cit. note 1.

11. Flavin and Lenssen, op. cit. note 4; Ernst von Weizsäcker, Amory B. Lovins, and Hunter L. Lovins, *Factor Four: Doubling Wealth, Halving Resource Use*, The New Report to the Club of Rome (London: Earthscan Publications Limited, 1997).

12. Nebojsa Nackicenovic, "Freeing Energy from Carbon," in Jesse H. Ausubel and H. Dale Langford, eds., *Technological Trajectories and the Human Environment* (Washington, DC: National Academy Press, 1997).

13. Shell International Limited, *The Evolution of the World's Energy Systems* (London: 1996).

14. W. Brian Arthur, *Increasing Returns and Path Dependence in the Economy* (Ann Arbor, MI: The University of Michigan Press, 1994); Michael Grubb, "Technologies, Energy Systems and the Timing of CO_2 Emissions Abatement," *Energy Policy*, February 1997; John S. Hoffman, U.S. Environmental Protection Agency, "The Potential of Institutional, Organizational, and Technological Change to Improve the Future Productivity of the Energy Economy," discussion paper (Washington, DC: 14 June 1996); Robert Repetto and Duncan Austin, *The Costs of Climate Protection: A Guide for the Perplexed* (Washington, DC: World Resources Institute, 1997).

15. Repetto and Austin, op. cit. note 14.

16. Robert T. Watson, Marufu C. Zinyowera, and Richard H. Moss, eds, *Technologies, Policies and Measures for Mitigating Climate Change*, IPCC Technical Paper 1 (Geneva: November 1996); Bruce, Lee, and Haites, op. cit. note 4.

17. Subsidy reforms and estimate of potential from World Bank, *Expanding the Measure of Wealth* (Washington, DC: June 1997); coal use and emissions reductions are Worldwatch estimates based on Boden, Marland, and Andreas, op. cit. note 2, and on BP, op. cit. note 2.

18. Greenpeace International, *Energy Subsidies in Europe*, prepared by Institute for Environmental Studies, Vrije University (Amsterdam: May 1997); IEA, *Energy Policies of IEA Countries, 1996 Review* (Paris: OECD, December 1996); Worldwatch estimate based on Boden, Marland, and Andreas, op. cit. note 2, and on BP, op. cit. note 2; World Bank, op. cit. note 17; Laurie Michaelis, *Reforming Coal and Electricity Subsidies*, Working Paper 2, Annex I Expert Group on the UN FCCC (Paris: July 1996); William G. Mahoney, "German Subvention at Record High; Coal Supports Blamed for Cost Hike," *The Solar Letter*, 12 September 1997; André de Moor and Peter Calamai, *Subsidizing Unsustainable Development: Undermining the Earth with Public Funds* (San José, Costa Rica, and The Hague: Earth Council and Institute for Research on Public Expenditure, 1997); Climate Network Europe (CNE) and US Climate Action Network (US CAN), *Independent NGO Evaluations of National Plans for Climate Change Mitigation, Fifth Review* (Washington, DC: US CAN, October 1997).

19. World Bank, op. cit. note 17.

20. De Moor and Calamai, op. cit. note 18.

21. European Conference of Ministers of Transport (ECMT), *Report on the Monitoring of Policies for Reduction of CO_2 Emissions* (Paris: 24 March 1997); Jane Holtz Kay, *Asphalt Nation: How the Automobile Took Over America and How We Can Take It Back* (New York: Crown Publishers, 1997); Dean Anderson, Michael Grubb, and Joanna Depledge, *Climate Change and the Energy Sector: A Country-by-Country Analysis of National Programmes, Volume 1: The European Union* (London: Financial Times Energy Publishing, 1997); John Pucher and Christian Lefevre, *The Urban Transport Crisis in Europe and North America* (London: MacMillan Press Ltd., 1996); CNE and US CAN, op. cit. note 18.

22. ECMT, op. cit. note 21; Laurie Michaelis, *Policies and Measures to Encourage Innovation in Transport Behavior and Technology*, Working Paper 13, Annex I Expert Group on the UN FCCC (Paris: March 1997); ECMT,

Sustainable Transport in Central and Eastern European Cities (Paris: OECD, 1996).

23. Richard Baron, *Economic Fiscal Instruments: Taxation*, Working Paper 3, Annex I Expert Group on the UN FCCC (Paris: July 1996); Watson, Zinyowera, and Moss, op. cit. note 16.

24. Baron, op. cit. note 23; "EC Tax Reform Group Revives Carbon/Energy Tax," ENDS Report 261, October 1996; IEA, *Climate Change Policy Initiatives, 1995–96 Update, Volume II, Selected Non-IEA Countries* (Paris: OECD, 1996); Costa Rica from Thomas E. Lovejoy, "Lesson from a Small Country," *Washington Post*, 22 April 1997.

25. ECMT, op. cit. note 21; U.K. tax from "Hot Air?" *Economist*, 9 August 1997.

26. Watson, Zinyowera, and Moss, op. cit. note 16; UN FCCC, *Report on the In-Depth Review of the National Communication of Austria* (Bonn: 10 December 1996).

27. Watson, Zinyowera, and Moss, op. cit. note 16.

28. Ibid.; Toyota Motor Corporation, "Toyota Launches the Revolutionary Prius Hybrid Passenger Vehicle," press release (Tokyo: 14 October 1997).

29. Laurie Michaelis, *Sustainable Transport Policies: CO_2 Emissions from Road Vehicles*, Working Paper 1, Annex I Expert Group on the UN FCCC (Bonn: July 1996); Matthew L. Wald, "U.S. Increasing Its Dependence on Oil Imports," *New York Times*, 11 August 1997.

30. IEA, *Voluntary Actions for Energy-Related CO_2 Abatement* (Paris: OECD, 1997); Michaelis, op. cit. note 29; "European Parliament Seeks Fuel Economy Standards," *Global Environmental Change Report*, 25 April 1997; John Duffy, *Energy Labeling, Standards and Building Codes: A Global Survey and Assessment for Selected Developing Countries* (Washington, DC: International Institute for Energy Conservation [IIEC], March 1996); Watson, Zinyowera, and Moss, op. cit. note 16.

31. Watson, Zinyowera, and Moss, op. cit. note 16.

32. Von Weizsäcker, Lovins, and Lovins, op. cit. note 11; UN FCCC, *Report on the In-Depth Review of the National Communication of the Netherlands* (Bonn: 31 July 1996); UN FCCC, *Report on the In-Depth Review of the National Communication of Germany* (Bonn: 21 July 1997); UN FCCC, *Report on the In-Depth Review of the National Communication of Japan* (Bonn: 28 June 1996).

33. UN FCCC, *Report on the In-Depth Review of the National Communication of Canada* (Bonn: 21 February 1996); National Air Issues Coordinating Committee, *1996 Review of Canada's National Action Program on Climate Change* (Ottawa: November 1996); Duffy, op. cit. note 30; Eric Jay Dolin, "EPA's Voluntary Pollution Prevention at a Profit," *Ecological Economics Bulletin*, Spring 1997; Bob Price and Caroline Hazard, "Voluntary Programs Catalyze Efficiency," *E-Notes*, March 1997; U.S. Department of State, "Second U.S. National Communication," Submitted Under the United Nations Framework Convention on Climate Change, Washington, DC, draft, 9 May 1997.

34. Duffy, op. cit. note 30; "Tax Incentives for Energy-Saving Goods, More Building of Efficient Housing Planned," *International Environment Reporter*, 2 October 1996.

35. Fiona Mullins, *Demand Side Efficiency: Energy Efficiency Standards for Traded Products*, Working Paper 5, Annex I Expert Group on the UN FCCC (Bonn: July 1996); Watson, Zinyowera, and Moss, op. cit. note 16; Matthew L. Wald, "New Energy Rules for Refrigerators, at a Cost," *New York Times*, 24 April 1997; CNE and US CAN, op. cit. note 18.

36. Mullins, op. cit. note 35; Duffy, op. cit. note 30; IIEC, *Examples in Action: Sustainable Energy Experiences in Developing and Transition Countries* (Washington, DC: 1996).

37. Mullins, op. cit. note 35; "More Power Consumption, Computer Use, Larger Cars Implicated in CO_2 Increase," *International Environment Reporter*, 10 July 1996; Global Environment Information Centre, *Choice by CO_2* (Tokyo: 1997).

38. Watson, Zinyowera, and Moss, op. cit. note 16; William R. Moomaw, "Industrial Emissions of Greenhouse Gases," *Energy Policy*, October/November 1996.

39. IEA, op. cit. note 30; Mark Storey, *Demand Side Efficiency: Voluntary Agreements with Industry*, Working Paper 8, Annex I Expert Group on the UN FCCC (Paris: December 1996).

40. IEA, op. cit. note 30; Ministry of Housing, Spatial Planning and the Environment, *Second Netherlands' National Communication on Climate Change Policies*, Prepared for the Conference of the Parties under the Framework Convention on Climate Change (The Hague: April 1997); UN FCCC, *Review of the Netherlands*, op. cit. note 32; Storey, op. cit. note 39; "Pacts Would Aim to Make Dutch Industries Most Energy-Efficient Performers in World," *International Environment Reporter*, 25 June 1997.

41. Bundesverband der Deutschen Industrie (BDI), *Updated and Extended Declaration by German Industry and Trade on Global Warming Prevention* (Cologne: July 1996); BDI, *CO_2 Monitoring* (Cologne: 26 February 1996); Storey, op. cit. note 39; IEA, op. cit. note 30; Klaus Rennings et al., *Voluntary Agreements in Environmental Protection—Experiences in Germany and Future Perspectives* (Mannheim, Germany: Zentrum fur Europaische Wirtschaftsforschung, March 1997); European Environment Agency, *Environment Agreements: Environmental Effectiveness* (Copenhagen: 1997).

42. IEA, op. cit. note 30; Storey, op. cit. note 39; "Japan Industry Vows CO_2 Reductions," *Global Environmental Change Report*, 19 March 1997; "MITI Asks Industry to Aim for Improvements in Energy Efficiency of 1 Percent Annually," *International Environment Reporter*, 19 March 1997; Jonathan Lloyd-Owen, "Climate Change Fence-Sitting," *Tomorrow*, October 1997.

43. UN FCCC, *Report on the In-Depth Review of the National Communication of the United States of America* (Bonn: 26 February 1996); IEA, op. cit. note 30; Storey, op. cit. note 39; U.S. Department of State, op. cit. note 33; U.S. General Accounting Office, *Global Warming: Information on the Results of Four of EPA's Voluntary Climate Change Programs* (Washington, DC: June 1997); Peter Tulej, "A Bright Light in Poland," *E-Notes*, August 1997; Ming Yang and Peter du Pont, "The Green Lights of China," *E-Notes*, March 1997.

44. IEA, op. cit. note 30; National Air Issues Coordinating Committee, op. cit. note 33; Pembina Institute for Appropriate Development, *Corporate Action on Climate Change 1996: An Independent Review* (Drayton Valley, Alberta, Canada: April 1997); Australia Institute, "Climate Change Policies in Australia," a briefing to a meeting of the Ad Hoc Group of the Berlin Mandate, Bonn, 5 August 1997; Storey, op. cit. note 39.

45. Price and Hazard, op. cit. note 33; IIEC, op. cit. note 36.

46. Watson, Zinyowera, and Moss, op. cit. note 16; Bruce, Lee, and Haites, op. cit. note 4.

47. IEA, *IEA Energy Technology R&D Statistics, 1974–1995* (Paris: OECD, 1997); IEA, *Renewable Energy Policy in IEA Countries* (Paris: OECD, 1997).

48. IEA, *Renewable Energy*, op. cit. note 47.

49. U.S. Office of Technology Assessment (OTA), *Renewing Our Energy Future* (Washington, DC: U.S. Government Printing Office, September 1995); IEA, *Renewable Energy*, op. cit. note 47; "Danish Turbine Industry Record," *Wind Directions*, October 1997; COGEN Europe, *European Cogeneration Review 1997* (Brussels: May 1997); UN FCCC, *Report*

on the In-Depth Review of the National Communication of Denmark (Bonn: 6 December 1996).

50. OTA, op. cit. note 49; California Energy Commission, Sacramento, CA, letter to author (Dunn), 17 October 1997; IEA, *Renewable Energy*, op. cit. note 47; Christopher Flavin, "Wind Power Growth Continues," in Brown, Renner, and Flavin, op. cit. note 4.

51. COGEN Europe, op. cit. note 49; OTA, op. cit. note 49; Ministry of Housing, Spatial Planning and the Environment, op. cit. note 40; "New Skyline for Dutch Coast," *Environmental News from the Netherlands,* February 1997.

52. IEA, *Renewable Energy*, op. cit. note 47; OTA, op. cit. note 49; Natural Resources Canada, *Renewable Energy Strategy: Creating a New Momentum* (Ottawa: October 1996).

53. IEA, *Renewable Energy*, op. cit. note 47; Flavin, op. cit. note 50; CNE and US CAN, op. cit. note 18.

54. Quote and Spanish policy from Andreas Wagner, "Feed-In Tariffs for Renewable Energies in Europe—An Overview," paper presented at EUROSOLAR Conference on Financing Renewable Energy (Bonn: September 1997); IEA, *Renewable Energy*, op. cit. note 47; Flavin, op. cit. note 50.

55. IEA, *Renewable Energy*, op. cit. note 47; UN FCCC, *Report on the In-Depth Review of the National Communication of the United Kingdom* (Bonn: 24 February 1997); U.K. Secretary of State for the Environment, *Climate Change: The UK Programme*, The United Kingdom's Second Report under the Framework Convention on Climate Change (London: February 1997).

56. OTA, op. cit. note 49; IEA, *Renewable Energy*, op. cit. note 47; The Ministry of Foreign Affairs, Government of Japan, *Global Environmental Problems—Japanese Approaches* (Tokyo: June 1997).

57. Brenda Biondo, "Pushing Solar Energy Through the Roof," *Solar Industry Journal,* Second Quarter 1997; Dean Anderson, Michael Grubb, and Joanna Depledge, *Climate Change and the Energy Sector: A Country-by-Country Analysis of National Programmes, Volume 2: Non-EU OECD Countries* (London: Financial Times Energy Publishing, 1997); "Japan to Boost Subsidies for Clean Energy Use," *Gallon Environment Letter,* 3 September 1997.

58. OTA, op. cit. note 49; Biondo, op. cit. note 57; White House, "President Clinton's Address to UN General Assembly Special Session," Washington, DC, 26 June 1997; Yih-huei Wan, *Net Metering Programs*, Topical Issues Brief, prepared for National Renewable Energy Laboratory (Boulder, CO: December 1996).

59. IIEC, op. cit. note 36; Government of Brazil, *The Brazilian Fuel Ethanol Program* (Brasilia: June 1997); Mary Miliken and Mara Lemos, "Brazil is Trying to Save Invention, Alcohol Power," *New York Times,* 27 June 1997; IIEC, op. cit. note 36; Flavin, op. cit. note 50.

60. F. Yang, D. Xin, and M.D. Levine, *The Role of Cogeneration in China's Energy System* (Berkeley, CA: Lawrence Berkeley Laboratory, 1997).

61. John T. Houghton et al., eds., *An Introduction to Simple Climate Models Used in the IPCC Second Assessment Report*, IPCC Technical Paper 2 (Geneva: February 1997).

62. Baron, op. cit. note 23.

63. Schipper, op. cit. note 6; IEA, op. cit. note 30.

64. IEA, *Renewable Energy*, op. cit. note 47.

65. John T. Houghton et al., eds., *Stabilization of Atmospheric Greenhouse Gases: Physical, Biological and Socio-economic Implications*, IPCC Technical Paper 3 (Geneva: February 1997).

66. Anderson, Grubb, and Depledge, op. cit. note 21.

67. Ibid.; Anderson, Grubb, and Depledge,

op. cit. note 57.

68. Anderson, Grubb, and Depledge, op. cit. note 57.

69. Ibid.

70. Walter V. Reid and Jose Goldemberg, *Are Developing Countries Already Doing as Much as Industrialized Countries to Slow Climate Change?* (Washington, DC: World Resources Institute, July 1997).

71. Hilary F. French, "Lessons from the Ozone Experience," in Lester R. Brown et al., *State of the World 1997* (New York: W.W. Norton & Company, 1997).

72. International Council for Local Environmental Initiatives, *Local Government Implementation of Climate Protection*, interim report to the Conference of the Parties (Toronto: July 1997).

Chapter 8. Curbing the Proliferation of Small Arms

1. The photograph appeared, among other places, in the *New York Times* on 23 March 1997.

2. Aaron Karp, "Small Arms—The New Major Weapons," in Jeffrey Boutwell, Michael T. Klare, and Laura W. Reed, eds., *Lethal Commerce: The Global Trade in Small Arms and Light Weapons* (Cambridge, MA: Committee on International Security Studies, American Academy of Arts and Sciences, 1995); 90 percent figure from Sverre Lodgaard, "Preface," in Estanislao Angel Zawels et al., *Managing Arms in Peace Processes: The Issues*, United Nations Institute for Disarmament Research (UNIDIR), Disarmament and Conflict Resolution Project (New York: United Nations, 1996).

3. Jeffrey Boutwell, Michael T. Klare, and Laura W. Reed, "Introduction," in Boutwell, Klare, and Reed, op. cit. note 2; Michael T. Klare, "The New Arms Race: Light Weapons

and International Security," *Current History*, April 1997.

4. "Small arms and light weapons" is the commonly accepted term in the literature. For convenience's sake, this chapter will use the terms "small arms" and "small weapons." Definitional issues are discussed by Michael Klare, "Stemming the Lethal Trade in Small Arms and Light Weapons," *Issues in Science and Technology*, Fall 1995, by Karp, op. cit. note 2, by Edward Laurance, *The New Field of Micro-Disarmament: Addressing the Proliferation and Buildup of Small Arms and Light Weapons*, BICC Brief 7 (Bonn: Bonn International Center for Conversion (BICC), September 1996), and by Swadesh Rana, *Small Arms and Intra-State Conflicts*, Research Paper No. 34 (New York: UNIDIR, 1995), Appendix I.

5. Klare, op. cit. note 4. If somewhat heavier arms, such as crew-served weapons like heavy machine guns and mortars, are included, the $3 billion figure could well double.

6. Ibid.

7. Laurance, op. cit. note 4; Christopher Smith, "Light Weapons and the International Arms Trade," in Christopher Smith, Peter Batchelor, and Jakkie Potgieter, *Small Arms Management and Peacekeeping in Southern Africa*, UNIDIR Disarmament and Conflict Resolution Project (New York: United Nations, 1996).

8. Rachel Brett and Margaret McCallin, *Children: The Invisible Soldiers* (Växjö, Sweden: Rädda Barnen [Swedish Save the Children], 1996); U.N. General Assembly, "Impact of Armed Conflict on Children. Note by the Secretary-General," New York, 26 August 1996; Thalif Deen, "Child Soldier Ranks Rise with Cheap, Easy Arms," *Jane's Defense Weekly*, 20 November 1996.

9. Natalie J. Goldring, British American Security Information Council (BASIC), "Bridging the Gap: Light and Major Conventional Weapons in Recent Conflicts,"

paper prepared for the annual meeting of the International Studies Association, Toronto, Ontario, 18–21 March 1997, <http://www.igc. apc.org/basic/isa97.html>, viewed 17 April 1997; Michael Klare, Hampshire College, e-mail message to author, 2 September 1997.

10. Smith, op. cit. note 7; Rana, op. cit. note 4; BICC, *Conversion Survey 1997: Global Disarmament and Disposal of Surplus Arms* (New York: Oxford University Press, 1997).

11. Figure 8–1 is based on Klaus Jürgen Gantzel and Torsten Schwinghammer, *Die Kriege nach dem Zweiten Weltkrieg 1945 bis 1992. Daten und Tendenzen* (Münster and Hamburg, Germany: Lit Verlag, 1995), and on Dietrich Jung, Klaus Schlichte, and Jens Siegelberg, *Das Kriegsgeschehen 1995. Daten und Tendenzen der Kriege und bewaffneten Konflikte im Jahr 1995* (Bonn: Stiftung Entwicklung und Frieden, 1996). Definitional and methodological questions, along with the lack of reliable information in some cases, explain why different analysts report slightly different numbers of armed conflicts in progress. Researchers at the University of Uppsala, Sweden—another widely used source—recorded 35 ongoing wars in 1995 and 36 in 1996; see Peter Wallensteen and Margareta Sollenberg, "Armed Conflicts, Conflict Termination and Peace Agreements, 1989–1996," *Journal of Peace Research*, vol. 34, no. 3 (1997); Margareta Sollenberg, ed., *States in Armed Conflict 1995*, Report No. 43 (Uppsala, Sweden: Uppsala University, Department of Peace and Conflict Research, 1996). Project Ploughshares, a Canadian research group, reports 44 armed conflicts for 1995; see Project Ploughshares, *Armed Conflicts Report 1996* (Waterloo, Canada: Institute of Peace and Conflict Studies, Conrad Grebel College, 1996).

12. Wallensteen and Sollenberg, op. cit. note 11; number of child soldiers from UNICEF, *The State of the World's Children 1996* (New York: Oxford University Press, 1996); conflicts with child soldiers from Brett and McCallin, op. cit. note 8, and from Project

Ploughshares, op. cit. note 11.

13. Wallensteen and Sollenberg, op. cit. note 11; war-related deaths computed from Ruth Leger Sivard with Arlette Brauer, Lora Lumpe, and Paul Walker, *World Military and Social Expenditures 1996* (Washington, DC: World Priorities, 1996). Figure 8–2 presents data in five-year periods because there is no reliable information on the annual death toll. It is a Worldwatch computation based on data in Sivard, op. cit. in this note. The data underlying the figure have been calculated on the basis of total number of persons killed in each individual war; where wars have straddled two or more five-year periods, the total number of deaths was divided into equal portions for the periods of time in question.

14. Dan Smith, *War, Peace and Third World Development*, Human Development Report Office, Occasional Paper No. 16 (New York: U.N. Development Programme, 1993); Jung, Schlichte, and Siegelberg, op. cit. note 11.

15. Michael T. Klare, "Light Weapons Diffusion and Global Violence in the Post–Cold War Era," in Jasjit Singh, ed., *Light Weapons and International Security* (Delhi: Indian Pugwash Society and BASIC, December 1995).

16. Michael Klare and David Andersen, *A Scourge of Guns: The Diffusion of Small Arms and Light Weapons in Latin America* (Washington, DC: Arms Sales Monitoring Project, Federation of American Scientists, August 1996); "The Backlash in Latin America," *Economist*, 30 November 1996; Jacklyn Cock, "A Sociological Account of Light Weapons Proliferation in Southern Africa," in Singh, op. cit. note 15.

17. Michael T. Klare, "The Global Trade in Light Weapons and the International System in the Post–Cold War Era," in Boutwell, Klare, and Reed, op. cit. note 2.

18. Daniel Gallik, ed., *World Military Expenditures and Arms Transfers*, electronic database, U.S. Arms Control and Disarmament

Agency, Washington, DC, computer diskette provided to author, 20 January 1997; Alex de Waal, "Contemporary Warfare in Africa," *IDS Bulletin*, vol. 27, no. 3 (1996).

19. Table 8–1 based on the following sources: James Brooke, "Police/Security Partnerships: Privatization Models that Impace [sic] Crime," *CJ Online The Americas*, <http://www.acsp.uic.edu/oicj/pubs/cja/090 211.htm>, viewed 22 July 1997; Mike Zielinski, "Armed and Dangerous: Private Police on the March," *Covert Action Quarterly*, <http://caq. com/CAQ54p.police.html>, viewed 21 July 1997; Les Johnston, *The Rebirth of Private Policing* (New York: Routledge, 1992); Cock, op. cit. note 16; Jeff Builta, Office of International Criminal Justice, "South Africa: Crime on the Increase," *CJ Online Europe*, <http://www.acsp.uic.edu/OICJ/PUBS/ CJE/060101.htm>, viewed 22 July 1997; United Nations, "The Fourth United Nations Survey of Crime Trends and Operations of Criminal Justice Systems," <http://www.ifs. univie.ac.at/~unjin/bpolice/totalpol.txt>, viewed 28 August 1997; Daniel Garcia-Peña Jaramillo, "Light Weapons and Internal Conflict in Colombia," in Boutwell, Klare, and Reed, op. cit. note 2; Gallik, op. cit. note 18. Firepower of private guards from Zielinski, op. cit. in this note.

20. Statement from "Ramos Orders Crackdown on Gun-runners," *The Straits Times Interactive*, 22 April 1997, <http://straits times.asia1.com/>.

21. United Nations, "Report of the Panel of Governmental Experts on Small Arms," New York, July 1997 (pre-publication version); "Russia: Kalashnikov Anniversary," *Omri Daily Digest*, 21 February 1997.

22. Prashant Dikshit, "Internal Conflict and Role of Light Weapons," in Singh, op. cit. note 15; United Nations, op. cit. note 21; "Russia: Kalashnikov Anniversary," op. cit. note 21; BICC, op. cit. note 10; "Counterfeit Weapons Flood World Arms Market," *The Press* (Christchurch, New Zealand), 3 July 1997.

23. Figure of 500 million from Singh, op. cit. note 15.

24. U.N. Commission on Crime Prevention and Criminal Justice, "Draft United Nations International Study on Firearm Regulation," Vienna, 25 April 1997, Table 2.7 and Figure 6.1.

25. Ibid.; Canada from John C. Thompson, *Misfire: The Black Market and Gun Control*, Mackenzie Institute Occasional Paper (Toronto: May 1995).

26. Number of gun dealers from Klare and Andersen, op. cit. note 16; number of McDonald's outlets from Customer Service Department, McDonald's Corporation Head Office, Oak Brook, IL, discussion with Daniel Schwartz, Worldwatch Institute, 3 September 1997; Justice Department from Pierre Thomas, "Study Finds Gun Ownership Common But Less Widespread," *Washington Post*, 6 May 1997; National Rifle Association, "1997 NRA Firearms Fact Card," <http://www. nra.org/research/NRA-FFACT.html>, viewed 2 August 1997; FBI from Katharine Q. Seelye, "NRA Turns to World Stage to Fight Gun Control," *New York Times*, 2 April 1997.

27. Figure 8–3 and availability from American Firearms Network (Amfire), "Civilian Firearms—Production, Import & Export 1899–1989," <http://www.amfire. com/afistatistics/production2.html>, viewed 2 August 1997, and from Amfire, "Firearms Production 1973–1994," <http://www.amfire. com/afistatistics/production.html>, viewed 2 August 1997; annual theft from Philip J. Cook and Jens Ludwig, "Guns in America: National Survey on Private Ownership and Use of Firearms," *NIJ Research in Brief*, May 1997; U.S. allowing assault weapons ownership from Jeff Brazil and Steve Berry, "Australia's Answer to Carnage: A Strict Law," *Los Angeles Times*, 27 August 1997; share of assault weapons from Jeff Brazil and Steve Berry, "Crackdown on Assault Weapons Has Missed Mark," *Los Angeles Times*, 24 August 1997.

28. Rise in firearm-related violence from Christopher Louise, *The Social Impacts of Light Weapons Availability and Proliferation*, Discussion Paper No. 59 (Geneva: U.N. Research Institute for Social Development, March 1995); comparisons of gun killings in the United States with other industrial countries from Brazil and Berry, "Australia's Answer," op. cit. note 27.

29. U.N. Commission, op. cit. note 24; Catherine Foster, "Nations Around the World Try to Get a Grip on Guns," *Christian Science Monitor*, 15 May 1996; "Drugs Make for Murder Metropolis," *Financial Times*, 10 April 1996.

30. Fred Weir, "Russians Arming Themselves," *Hindustan Times*, 12 March 1997; "Russia: Interior Minister Advocates Tighter Army Gun Control," Moscow Radiostantsiya Ekho Moskvy, in Foreign Broadcast Information Service (FBIS), *FBIS Daily Report*, 18 April 1997; Mitchell Landsberg, "Gun Ownership Soars in Russia," Associated Press, 12 May 1997.

31. Salvadorans killed since 1992 from Klare and Andersen, op. cit. note 16; people killed during the war from Sivard, op. cit. note 13.

32. *Dialogo Centroamericano*, January 1997 (newsletter published by the Centro para la Paz of the Arias Foundation for Peace and Human Progress, San José, Costa Rica); Klare and Andersen, op. cit. note 16; Laurance, op. cit. note 4.

33. Larry Rohter, "In U.S. Deportation Policy, a Pandora's Box," *New York Times*, 10 August 1997.

34. Cock, op. cit. note 16.

35. Ibid.; Smith, op. cit. note 7.

36. "Mozambique is Drowning in the Weapons of Decades of War," *The Cape Town Star*, 24 March 1997; Brian Latham, "Mozambique: Illegal Weapons Trade Threatens Security," *Africa Information Afrique*, 6 March 1995; Cock, op. cit. note 16; Suzanne Daley, "In Mozambique, Guns for Plowshares and Bicycles," *New York Times*, 2 March 1997.

37. "Police Carry Out Civilian Disarmament Operation in Luanda," Luanda Radio Nacional Network, in FBIS, *FBIS Daily Report*, 7 February 1997; Gumisai Mutume, "Haven of Peace Threatened by Arms," *Electronic Mail & Guardian* (South Africa), 26 January 1997, <http://www.mg.co.za/mg/news>.

38. Rana, op. cit. note 4; nonstate groups from Stephanie G. Neuman, "The Arms Trade, Military Assistance, and Recent Wars: Change and Continuity," *The Annals of the American Academy*, September 1995, and from Smith, op. cit. note 7.

39. Klare, op. cit. note 15.

40. Goldring, op. cit. note 9; Klare, op. cit. note 3.

41. Klare, op. cit. note 17; Klare, op. cit. note 3.

42. Klare, op. cit. note 17; Klare, op. cit. note 3. Table 8–2 is based on the following sources: William Reno, "The Business of War in Liberia," *Current History*, May 1996; Smith, op. cit. note 7; Elizabeth Rubin, "An Army of One's Own," *Harper's*, February 1997; Neuman, op. cit. note 38; Cock, op. cit. note 16; "Still Waiting for Peace," *Economist*, 29 March 1997; "Demobilizing but Still Divided," *Economist*, 14 September 1996; Suzanne Daley, "Tensions Threaten Angola's 3-Year Peace," *New York Times*, 1 August 1997; Eric Berman, *Managing Arms in Peace Processes: Mozambique*, UNIDIR Disarmament and Conflict Resolution Project (New York: United Nations, 1996); Jasjit Singh, "Light Weapons and Conflict in Southern Asia," and Tara Kartha, "Southern Asia: The Narcotics and Weapons Linkage," both in Singh, op. cit. note 15; Klare and Andersen, op. cit. note 16; Pierre Thomas and John Ward Anderson, "Mexico Asks U.S. to Track Guns Being Imported by Drug

Cartels," *Washington Post*, 5 November 1996. Quote from R.T. Naylor, "The Structure and Operation of the Modern Arms Black Market," in Boutwell, Klare, and Reed, op. cit. note 2.

43. Latin America and former Yugoslavia from Klare, op. cit. note 3; Algeria and Somalia from Smith, op. cit. note 7; Sierra Leone and Cambodia from Neuman, op. cit. note 38; South Africa from Cock, op. cit. note 16, and from Smith, op. cit. note 7.

44. Estimates of weapons seized from "Albania: Interior Ministry Reports 8 Deaths in Past 24 Hours," Paris AFP, in FBIS, *FBIS Daily Report*, 24 March 1997, and from "Anarchy in Albania: Collapse of European Collective Security?" *BASIC Papers*, no. 21, June 1997; bullets from Jane Perlez, "Arrest of Gang Gives Albanians Hope That Chaos Is Ending," *New York Times*, 17 August 1997; "Albania: TV To Broadcast UNICEF Message to Children About Weapons," Paris AFP, cited in FBIS, *FBIS Daily Report*, 14 March 1997; gun smuggling to neighboring countries from "Albania Village Finds Boom in Gun-Running," *New York Times*, 24 April 1997, and from "Albanian Arms Trafficking Increases," Agence France-Presse, Association for Progressive Communications (APC) (archived by Institute for Global Communications, San Francisco) computer conference <igc:disarm.armstra>, posted 31 July 1997.

45. Ksenia Gonchar and Peter Lock, "Small Arms and Light Weapons: Russia and the Former Soviet Union," in Boutwell, Klare, and Reed, op. cit. note 2; conscript quoted in Sarah Brown, "Modern Tales of the Russian Army," *World Policy Journal*, spring 1997.

46. China from Foster, op. cit. note 29; Pentagon from Gordon Witkin, "Handgun Stealing Made Real Easy," *U.S. News & World Report*, 9 June 1997.

47. Figure of 3 million firearms from John Mintz, "Amendment Could Bring Flood of Guns Into U.S.," *Washington Post*, 31 July 1997;

Michael Brzoska and Herbert Wulf, "Clean Up the World's Glut of Surplus Weapons," *International Herald Tribune*, 5 June 1997.

48. BICC, op. cit. note 10; Turkey from Klare, op. cit. note 15.

49. Goldring, op. cit. note 9.

50. Chris Smith, "Light Weapons and Ethnic Conflict in South Asia," in Boutwell, Klare, and Reed, op. cit. note 2; estimates of value of weapons can be found in Singh, op. cit. note 15, and in Smith, op. cit. note 7.

51. Singh, op. cit. note 42; Kartha, op. cit. note 42; Smith, op. cit. note 7.

52. North West Frontier Province, India, and Kashmir from Smith, op. cit. note 50, and from Smith, op. cit. note 7; Tajikistan from Jo L. Husbands, "Controlling Transfers of Light Arms: Linkages to Conflict Processes and Conflict Resolution Strategies," in Boutwell, Klare, and Reed, op. cit. note 2; Algeria, Myanmar, and Sri Lanka from Brzoska and Wulf, op. cit. note 47.

53. Secondhand markets from Naylor, op. cit. note 42, and from Smith, op. cit. note 7.

54. Zawels et al., op. cit. note 2; Paulo Wrobel, *Managing Arms in Peace Processes: Nicaragua and El Salvador*, UNIDIR Disarmament and Conflict Resolution Project (New York: United Nations, 1996); Laurance, op. cit. note 4; Peter Batchelor, "Disarmament, Small Arms, and Intra-State Conflict: The Case of Southern Africa," in Smith, Batchelor, and Potgieter, op. cit. note 7; Berman, op. cit. note 42; Smith, op. cit. note 7; Daley, op. cit. note 36; Clement Adibe, *Managing Arms in Peace Processes: Somalia*, UNIDIR Disarmament and Conflict Resolution Project (New York: United Nations, 1995); David Cox, "Peacekeeping and Disarmament: Peace Agreements, Security Council Mandates, and the Disarmament Experience," in Zawels et al., op. cit. note 2; Jianwei Wang, *Managing Arms in Peace Processes: Cambodia*, UNIDIR Disarmament and Conflict Resolution Project (New York: United Nations,

1996).

55. Laurance, op. cit. note 4; Batchelor, op. cit. note 54; Smith, op. cit. note 7; Fred Tanner, "Consensual Versus Coercive Disarmament," in Zawels et al., op. cit. note 2.

56. Need for swift disarmament from Sverre Lodgaard, "Demobilization and Disarmament: Experiences to Date," *UNIDIR Newsletter*, no. 32, 1996; the trade-offs between consensual and coercive disarmament are discussed in Tanner, op. cit. note 55.

57. Table 8–3 is based on the following sources: Laurance, op. cit. note 4; Armadeo Cabrera, "Arranca de Nuevo Campaña Bienes por Armas de Fuego," *La Prensa Grafica*, 6 March 1997; "Mas de 500 Armas Recolectadas el Fin de Semana," *La Nacion*, 8 April 1997; "Urgen Ley para Control de Armas de Fuego," *El Diario de Hoy*, 3 April 1997; Douglas Farah, "Cash for Cached Weapons," *Washington Post*, 1 November 1996; Daley, op. cit. note 36; Warren Hoge, "Arms Ban Leaves Owners Feeling Pistol-Whipped," *New York Times*, 17 July 1997; "Handgun Ban in Britain Passes Crucial Test," *New York Times*, 12 June 1997; Sarah Lyall, "Britain May Forbid Private Gun Ownership of Most Handguns," *New York Times*, 17 October 1996; "Gun Control Report Due to be Studied by Committee," *Otago Daily Times* (New Zealand), 1 July 1997; Brazil and Berry, "Australia's Answer," op. cit. note 27; David Elias, "Farewell to Arms, Gun by Gun," *The Age Online*, 20 September 1997, <http://www.theage.com.au:80/daily/970920/news/news1.htm>; "600,000 Guns Turned in During Australian Gun Amnesty," 30 September 1997, <http://www.nando.net/newsroom/ntn/world/093097/world16_20836.html>.

58. Laurance, op. cit. note 4.

59. Lodgaard, op. cit. note 56; Batchelor, op. cit. note 54.

60. Lodgaard, op. cit. note 56; amnesty programs from "Prime Minister Offers Pardon for 'Unlawful' Firearms," Maseru Radio Lesotho in FBIS, *FBIS Daily Report*, 30 October 1996, from "Sri Lanka Sets Arms Deadline," *World News*, 2 February 1997, and from United Kingdom Home Office, "22,939 Guns Collected in the Firearms Amnesty," press release (London: 23 July 1996).

61. Klare, op. cit. note 3.

62. Susannah L. Dyer and Natalie J. Goldring, "Analysing Policy Proposals to Limit Light Weapons Transfers," in Singh, op. cit. note 15.

63. Stephen Kinzer, "Nobel Peace Laureates Draft a Plan to Govern Arms Trade," *New York Times*, 6 September 1995; "Speech by Dr. Oscar Arias at Capitol Hill Symposium," Washington, DC, 15 December 1995, APC computer conference <igc:disarm.armstra>, posted 19 December 1995; "Nobel Laureates' International Code of Conduct on Arms Transfers," <http://www.igc.apc.org/basic/code_itl.htm>, viewed 25 September 1997.

64. Michael S. Lelyveld, "Bill Backed by Rights Groups Has Weapons Exporters Up in Arms," *Journal of Commerce*, 28 April 1997; "Banning Arms for Dictators" (editorial), *New York Times*, 20 June 1997; Jordana Friedman, Campaign Coordinator, The Year 2000 Campaign to Redirect World Military Spending to Human Development, "Endorsement, Media, and Legislative Update," New York, 1 August 1997; "Fate of Code Unclear," *Arms Trade News*, August/September 1997.

65. "Arias Introduces Code of Conduct," *Arms Trade News*, June 1997; "Banning Arms for Dictators," op. cit. note 64; BASIC, "Codes of Conduct on Arms Transfers: An Opportunity for the United States and its European Allies to Work Together," <http://www.igc.apc.org/basic/basic_sw.htm>, viewed 25 September 1997; Organization on Security and Cooperation in Europe, "Criteria on Conventional Arms Transfers," November 1993, <http://www.igc.apc.org/basic/osce-code.htm>; United Kingdom from Alan

Wheatley, "Britain Tightens Curbs on Arms Exports," <http://www.yahoo.com/headlines /970728/international/stories/weapons_ 2.hml>, 28 July 1997.

66. Karp, op. cit. note 2; Laurance, op. cit. note 4.

67. Klare, op. cit. note 3; Goldring, op. cit. note 9; Lora Lumpe, Federation of American Scientists, "Preliminary Policy Options for Monitoring/Restricting Exports of Light Arms," <http://www.fas.org/light_weapons/ light2.htm#head6>, viewed 28 May 1997.

68. Mexico from Howard LaFranchi, "Mexicans Too Have a Problem: Awash in U.S. Guns," *Christian Science Monitor*, 20 April 1997; for the OAS agreement, known as the Draft Inter-American Convention Against the Illicit Manufacturing of and Trafficking in Firearms, Ammunition, Explosives and Other Related Materials, see United Nations, op. cit. note 21; Central America from Sarah Meek, *United Nations Report on Firearms Regulation*, Institute for Security Studies Occasional Paper no. 23 (South Africa: June 1997); tripartite agreement from Batchelor, op. cit. note 54; South Africa-Mozambique agreement from Cock, op. cit. note 16, from "Police in Mozambique Destroy Cache of Arms," *New York Times*, 12 August 1997, and from Alex Belida, "SAF/ Mozambique," *Voice of America*, 12 August 1997, <gopher://gopher.voa.gov:70/00/newswire/ tue/SAF_-_MOZAMBIQUE>; "The EU Programme for Preventing and Combating Illicit Trafficking in Conventional Arms," *International Security Digest*, July 1997.

69. Naylor, op. cit. note 42.

70. Problem of lack of restrictions in one country affecting others from Sarah Brady, "Our Nation's Claim to Shame: United Nations Study Finds U.S. Is a Leading Source of Firearms for International Gun Smugglers," press release, Handgun Control, Inc., Washington, DC, 5 May 1997.

71. Raymond Bonner, "How a Group of Outsiders Moved Nations to Ban Land Mines," *New York Times*, 20 September 1997; U.S. Campaign to Ban Landmines, *Ban Treaty News*, APC computer conference <igc:disarm.arm-stra>, posted 16 September 1997.

Chapter 9. Assessing Private Capital Flows to Developing Countries

1. See Chapter 33 in United Nations, *Agenda 21: The United Nations Programme of Action from Rio* (New York: U.N. Publications, 1992); aid numbers from World Bank, *Global Development Finance 1997: Volume 1* (Washington, DC: 1997); 1996 numbers are preliminary World Bank estimates; reasons for aid's decline from Organisation for Economic Cooperation and Development (OECD), *Development Cooperation: 1996 Report* (Paris: 1997).

2. The World Bank defines developing countries as "all low and middle-income countries," which includes all of Africa and Latin America, and selected countries in Asia and the Pacific, the Caribbean, Eastern Europe and the Middle East; data and Figure 9–1 based on World Bank, op. cit. note 1 (1996 numbers are preliminary), and on World Bank, *Debtor Reporting System*, electronic database, Washington, DC, as of 30 July 1997; Institute of International Finance, Inc. (IIF), *Capital Flows to Emerging Market Economies: Update*, biannual report (Washington, DC: 11 September 1997). Of course, developing countries still receive only a relatively small share of total international private capital flows—37 percent of all foreign direct investment (FDI) inflows in 1996, per United Nations Conference on Trade and Development (UNCTAD), *World Investment Report 1997* (New York: United Nations, 1997).

3. World Bank, *Private Capital Flows to Developing Countries* (New York: Oxford University Press, 1997).

4. Major source countries from UNCTAD, op. cit. note 2, and from David Hedley, IIF, dis-

cussion with Payal Sampat, Worldwatch Institute, 18 September 1997; IIF, op. cit. note 2; Jacques de Larosière, "Financing Development in a World of Private Capital Flows: The Challenge for Multilateral Development Banks in Working with the Private Sector," The Per Jacobsson Lecture, Washington, DC, 29 September 1996; World Bank, op. cit. note 3.

5. World Bank, op. cit. note 3; China numbers from World Bank, *World Development Indicators on CD-ROM* (Washington, DC: 1997); growth rates in developing and industrial worlds from International Monetary Fund (IMF), *World Economic Outlook, October 1996* (Washington, DC: 1996).

6. Combating poverty is essential to meeting the needs of the present, and is thus fundamental to the concept of sustainable development. However, the question of how rising private capital flows affect poverty alleviation is for the most part beyond the scope of this chapter, which focuses primarily on the environmental dimensions of sustainable development. For information on the impact of economic globalization on poverty, see United Nations Development Programme (UNDP), *Human Development Report 1997* (New York: Oxford University Press, 1997).

7. Private flows based on World Bank, op. cit. note 5, and on World Bank, op. cit. note 1; reduction of poverty rates from UNDP, op. cit. note 6.

8. Richard J. Barnet and John Cavanagh, *Global Dreams: Imperial Corporations and the New World Order* (New York: Simon and Schuster, 1994); OECD, *Economic Globalization and the Environment* (Paris: 1997).

9. World Bank, *Annual Report 1997* (Washington, DC: 1997).

10. De Larosière, op. cit. note 4; World Bank, op. cit. note 1; IIF, op. cit. note 2.

11. FDI numbers from World Bank, op. cit. note 1 (total excludes some countries for which no data are given); gross domestic investment numbers based on World Bank, op. cit. note 5; attributes of FDI discussed in Theodore Panayotou, "The Role of the Private Sector in Sustainable Infrastructure Development," in Luis Gomez-Echeverri, ed., *Bridges to Sustainability: Business and Government Working Together for a Better Environment*, Yale School of Forestry and Environmental Studies Bulletin Series, Number 101 (New Haven, CT: Yale University, 1997).

12. UNCTAD, op. cit. note 2; share of holdings in developing world from Exxon *Annual Report 1996*, <http://www.exxon.com/exxon corp/shareholder_info/annual_96>, viewed 24 September 1997; Royal Dutch/Shell *Annual Report 1996*, <http://194.93.128.253/Annual_Report/index.html>, viewed 24 September 1997.

13. UNCTAD, op. cit. note 2.

14. Ibid.; World Bank, op. cit. note 1. The "services" sector is also known as the "tertiary" sector.

15. Indonesia data based on Investment Coordinating Board, *Statistics on Investment*, various issues, supplied by Masataka Fujita, UNCTAD, letter to Yumi Katagiri, Worldwatch Institute, 3 March 1997; Chile from Inter-American Development Bank/Institute for European-Latin Relations, *Latin America: The New Economic Climate* (Madrid: IRELA, 1996), cited in Pamela Stedman-Edwards et al., *The Private Sector in Latin America: Implications for the Environment and Sustainable Development* (Washington, DC: World Wildlife Fund, July 1997); Botswana from "African Investment: New Signs of Vitality," press release (Geneva: UNCTAD, 1 May 1997); Tunisia from World Bank, *World Debt Tables 1996, Volume 1* (Washington, DC: 1996), and from UNCTAD, *Foreign Direct Investment in Africa 1995* (New York: United Nations, 1995).

16. World Bank, op. cit. note 1; sectors from various investment fund prospectuses; de Larosière op. cit. note 4; Asian and Mexican crashes referred to in IIF, op. cit. note 2.

17. World Bank, op. cit. note 1; IIF, op. cit. note 2.

18. Minerals exploration numbers based on Metals Economic Group, "Major Increase in Junior Exploration Spending," press release (Halifax, NS, Canada: 14 October 1994), on Metals Economics Group, "Latin America Tops Exploration Spending for the Fourth Year," press release (Halifax, NS, Canada: 16 October 1997), and on Steve Kral, "Conference Explores Mining Possibilities," *Mining Engineering,* August 1997; gold exploration figures from Project Underground, "Global Gold Fever," from <http://www.moles.org/alerts/gold.html>, viewed 29 October 1997; William C. Symonds, "All that Glitters is Not Bre-X," *Business Week,* 19 May 1997.

19. Christine A. Adamec, "Face Forward," *Mining Voice,* May/June 1996; 70 countries from Symonds, op. cit. note 18; gold-to-waste ratio from John E. Young, "Gold Production at Record High," in Lester R. Brown, Hal Kane, and David Malin Roodman, *Vital Signs 1994* (New York: W.W. Norton & Company, 1994), based on U.S. Bureau of Mines data; indigenous peoples figure from Project Underground, op. cit. note 18. For more on the environmental and social impacts of mining around the world, see John E. Young, *Mining the Earth,* Worldwatch Paper 109 (Washington, DC: Worldwatch Institute, July 1992).

20. Oil and gas reserves from Hossein Razavi, "Financing Oil and Gas Projects in Developing Countries," *Finance and Development,* June 1996; regions from Jonathan Friedland, "Oil Companies Strive to Turn a New Leaf to Save Rain Forest," *Wall Street Journal,* 17 July 1997, from Patricia M. Carey, "Prospecting for Project Finance," *Infrastructure Finance,* April/May 1995, and from Geoff B. Kleburtz et al., Salomon Brothers Inc., "97 E&P Spending: Strongest Outlook in Nine Years," *World Oil,* February 1997.

21. Popovich quoted in Robin Bulman, "'Green Harassment' Spurs Overseas Quest," *Journal of Commerce,* 24 October 1996; Jonathan

Friedland, "Troubled at Home, Asian Timber Firms Set Sights on Amazon," *Wall Street Journal,* 11 November 1996; Environmental Investigation Agency, *Corporate Power, Corruption & The Destruction of the World's Forests* (Washington, DC: September 1996); Nigel Sizer, *Profit Without Plunder: Reaping Revenue from Guyana's Tropical Forests Without Destroying Them* (Washington, DC: World Resources Institute, September 1996); Julia Preston, "It's Indians vs. Loggers in Nicaragua," *New York Times,* 25 June 1996; Paul Adams, "Nigerian Logging Scheme Hits a Logjam," *Financial Times,* 1 October 1996; Nigel Sizer and Richard Rice, *Backs to the Wall in Suriname: Forest Policy in a Country in Crisis* (Washington, DC: World Resources Institute, April 1995).

22. Jeffrey D. Sachs and Andrew M. Warner, *Natural Resource Abundance and Economic Growth,* Development Discussion Paper No. 517a (Cambridge, MA: Harvard Institute for International Development, October 1995); linkages from Philip Daniel, "Economic Policy in Mineral-Exporting Countries: What Have We Learned?" in John E. Tilton, ed., *Mineral Wealth and Economic Development* (Washington, DC: Resources For the Future, 1992); Papua New Guinea and jobs from Danny Kennedy, "Drilling Papua New Guinea: Chevron Comes to Lake Kutubu," *Multinational Monitor,* March 1996; share of minerals exports in gross domestic product from Travis Q. Lyday, "The Mineral Industry of Papua New Guinea," in U.S. Geological Survey, *Minerals Information* (Washington, DC: 1996).

23. Walter V. Reid et al., *Biodiversity Prospecting: Using Genetic Resources for Sustainable Development* (Washington, DC: World Resources Institute, May 1993).

24. Ibid.; Jeffrey A. McNeely, "Achieving Financial Sustainability in Biodiversity Conservation Programs," in *Investing in Biodiversity Conservation,* Workshop Proceedings, Inter-American Development Bank, July 1997; Julie M. Feinsilver, "Biodiversity Prospecting: A

New Panacea for Development?" *Cepal Review 60*, December 1996; Layla Hughes, Conservation International, letter to Payal Sampat, Worldwatch Institute, 1 October 1997.

25. Sizer, op. cit. note 21; export revenue figures from Douglas Southgate, *Alternatives for Habitat Protection and Rural Income Generation* (Washington, DC: Inter-American Development Bank, March 1997); role for international investment in ecotourism from Katrina Brandon, *Ecotourism and Conservation: A Review of Key Issues* (Washington, DC: World Bank, April 1996).

26. Rainforest Alliance, "SmartWood List of Certified Operations," factsheet (New York: September 1997); Rainforest Alliance, Smart-Wood Program, "Public Certification Summary Report for Natural Forest Assessment of Mil Madeireira Itacoatiara Ltd." (New York: August 1997); Cheri Sugal, "Labeling Wood," *World Watch*, September/October 1996.

27. For the conventional view, see World Bank, *The East Asian Miracle: Economic Growth and Public Policy* (New York: Oxford University Press, 1993). However, see also Albert Fishlow et al., *Miracle or Design? Lessons From the East Asian Experience* (Washington, DC: Overseas Development Council, 1994); Paul Krugman, "First: Whatever Happened to the Asian Miracle?" *Fortune*, 18 August 1997; and Peter Montagnon, "Economies: Asia's Endangered Tigers," *Financial Times*, 30 August 1997.

28. The U.S. Department of Commerce includes food products, chemicals, machinery, paper products, electronics equipment, and several other industries in its category of manufacturing, per *Survey of Current Business*, March 1995. The United Nations Industry and Development Organization (UNIDO) uses a similar definition, per UNIDO, *Industrial Development: Global Report 1996* (Oxford: Oxford University Press, 1996). Information on relative labor intensity and environmental sensitivity of various industries from Michael Renner, *Jobs in a Sustainable Economy*, Worldwatch Paper 104 (Washington,

DC: Worldwatch Institute, September 1991).

29. Share of developing countries in production of various industries from UNIDO, data provided by Gerhard Magreiter, UNIDO, letter to Payal Sampat, Worldwatch Institute, 3 October 1997.

30. World Bank, op. cit. note 1; U.S. Department of Commerce, *Survey of Current Business*, September 1997.

31. Howard Hu, "Exporting Hazardous Industries, Products, and Wastes," *Our Planet*, vol. 8, no. 6 (1997); Carlos Plazola, Silicon Valley Toxics Coalition, "The Globalization of High Tech: Environmental Injustices Plague Industry," <http://www.corpwatch.org/feature/hitech/global.html>, viewed 15 September 1997.

32. Bradford S. Gentry and Daniel C. Esty, "Private Capital Flows: New and Additional Resources for Sustainable Development," in Gomez-Echeverri, op. cit. note 11; OECD, op. cit. note 8.

33. For a full though somewhat dated discussion of the role of environmental factors in companies' location decisions, see H. Jeffrey Leonard, *Pollution and the Struggle for the World Product* (Cambridge, U.K.: Cambridge University Press, 1988); on North American Free Trade Agreement (NAFTA) debate's focus on the border area, see, for example, John Holusha, "Trade Pact May Intensify Problems at the Border," *New York Times*, 20 August 1992; number of manufacturing plants from Gary Clyde Hufbacher and Jeffrey J. Schott, *North American Free Trade: Issues and Recommendations* (Washington, DC: Institute for International Economics, 1992); Mexicali from Roberto Sanchez, "Health and Environmental Risks of the Maquiladora in Mexico," *Natural Resources Journal*, Winter 1990.

34. Jason Abbott, "Export Processing Zones and the Developing World," *Contemporary Review*, vol. 270, no. 1576 (1997); Cavite information from Keith B. Richburg, "Under

Southeast Asia's Haze: More Bad Air," *Washington Post*, 5 October 1997; Chinese accusation from Xia Guang, "Pollution by Foreign Firms Rises," *China Environment News*, 15 February 1997.

35. Keith Bradsher, "In the Biggest, Booming Cities, A Car Population Problem," *New York Times*, 11 May 1997; Rebecca Blumenstein, "GM is Building Plants in Developing Nations to Woo New Markets," *Wall Street Journal*, 8 August 1997; Manjeet Kripalani, "A Traffic Jam of Auto Makers," *Business Week*, 5 August 1996.

36. David Wheeler and Paul Martin, "Prices, Policies, and International Diffusion of Clean Technology: The Case of Wood Pulp Production" in Patrick Low, ed., *International Trade and the Environment*, World Bank Discussion Papers (Washington, DC: World Bank, 1992); Stedman-Edwards et al., op. cit. note 15; Bradford S. Gentry, *Private Investment and the Environment*, Discussion Paper 11 (New York: UNDP, undated); Bradford S. Gentry and Lisa Fernandez, "Mexican Steel," in Bradford S. Gentry, ed., *Changing Roles: Private Capital Flows and the Environment in Latin America* (New Haven, CT: Center for Environmental Law and Policy, Yale University, pre-publication draft, 1997).

37. Steven Nadel et al., *Lighting Energy Efficiency in China—Current Status: Future Directions* (Washington, DC: American Council for an Energy-Efficient Economy, May 1997).

38. Rakesh Bakshi, "Country Survey: India," *Wind Directions*, April 1997; Christopher Flavin, "Wind Power Growth Continues," in Lester R. Brown, Michael Renner, and Christopher Flavin, *Vital Signs 1997* (New York: W.W. Norton & Company, 1997).

39. Services sector definitions based on UNCTAD, *World Investment Directory, Volume V: Africa* (New York: United Nations, 1997), on U.S. Department of Commerce, op. cit. note 28, and on Central Bank of the Philippines, Reserve Bank of India, and others.

40. Safe water from UNDP, op. cit. note 6; electricity from World Bank, *Rural Energy and Development: Improving Energy Supplies for Two Billion People* (Washington, DC: 1996); sanitation from UNICEF, *The Progress of Nations 1997* (New York: United Nations, 1997).

41. International Finance Corporation (IFC), *Financing Private Infrastructure* (Washington, DC: World Bank and IFC, 1996); World Bank, op. cit. note 1.

42. Asian Development Bank (ADB) *Emerging Asia: Changes and Challenges* (Manila: May 1997); Alex Wilks, "The World Bank's Promotion of Privatisation and Private Sector Development: Issues and Concerns," Bretton Woods Project, London, February 1997; Theodore Panayotou, "Asia in the 21st Century: Can it Grow Cleaner as it Grows Richer?" unpublished paper based on "Environment and Natural Resources" draft in ADB, op. cit. in this note.

43. Growth of developing-country power sector from International Energy Agency, *World Energy Outlook: 1996 Edition* (Paris: OECD, 1996).

44. Interest of international investors from Craig S. Smith, "China Experiments with Open Bidding to Break Logjam on Power Projects," *Wall Street Journal*, 6 December 1996, and from Henny Sender, "Fired Up," *Far Eastern Economic Review*, 16 January 1997; number of power plants to be built based on projections provided by Shi Dazhen, President of The State Power Corporation of China, in "Reform and Development of China's Power Industry," presented to CERA Global Power Forum Summit, February 13, 1997; "Authorities Reveal 3 Million Deaths Linked to Illness from Air Pollution," *International Environment Reporter*, 30 October 1996; China carbon emissions from Seth Dunn, "Carbon Emissions Set New Record," in Brown, Renner, and Flavin, op. cit. note 38, based on data from Oak Ridge National Laboratory and British

Petroleum; projections for 2010 are a Worldwatch estimate based on current carbon emissions growth rates.

45. "Survey: Power Generation," *Financial Times,* 19 June 1997; N. Vasuki Rao, "Power Transmission Open to Private Funds in India," *Journal of Commerce,* 24 January 1997; Kevin G. Hall, "El Salvador Set to Launch Bidding on Power Grids," *Journal of Commerce,* 20 February 1997; Kenneth Cooper, "Wattage to India," *Washington Post,* 5 February 1996; "Indonesia Picks Gas over Nuclear," *Journal of Commerce,* 7 August 1997; Jeremy Grant, "Vietnam Faces the Prospect of Power Crunch Next Year," *Financial Times,* 25 July 1997; Atossa Soltani and Tracey Osborne, *Arteries for Global Trade, Consequences for Amazonia,* (Malibu, CA: Amazon Watch, April 1997); quote from Jonathan Friedland, "In this 'Great Game,' No Holds Are Barred," *Wall Street Journal,* 14 August 1996; Michael S. Lelyveld, "Central Asia, Mideast Generate Gas, Power Deals," *Journal of Commerce,* 26 February 1997; "Thai National Environment Board Approves EIA for Gas Pipeline, With Conditions," *International Environment Reporter,* 2 April 1997.

46. Electricity to be supplied from James Harding, "China: More Winners Emerge in Three Gorges Scramble," *Financial Times,* 20 August 1997; flooding and resettlement numbers are U.S. Export-Import Bank estimates cited in "Ex-Im Bank Turns Down Requests to Consider Three Gorges Lending," *International Environment Reporter,* 12 June 1996; bond sales from Joe Studwell, "China is Confident on Dam Project, Rebuffs Skeptics," *Journal of Commerce,* 10 March 1997; "Contest Hots Up for Huge Yangtze Power Contracts," *Financial Times,* 25 July 1997.

47. Casper Henderson, "The Solar Revival," *Financial Times,* 3 July 1996; Enron Corp., "Amoco/Enron Solar Wins Contract to Build Largest Photovoltaic Solar Power Plant in the United States," press release (Houston, TX: 28 October 1996); Carol Hensley, spokesperson, Enron Corp., discussion with

Payal Sampat, Worldwatch Institute, 24 October 1997; Triodos Bank from Christopher Flavin and Molly O'Meara, "Financing Solar Electricity," *World Watch,* May/June 1997.

48. Figure of $600 billion from Ismail Serageldin, *Toward Sustainable Management of Water Resources* (Washington, DC: World Bank, 1995); Sandra Postel, *Last Oasis,* rev. ed. (New York: W.W. Norton & Company, 1997); Gentry, *Private Investment,* op. cit. note 36.

49. Postel, op. cit. note 48; Carl Frankel, "Heaven Can Wait," *Tomorrow,* September/October 1997; IFC, op. cit. note 41.

50. Michelle Chan, *Anatomy of a Deal: A Handbook of International Project Finance* (Washington, DC: Friends of the Earth, April 1996).

51. For example, for a description of World Bank environmental policies and guidelines, see World Bank, *Environment Matters: Annual Review* (Washington, DC: Fall 1996).

52. Peter Busowski, "OPIC Case Against U.S. Firm in Indonesia Raises Question of Authority, Project Scope," *International Environment Reporter,* 29 November 1995; $60 billion from Robert Bryce, "Environment: Struck By A Golden Spear," *The Guardian* (London), 17 January 1996; Stewart Yerton, "Mine Venture: Battle Between Ecology, Profits," *The Plain Dealer* (Cleveland), 28 January 1996; Janine Robers, "UK Cash Props Up Terror Mine," *The Independent* (London), 26 November 1995.

53. "Business Brief—Freeport-McMoran Copper & Gold Inc.: Federal Agency Reinstates Insurance on Firm's Project," *Wall Street Journal,* 22 April 1996; "Freeport-McMoran Copper & Gold Cancels Government Policy," *Wall Street Journal,* 23 September 1996.

54. John H. Cushman, "Ex-Im Bank Refuses Loan Backing for Big China Dam," *New York Times,* 31 May 1996; Tony Walker, "Power Hungry on the Gorges," *Financial*

Times, 17 February 1997; Office of the Press Secretary, The White House, "Remarks by the President in Address to the United Nations Special Session on Environment and Development," 26 June 1997.

55. Description of World Bank private-sector operations from World Bank, *The World Bank: Annual Report 1997* (Washington, DC: 1997); ratio of loans to private funds from IFC, "Investing in Development," Corporate Relations Office Slide Presentation, Washington, DC, 1997; Paul Lewis, "New World Bank: Consultant to Third World Investors," *New York Times,* 27 April 1995; MIGA numbers from Shaila Fernandes, Multilateral Investment Guarantee Agency, letter to Jennifer Mitchell, Worldwatch Institute, 14 March 1997.

56. IFC, "FY97 IFC Financing by Sector," Corporate Relations Office Slide Presentation, Washington, DC, 1997; Friends of the Earth-U.S., "IFC Investments in Latin America and Caribbean," "IFC Investments in Central Asia, Middle East, North Africa," "IFC Investments in Asia," and "IFC Investments in Sub-Saharan Africa," fact sheets (Washington, DC: undated); "Freeport McMoran Cancels MIGA Contract," *BankCheck Quarterly,* December 1996/January 1997.

57. IFC, op. cit. note 41; IFC, *World Bank Environmental Policy* (Washington, DC: 17 April 1994); IFC, "Environmental Requirements for Project Sponsors," undated; Ronald Anderson, IFC, discussion with author, 29 June 1995; Bruce Rich, *Mortgaging the Earth* (Boston: Beacon Press, 1994); Bruce Rich, "The Smile on a Child's Face," Epilogue to *Mortgaging the Earth* (Washington, DC: Environmental Defense Fund, unpublished, 1997).

58. "A New Environmental Sensitivity at the World Bank," Highlights from World Bank President James Wolfensohn's Speech at a World Resources Institute Dinner in Washington, DC," *International Perspectives on Sustainability,* World Resources Institute, March 1996; James D. Wolfensohn, remarks to Bank Group Seminar for NGOs on Private Sector Development and the Role of the Bank Group, Washington, DC, June 6, 1996; "World Bank Agency Challenged on Loan for Chilean Dam," press release (Berkeley, CA: International Rivers Network, 17 November 1995); Leslie Crawford, "Chile Dam Row Shows IFC's Problems with Projects," *Financial Times,* 8 August 1997.

59. World Bank, op. cit. note 51; $15 million from Mark Constantine, Manager of Corporate Relations, IFC, discussion with Payal Sampat, Worldwatch Institute, 23 October 1997; small loans from "EEAF Investments Up to February, 1997," information sheet (Arlington, VA: Environmental Enterprises Assistance Fund, Inc., 1997).

60. World Bank, op. cit. note 51; World Bank, "Private Sector Information Kiosk," from <http://www.worldbank.org/html/gef/private/priv.htm>, viewed 17 September 1997; Douglas Salloum, Small and Medium Enterprises Program Manager, IFC, discussion with Payal Sampat, Worldwatch Institute, 29 October 1997 ; IFC, *Annual Report 1997* (Washington, DC: 1997); Wilks, op. cit. note 42.

61. Michelle Chan-Fishel, "Risk Exposure: Revealing Environmental and Political Risk to Private Financiers," draft report (Washington, DC: Friends of the Earth, 11 May 1996); Gentry, *Private Investment,* op. cit. note 36; Schmidheiny and Zorraquín op. cit. note 42; "Bankers Urged to Include Assessments of Environmental Risk in Lending Decisions," *International Environment Reporter,* 14 May 1997.

62. Gentry, *Private Investment,* op. cit. note 36; John T. Ganzi and Julie Tanner, "Global Survey on Environmental Policies and Practices of the Financial Services Industry: The Private Sector," sponsored by National Wildlife Federation, Washington, DC, produced by Environment & Finance Enterprise, 16 May 1997.

63. Mark A. Cohen, Scott A. Fenn, and Jonathan S. Naimon, *Environmental and Financial Performance: Are They Related?*

(Washington, DC: Investor Responsibility Research Center, April 1995); Stanley J. Feldman, Peter A. Soyka, and Paul Ameer, *Does Improving a Firm's Environmental Management System and Environmental Performance Result in a Higher Stock Price?* (Fairfax, VA: ICF Kaiser International, Inc., November 1996). See also Jerald Blumburg, Åge Korsvold, and Georges Blum, *Environmental Performance and Shareholder Value* (Geneva: World Business Council for Sustainable Development, undated), and "Environmentally Responsible Investments Outperform Others," *Business and the Environment*, July 1997.

64. Social Investment Forum, *Responsible Investing Trends in the United States* (Washington, DC: 1997); "Green Investing Picks Up Steam," *EHS Management*, 4 August 1997; Chan, op. cit. note 50; "1996 SRI Industry Highlights & Changes," and "Mutual Fund Returns," *Green Money Journal*, Spring 1997; Domini 400 Index from Peter Kinder, President, Kinder, Lydenberg and Domini Co., Inc. (KLD), discussion with Payal Sampat, Worldwatch Institute, 22 October 1997, and from "Domini 400 Social Index Gains 5.53% in September, S&P 500 Gains 5.45%," news release (Cambridge, MA: KLD, 17 October 1997); Michelle Chan-Fishel, "International SRI," *GreenMoney Journal* online, <http://www.greenmoney.com/gmj/spr97/chan.htm>. For a list of socially responsible mutual funds, see the Social Investment Forum at <http://www.socialinvest.org/>.

65. "The Global Environment Fund Group," information sheet (Washington, DC: September 1996); Greg Nagler, Investment Analyst, Global Environment Fund, discussion with Payal Sampat, Worldwatch Institute, 30 October 1997; IFC, op. cit. note 60.

66. James Kynge, "Malaysia Appeal Court Clears Way for Dam Project," *Financial Times*, 18 February 1997; "Financial Backers of Bakun Dam Agree to Cancel Share Rights Issue," *International Environment Reporter*, 25 June 25, 1997.

67. See, for example, "The World Economy: The Future of the State," *The Economist*, 20 September 1997, and Peter F. Drucker, "The Global Economy and the Nation-State," *Foreign Affairs*, September/October 1997.

68. Stephan Schmidheiny and Federico J.L. Zorraquín, with the World Business Council for Sustainable Development, *Financing Change* (Cambridge, MA: The MIT Press, 1996); UNCTAD, *Self Regulation of Environmental Management: An Analysis of Guidelines Set by International Industry Associations for Their Member Firms* (New York: United Nations, 1996); Control Risks Group, *No Hiding Place: Business and the Politics of Pressure* (London: July 1997); "Lawyers See Rise in Court Cases Attempting to Apply U.S. Laws Outside Borders," *International Environment Reporter*, 25 June 1997.

69. On ISO certification see, for example, "Certification under ISO 14001 Expected for a Dozen Thai Firms in 1997," *International Environment Reporter*, 16 April 1997, "Czech Chemical Firm First to be Certified under 14001 in Former Eastern Bloc Country," *International Environment Reporter*, 5 March 1997, and "Environmental Management Systems: ISO Standard 14000," *International Environment Reporter*, 7 August 1996; "ISO 14001, 14004 Standards Finalized; U.K. To Withdraw Its Measure in March," *International Environment Reporter*, 2 October 1996; Benchmark Environmental Consulting, Portland, Maine, "ISO 14001 An Uncommon Perspective," November 1995, reprinted February 1996, <http://www.envirocom.com:80/standards/iso/14001/info.htm>, viewed 10 February 1997.

70. Pierre Hauselmann, *ISO Inside Out: ISO and Environmental Management*, WWF International Discussion Paper (Gland, Switzerland: June 1996); Sugal, op. cit. note 26; Anne Platt McGinn, "A Private-Sector Sustainable Fishing Initiative," *World Watch*, September/October 1996.

71. "North American Agreement on Environmental Cooperation, 1993," in *NAFTA Supplemental Agreements* (Washington, DC: U.S. Government Printing Office, 1993); Daniel Magraw, "NAFTA's Repercussions: Is Green Trade Possible?" *Environment,* March 1994; environmental benefits of NAFTA listed in U.S. Government, *Study on the Operation and Effects of the North American Free Trade Agreement,* 1997, <http://www.ustr.gov/reports/index. html>, viewed 8 October 1997; for an independent assessment, see Justin R. Ward, *The Greening of North American Trade, Four Years Later: A Summary and Report Card on Implementation of the NAFTA Environmental Package* (Washington, DC: Natural Resources Defense Council, 10 September 1997); 44 tons from Alberto Bustani, "Environmental Needs and Infrastructure in Mexico," 21 April 1995, cited in David W. Eaton, "NAFTA and the Environment; A Proposal for Free Trade in Hazardous Waste Between the United States and Mexico," *St. Mary's Law Journal,* vol. 27, no. 4 (1996).

72. Molly O'Meara, "Riding the Dragon," *World Watch,* March/April 1997; Asia-Pacific Economic Cooperation, *Implementing the APEC Vision,* Third Report of the Eminent Persons Group (Singapore: August 1995).

73. *The OECD Multilateral Agreement on Investment,* WWF (International) Briefing (Gland, Switzerland: March 1997); "The OECD Multilateral Agreement on Investment (MAI): Examples of Laws that Would Conflict with the MAI," <http://www.foe.org/ga/ exshort. html>, viewed 23 October 1997; Mark Vallianatos, Friends of the Earth, "Update on Negotiations for a Multilateral Investment Agreement (MAI)," memo to international activists (Washington, DC: 4 August 1997); International Non-Governmental Organisations, "Global Investment Treaty Challenged by International Coalition of NGOs," press release, 27 October 1997, <csdgen@nygate. undp.org>, posted 24 October 1997; International Institute for Sustainable Development, "WTO Ministerial Conference, 9–13 December 1996," *Sustainable Developments,* vol. 3, no. 6 (1996).

74. UNEP sectoral task forces described in "UNEP's Past Two Years; A Period of Significant Accomplishments," information sheet (New York: United Nations Environment Programme, May 1997); influence of World Bank guidelines from "Attorney Says Environmental Trends Abroad Will Have Far-Reaching Impact on U.S. Firms," *International Environment Reporter,* 1 November 1995.

75. Smitu Kothari, "Rising from the Margins: The Awakening of Civil Society in the Third World," *Development,* no. 3, 1996; Jonathan Friedland, "Across Latin America, New Environmentalists Extend Their Reach," *Wall Street Journal,* 26 March 1997; Lisa Jordan (Bank Information Center, Washington, DC) and Peter van Tuijl (Consultant, Novib, Amsterdam, Netherlands), "Political Responsibility in NGO Advocacy: Exploring Emerging Shapes of Global Democracy," unpublished paper, June 1997; Chan, op. cit. note 50; Leyla Boulton, "Activists Take Up Sharper Arrows," *Financial Times,* 13 May 1997.

76. Control Risks Group, op. cit. note 68; Control Risks Group description from <http://www.crg.com/ControlRisks/crg/inde x.html>, viewed 13 October 1997.

Chapter 10. Building a New Economy

1. Historic data from Herbert R. Block, *The Planetary Product in 1980: A Creative Pause?* (Washington, DC: U.S. Department of State, 1981); current data from International Monetary Fund (IMF), *World Economic Outlook, May 1997* (Washington, DC: 1997).

2. Current global output from IMF, op. cit. note 1.

3. Population increase from United Nations, *World Population Prospects: The 1996 Revision* (New York: forthcoming); informa-

tion on idled cropland from K.F. Isherwood and K.G. Soh, "Short Term Prospects for World Agriculture and Fertilizer Use," presented at 21st Enlarged Council Meeting, International Fertilizer Industry Association, Paris, 15–17 November 1995, and U.S. Department of Agriculture (USDA), Foreign Agricultural Service (FAS), *World Agricultural Production* (Washington, DC: October 1995); grain stocks data from USDA, *Production, Supply, and Distribution* (PS&D), electronic database, Washington, DC, updated May 1997, and from USDA, FAS, *Grain: World Markets and Trade* (Washington, DC: September 1997).

4. Sandra Postel, *Last Oasis,* rev. ed. (New York: W.W. Norton & Company, 1997); grain import data from USDA, PS&D, op. cit. note 3.

5. Postel, op. cit. note 4; Thomas F. Homer-Dixon, Jeffrey H. Boutwell, and George W. Rathjens, "Environmental Change and Violent Conflict," *Scientific American,* February 1993.

6. IMF, *International Financial Statistics* (Washington, DC: 1996).

7. "Tension in Jordan After Bread Riots," Reuters, 17 August 1996; Jamal Halaby, "More Jordanians Riot In Bread Price Protest," *Washington Post,* 18 August 1996; Serge Schmemann, "In Jordan, Bread-Price Protests Signal Deep Anger," *New York Times,* 21 August 1996; Pakistan information from "Surge in Wheat Imports by Several Nations Offset China and Russia Declines," in USDA, FAS, *Grain: World Markets and Trade* (Washington, DC: August 1997).

8. Paul McKeague, "Nation's Environment Abuse Decried," *Southam Newspapers,* 1 April 1997.

9. Population from United Nations, op. cit. note 3; grain data and Figure 10–1 from USDA, PS&D, op. cit. note 3.

10. Example of "leapfrogging" to cellular phones in "Can China Reform?" *Business Week,* 29 September 1997.

11. Scrap recycling data for 1996 from William Heanan, Steel Recycling Institute, discussion with author (Mitchell), 12 August 1997; Steel Recycling Institute, "The Inherent Recycled Content of Today's Steel," fact sheet (Pittsburgh, PA: July 1997); energy savings from Nicholas Lenssen and David Malin Roodman, "Making Better Buildings," in Lester R. Brown et al., *State of the World 1995* (Washington, DC: W.W. Norton & Company, 1995).

12. Jerry Powell, "The Coming Crisis In Steel Recycling: The Rising Role of Scrap Substitutes," *Resource Recycling,* July 1997; Steel Recycling Institute, op. cit. note 11.

13. Maureen Smith, *The U.S. Paper Industry* (Cambridge, MA: The MIT Press, 1997).

14. Brenda Platt and David Morris, *The Economic Benefits of Recycling* (Washington, DC: Institute for Local Self-Reliance, January 1993).

15. Data on jobs from ibid.; German data from "Green Dot Recycling Program Reports Rise in Level of Packaging Waste Collected in 1996," *International Environment Reporter,* 14 May 1997, and from "Government to Try Again to Get Parliament to Approve Changes to Packaging Ordinance," *International Environment Reporter,* 11 June 1997.

16. "Industrial Ecology: Case Histories," Indigo Development, Competitive Industries in Sustainable Communities Through Industrial Ecology, CA, <http://www.indigodev.com/Cases.html>, viewed 31 July 1997; Nicholas Gertler, "Industrial Ecosystems: Developing Sustainable Industrial Structures," Master's Thesis, Massachusetts Institute of Technology, Cambridge, MA, 1995.

17. "Industrial Ecology: Case Histories," op. cit. note 16; Gunter Pauli, Executive Director, Zero Emissions Research Institute, discussion with author (Brown), Tokyo, Japan, 15 September 1997.

18. Information on the Conservation

Reserve Program from Isherwood and Soh, op. cit. note 3, and from USDA, Natural Resources Conservation Service, *America's Private Land: A Geography of Hope* (Washington, DC: December 1996).

19. Information on Japan from Noel Grove, "Rice, The Essential Harvest," *National Geographic*, May 1994, and from USDA, PS&D, op. cit. note 3; "Chinese Reform Burial Customs," *Mazingira*, March 1984; information on Viet Nam from "South Korean Golf Course Exempted from Decree on Rice Fields," *New Frontiers*, June 1995.

20. Gary Gardner, *Shrinking Fields: Cropland Loss in a World of Eight Billion*, Worldwatch Paper 131 (Washington, DC: Worldwatch Institute, July 1996); Lester Brown, "Higher Crop Yields?" *World Watch*, July/August 1997.

21. Sandra Postel, *Dividing the Waters: Food Security, Ecosystem Health, and the New Politics of Scarcity*, Worldwatch Paper 132 (Washington, DC: Worldwatch Institute, September 1996).

22. Ibid.; Postel, op. cit. note 4; shifting land from USDA, PS&D, op. cit. note 3.

23. Grain-to-poultry ratio derived from Robert V. Bishop et al., *The World Poultry Market—Government Intervention and Multilateral Policy Reform* (Washington, DC: USDA, 1990); grain-to-beef conversion ratio based on Allen Baker, Feed Situation and Outlook Staff, Economic Research Service (ERS), USDA, Washington, DC, discussion with author (Brown), 27 April 1992; Figure 10–2 from USDA, PS&D, op. cit. note 3, and from USDA, FAS, *Livestock and Poultry: World Markets and Trade* (Washington, DC: March 1997).

24. United Nations, op. cit. note 3; water needed based on Wulf Klohn and Hans Wolter, "Perspectives of Food Security and Water Development," unpublished paper, and on Postel, op. cit. note 4; grain needed based on USDA, PS&D, op. cit. note 3. Water calculation assumes that 40 percent of the water required to produce the additional grain comes from irrigation.

25. United Nations, op. cit. note 3.

26. U.S. Bureau of the Census, *International Data Base*, Suitland, MD, 10 October 1997; John Cleland and Louisiana Lush, "Population and Policies in Bangladesh, Pakistan," *Forum For Applied Research and Public Policy*, Summer 1997; Figure 10–3 from United Nations, op. cit. note 3.

27. United Nations, op. cit. note 3.

28. John Bongaarts, "Population Policy Options in the Developing World," *Science*, 11 February 1994; Barbara Shane, *Family Planning Saves Lives* (Washington, DC: Population Reference Bureau, January 1997).

29. Nada Chaya, "Contraceptive Choice: Worldwide Access to Family Planning," wall chart (Washington, DC: Population Action International, 1997); Macro International, *Contraceptive Knowledge, Use, and Sources: Comparative Studies Number 19* (Calverton, MD: 1996).

30. "Pakistan: Family Planning with Male Involvement Project of Mardan," in *Family Planning Programs: Diverse Solutions For a Global Challenge*, package by Population Reference Bureau, Washington, DC, November 1993; information on spousal consent from John A. Ross, W. Parker Mauldin, and Vincent C. Miller, *Family Planning and Population: A Compendium of International Statistics* (New York: The Population Council, 1993), and from "Zambia: New Family Planning Policy Applauded," *Comtex Newswire*, 6 October 1997. In some countries, it may be beneficial for a woman to receive her husband's consent for sterilization so that her inability to reproduce is not used against her in the future.

31. G. Tyler Miller, "Cops and Rubbers Day in Thailand," in *Living In The Environment*, 8th ed. (Belmont, CA: Wadsworth Publishing Company, 1994); growth rates from United Nations, op. cit. note 3.

32. Bongaarts, op. cit. note 28.

33. David Bornstein, "The Grameen Bank—Trying to Put Poverty in Museums," *Why*, Summer 1997.

34. Macro International, *Bangladesh Demographic and Health Survey, 1996–97*, Preliminary Report (Calverton, MD: June 1997).

35. Shane, op. cit. note 28.

36. Ann Austin, "State of Grace," *Earthwatch*, March/April 1993.

37. Bongaarts, op. cit. note 28.

38. Ibid.

39. "Bangladesh: National Family Planning Program," in *Family Planning Programs: Diverse Solutions For a Global Challenge*, package by Population Reference Bureau, Washington, DC, February 1994.

40. United Nations Population Fund (UNFPA), "Meeting The Goals of The ICPD: Consequences of Resource Shortfalls up to the Year 2000," paper presented to the Executive Board of the U.N. Development Programme and the UNFPA, New York, 12–23 May 1997.

41. Ibid.; Michael Vlassoff, UNFPA, conversation with author (Mitchell), 28 October 1997.

42. UNFPA, op. cit. note 40.

43. Sharon L. Camp, "Population: The Critical Decade," *Foreign Policy*, Spring 1993.

44. Global temperatures from James Hansen et al., Goddard Institute for Space Studies Surface Air Temperature Analyses, "Table of Global Mean Monthly, Annual and Seasonal Land Ocean Temperature Index, 1950–Present," <http://www.giss.nasa.gov/Data/GISTEMP>, 19 January 1996; information on the insurance industry from Michael Tucker, "Climate Change and the Insurance Industry: The Cost of Increased Risk and the Impetus for Action," *Ecological Economics*, no.

22, 1997.

45. World Resources Institute et al., *World Resources 1996–97* (New York: Oxford University Press, 1996).

46. Bicycle data from United Nations, *Industrial Commodity Statistics Yearbook 1994* (New York: 1996); automobile statistics from American Automobile Manufacturers Association (AAMA), *World Motor Vehicle Data*, 1996 ed. (Detroit, MI: 1996), from AAMA, *Motor Vehicle Facts and Figures 1996* (Detroit, MI: 1996), and from DRI/McGraw-Hill, *World Car Industry Forecast Report* (London: November 1996).

47. China bicycle data from "World Market Report," *1997 Interbike Directory* (Newport Beach, CA: Primedia, Inc. 1997); Figure 10–4 from United Nations, op. cit. note 46, from "World Market Report," op. cit. this note, from AAMA, *World Motor Vehicle Data*, op. cit. note 46, from AAMA, *Facts and Figures 1996*, op. cit. note 46, and from DRI/McGraw-Hill, op. cit. note 46; Amsterdam information from "Civilized Servants," *IBF News* (International Bicycle Fund, Seattle), no. 2, 1995; Lima information from Deike Peters, "Bikeways Come to Lima's Mean Streets," *Sustainable Transport*, Winter 1997; U.K. information from "Government Sets Target to Quadruple Bicycle Use," *ENDS Report 258*, July 1996.

48. Toni Nelson, "Sales of Compact Flourescents Soar," in Lester R. Brown, Christopher Flavin, and Hal Kane, *Vital Signs 1996* (New York: W.W. Norton & Company, 1996); David Malin Roodman, "Compact Fluorescents Remain Strong," in Lester R. Brown, Nicholas Lenssen, and Hal Kane, *Vital Signs 1995* (New York: W.W. Norton & Company, 1995). Figure 10–5 has 1988 data from Evan Mills, Lawrence Berkeley Laboratory, Berkeley, CA, per discussion with David Malin Roodman, Worldwatch Institute, 3 February 1993; 1989–92 data from Nils Borg, "Global CFL Sales," *International Association for Energy-Efficient Lighting (IAEEL) Newsletter*, Stockholm, Sweden, April 1994; and 1993–95 data from Nils Borg, IAEEL/National Board

for Industrial and Technical Development, Stockholm, Sweden, discussion with Toni Nelson, Worldwatch Institute, 5 February 1996.

49. Firewood data from U.N. Food and Agriculture Organization, *State of the World's Forests 1997* (Oxford, U.K.: 1997); hydropower data from Energy Information Administration, *International Energy Annual 1995* (Washington, DC: Department of Energy, December 1996); installed wind generating capacity is a preliminary Worldwatch estimate based on Christopher Flavin, "Wind Power Growth Continues," in Lester R. Brown, Michael Renner, and Christopher Flavin, *Vital Signs 1997* (New York: W.W. Norton & Company, 1997), on *The Solar Letter*, various issues, and on *Windpower Monthly*, various issues; California wind farms from Mike Batham, California Energy Commission, Sacramento, CA, discussion with Christopher Flavin, Worldwatch Institute, 7 April 1994; Figure 10–6 from Birger Madsen, BTM Consult, "International Wind Energy Development" (Ringkobing, Denmark: 17 January 1997), from Paul Gipe and Associates, Tehachapi, CA, discussion with Christopher Flavin, Worldwatch Institute, 19 February 1996, and from Knud Rehfeldt, Deutsches Windenergie-Institut, letter to Christopher Flavin, Worldwatch Institute, 13 January 1997.

50. D.L. Elliott, L.L. Windell, and G.L. Gower, *An Assessment of the Available Windy Land Area and Wind Energy Potential in the Contiguous United States* (Richland, WA: Pacific Northwest Laboratory, 1991); China data from Christopher Flavin, "Worldwide Growth of Wind Energy," *World Watch*, September/October 1996.

51. Christopher Flavin, "Clean as a Breeze," *Time Special Issue*, November 1997.

52. Neville Williams, Solar Electric Light Fund, Washington, DC, discussion with Christopher Flavin, Worldwatch Institute, 29 January 1997.

53. Flavin, op. cit. note 51; information on Japan from "Japanese PVPS Would Go Further," *The Solar Letter*, 9 May 1997.

54. Enron Corp, "Enron Forms Enron Renewable Energy Corp: Acquire Zond Corporation, Leading Developer of Wind Energy Power," press release (Houston, TX: 6 January 1997); Martha M. Hamilton, "Energizing Solar Power," *Washington Post*, 26 August 1997.

55. Hamilton, op. cit. note 54; Robert Corzine, "Shell: £300m Spend on Renewable Energy," *Financial Times*, 17 October 1997; Flavin, op. cit. note 51.

56. Table 10–2 from the following sources: Sweden descriptions from P. Bohm, "Environment and Taxation: The Case of Sweden," in Organisation for Economic Co-operation and Development (OECD), *Environment and Taxation: The Cases of the Netherlands, Sweden and the United States* (Paris: 1994); Sweden quantity (14.4 billion Swedish kronor) from Nordic Council of Ministers, *The Use of Economic Instruments in Nordic Environmental Policy* (Copenhagen: 1996), cited in Stefan Speck, Keele University, Department of Economics, Keele, Staffordshire, U.K., e-mail message to David Roodman, Worldwatch Institute, 11 February 1997; Denmark 1994 description and quantity (12 billion Danish kroner) from Mikael Skou Andersen, "The Green Tax Reform in Denmark: Shifting the Focus of Tax Liability," *Journal of Environmental Liability*, no. 2, 1994; Denmark 1996 description and quantity (2.675 billion kroner) from Ministry of Finance, *Energy Tax on Industry* (Oslo: 1995); Netherlands description from Ministry of Housing, Spatial Planning, and Environment, *The Netherlands' Regulatory Tax on Energy: Questions and Answers* (The Hague: 1996); Netherlands quantity (2.2 billion florins) from Koos van der Vaart, Ministry of France, the Hague, discussion with David Roodman, Worldwatch Institute, 18 December 1995; Spain description from Thomas Shroder, "Spain: Improve Competitiveness through an

ETR," *Wuppertal Bulletin on Ecological Tax Reform* (Wuppertal Institute for Climate, Environment, and Energy), summer 1995; Spain quantity (47.47 billion pesetas) from Juan-Jose Escobar, Ministry of Economy and Finance, Madrid, letter to David Roodman, Worldwatch Institute, 29 January 1997; United Kingdom description and quantity (450 million pounds) from "Landfill Tax Regime Takes Shape," *ENDS Report* (London: Environmental Data Services), November 1995; total tax revenues for all countries from OECD, *Revenue Statistics of OECD Member Countries 1965–1995* (Paris: 1996).

57. Malaysia from David Malin Roodman, *Getting the Signals Right: Tax Reform to Protect the Environment and the Economy*, Worldwatch Paper 134 (Washington, DC: Worldwatch Institute, May 1997); Germany from European Environment Agency (EEA), *Environmental Taxes: Implementation and Environmental Effectiveness* (Copenhagen: 1996); Hans Th. A. Bressers and Jeannette Schuddeboom, "A Survey of Effluent Charges and Other Economic Instruments in Dutch Environmental Policy," in OECD, *Applying Economic Instruments to Environmental Policies in OECD and Dynamic Non-member Economies* (Paris: 1994).

58. "Two Birds With One Stone," *Acid News*, 1 April 1997.

59. Barbara Crossette, "Subsidies Hurt Environment, Critics Say Before Talks," *New York Times*, 23 June 1997.

60. EEA, op. cit. note 57; U.S. polling result is based on a sample of 1,000 adults taken in January 1993 by Greenberg-Lake/The Analysis Group, Washington, DC, and The Tarrance Group, Alexandria, VA, cited in Kate Stewart, Belden & Russonello, Washington, DC, letter to David Roodman, Worldwatch Institute, 10 March 1997.

61. Ross Gelbspan, *The Heat Is On* (New York: Addison-Wesley Publishing Company, Inc., 1997).

62. Teresa Watanbe, "In Historic Vote, Japanese Town Rejects Nuclear Plant," *Los Angeles Times*, 5 August 1997; Lester R. Brown, "We Are All Rubber Tappers," *World Watch*, March/April 1989; Yul Choi, Secretary General of the Korean Federation for Environmental Movement, discussion with authors, 6 October 1997; National Wildlife Federation, *1996 Annual Report* (Washington, DC: 1996); *United Nations Environment Programme (UNEP) Source of Funds, 1992–1996*, provided by Jim Sniffen, UNEP, New York, discussion with Hilary French, Worldwatch Institute, 19 February 1997.

63. Lester R. Brown, *Who Will Feed China?* (New York: W.W. Norton & Company, 1995).

64. "Surgeon General's Reports," Office of Smoking and Health, Centers for Disease Control and Prevention, http://www.cdc.gov/nccdphp/osh/sgrpage.htm, viewed 27 October 1997.

65. J.T. Houghton et al., eds. *Climate Change 1995: The Science of Climate Change*, Contribution of Working Group I to the Second Assessment Report of the International Panel on Climate Change (Cambridge, U.K.: Cambridge University Press, 1996); Colin D. Woodroffe, "Preliminary Assessment of the Vulnerability of Kiribati to Accelerated Sea Level Rise," in Joan O'Callahan, ed. *Global Climate Change and the Rising Challenge of the Sea*, Proceedings of the IPCC Workshop held at Margarita Island, Venezuela, March 9–13, 1992 (Silver Spring, MD: National Oceanic and Atmospheric Administration, 1992).

66. Gerhard A. Berz, Muchener Ruckversicherungs-Gesellschaff, press release (Munich, Germany: 23 December 1996); UNEP Insurance Initiative, *Position Paper on Climate Change* (Geneva: UNEP, 9 July 1996).

67. Ken Lay, Chairman and Chief Executive Officer, Enron, USA, "Too Hot For Business? The Implications of Global

Warming?" lunch session at the World Economic Forum Annual Meeting, Davos, Switzerland, 1 February 1997.

68. John Browne, Group Chief Executive, British Petroleum (BP America), Climate Change Speech, Stanford University, 19 May 1997.

69. Patrick E. Tyler, "China's Transport Gridlock: Cars vs. Mass Transit," *New York Times*, 4 May 1996.

70. Shapiro quoted in Joan Magretta, "Growth Through Global Sustainability," *Harvard Business Review*, January-February 1997; EBARA information from Pauli, op. cit. note 17.

71. Monsanto in Magretta, op. cit. note 70.

72. United Nations, op. cit. note 3; USDA, PS&D, op. cit. note 3; information on Denmark's restriction of coal-fired power plants from Climate Network Europe and US Climate Action Network (US CAN), *Independent NGO Evaluations of National Plans for Climate Change Mitigation, Fifth Review*

(Washington, DC: US CAN, November 1997); wind power data from Madsen, op. cit. note 49.

73. United Nations, op. cit. note 3; Saudi data from Seth S. Dunn, "The Geneva Conference: Implications for U.N. Famework Convention on Climate Change," *International Environment Reporter*, 2 October 1997.

74. United Nations, op. cit. note 3.

75. Stephen H. Schneider, "Global Warming Balance Sheet: What Do We Really Know," *Christian Science Monitor*, 8 August 1997; Howard Kurtz, "The White House Hopes To Warm Up TV Weathercasters," *Washington Post*, 18 September 1997.

76. For more on this, see Peter M. Vitousek et al., "Human Domination of Earth's Ecosystems," *Science*, 25 July 1997.

77. David Rohde, "Ted Turner Plans a $1 Billion Gift For U.N. Agencies," *New York Times*, 19 September 1997; John Goshko, "For United Nations, $1 Billion Is a Good Round Figure," *Washington Post*, 20 September 1997.

Index

Abbey, Edward, 4
Afghanistan, 142–43
Africa
    cropland productivity, 85
    endangered species, 47–49,
        51, 56
    fertilizer use, 101
    fisheries, 70
    foreign investment, 150
    grain imports, 94, 98
    soil erosion, 9
    see also specific countries
agriculture
    aquaculture, 5, 15, 60, 73
    bioinvasion, 45, 49, 54
    climate change effects, 10-11,
        92
    cropland loss, 8–9, 19, 80–81,
        172
    farm waste management, 97,
        109–10
    irrigation, 84–86, 173
    Organic Farming Research
        Foundation, 112
    organic materials flow, 96–99,
        110–12
    pesticide use, 43, 46
    Pioneer Hybrid seed
        company, 82–83
    Rodale Institute, 100
    soil management, 8–10, 19
    urban agriculture, 103
    water scarcity, 5–6, 168–69,
        173
    see also cropland productivity;
        fertilizer; forest products;
        forests; grain; livestock
aid, *see* food, aid; foreign
    investment
air pollution, 10–11, 14, 159, 172
Alliance of Small Island States,
    184
Amazon basin, 25–26, 30
Amoco, 160
amphibians, 49–52
Anglo-Dutch Unilever, 78
aquaculture, 5, 15, 60, 73

aquifer depletion
    accelerated water use, 4–6
    deforestation effects, 10
    economic effects, 18, 169
    land productivity, 95
Argentina
    cropland productivity, 88, 91
    endangered species, 46
    foreign investment, 156, 160
Arias, Oscar, 146
arms, *see* small arms proliferation
Asia-Pacific Economic
    Cooperation, 166
Asian Development Bank, 159
Association of South East Asian
    Nations, 146
Australia
    cropland productivity, 84
    endangered species, 49, 51
    energy policy, 117, 123, 129
    fisheries, 74
    small arms proliferation, 145
automobiles, 13–14, 115–16, 120,
    178

Bangladesh
    cropland productivity, 86
    economic growth, 15
    population stabilization, 174
        77
    water scarcity, 7–8
Bechtel, 180
beef, *see* livestock
bicycles, 178
biodiversity, 41–58
    amphibians, 49–52
    bioinvasion, 45, 49, 54
    birds, 43–46
    economic value, 11–12, 42, 57
    fish, 52–54
    indigenous people, 57–58,
        151, 162
    mammals, 46–49
    management, 54–58
    measurement, 41–43
    protected areas, 56–57
    reptiles, 49–52

sustainable forest
    management, 33–34, 39
    see also endangered species
biogas, 101, 108
bioinvasion, 45, 49, 54
bioprospecting, 32, 36, 155
biotechnology, 82–83, 89
birds, 43–46
Bongaarts, John, 175–76
Bonn International Center for
    Conversion, 142
Brazil
    cropland productivity, 88–89
    deforestation, 25, 28, 30
    energy policy, 117, 127
    fisheries, 64
    grain imports, 94
    illegal logging, 30
    logging waste, 36
    small arms proliferation, 137
Bristol Myers Squibb, 155
British American Security
    Information Council, 142
British Petroleum, 180, 185
Browne, John, 185
building efficiencies, 120–21

Cable News Network, 187
Cambodia
    illegal logging, 30–31
    small arms proliferation, 141
    sustainable forest
        management, 40
Camp, Sharon, 177
Canada
    cropland productivity, 88
    energy policy, 117, 123, 126,
        129
    fisheries, 59–61, 71, 73
    forest management, 27, 31, 38
    Sierra Legal Defense Fund, 31
    small arms proliferation, 138
    transportation policy, 120
carbon emissions
    carbon dioxide, 10, 19,
        113–17
    chlorofluorocarbons, 130

carbon emissions *(continued)*
  costs, 117–19
  energy policies, 117–19, 127
    30, 159
  methane, 101, 108
  stabilization, 119–23, 127–30,
    185
  subsidies, 114, 117–19, 128
  taxes, 111–19, 128, 181–83
  see also climate change
Caterpiller, 161
China
  air pollution, 14, 159
  aquifer depletion, 7
  automobile use, 13–14, 185
  cropland loss, 80, 86–90, 172
  economic growth, 3, 12–15
  energy policy, 123, 127, 179
  fertilizer use, 16
  foreign investment, 158–59,
    161
  grain consumption, 12–13,
    15
  grain production, 7
  grain trade, 92, 94
  human waste management,
    104, 108
  industrialization, 13–14, 80
  livestock consumption, 13,
    15
  Ministry of Heavy Industry,
    13
  National Environmental
    Protection Agency, 14,
    157
  oil consumption, 13–14
  population stabilization, 184
  small arms proliferation, 141
  water pollution, 11
  water scarcity, 7
Chinese Academy of Sciences, 14
chlorofluorocarbons, 130
Christy, Francis, 68
climate change, 113–30
  crop damage, 10–11, 92
  ecological effects, 10–11, 19,
    55, 63
  Framework Convention on
    Climate Change (Rio), 39
  Intergovernmental Panel on
    Climate Change, 63, 113,
    117–24, 184
  Kyoto meeting, 113, 127–30
  stabilization strategies, 113–
    14, 127–30, 177–81
  storms, 10
  see also carbon emissions
Clinton, Bill, 127, 187
Clinton administration, 186–87
coal, 115, 117–19, 159, 179

Cock, Jacklyn, 138
Code of Conduct for
  Responsible Fishing, 75
cogeneration, 124–25, 159
Colombia, 138, 145
Community Recycling, 104
compact fluorescent lights, 179
Compagnie Générale des Eaux,
  160
composting, 102–04, 107, 112
composting toilets, 102, 107–08
Congo, Democratic Republic of,
  48, 55
conservation
  energy reform, 119–30, 173,
    179
  forest management, 4, 24–40
  land management, 80, 172
  soil management, 8
  World Conservation Union,
    35, 43–52, 55–56
  see also biodiversity;
    endangered species;
    waste management
Conservation International, 155
Conservation Reserve Program
  (U.S.), 80, 172
Control Risks Group, 167
Cooke, G.W., 99
corn, *see* grain
Costa Rica
  energy policy, 119
  foreign investment, 154
Costanza, Robert, 37
Côte d'Ivoire, 9
cropland loss
  erosion, 8–9, 19, 81
  land-use zoning, 172
  nonfarm use, 80–81, 172
  urbanization, 80
cropland productivity, 79–95
  assessment, 79–81
  biotechnology, 82–83, 89
  commercial fertilizer, 16, 82
    83, 88, 95
  compost use, 102–04, 107,
    112
  environmental factors, 10,
    84–88, 92
  global trends, 88–95
  irrigation, 84–86, 173
  mechanization, 83–84, 89–90
  nonfarm use, 80–81

Daley, Suzanne, 139
dams
  foreign investment, 160, 162
  habitat loss, 52, 162, 164
deforestation, 9–10, 22–30, 154
demilitarization, *see* small arms

  proliferation
Denmark
  energy policy, 124, 129, 181
  fisheries, 61
  industrial ecology, 172
  population stabilization, 186
  transportation policy, 118
developing countries
  aid, *see* foreign investment
  air pollution effects, 10–11
  carbon emissions, 115–16
  cropland productivity, 85
  energy policy, 116, 122
  fisheries, 67, 70–71, 73
  fuelwood consumption,
    9–10, 23–24, 37, 179
  industrialization, 14, 115,
    171–72
  infrastructure development,
    158–60
  small arms proliferation,
    133–36, 144–45
  see also specific countries
diet, *see* food
disarmament, *see* small arms
  proliferation
Duvick, Don, 82–83

Earth Summit, 149
economy
  aquifer depletion effects, 18,
    169
  biodiversity value, 11–12, 42,
    57
  carbon emission costs,
    117–19
  ecological impact, 4–12,
    153–56, 168–87
  economic zones, 157
  energy costs, 117–19
  exclusive economic zones,
    67, 75
  fertilizer costs, 99–102
  fisheries value, 67–71
  food scarcity consequences,
    14–17, 91–95, 169
  forest products trade, 26,
    39–40, 154
  gross domestic investment,
    152
  growth consequences, 3–20,
    168–69
  industrialization, 12–14, 115,
    171–72
  international trade, 26,
    39–40, 91–95, 157
  recycling value, 99–102,
    170–72
  reform policy, 181–83
  sustainable development,

4–9, 17–20, 168–87
see also foreign investment;
grain; subsidies; taxes
ecosystems
economic growth impact,
4–9, 11–12, 153–56
economic value, 37
habitat loss, 22–29, 44–55
organic materials flow, 96–99,
110–12
sustainable forest
management, 4, 31–40
wetlands, 53, 106–08
see also biodiversity;
freshwater ecosystems
ecotourism, 155
Egypt, 7, 8, 88
El Salvador, 138, 145
employment, *see* jobs
endangered species, 41–58
amphibians, 49–52
bioinvasion, 45, 49, 54
birds, 43–46
economic growth effects,
11–12
fish, 11, 52–54
mammals, 46–49
reptiles, 49–52
sustainable forest
management, 4, 31–40
see also biodiversity
Endangered Species Act (U.S.),
74
energy
costs, 117–19
efficient use, 119–23, 173, 179
foreign investment, 158–60
International Energy Agency,
115
policy, 127–30
Tata Energy Research Institute
(India), 11
see also carbon emissions;
fossil fuels; renewable
energy
Enron, 160, 180, 185
environmental education, 57
environmental policy, 151,
153–56, 160–67
erosion, 8–9, 19, 81
European Commission, 119–20
European Council of Ministers,
146–47
European Union
energy policy, 121
fisheries, 5, 61, 69–70, 73
grain exports, 92–93
population stabilization, 170
water pollution, 100
see also specific countries

Evans, L.T., 82
exclusive economic zones, 67, 75
exotic organisms, *see* bioinvasion
extinction, *see* biodiversity;
endangered species
Exxon, 152

family planning, 175–77
farmland, *see* cropland loss;
cropland productivity
Federation for Environmental
Movement (Korea), 184
fertilizer
compost use, 102–04, 107, 112
costs, 99–102
cropland productivity, 16,
82–83, 88, 95
nutrient flow, 96–99, 110–12
overfertilization, 96, 99
runoff, 53, 62, 96, 98–100
sewage sludge, 104–08
fisheries, 59–78
aquaculture, 5, 15, 60, 73
bycatch, 64, 74
capacity, 65–69
catch, 5, 61–62
climate change effects, 63
Code of Conduct for
Responsible Fishing, 75
cyanide fishing, 64, 74
decline, 60–67
economic value, 67–71
endangered species, 11, 52–54
exclusive economic zones, 67,
75
fishing gear effects, 63–65
individual transferable quotas,
72–73
International Center for
Living Aquatic Resources
Management, 62–63
international conflicts, 59–60,
66
job losses, 59–60, 71
Marine Stewardship Council,
165
overfishing, 60–67
pollution effects, 62
regulation, 59–60, 66, 70–75
social effects, 69–71
South Pacific Forum Fisheries
Agency, 74
subsidies, 65, 67, 69
sustainable management, 4–5,
13, 18, 75–78
Five College Program in Peace
and World Security
Studies, 134, 139–40
floods, 26, 29
food

aid, 93
economy effects, 14–17
global stabilization, 172–74
scarcity, 14–17, 91–95, 169
see also agriculture; cropland
productivity; fisheries;
grain; livestock; waste
management
Food and Agriculture
Organization (U.N.)
fisheries report, 5, 60, 64,
67–68, 74–75
forest assessment, 23–24, 36,
40
grain stock projections, 94
Ford Motor Company, 152, 157
foreign investment, 149–67
commercial bank loans,
151–52
commodities, 153
environmental policy effects,
151, 153–56, 160–67
governmental aid, 151–52
infrastructure investment,
158–60
investment power, 160–64
manufacturing, 156–58
natural wealth, 153–56
portfolio equity investments,
153
private investment, 149–53,
161–62
stocks, 163–64
see also subsidies
Forest Practices Code (Canada),
31
forest products
demand, 9, 21, 24
economic value, 24, 27–32,
35–38
international trade, 26, 39–40,
154
nontimber forest products, 27,
32–33, 36, 155
paper consumption, 24, 36–37
production management,
35–36
Forest Stewardship Council,
33–35, 156, 165
forests, 21–40
area, 22–23
deforestation, 9–10, 22–30,
154
foreign investment, 154–56
fuelwood, 9–10, 23–24, 37,
179
illegal logging, 30–31, 38
International Tropical Timber
Agreement, 39–40
management, 24–25, 27–40

forests *(continued)*
    national policies, 27–31,
        38–40
    plantations, 23, 33
    quality, 22–23
    rehabilitation, 35–40
    subsidies, 24, 27–28, 31,
        37–38
    sustainable forest
        management, 4, 31–40
fossil fuels
    consumption, 13–14, 115–19
    efficient use, 119–23
    foreign investment, 151–54,
        159
    subsidies, 114, 117–19, 128,
        183
    taxes, 111–19, 128
    see also carbon emissions;
        renewable energy
France
    carbon emissions, 115
    cropland productivity, 84, 90
    fisheries, 64
    transportation policy, 118
Franklin, Jerry, 32
Freeport McMoran Copper and
        Gold, 161–62
freshwater ecosystems
    Amazon River basin, 25–26,
        30
    Colorado River, 53
    Comprehensive Freshwater
        Assessment, 102
    dam effects, 52, 160, 164
    fertilizer runoff, 53, 62, 96,
        98–100
    fish extinctions, 52–54
    floods, 26, 29
    Ganges River, 7–8, 26
    Huang He River, 7, 85
    Lake Victoria, 53
    management, 54
    Mississippi River basin, 53,
        100
    Nile River, 8
    Tonle Sap, 30
    wetlands, 53, 106–08
    Yangtze River, 160–61
Friends of the Earth, 161, 184
fuelwood consumption, 9–10,
        23–24, 37, 179
Fujimura, Hiroyuki, 185

Gelbspan, Ross, 183
General Motors, 152, 157
Gentry, Bradford, 163
Germany
    carbon emissions, 115, 181
    energy policy, 122, 126–27,

        129, 180
    recycling projects, 171–72
    small arms proliferation, 142
    toxic waste, 181
    transportation policy, 118
Global Environment Facility, 58,
        69, 162–64
Global Environment Fund, 164
global warming, *see* climate
        change
Goldring, Natalie, 142
Gonchar, Ksenia, 140–41
grain
    biotechnology, 82–83, 89
    carryover stocks, 16, 79, 91,
        95
    consumption, 12–16, 79,
        91–95, 168
    environmental effects, 10,
        84–88, 92
    feedgrain use, 15, 80, 98, 173
    international trade, 91–95,
        98, 109
    prices, 16–17, 91, 94–95, 169
    subsidies, 6, 90
    yields, *see* cropland
        productivity
Grameen Bank, 176
greenhouse gases, *see* carbon
        emissions; climate
        change; specific gas
Greenpeace, 184
guns, *see* small arms
        proliferation

Hardin, Garrett, 65
Hasan, Bob, 31
hazardous waste, 105–06, 156,
        181
Hoitink, Harry, 102
Holdren, John, 115
hunger, *see* food
hydrogen fuel, 180–81, 185

ICF Kaiser, 163
IMAZON, 36
India
    air pollution effects, 11
    composting facilities, 104
    cropland productivity, 84, 86
    economic growth, 15
    endangered species, 48, 53,
        56
    energy policy, 117, 127
    family planning, 176
    foreign investment, 157–58,
        160
    forest management, 38
    fuelwood consumption, 10
    grain imports, 94

    human waste management,
        107
    National Environmental
        Engineering Research
        Institute, 6
    small arms proliferation, 143
    water scarcity, 6–7, 18
indigenous people, 29, 57, 151,
        154, 162
individual transferable quotas,
        72–73
Indonesia
    deforestation, 25–27
    economic growth, 15
    foreign investment, 153
    forest fires, 25–26
    forest management, 27–32,
        38
    transmigration program,
        28–29
industrialization, 12–14, 115,
        171–72
Institute for Soil Management
        (Kazakhstan), 8
Institute of International
        Finance, 149
International Center for Living
        Aquatic Resources
        Management, 62–63
International Council for the
        Exploration of the Seas,
        61
International Finance
        Corporation, 161–64
International Monetary Fund, 3,
        17, 40
International Organization for
        Standardization, 165
International Peace Research
        Institute, 134
Investor Responsibility Research
        Center, 163
Iran, 7–8
irrigation
    cropland productivity
        enhancement, 84–86, 173
    ecological damage, 8
    nonfarm use, 7

Japan
    cropland productivity, 81–86,
        90
    energy policy, 121–23, 127,
        129, 179–80
    fisheries, 13, 66, 70, 74
    foreign investment, 150
    forest products consumption,
        26, 34
    grain imports, 93
    land–use zoning, 172

jobs
  fisheries decline, 59–60, 71
  industrialization, 13–14, 80
  wind generation, 126

Kazakhstan, 8, 80, 84
Khmer Rouge, 30
Khush, Gurdev, 87
Klare, Michael, 134–35, 139–40
Kohm, Kathryn, 32
Kyoto meeting on climate
    change, 113, 127–30

Lal, Rattan, 9
land, *see* cropland loss; cropland
    productivity; rangeland
Laurance, Edward, 138, 144
Law of the Sea, 60, 67
Lay, Ken, 185
Liberia, 141
Lien, Jon, 71
life expectancy, 3
livestock
  consumption, 13, 15
  farm waste management, 97,
    109–10
  feedgrain use, 15, 80, 98, 173
  grazing practices, 8
Lock, Peter, 140–41
logging, *see* forest products;
    forests
Lubchenco, Jane, 19
Lyonnaise des Eaux, 160

Malaysia
  economic growth, 15
  energy policy, 181
  foreign investment, 156
mammals, 46–49
manufacturing
  foreign investment, 156–58
  recycle economy, 171–73
Marcos, Ferdinand, 29–30
Mathe, Lazaro, 138
McQuaid, John, 70
Mercedes–Benz, 157
Merck and Company, 155
methane, 101, 108
methyl bromide, 102
Mexico
  cropland productivity, 85–86,
    88, 90
  fisheries, 74
  foreign investment, 153, 157,
    160
  grain imports, 94
  human waste management,
    106–08
  small arms proliferation, 138,
    141
Milazzo, Matteo, 68–69

Miller, David, 74
mining, 154, 161–62
Missouri Botanical Gardens, 155
Monsanto, 185–86
Monterey Institute of
    International Studies, 138
Mozambique, 138–39, 145
Multilateral Investment
    Guarantee Agency, 161–62
Myers, Norman, 37

National Rifle Association (U.S.),
    137
National Wildlife Federation
    (U.S.), 108, 163, 184
natural gas, 159
natural resources
  degradation, 22–24, 27–30,
    154
  foreign investment, 153–56
  mining, 154, 161–62
  see also biodiversity;
    endangered species;
    fisheries; forests; fossil
    fuels; renewable energy;
    water
Naylor, R.T., 140, 147
Netherlands
  energy policy, 125, 128–29,
    181
  livestock waste management,
    109, 112
  transportation policy, 118–19
New Zealand, 45, 49, 74
North American Free Trade
    Agreement, 157, 165
North Atlantic Treaty
    Organization, 142

oceans, *see* fisheries
oil, 13–14, 151–54
Organic Farming Research
    Foundation, 112
organic materials, *see* recycling;
    waste management
Organisation for Economic
    Co-operation and
    Development, 73, 100, 102,
    118, 166
Organization of American States,
    146–47
Organization on Security and Co-
    operation in Europe, 146
ozone depletion, 116

Pakistan
  economic growth, 15
  food scarcity, 169
  grain imports, 94
  population stabilization,
    174–75

small arms proliferation,
    142–43
paper
  consumption, 24, 36–37
  recycling, 36–37, 171
Philippines
  cropland productivity, 87
  endangered species, 45
  fisheries, 72, 76
  forest management, 29–30
  forest product imports, 9
Pioneer Hybrid seed company,
    82–83
policy
  economic reform, 181–83
  energy, 119–30, 173, 179
  environment, 151, 153–56,
    160–67
  fisheries management, 4–5,
    13, 18, 75–78
  forest management, 4, 31–40
  freshwater ecosystems, 54
  transportation, 118–20
pollution
  air pollution, 10–11, 14, 159,
    172
  fertilizer runoff, 53, 62, 96,
    98–100
  manufacturing, 156–58
  manure runoff, 109–10
  pesticides, 43, 46
  species extinction, 46, 52, 54
  see also water pollution
Popovich, Luke, 154
Population and Community
    Development Association
    (Thailand), 175
population growth
  family planning, 175–77
  grain demand, 79–80, 94–95,
    168
  stabilization, 170, 174–77,
    186
Porter, Gareth, 69
poverty, 150
Precious Woods Management
    Ltd., 156
private investment, *see* foreign
    investment
private security forces, 135–36

Rainforest Alliance, 156
rangeland, 8, 15, 173
recycling, 96–122
  Community Recycling, 104
  costs, 99–102
  economic stabilization,
    170–72
  farm waste management, 97,
    109–10

recycling *(continued)*
　human waste management,
　　97, 101, 104–08
　landfills, 101–02, 111, 171–72
　organic materials flow, 96–99,
　　110–12
　paper, 36–37, 171
　urban garbage composting,
　　102–04
Rees, William, 169
renewable energy
　alternative sources, 37, 114,
　　123–27, 177–81
　biogas, 101, 108
　cogeneration, 124–25, 159
　ethanol, 127
　foreign investment, 158–60
　hydroelectric, 160, 162
　hydrogen fuel, 180–81, 185
　solar, 123–27, 158–60, 180–81
　tax incentives, 119–30
　wind, 124–27, 179–80, 186
Repetto, Robert, 116
reptiles, 49–52
rice, *see* grain
Riso National Laboratory
　(Denmark), 124
rivers, *see* floods; freshwater
　ecosystems; water
road subsidies, 117–18
Rodale Institute, 100
Royal Dutch Shell, 116, 152, 180,
　185
Russia
　carbon emissions, 115
　energy policy, 117, 121
　fisheries, 66
　small arms proliferation, 136,
　　140–41, 143

Sachs, Jeffrey, 155
Scripps Institute of
　Oceanography, 63
sewage treatment, *see* waste
　management
Shapiro, Robert, 185–86
Sierra Legal Defense Fund
　(Canada), 31
Silicon Valley Toxics Coalition,
　156
Sinclair, Thomas R., 89
SIRDO, 107–08
small arms proliferation, 131–48
　children soldiers, 133–34
　code of conduct, 146
　disarmament, 143–46
　Institute for Disarmament
　　Research, 139
　privatized violence, 132–36
　sources, 136–43

SmartWood, 156
Smith, Chris, 142
Smith, Dan, 134
Social Investment Forum, 164
Soeharto, 31
soil, *see* cropland loss; cropland
　productivity; erosion
solar energy, 123–27, 158–60,
　180–81
Solarex, 180
South Africa, 138–40
South Korea
　cropland productivity, 86
　economic growth, 15
　energy policy, 120
　Federation for Environmental
　　Movement, 184
　forest products consumption,
　　26
　grain imports, 93
Soviet Union (former)
　carbon emissions, 115
　cropland productivity, 83,
　　88–89
　small arms proliferation,
　　139–40, 142
stabilization ponds, 106–08
subsidies
　carbon emissions, 114,
　　117–19, 128
　fisheries, 65, 67, 69
　forest use, 24, 27–28, 31,
　　37–38
　grain, 6, 90
　renewable energy, 119–30
　water use, 6
Suriname, 26, 27, 30, 155
sustainable development
　economic development, 4–9,
　　17–20, 168–87
　forest management, 4, 31–40
Sweden, 119, 121, 126, 182
Switzerland, 121, 126, 180

Taiwan, 93, 109
Tata Energy Research Institute
　(India), 11
taxes
　carbon emissions, 111–19,
　　128, 181–83
　economic reform policy,
　　181–83
　land use, 28, 172
　landfills, 111
　renewable energy incentives,
　　119–30
　timber, 28
Terra Capital Fund, 164
Thailand
　economic growth, 15

family planning, 175
fisheries, 70
forest management, 29
forest product imports, 9
Third World, *see* developing
　countries
Three Gorges Dam (China),
　160–61
Tomen, 179–80
toxic waste, 105–06, 156, 181
trade, *see* economy
TRAFFIC, 51
transportation
　automobiles, 13–14, 115–16,
　　120, 178
　bicycles, 178
　foreign investment, 158–60
　public transportation, 118–19
　road subsidies, 117–18
Trillium Corporation, 166
Triodos Bank, 160
Truman Proclamation, 66
Turner, Ted, 187

unemployment, *see* jobs
UNIDIR, 143
United Kingdom
　carbon emissions, 115
　certified wood products,
　　33–34
　cropland productivity, 90
　energy policy, 117, 126
　landfills, 101, 111
　paper consumption, 36
　small arms proliferation,
　　145–46
　transportation policy, 118–19
United Nations
　Commission on Crime
　　Prevention and Criminal
　　Justice, 136
　Commission on Forests and
　　Sustainable Development,
　　39
　Commission on Sustainable
　　Development, 75
　Comprehensive Freshwater
　　Assessment, 102
　Conference on Environment
　　and Development, 149
　Conference on Trade and
　　Development, 152
　Convention on Biological
　　Diversity, 39, 55, 58, 75,
　　155
　Convention on Highly
　　Migratory and Straddling
　　Stocks, 75
　Convention on International
　　Trade in Endangered

Species of Wild Flora and Fauna, 40, 51, 55
Convention on the Law of the Sea, 60, 67
Development Programme, 162
Environment Programme, 162, 166, 184
Framework Convention on Climate Change (Rio), 39
Institute for Disarmament Research, 139
Intergovernmental Panel on Climate Change, 63, 113, 117–24, 184
Intergovernmental Panel on Forests, 39
International Conference on Population and Development (Cairo), 177
International Energy Agency, 115
International Labour Organization, 166
International Tropical Timber Agreement, 39–40
Kyoto meeting on climate change, 113, 127–30
Population Fund, 177
Register of Conventional Arms, 146
World Health Organization, 106
see also Food and Agriculture Organization
United States
Agency for International Development, 70
Centers for Disease Control and Prevention, 137
Central Intelligence Agency, 142
composting facilities, 103–04
Conservation Reserve Program, 80, 172
cropland productivity, 80–84, 87–90
Department of Agriculture, 89–90, 112
endangered species, 44–45, 50–51, 74
Endangered Species Act, 74

energy policy, 117–29, 179, 183
Environmental Protection Agency, 101, 109–10
Export-Import Bank, 161
Federal Bureau of Investigation, 137
fisheries, 59–60, 63–68, 73–74
foreign investment, 150, 156–61
forest management, 27–28, 30, 34
General Accounting Office, 141–42
grain production, 10, 16, 80–90
human waste management, 106–07
Justice Department, 137
landfills, 101, 111
livestock waste management, 109–10
National Marine Fisheries Service, 68–69
Overseas Private Investment Corporation, 161, 164
paper consumption, 36–37
road subsidies, 117–18
small arms proliferation, 136–37, 140, 145–46
transportation policy, 118–20
water pollution, 53, 100
water scarcity, 7
Urban Institute, 137

Viet Nam, 15, 92, 172
Viravidaiya, Mechai, 175

Wagner, Andreas, 126
war, *see* small arms proliferation
Warner, Andrew, 155
waste management, 96–112
biogas production, 101, 108
composting, 102–04, 107, 112
composting toilets, 102, 107–08
hazardous materials, 105–06, 156, 181
landfills, 101–02, 111, 171–72
livestock waste, 109–10
sewage treatment plants, 97, 101, 104–08

SIRDO, 107–08
stabilization ponds, 106–08
see also recycling
water
aquaculture, 5, 15, 60, 73
nonfarm use, 7
scarcity, 5–6, 168–69, 173
subsidies, 6
see also aquifer depletion; freshwater ecosystems; wetlands
water pollution
fertilizer runoff, 53, 62, 96, 98–100
industrialization effects, 11
manure runoff, 109–10
wetlands
endangered species, 53
waste management, 106–08
see also freshwater ecosystems
wheat, *see* grain
Wilson, Edward O., 42
wind energy, 124–27, 179–80, 186
Wolfensohn, James, 162
World Bank
carbon emission projections, 117
composting study, 103
development assistance, 151
economic growth projections, 12
environmental policies, 162, 164
fisheries management, 66
foreign investment analysis, 149, 153, 156–62
forest assessment, 28
grain prices, 17, 81, 94
sustainable forest management, 35, 40
World Conservation Union, 35, 43–52, 55–56
World Food Summit (Rome), 95
World Wide Fund for Nature, 35, 56, 78, 184

Zaire, *see* Congo, Democratic Republic
Zero Emissions Research Initiative, 172
Zond, 180

Now you can import
all the tables
and graphs from
State of the World 1998
and all other Worldwatch
publications into your
spreadsheet program,
presentation software,
and word processor
with the...

1998 WORLDWATCH DATABASE DISK

The Worldwatch Database Disk gives you current data from all Worldwatch publications, including the *State of the World* and *Vital Signs* annual book series, *World Watch* magazine, Worldwatch Papers, and Environmental Alert series books.

The disk covers trends from mid-century onward...much not readily available from other sources. All data are sourced, and are accurate, comprehensive, and up-to-date. Researchers, professors, reporters, and policy analysts use the disk to ...

- Design graphs to illustrate newspaper stories and policy reports
- Prepare overhead projections on trends for policy briefings, board meetings, and corporate presentations
- Create specific "what if?" scenarios for energy, population, or grain supply
- Overlay one trend onto another, to see how they relate
- Track long-term trends and discern new ones

Order the 1998 Worldwatch Database Disk for just $89 plus $4 shipping and handling. To order by credit card (Mastercard, Visa, or American Express), call 1-800-555-2028, or fax to (202) 296-7365. Our e-mail address is wwpub@worldwatch.org. You can also order by sending your check or credit card information to:

Worldwatch Institute
1776 Massachusetts Ave., NW
Washington, DC 20036